Becoming the Ex-Wife

— *By* —

Ursula Parrott

who, although still in her twenties, has been mar-
ried, divorced, has a five-year-old son, and is the
author of " Ex-Wife" and " Strangers May Kiss."
She was born in Boston, a doctor's daughter, studied
at Radcliffe, and now lives in New York City where
she is working on movie and magazine material and
on a new novel soon to be published.

After the publication of her first book, *Ex-Wife*, in 1929, descriptions of Ursula Parrott always led with her marital status and often with her parental status as well, as was the case when she published "Meeting at Midnight" in *Liberty*'s May 23, 1931, issue.

Becoming the Ex-Wife

THE UNCONVENTIONAL LIFE
AND FORGOTTEN WRITINGS OF URSULA PARROTT

Marsha Gordon

UNIVERSITY OF CALIFORNIA PRESS

*The publisher and the University of California Press
Foundation gratefully acknowledge the generous support of
the Kenneth Turan and Patricia Williams Endowment Fund
in American Film.*

University of California Press
Oakland, California

Library of Congress Cataloging-in-Publication Data
Names: Gordon, Marsha, 1971– author.
Title: Becoming the ex-wife : the unconventional life and forgotten writings
    of Ursula Parrott / Marsha Gordon.
Description: Oakland, California : University of California Press, [2023] |
    Includes bibliographical references and index.
Identifiers: LCCN 2022026738 (print) | LCCN 2022026739 (ebook) |
    ISBN 9780520391543 (cloth) | ISBN 9780520391550 (ebook)
Subjects: LCSH: Parrott, Ursula, 1899–1957—Biography. | Authors—20th
    century—Biography. | Women—Social conditions—20th century.
Classification: LCC PS3531.A666 Z68 2023 (print) | LCC PS3531.A666
    (ebook) | DDC 810.9/005—dc23/eng/20220927
LC record available at https://lccn.loc.gov/2022026738
LC ebook record available at https://lccn.loc.gov/2022026739

Manufactured in the United States of America

32 31 30 29 28 27 26 25 24 23
10 9 8 7 6 5 4 3 2 1

CONTENTS

ILLUSTRATIONS

A NOTE ON NAME USAGE

Katherine Ursula Towle went by many names over the course of her life. In the first part of the book, I refer to her as Kitty (her lifelong nickname) or Katherine. After she married her first husband, Lindesay Marc Parrott, in 1922, I use Parrott, Katherine, or Kitty. When she began publishing in late summer 1929, her middle name became the name by which she was known to the public, so I use Ursula or Parrott thereafter (her intimates continued to call her Kitty). Even though she adopted some of her later husbands' last names in her personal life, she always used Parrott as her publishing name, so that is the surname I use throughout, even in the earlier part of the book.

"Maxims in the Copybook of Modernism"

Her words are important to the modern woman.
She faces squarely the vital problems of this new existence.

August 1931 Photoplay *profile of Ursula Parrott,*
"Should Women Work?"

In mid-August 1929, the soon-to-be-very-famous author Ursula Parrott reached nearly one hundred years into the future to offer her advice on the writing of the book you are now reading. She wrote her message just after her first novel, *Ex-Wife,* was published and less than three months before the diametrically opposed coincidences of the stock market crash, which triggered the United States' slide into the Great Depression, and the arrival of the novice author's first big paycheck. Her letter had a purpose: to convince her lover not to end their affair. But halfway down the first of seven single-spaced pages, Parrott took a detour, declaring, "If I, by accident became sufficiently important, ever, to have a biographer, he might say about me, 'The publication of her first book coincided with the final rupture of her heart.' (Providing he was writing in a sentimental decade that took things that happen to the heart, seriously.)"[1]

Although I was not the intended recipient of this letter, I am sympathetic to Ursula Parrott's ambitions to become "sufficiently important" as well as to her anguish—more so, it seems, than the man for whom these sentiments were intended. Parrott stands at one end of modernity, struggling to find her way during its untrodden novelty stage, and I stand at another, with a road made easier because so many, Parrott among them, forced the culture to reckon with women defying tradition and emerging from the confines of the home to explore what Parrott described as the wide, wide world.

The publication of Ursula Parrott's first book coincided not only with her personal heartbreak but also with a cultural rift: a fault line dividing the

Victorian age, into the tail end of which she was born, from what we might call the modern age. Parrott's formative years were colored by the traumatic upheavals of the deadly influenza epidemic of 1918 and the Great War, which endowed her generation with a sense of life's fragility, easily evidenced in the "omnipresence of death from every daily paper's casualty lists," as the narrator puts it in her sixth novel, *Next Time We Live*. In the postwar era, she observed her generation indulging in a host of hedonistic impulses, squeezing life out of every waking moment in case tomorrow never came. Those who lived by this ethos, Ursula eventually among them, often found that their pursuits were a recipe for exhaustion as they muddled through missteps made in the spirit of free living.

Although she is almost entirely unknown today, Ursula Parrott spent a high-profile career exploring what she called "maxims in the copybook of modernism."[2] From the late 1920s through the late 1940s, she published twenty books, several of them best sellers, and over one hundred short stories, articles, and novel-length magazine serials. Parrott made and spent astronomical sums of money during the height of the Depression through the post–World War II years, some of which she earned during brief but lucrative stints in Hollywood. Her movie and book deals, as well as her divorces and run-ins with the law, regularly generated newspaper headlines. She was a world traveler, a partner in a rural Connecticut newspaper, an informant in a federal drug investigation, and a pilot in the Civil Aeronautics Administration during World War II. She navigated a wildly fluctuating career and personal life, including four husbands and as many exes. For the most part she was a single—or unmarried, as it was usually termed—mother with strong beliefs about child-rearing, which she shared with the reading public whenever given the opportunity to do so.

Starting with her debut best seller in 1929, Ursula Parrott wrote thousands of pages about modern life and especially about the modern woman, probing the perplexing times in which she lived. Her experiences—with marriages, divorces, and raising a child; with career ambitions and loneliness; with birth control and abortions; with alcohol and depression—made their way into the pages of her stories, which are about how women broke with much of what had previously both constrained and protected them. Ursula frequently bemoaned her imperfect balancing acts as she tried to find the right mate to copilot the ship of life while balancing a demanding writing career that supported her unconventional family and lifestyle. She became a voice of alarm about what was happening to women like her—white, educated, city dwelling, and economically privileged by birth, career, or marriage—who were caught between a push for "equal everything," as she put it, and an uphill battle to succeed on so many fronts at a time when men's interests were often at odds with women's ambitions. "I'm not important," she once declared; but the story she was writing at any given moment "might be a comfort to" her readers.[3] She described the sticky situations in which women found themselves with the hope that greater understanding would lead, eventually, to less disappointment, especially if and when men accepted women's "new existence" on equal terms with what they expected for themselves.

After publishing *Ex-Wife*—a bold book about a young married woman who becomes, against her wishes, a divorcée—the exploration of male-female relations became Parrott's *raison d'être*. Parrott's autobiographically inspired first novel also became the blessing and curse that defined her, personally and professionally, for the rest of her life. When it was published in 1929, the *New York Times* credited Parrott with creating the category of the ex-wife, which they described as "a new descriptive tag to the American language." Although the term *ex-wife* had been in circulation for years, Parrott endowed it with a vivid new life at a moment of widespread curiosity about what was happening to society in an age of marital impermanence. Many years and marriages later, the *Boston Herald* proclaimed that "'Ex-Wife' is more than a best seller to Ursula Parrott; it's a state of mind!," and the *Los Angeles Times* called her "the logical candidate for the presidency of the 'Ex-Wives' Association of America."[4] Ursula's debut novel branded her in ways that were simultaneously profitable and impossible to shake (see figure 1).

Parrott became known as a specialist in "'the maladjustment emotionally' of women whose marriages had gone on the rocks" at a time when the number of women who fit this description was growing. If a journalist in the 1930s was writing an article about women's careers or the institution of marriage, they often called Ursula Parrott for an expert opinion, as Helen Welshimer did for "What the Best Known 'Ex-Wife' Thinks of Marriage," one of many like-minded (and like-titled) articles published in this era.[5] Ursula became a spokeswoman about life in a period of dizzying change in part because she expressed the contradictions of her own moment with great candor and lucidity.

Parrott published her stories in commercial magazines—the likes of *Cosmopolitan*, *Redbook*, *Ladies' Home Journal*, *American Magazine*, and *Good Housekeeping*—which had enormous circulations and paid extravagantly, even during the Depression. Her words became, as Hollywood's *Photoplay*

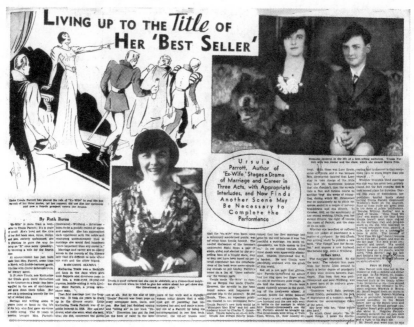

FIGURE 1. The profile that ran in Parrott's hometown newspaper nicely sums up her public persona, including her association with the subjects of marriage and divorce, her outspokenness about modern methods for raising her son, and her commitment to writing about the plight of women in a changing America. "Living Up to the Title of Her 'Best Seller,'" *Boston Herald*, March 5, 1939.

magazine put it in 1931, "important to the modern woman": she told tales about failed marriages, work-life balance, the dilemmas of single mother-hood, and the seemingly incompatible desires for independence and secu-rity. Parrott dramatized contradictions about modern life that remain unre-solved, especially regarding women's roles at work and at home. She exposed dilemmas that Betty Friedan would describe in *The Feminine Mystique* in 1963, that Helen Gurley Brown would imagine pushing past in *Having It All* in 1982, and that Sheryl Sandberg would encourage women to transcend in her 2013 *Lean In*. She wrote about women stumbling through frustrating rituals of modern courtship and proto hookup culture; paying bills and keep-ing things together when their lovers or husbands failed to hold up their end of the bargain; raising children whose fathers were absent because their "lib-erated" views allowed them to shirk responsibility; and numbing themselves from the miseries of modernity with alcohol. It is easy to see reflections of her life in her fiction; she wrote about what she knew.

Her stories rarely have happy endings. After pages that point to numerous paths to contentment, Parrott's smart and savvy female characters leave or are left, accept their loneliness with resignation, compromise their moral standards to have affairs instead of marriages, soldier on unaccompanied, or die. If they are not disillusioned on the first page, they are almost always disappointed by the last. Her stories regularly conclude with an emptiness reminiscent of her contemporaries, like F. Scott Fitzgerald and Ernest Hemingway, delivered with the kind of wisecracking wit practiced by Dorothy Parker. Like these benchmark figures of twentieth-century American literature, Parrott was committed to writing with "terrible honesty," the phrase historian Ann Douglas uses to describe the ethos shared by New York writers of this period. Parrott wrote about romance but was not just a romance writer, though she was widely perceived as one during her lifetime. She did, however, write about the consequences of romance and sex in a newly liberated age. Parrott once said that she confined her "literary attention to women who understand the meaning of life," possessed of real-world problems and survival skills built on a track record of letdowns, as well as sexual experience, often outside the safe confines of a marriage.[6]

Feminists in the early years of the twentieth century advocated for things that liberated women from the limited options of marriage, family, and home. Margaret Sanger inadvertently led the way as an advocate for birth control, which made it possible to imagine cleaving sex from reproduction. This was amplified by easy—though, of course, not legal—access to abortionists, at least in a metropolis like New York City, where Parrott lived most of her adult life. Ursula availed herself of their services numerous times, with serious physical and psychological consequences, and knew firsthand what it was like to risk her life for the "felicities," as she referred to them, of sexual intimacy. She saw women's sexual liberation as a mixed bag, characterizing some of her own encounters as "a tawdry business, mixed up with permitting one's self to be mauled in a taxi-cab," and others as "a very beautiful thing." Her stories depict what women living in a less rulebound age often had to face alone: pregnancies, decisions to have abortions or not, childbirth, and child-rearing. As she would have known from her father's recounting of the postchildbirth death of his first wife, pregnancy was risky. In the late 1920s, more women in the United States died each year as a result of childbirth than all other causes outside of tuberculosis.[7]

Ursula Parrott blamed the "Equal-*Everything*" feminists for many of her generation's difficulties. "I am not a feminist," she told an interviewer. "In fact, I resent the feminists—they are the ones who started all this. I wonder if they realized what they were letting us all in for." She believed that young women of her generation inherited a drive for equality—for the vote, at first, but subsequently in the realms of education, work, and marriage— that made their lives harder, and her stories dramatized the consequences of this unwanted bequest. She was twenty-one when women got the vote in 1920, so she was aware of the fight it took to earn the right. However, by the mid-1920s, with the suffrage victory behind them, a sense of battle fatigue for the old guard of the women's movement set in just as a younger generation started to reject many of the movement's ideals. Some "ex-feminists" began speaking out about their husbands' resentment toward them, debunking the optimism that carried them through the suffrage years; what they had fought for in theory, they could not execute with satisfaction in practice. Scholar Elaine Showalter describes this postsuffrage era as a "feminist crash." Women who wanted to work, marry, and have children were finding "that such a life was still unattainable, and they interpreted their inability to find exciting jobs and reliable child care as personal failures, rather than challenging the patriarchal assumptions of American society."[8]

Despite her alleged disregard for feminism, challenging patriarchal assumptions turned out to be Ursula Parrott's specialty. She observed what we would now call structural inequalities, complaining that women "don't earn quite as much" as men despite the fact that "it costs them just as much to live (savings in food offset by greater clothes' expense), so they're more likely than young men to be in recurrent jams." She called out instances of sexual harassment, describing her first publisher, Jonathan Cape, twenty years her senior, as a "white-haired sturdy ambitious man" who "mauled [her] between calls." "He's a grand person," Parrott proclaimed flippantly and with a qualifier, "if he'd keep his hands where they belong." She was even more indignant when a banker told her she "should always borrow from his bank, by suggesting payment in kind-ness." "I refused to do anything about it," Parrott proudly declared, "and he never suggested it again," the outcome of which was that "I pay 'em six percent interest, like all the men who borrow from them."[9] Had she been alive today, instead of writing letters in which she complained about these matters privately, Ursula might have Tweeted about them with the #MeToo hashtag and the rallying cry "Time's Up."

Parrott's stories collectively offer an argument about how much women's lives were changing during the first decades of the twentieth century, and what a bad job men were doing dealing with these changes. Her male characters tend to be fragile and insecure, falling apart in the face of women who are more independent and ambitious than they are. These men try to marry ambitious women away from their work or lash out at their girlfriends and wives when they are more successful, as is almost always the case. They drink themselves into oblivion and sexual misconduct, seeking out other women, young or without career aspirations, to make them feel powerful after their wives or lovers outpace them in talent, fame, or fortune. They shield themselves from self-scrutiny by blaming their demise on women who are unerringly—and sometimes embarrassingly—dedicated to them. Virtually no Parrott heroine overcomes the disequilibrium between them and the men who come to resent them. An advertisement for the 1936 movie based on Parrott's novel *Next Time We Live*, starring Jimmy Stewart and Margaret Sullivan, sums up the dilemma that Parrott saw as the pathology of her age: "What happens to romance when the wife becomes the breadwinner and the husband becomes the housemaid?"[10] Spoiler alert: it does not go well.

Ursula Parrott came out of the publishing gate with an argument about what was wrong with modern life: while men had never had it better, these were confusing and anxious times for women. In her first nonfiction article, published in December 1929, "Leftover Ladies," Parrott summed up the crisis with an unexpected twist: her generation "are all Free Women, free to work, to vote, to experiment with alcohol and extramarital arrangements, or what they choose. And their grandmothers had more actual freedom than they have" (see figure 2). In comparison to past generations when men were, for the most part, husbands and economic providers and women were, for the most part, wives and mothers, impermanence had become the governing principle of the times, inseparable from its inherently negative twin, instability. As one of Parrott's pitiable male characters says to the successful woman he's convinced to be his mistress instead of his wife, "So few things or people in the world we know are really permanent. It's—it's almost impossible to be permanent about anything."[11]

Without indulging in naïve enthusiasm or uncomplicated nostalgia, Parrott argued that women of earlier generations who had little choice except to focus their energies on the home had a sense of clarity and security that was now in short supply. Since women of her generation could have careers and earn their own wages, men no longer felt obliged to care for them, freeing husbands from "so many restraints and responsibilities." As she put it,

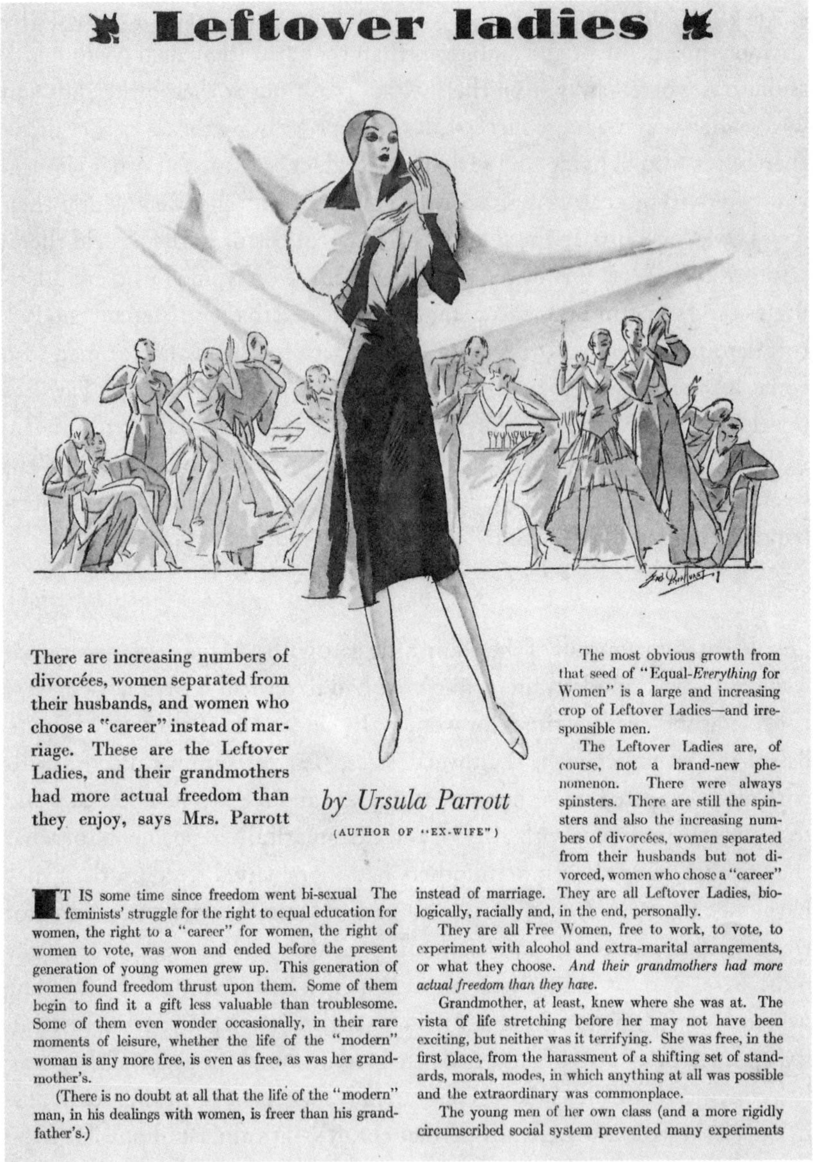

🦇 Leftover ladies 🦇

There are increasing numbers of divorcées, women separated from their husbands, and women who choose a "career" instead of marriage. These are the Leftover Ladies, and their grandmothers had more actual freedom than they enjoy, says Mrs. Parrott

by Ursula Parrott
(AUTHOR OF "EX-WIFE")

IT IS some time since freedom went bi-sexual The feminists' struggle for the right to equal education for women, the right to a "career" for women, the right of women to vote, was won and ended before the present generation of young women grew up. This generation of women found freedom thrust upon them. Some of them begin to find it a gift less valuable than troublesome. Some of them even wonder occasionally, in their rare moments of leisure, whether the life of the "modern" woman is any more free, is even as free, as was her grandmother's.

(There is no doubt at all that the life of the "modern" man, in his dealings with women, is freer than his grandfather's.)

The most obvious growth from that seed of "Equal-*Everything* for Women" is a large and increasing crop of Leftover Ladies—and irresponsible men.

The Leftover Ladies are, of course, not a brand-new phenomenon. There were always spinsters. There are still the spinsters and also the increasing numbers of divorcées, women separated from their husbands but not divorced, women who chose a "career" instead of marriage. They are all Leftover Ladies, biologically, racially and, in the end, personally.

They are all Free Women, free to work, to vote, to experiment with alcohol and extra-marital arrangements, or what they choose. *And their grandmothers had more actual freedom than they have.*

Grandmother, at least, knew where she was at. The vista of life stretching before her may not have been exciting, but neither was it terrifying. She was free, in the first place, from the harassment of a shifting set of standards, morals, modes, in which anything at all was possible and the extraordinary was commonplace.

The young men of her own class (and a more rigidly circumscribed social system prevented many experiments

FIGURE 2. On the heels of *Ex-Wife,* Parrott published her first magazine article and coined a new concept, "Leftover Ladies," in *The Mentor*'s December 1929 issue. (Author's collection.)

"New Freedom for Women left men free to leave." The legs were being pulled out from under the venerable institution that relied on an oft-spoken phrase uttered by millions of people who casually proceeded to defy it: "as long as we both shall live."

Of course, that pertained only to those who opted for marriage, which was not always the case now since sex was no longer restricted to the post-marital bed. Young women of Ursula's generation were torn between the uncertainties of behaving adequately modern or the embarrassment of clinging to prudish, Victorian-era sensibilities. When a female character experiences jealousy in *Ex-Wife* and mocks herself by declaring that she is "being 1880," Parrott draws attention to something that the character needs to get over to survive in the twentieth century, despite it being an otherwise perfectly understandable reaction.

Parrott used "Leftover Ladies" to issue a complaint: there was now relentless pressure to behave like "women of their time" with marriages, divorces, children, careers, and even dalliances that drove them to physical, mental, and moral exhaustion. In the past, husbands might have had affairs, but wives knew the solid ground on which they stood since they were wives for life with no need to worry about paying bills, suffering from perpetual loneliness, or buckling under the pressure of trying to look forever twenty-one to facilitate the next stroll down the aisle. Between "skillful makeup to hide any ravages of time and disillusionment," "flippancy to serve her in the place of sincerity," and "gaiety instead of kindliness," Parrott described women of her generation, herself included, turning to the bottle as "a fairly sure solace against taking anything too seriously."

Parrott strongly believed the deck was stacked against women like her, especially when it came to marriages. "Not only has a wife to be a combined Madonna and Cleopatra, but she has often to be a business woman, sharing a fifty percent economic burden with her man, as well as a fairly good athlete, a perfect listener, and—if she hopes to hold her man, she must also put on a 'clinging vine' act. She must never appear too capable or self-sufficient." It would take over thirty years for Helen Gurley Brown to put a different spin on this situation in *Sex and the Single Girl*, which celebrated unattached working women: "Economically she is a dream. She is not a parasite, a dependent, a scrounger, a sponger or a bum. She is a giver, not a taker, a winner and not a loser."[12] Brown's message was that women should enjoy being single, wait to marry, and enjoy "having it all"; but Parrott had no confidence that such a happy outcome could come to pass. Instead, she saw a growing number of "Leftover Ladies," divorcées as well as unmarried career women, struggling to navigate a significantly changed world.

With its catchy title and often counterintuitive messaging, "Leftover Ladies" was typical of Ursula Parrott, who became both a symbol of her freewheeling age and a determined slayer of its fictions. She signed off her awareness-raising manifesto wondering if "Leftover Ladies—may become a Great Moral Lesson yet, Lesson to a still younger generation—that freedom in itself is just a word that a good many people have used recklessly, that it may mean something very wonderful—or just something very wearying."

Ursula Parrott became "sufficiently important," and then she was forgotten. Widely read and highly sought after in her heyday, she suffered the fate of many women authors of her time, dismissed as a money-writer churning out romantic pablum for undiscerning female readers. Yes, she wrote many a romantic storyline—but she used most of these to critique a culture unwilling to grant women real equality, or to point out how impossible it was for women to try to do it all. While she also wrote to earn money, especially during financially exigent times, so did all writers of her time who had to survive without inherited wealth or patronage; after all, she had a family to support.[13]

Becoming the Ex-Wife: The Unconventional Life and Forgotten Writings of Ursula Parrott tells the story of this once-famous woman. It also explores how readers and moviegoers were introduced to new ideas about marriage and divorce, ex-wives and unmarried mothers, and career women. Once the best-known ex-wife in the United States, Ursula Parrott participated in a larger conversation about the modern woman during a rocky transformative period, a conversation taking place on pages and movie screens, in barrooms, bedrooms, and courtrooms. Writing to her longtime literary agent, George Bye, about a missed deadline, Parrott blamed "one of those GREAT TRAGEDIES which seem to punctuate the lives of female authors (and may be traced in their plots, a couple of years after the event, for thus the young women turn life's losses into life's gains, which is damn sensible of them)."[14] True to this witty remark, Ursula Parrott made a career out of turning her experiences and observations into salable tales about women's uncertain fate in a complicated age.

ONE

The Limited Life of a Dorchester Girl

Katherine Ursula Parrott was thirty years old when she published *Ex-Wife* and became a public figure, but nobody outside of her closest family members would have known. Like many women of her generation, she was extremely age-conscious and considered thirty to be well past the peak of life. In fact, when New York began its 1925 state census, Secretary of State Florence Knapp—who, as a woman herself, was wise in such matters—appealed directly "to all residents to give their ages honestly," inspiring one newspaper to only half-jestingly editorialize, "Does she really expect the ancient flappers to enumerate all the long, hard winters?"[1]

Although she was born on March 26, 1899, Katherine Ursula Towle— Kitty to her intimates—was so successful at the art of age reduction that even her Federal Bureau of Investigation file, which she earned later in life, incorrectly recorded her birth year as 1902. Her father, Henry Charles Towle, hailed from Paterson, New Jersey, born in 1853 to Irish immigrant parents. His father was a blacksmith who moved his family from New Jersey to Boston's South End, where Henry grew up a few miles away from where he later raised his own children. Henry deepened his family's roots in Boston with the benefit of social progress that had been hard won by Irish Americans over the course of the nineteenth century. As was often the case with children of European immigrants, he had greater opportunities than his father, starting with education, which provided a path away from the trades: thirteen-year-old Henry entered Jesuit-founded Boston College in 1865, just one year after it opened and at a time when it was customary for students to obtain many years of education within the school's walls. He was part of the college's first graduating class in 1877 and went on to obtain an MD degree from New York Medical College.[2]

Dr. Henry Towle, who was described in the press as "one of the last of Dorchester's old family doctors," spent his life working as a physician in the predominantly Irish neighborhood of Dorchester, a six-square-mile suburb that was incorporated into Boston in 1870, located a few miles south of the Boston Common. Ursula Parrott (the name she would adopt under the combined influences of her first husband, who gave her the name Parrott, and her first publisher, who preferred her middle name over her first) characterized her father as having what amounted to two practices: one a "small very high-hat practice as a consultant and obstetrician" alongside "a large G.P. [general practitioner] practice among the Irish poor, who adored him, but seldom paid him."[3] In addition to serving the poor and working-class Boston Irish community, Dr. Towle was active in the Catholic church and was a founding member of the Irish Clover Club.

Dr. Towle's first marriage, to Boston-born Elizabeth "Lizzie" Mooney on April 12, 1883, was short-lived for reasons that were typical in the era. Almost nine months after their wedding day, on January 5, 1884, Elizabeth gave birth to a daughter, Margaret, named after Dr. Towle's mother. Two days after the delivery, Elizabeth developed a severe fever that persisted for two weeks before she died of cardiac failure at the age of twenty-seven. Her death must have been especially devastating given Dr. Towle's work, which eventually included the delivery of almost 6,000 babies.[4] The young doctor was now a widower with a baby girl.

It seems unlikely that Margaret was brought up under the same roof as the children of Dr. Towle's eventual second marriage. Perhaps Dr. Towle sent Margaret—who as an adult looked every bit a Towle, with dark hair, oval face, fair skin, and delicate lips—to live with relatives or in a Catholic home. Even though they appear to have had little, if any, relationship with one another, Margaret's life both dovetailed with and diverged from her half-sister Katherine's in a number of intriguing ways.

Margaret had a flare for drama and unconventionality. She was an ardent suffragist who married in 1916, divorced in 1919, and cast off her birth name to become stage actress Madge Tyrone, keeping only her initials intact (see figure 3). After a slow but steady ascent on the stage, Madge made the leap to the silver screen, acting in movies until undertaking work as a scenarist and movie editor with Louis B. Mayer, the future founder of Metro-Goldwyn-Mayer (MGM). Deemed "one of filmdom's cleverest subtitlers," Tyrone wrote for silent films less than a decade before her half-sister arrived in Hollywood.[5] Tyrone's film career was, however, interrupted by an accident in which she

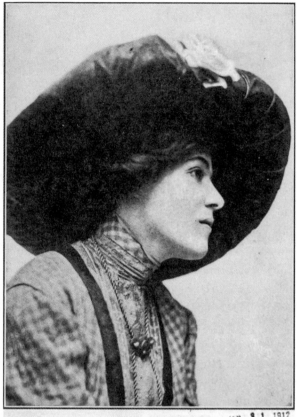

MADGE TYRONE *m.g.m.* ᴵᴬᴺ 3 1 1912

FIGURE 3. Katherine Ursula Towle's older half-sister Margaret looks every bit a Towle in this portrait taken circa 1912 during her theatrical stage career as Madge Tyrone. (Courtesy of the Billy Rose Theatre Division, New York Public Library, New York Public Library Digital Collections.)

sustained "a severe injury" when her "automobile skidded and turned turtle in an attempt to avoid collision with another car."[6] One of several car accidents experienced by people in Katherine's circle, the future author became so obsessed with automobile wrecks that they occur in almost two dozen of her stories, usually with fatal consequences.

Almost four years after his first wife's death, Dr. Towle married Mary Catherine Flusk on September 27, 1887. The Towles purchased a house at 1428 Dorchester Avenue in an area known as Fields Corner, where they lived for the duration of their marriage and where Dr. Towle resided until

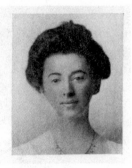

FIGURE 4. Katherine's older sister Lucy Inez Towle's entry in "The Microcosm," Simmons College 1911 yearbook. (Courtesy of the Simmons University Archives.)

his death. Dorchester, and other neighborhoods like it, had become a sign of Irish ascension in Massachusetts as well as a refuge from discrimination. When Dr. Towle was raising his children, downtown Boston shops still displayed signs that read "No Irish Need Apply."[7]

Their first daughter, Lucy Inez Towle, was born within a year. Lucy was studious and well positioned to take advantage of new opportunities available for young women coming of age at the turn-of-the-century. After graduating from Dorchester High School, she enrolled at nearby Simmons College, a women's college whose doors had been open less than a decade. In her college yearbook picture, Lucy looks like a textbook young Victorian woman, as do her classmates (see figure 4). For her senior quotation, she selected a line from the seventeenth-century English poet John Dryden: "Her wit was more than man, her innocence a child." Lucy's appearance and literary proclivities signal the decade that separated her from her ten-years-younger sister, with shifts as visible as the one that would transform the buns of Lucy's college yearbook to the bobs of Katherine's and replace Dryden with the racy musings of John Galsworthy. Although Lucy graduated from Simmons in 1911 with a degree in general science "designed for students who wish to prepare themselves to teach science, to serve as research assistants in Chemistry or Biology, or to fill certain positions which involve the application of these sciences in the arts," she never undertook a career, instead spending her never-married adult life juggling charitable service, club activities, and—first and foremost—family obligations.[8]

In March 1899, ten years after Lucy's birth, Dr. Towle and his second bride welcomed Katherine Ursula Towle into the world. Her arrival was bookended by two other children who died young: Gertrude at eleven days old, of a gastric hemorrhage in 1898, and Agnes at two days old, after a very premature birth in September 1899. Given the fate of the two baby girls whose deaths surrounded hers, Kitty was fortunate to have survived.[9]

Although she would eventually stray far from her Catholic upbringing, Katherine never forgot her Boston Irish roots nor her father's role in shaping her intellectual life. Because education had been so important to him, he took it upon himself to teach his daughters to read, something Katherine later recalled with gratitude. The acquisition of knowledge had changed his life, and his daughters were given similar advantages with which to approach theirs.[10] This was modern thinking, indicative of a new age that granted young women the right to an intellectual life even if their efforts might still be largely or entirely focused on husband and home.

Katherine adored her mother Mary but remembered her primarily for her fragility. Mary took her on an annual southward trip "for ten days before Easter" to stay at Haddon Hall, a hotel on Atlantic City's Boardwalk, where Katherine played tag with a "small pale blonde girl" and rode ponies on the beach, the start of a lifelong interest in horseback riding. "Once I fell off in the water," Katherine recalled of the first of what would be several riding accidents. But most memorable from these vacations was her mother's tenuous health. "Mother wasn't well," she later recalled, "and used to have to be wheeled along in bath chairs, with the mamma of the blonde child." Later in life Katherine once contemplated returning to Atlantic City for "an unmoral week-end there, but changed [her] mind, and came back the same afternoon." What remained of her Catholic guilt had percolated to the surface. "The ghost of the child who thought it was a heavenly place troubled [her] too much," so she pulled the plug on her tryst.[11]

Despite their mother's protestations about them missing class, Dr. Towle regularly pulled his daughters out of school for fall road trips. The family would set off from Boston to drive "through the glowing New England autumn country" to Gloucester, Portsmouth, Portland, and points as far west as Fort Ticonderoga on the edge of Lake George. Katherine spent "week ends on father's farm" in northeastern Massachusetts: "I put on awful old clothes and went splashing happily along muddy lanes—meditating on the extraordinary things I would do when I grew up—and sitting in the lee of some storm wall or other to smoke a cigarette because it tasted so good in the rain, and getting my face all scratched climbing trees for cherries."[12] The Towle farm gave Katherine a taste for country living that manifested, years later, in the acquisition of her own Connecticut estates. Her recollection about smoking, however, points to the trouble she would eventually stir up in her conservative Dorchester environs. In *Ex-Wife*, when Katherine's stand-in, Patricia, goes to Boston for a surprise visit with her father, who is (not coincidentally) a retired doctor in his seventies, he answers the door, and Pat, a grown woman already married and divorced, holds her breath "to conceal the scent of [her] last cigarette in the cab."

The busy doctor and his infirm wife needed help raising their children so hired two important caretaking members of the household, Mary Bartley and Mary Donahue, who stayed with the family the entirety of their working lives. "Old Mary" Donahue was the "dean of a coterie of Irish servants in Boston and its suburbs."[13] Kitty nicknamed her "Dado" because she could not properly pronounce "Donahue" as a child, describing her affectionately as "the lap to be climbed upon at will, the arms in which was immediate safety from nightmares (consequent on the chocolate cake stolen after supper, as Dado pointed out, but gently)." Whenever she "wanted counsel," Kitty shared her troubles as Dado rocked in her rocking chair and slid rosary beads through her fingers. Dado regularly took her ward on visits with her housekeeping friends in kitchens throughout the city, where the young girl admired the "shining, black, silver-trimmed stoves," took in "the wonderful fragrance of Parker House rolls or gingerbread baking," and got to peek into the "housekeeper's rooms," always complete with photographs of children and sweethearts alongside pictures of "theinfantjesus" and "theholymother."

In *Ex-Wife*, Patricia visits her Irish domestic, named Nellie (instead of Mary), on a trip to Boston. Patricia looks at the photos on Nellie's wall, of "mother, and of the babies who died, and at least eight of me because I was the last child and was 'her' baby." Katherine wrote a letter about a similar visit to Dado's room during a 1928 trip to Boston, in which she detailed a wall of photographs almost exactly as she later wrote the scene in *Ex-Wife*: "of my mother, and Lucy, and the two babies that died, and at least a dozen of me, because I was 'her' baby—the last one." But in Katherine's letter, there is an additional detail: Dado tells Katherine that she is growing "more and more to look like my-mother-who-was-a-saint" and asks if she is going "to communion regularly." She did not record her answer, though we can deduce what her honest response would have been: in her surviving letters, Katherine mentions churchgoing only once—on Good Friday 1929 when, severely hungover after a night of too many speakeasies, she swore off drinking.[14] Her oath of abstinence was short-lived.

Looking back at her childhood, Katherine described her upbringing as conventional, her world claustrophobic. As she sat on that farm fence in the country or in her Dorchester home, she developed ambitions to escape. "All my youth in Boston, I looked forward to going to live in Greenwich Village, wherever one was clever and gay and young…and talked about 'Things that Mattered' 'stead of church and successful marriage, and the babies people had or didn't have." As her desire for secular urbanity took hold, Katherine often found herself at odds with her father, who had not let her "go to din or anything with men I knew when I was a child, in Boston": "he's that Catholic." If he had his way, she would have stayed nearby, like her older sister Lucy, who dedicated her life to church and community. But Katherine wanted more. She had a yen for adventure that made her take risks, which strained her relationship with her father. Later in life she expressed regret, wishing she had "been nicer" to her father, "but in my late 'teens we fought like hell."[15]

She also blamed him for what eventually became her debilitating inability to manage money. "He made plenty," she recalled, but was not "any good" about it.[16] However, from ages sixteen to twenty, Katherine did in fact manage "the various apartment houses father had." As the youngest daughter in a family without sons, she was a fallback to tend to this business.[17] But Dr. Towle certainly schooled his daughter on the basics of bookkeeping, just as he ensured that she had the best education available to a young woman at the time. From 1912 to 1916 Katherine attended the prestigious public Girls' Latin School where she received a classical education as good as any in the country. Located in a newly constructed 17,000 square foot building on Huntington Avenue in Boston, it was part of a complex that included the Normal School (future Teachers College), just a block away from Isabella Stewart Gardner's recently completed Fenway Court. The female offshoot of the venerable, male-only Boston Latin School opened its doors in 1878, a year before the Harvard Annex, which eventually became Radcliffe, began providing college instruction to women. Girls' Latin School was one of several progressive Northeastern educational institutions founded to provide women educational opportunities comparable to those available to men. Applications to the school were only considered if they came with "written assurance from the parents or guardians that it is their purpose to send the applicant to college."[18]

The Boston Girls' Latin School announced its purpose in limestone blocks bearing the school's motto: "Let thy life be sincere." The curriculum was rigorous. Students memorized prose and poetry; learned Latin and Greek translation, as well as reading and speaking in German and French; studied the Constitution and botany; learned the metric system, algebra, and observational geometry; studied map drawing and world geography; and practiced gymnastics and singing. Before graduating, students had to translate at least five hundred lines of Ovid and four books of Virgil's *Aeneid*, both orally and in writing. The curriculum included moral training, including the virtues outlined by the Revised Laws of Massachusetts: "principles of piety and justice, and a sacred regard for truth, love of their country, humanity and universal benevolence, sobriety, industry, and frugality, chastity, moderation, and temperance." The school singled out a particular value that it was required by statute to teach: "the subject of Thrift."[19] As her later life would indicate, Katherine did not abide by many of these early teachings. But they were part of her formal education, much of which she broke with as she made her way in the world.

During her high school years, Katherine showed significant academic promise, though her potential exceeded her performance. Under the leadership of the notoriously strict Headmaster "Happy" Hapgood, Girls' Latin School expected its students to strive for excellence. Hapgood recorded all student transgressions, which were erased only when good behavior warranted reconsideration. But he was also prejudiced, in ways that would have been typical for the time, about the Irish infiltration of Boston society. For example, Hapgood would not consider the future poet Louise Bogan, who overlapped with Katherine for three years of her studies, for the editorship of the student newspaper because "*no Irish girl* could be editor of the school magazine."[20]

Headmaster Hapgood assessed Katherine's scholarly record and likelihood for future success as part of her application to Radcliffe College. Focusing on her grades from her senior year in 1915–16, he described her as a good student in all areas except for advanced Greek, for which she received a "C." Katherine's highest grade that year came in physics, for which she earned a "B," though Hapgood failed to mention this in his letter, no doubt because a future in physics for a young woman would have been virtually unthinkable at the time. He noted that Katherine possessed "a fair record in attendance and punctuality," was in "excellent health," and was "moderately attractive in personal appearance," a standard for which the headmaster provided no explanation. One reason for Katherine receiving a tentative mark for per-

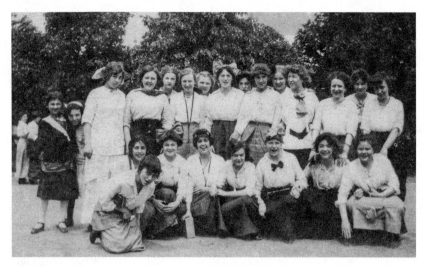

FIGURE 5. Nobody is identified on the back of this 1916 photo of students at the Boston Girls' Latin School. However, it seems likely that the young woman in the front with the cropped hair standing out from her Gibson Girlesque peers is Katherine Ursula Towle. (Courtesy of Schlesinger Library, Harvard Radcliffe Institute, Girls' Latin School/Boston Latin Academy Association collection.)

sonal appearance might be detected in a 1916 photograph of students at the Girls' School (figure 5). Although the subjects in this candid photograph are not identified, it seems likely that the perfectly out of place young woman sporting a version of what would become her signature cropped hairstyle, at a time when her classmates looked more Gibson girl than future flapper, is Katherine Ursula Towle.

Assessing her moral character, Hapgood decreed that "her honesty is unquestioned and her standards of conduct have been fairly satisfactory." He was compelled to acknowledge, however, that Katherine "has made only a fair effort throughout her course. Her teachers feel that with her ability she could have attained a considerably higher rank" than "among the leaders of the second third of her class of 96." At times, however, "her performances are brilliant."[21] This was Katherine's nature and her curse: effortlessly gifted, she had both lazy and rebellious streaks that would end up complicating every aspect and phase of her life.

At the end of Katherine's senior year of high school, her mother died suddenly at the age of fifty-six. They had just spent the day shopping together, mother and daughter getting excited over her "new frocks," and then

"Mother went out of this world one evening without time for any good-by." Her mother had long suffered from an illness she never discussed with her daughters, who only knew that she was sent south every winter for "a bit of a holiday" and needed more than usual help around the house. Katherine had always been told, "You are strong like your father's people. Your mother needs more vacations to stay strong." She recalled that when her mother arrived home from one of these vacations, the family headed to the shore. Sister Lucy and Dr. Towle swam, she stood deep in the water with Dado, and "Mother sat on a blanket on the sand, applauding us."[22]

At the time of her mother's passing, Katherine's father was in bad shape himself. Dr. Towle was on the "danger list" in the City Hospital and had been ill for a month—perhaps a first stroke, the recurrence of which would eventually claim his life. The pastor of St. Ambrose church was dispatched to City Hospital to break the news of his wife's death to the doctor, despite concerns that "the shock might prove fatal." Dr. Towle took the news "bravely," exclaiming, "I've got to live now. I've got to live."[23]

Over twelve hundred people, "including most of the doctors of Dorchester," attended Mary Towle's funeral on June 28, 1916, at St. Ambrose church. By all accounts, Mrs. Towle was a much-loved, "kind, thoughtful lady" who was "prominent in charitable and social circles."[24] High mass was followed by her burial at Holyhood Cemetery in Brookline, where Dr. Towle's first wife had already been laid to rest. He was on his own again. He certainly could not have imagined that just a decade later he would be helping to raise his youngest daughter's child in the family home while she was off in Greenwich Village collecting notes on the trials and tribulations of life as a newly minted ex-wife.

In the fall of 1930, just a year after Ursula became the most famous divorcée in the United States, Dr. Towle passed away following a cerebral hemorrhage at age seventy-seven. His obituary—which bore the subheading "Father of Ursula Parrott, Author of 'Ex Wife,' Dies in Boston"—explained that he "died before his authoress daughter and her sister, Lucy, could reach home from New York. Another daughter, Margaret, was at the bedside." Although her younger half-sister would steal the headline, it was Margaret who was with Dr. Towle in his final hours. When Margaret died on April 13, 1955, her brief *New York Times* obituary used an aptly hybrid name, Madge Tyrone Towle, to announce her requiem mass and interment at the Catholic Gate of Heaven Cemetery in New York. For reasons unknown, Dr. Towle's first born was not interred in the Towle family plot at the Holyhood Cemetery in Brookline, Massachusetts, where her mother, father, and stepmother had been laid to rest and her half-sisters, Lucy and Katherine, would eventually be buried.[25]

TWO

At Radcliffe

"A PUSHY LACE-CURTAIN IRISH GIRL FROM DORCHESTER"

Katherine Ursula Towle was one of seventeen girls from her 1916 class at Girls' Latin School to take honors in her Radcliffe entrance examinations, demonstrating promising intellectual abilities despite a lackluster work ethic and mediocre grades. Twenty of her Latin School classmates joined her at Radcliffe, and the remainder pursued degrees at Vassar, Smith, Mount Holyoke, Wellesley, Barnard, and Bryn Mawr, a group of women's colleges nicknamed the Seven Sisters because of their affiliations with Ivy League men's colleges. Radcliffe began granting degrees in 1893, making the future Ursula Parrott one of a select but growing number of women who could obtain an education comparable with what was offered by the country's most venerable private university. Katherine was actually not, however, the first Towle to attend Radcliffe; she was preceded by Margaret, who attended from 1901–1904 but did not complete her degree, earning Cs, Ds, Es, and Fs in all of her classes except for German.[1] Katherine may have followed in her half-sister's wake, but she had a better outcome despite some rather dubious methods.

Katherine majored in English. As might have been expected given her academic performance at Girls' Latin School, her college experience was not without incident, for reasons that would not have surprised Headmaster Hapgood. A spring 1917 issue of the *Radcliffe News* published the names of young women whose records of tardiness had been most egregious during the prior semester. The column's author, Elizabeth Woodworth, led her scolding by declaring faith in the average Radcliffe girl: she had hoped to publish a list of students "who have not been late in a single class this year," but that was impossible because "the list would be much too long to print." The more succinct list compiled students who had been late over twelve times during the fall semester, of which there were only a dozen, among them Katherine Towle, class of 1920, weighing it at fourteen late slips. Woodworth concluded her public shaming with some encouragement: "I hope that with a new term beginning, there will be a marked improvement that will last until June." Woodworth's optimism was, for the most part, warranted. In the spring of 1918, when the *Radcliffe News* published its new list of chronically late students, there was only one recidivist from the prior year: "K. Towle, '20" who had at least improved somewhat in her record, having been marked late only nine times.[2]

There were many rules guiding the college experience for young women attending Radcliffe in Katherine's time, no doubt intended to limit opportunities for hanky-panky and other unladylike behavior. These included qualifications for moviegoing ("upperclassmen" could go "with a man" if they returned home immediately after); attending concerts, lectures, or the theater (fine with a "group of five girls—among whom is a Senior," but only "if they come directly home" after); and "staying at the Boston Public Library till the closing hour, if they come directly home." The university also published a list of reputable Cambridge and Boston restaurants at which Radcliffe girls "may dine with a man," including The Brattle Inn, The Parker House, and Dergon and Park's at Faneuil Hall.[3]

While at Radcliffe, Katherine remained under her father's watchful eye. She described herself as "very restless" in these years, during which she had ongoing "contests with father." Like many young women of her generation, she wanted to support the boys being sent overseas to fight in the Great War, an event she would later consider the defining one for her generation. With an escape from mundane Boston life on her mind, she landed on the notion that she would volunteer as a nurse's assistant overseas. "At the last moment," however, her father "refused to let me go with the City Hospital unit," an adventure she deeply regretted missing.[4]

The battle Katherine considered the most significant during her college years, however, occurred when she wanted to drop out of Radcliffe in her junior year to "go into medicine and specialize in obstetrics." "I always had the idea, after that obstetrical incident I ran into during the war," she recalled without specifying what the episode was, "that it was pretty awful for any woman to have to have a man doctor around during all that messiness. I still think that, too." Her father, however, "refused flat to let [her] go to medical college—said the profession was no place for women, that they lost all their delicacy and fastidiousness, and morals and what all." Being a doctor was "not a modest occupation for a woman," chides one of Parrott's characters, in an echo of her father's rejection of this career path. Dr. Towle resorted to a bribe to convince his daughter to stay the course of her studies at Radcliffe: he bought her a new car and let her "keep it around college most of the time, and a few odds and ends like that." In retrospect, she was glad to have been steered away from a possible gynecological career. However, "for six months or so, I guess I was fairly dismal."[5]

The widower was trying to lead his daughter down a morally correct path during these years, including failed attempts to orchestrate her romantic life. Katherine recalled going on any number of "normal" dates in these years, referring to the mannered courtship that her father approved of instead of the hookup culture that ended up becoming part of her generation's pursuit of uninhibited pleasures. When she was "seventeen or somesuch," her "first admirer" took her "to Sunday supper and to Keith's [vaudeville theater]— which used to be the conventional thing to do Sunday evenings in Boston." But such quaint rituals, with good Irish Catholic boys in particular, seemed not much fun for a young woman who was already looking for thrills and itching to buck conventionality.[6]

While she was home from college one summer, her father forbade her from seeing one particular boy, Bill Murphy, whom she had a special fondness for. Although Catholic and Irish, Bill was also older and had an air of danger about him—right up Katherine's alley. Dr. Towle was unhappy about her spending time with someone who seemed bold and careless, judging Murphy too "wild." He told his daughter that she was "forbidden to have anything to do with him." So, Parrott later bragged, "Of course I saw him every day that I was home from college."

Bill drove a Stutz motor car, "was God-awful handsome and had money, and occasionally took telephone operators for a ride (in several senses) when he was being low-life." "But," Parrott added, "he never let [the telephone operators] drive." Bill did, however, let Katherine drive, and much to her delight even said she was good at it. One time, when she and Bill were on an excursion, they "got pinched" for reckless driving "in Hingham, a town [about twenty miles south of Boston] where he couldn't fix anything. So there were four or five lines about it in the papers." Not surprisingly for the daughter of an Irish Catholic Boston doctor, her "family raised hell," and for good reason given legitimate concerns for her reputation and safety. Automobiles were becoming associated not only with freedom and mobility but also sexual misconduct and danger. As one 1920s study reported, more than

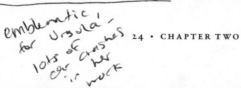

emblematic!
for Ursula,
lots of crashes
car in her work

two-thirds of girls charged with sex crimes in a small midwestern city had committed their transgressions in an automobile.[7]

As it turned out, Dr. Towle was right to be concerned. In 1921, Bill Murphy was driving drunk with a "vaudeville girl" in the passenger seat when he crashed his car and the "steering wheel went right through his tum," as Parrott put it in a morbidly frank remembrance of her friend's fatal stomach wound. What happened after the accident indicates something solid about young Katherine's character, an admirable side to her lack of regard for convention, even in a place as socially rigid as Boston. "Almost nobody respectable went to his funeral," Parrott explained. She knew this because she was there. "His father and three brothers all came up to me at the grave and thanked me for going."[8]

Perhaps it is not surprising, given this early and memorable loss combined with Margaret's California car wreck, that more Parrott characters die from car crashes than any other cause.

Like any teenager, Katherine was finding her way in the world. She looked for kicks as well as purpose. When she was fishing for causes during college, Dr. Towle tried to steer her down a path aligned with his morals by proposing that she "take an interest in the people to whom [he'd] devoted most of [his] life": "the very poor Irish."[9] He had helped to establish "a number of chapters of the Massachusetts Catholic Order of Foresters," a benevolent society that provided "a thousand dollars when you die, and free medical service, and that kind of thing." Dr. Towle persuaded his daughter to join the Foresters and experience firsthand what it was like to perform good works for their community, since "so few of them had any education." Besides, her father promised, "he'd see that [she] got to be an officer right away, and then [she] could go make speeches at state conventions, and tell 'em all about how to live healthily, and bring up their children according to Social Hygiene." Katherine tried to please her father on this occasion, feeling "touched" by his hope that she might "carry on his work." Besides, she recalled: "I thought I could do a lot of advocating of Liberal Club principals," referring to the left-wing political organization she had gotten involved with at Radcliffe, "among the poor uninstructed people who knew nothing of the Socialistic state." Katherine was being both playfully sarcastic and fashionably radical in her flirtation with political ideas that ran to the liberal end of the spectrum.

As with the other conventional pursuits she undertook, however, Katherine was immediately bored. It took a lot of effort to do good. There was too much praying. There was too much initiating. Within three months she was "nominated for Vice Chief Whatnot, due to father's drag." Now she had a campaign to run before an election that would determine her future in the organization. Her prospects, however, were mixed. Although she was admired by the older members of the Foresters, she was hated by "all the young women, telephone operators and what not" because she "went to Radcliffe, and talked with a Hahvahd drawl, and said 'Well, r-eally, you know, it just isn't done.'" Perhaps it was a relief, then, that she lost the election, after which she "wouldn't go to their damn meetings any more." "I did," she recalled, "make them a speech though, explaining the Liberal Club, before I stopped going." It seems unlikely that the working-class telephone operators much enjoyed hearing about the Liberal Club from Dr. Towle's beautiful, bobbed daughter in her snooty Harvard accent before she returned to her halfhearted studies in the car her father had bought for her.

If Katherine had not been popular with the working-class telephone operators of the Foresters, she was also not particularly welcome in the realm of Radcliffe's social elite. She stood out from the other Radcliffe girls and struggled to find her place. Nor did she possess the wherewithal to create or sustain meaningful friendships with her classmates, using a literary metaphor to explain that "they were no more than short stories one read and was done with." Later in life, her only son wondered if some of his mother's "showoff traits, some charming, some very dangerous, derived from the snubbing she took in Cambridge as a pushy lace-curtain Irish girl from Dorchester."[10] That she was different from her classmates would become even more apparent in her postcollege years, evident in the college alumni bulletin's occasional updates involving her string of moves and marriages, a stark contrast to the longitudinal stability—and largely mundane lives—of her classmates.

While at Radcliffe, Katherine did explore "doing some good in the world" and pursued an eclectic mix of club memberships befitting an exploratory mind (see figure 6). She was "active in the new Liberal Club at college, and taught in a settlement, and read [Immanuel] Kant." She was in the Debating, Civics, Socialist, and Catholic clubs, though her membership in two clubs lasted only one year—Suffrage and Socialist, which she abandoned in 1918 (two years before women got the vote) and 1920 respectively. During her senior year, Katherine might have gone on a weekly charitable visit to the Holy Ghost Hospital or listened to a lecture such as "Higher Criticism of the Bible" with the Catholic Club; attended the Intercollegiate Socialist

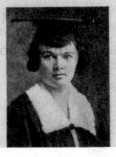

KATHARINE URSULA TOWLE

1428 Dorchester Avenue, Boston.
Born March 26, 1899, Dorchester, Mass.
School and year of graduation: Girls' Latin School, 1916.
College Concentration: English.
     Civics Club 1916-1920. Debating Club 1917-1920. Suf-
     frage Club 1917-1918. Socialist Club 1919-1920. Catholic
     Club 1917-1920.
            "*Cut, and come again.*"

FIGURE 6. Katherine Ursula Towle's Radcliffe College yearbook photo, 1920, lists the clubs she explored during her studies, including her short-lived membership in the Suffrage Club. (Courtesy of Schlesinger Library, Harvard Radcliffe Institute.)

Convention in New York City or an illustrated lecture about Russia with the Socialist Club; listened to lectures on the British Labour Party or "Law and Order" with the Civics Club; or helped her team to argue the affirmative side of the question of whether or not "Recognition of Labor Unions Is Essential to Collective Bargaining" with the Debating Club.[11] Of course, given her attendance record, she might have skipped out on most or all of these club activities as well.

Parrott recalled that the Liberal Club, a campus version of the radical Greenwich Village organization, got "a hell of a lot of publicity" when they asked anarchist and feminist "Emma Goldman to speak, or planned a protest rally because she'd been deported" (reminiscing about it later in life, she could not precisely recall which). Goldman was a labor organizer, admired as well as feared, and a fierce advocate for birth control's essential role in women's liberation. Because of the Goldman incident on campus, some Liberal Club members "got kicked out, and some suspended" as concerns circulated that Radcliffe was becoming a "hotbed of Bolshevism."[12] Katherine's fate was not so consequential, though she did get her name in the papers because of her involvement. "Poor Father!" she proclaimed when recalling the incident.

In *The Tumult and the Shouting*, Parrott's 1933 novel about a Boston Irish family modeled on her own, she imagined how scandalous newspaper publicity might have affected someone unmistakably like her father. In it, aging but deeply revered Boston doctor Michael Gavin's daughter lives a reckless life as a New York city dancer and actress. Instead of marrying, Carol has affairs, including with married men, the consequences for which include being publicly accused of breaking up a marriage. The "*flop* of the newspaper against the front door" at the doctor's Boston home ushers in the unwelcome delivery of a front-page headline: "Boston Dancer Named as Co-Respondent." Looking at the paper, Dr. Gavin's sister cries, blurring the "big picture of Carol on the front page," before declaring, "It would be better if she were dead." The doctor rushes to New York to try to bring his daughter back to a respectable life in Boston but is baffled to find Carol hosting a party and making light of the headlines. Returning home in a ferocious storm, the doctor is immediately called to tend to a critically ill patient. Soon after, Dr. Gavin sickens and dies. Parrott surely wrote this story with her recently deceased father in mind as she considered how her ample newspaper publicity—which was off to a good start in her high school and college years—might have hastened his decline.

Midway through her studies at Radcliffe, there were signs beyond her attendance record and brushes with scandal that Katherine was veering offtrack, continuing a pattern that would recur throughout her life of success interwoven with disappointment or scandal. A letter from the university to her father reported that Katherine's 1917–18 record had recently been submitted for review to the chairman of the academic board. Dr. Towle was issued a stern warning: Katherine "must make a marked improvement in her record for the remainder of her college course if she hopes to get her degree with her class." While she had potential, her academic performance indicated distraction and disinterest. The letter continues condescendingly: "You realize, do you not, that in order to get the degree from Radcliffe, a student must pass in at least seventeen courses with grades above 'D' in two-thirds of them." During her freshman and sophomore years, Katherine earned Ds in German, history, botany, and English—seemingly following in Margaret's subpar academic footsteps. Henry Towle had been an extremely serious student at Boston College, so witnessing his daughter's squandering of her Radcliffe education was surely a letdown. The letter concluded with a suggestion that doubled as a warning: "She should make every effort to improve her record for next year."[13]

Dr. Towle must have made his displeasure adequately known since his daughter turned things around enough to successfully earn her English degree on June 23, 1920. Even this success, however, was tainted by Katherine's questionable behavior. In Radcliffe's 1920 yearbook, the student body president endowed humorous class gifts in verse upon each graduate. Hers began, "I don't suppose Katharine [sp] Towle is here; she is probably cramming at the Widow's." For her gift, she received a "Widow's veil" along with the following bit of doggerel:

> She cut classes all during the year,
> Her finals then filled her with fear.
> At the Widow's she learned
> What from profs, she had spurned,
> A proceeding most queer.

This mockery targeted Katherine's use of "The Widow's," the nickname for Harvard graduate William Whiting Nolen's "cram parlor," which sold notes from classes, provided ethically questionable test preparation, and offered ghostwritten papers for Harvard and Radcliffe students.[14] The Widow's was an open secret, and Katherine's use of it to make up for her inattention and truancy was memorialized in her college yearbook.

After receiving her Radcliffe degree in 1920, Katherine got into another skirmish with her father, who "wanted [her] to stay home and teach English in a convent." It is almost impossible to imagine the spirited, defiant, increasingly secular Katherine entering the world of the convent. "I won that" battle, she boasted, "by getting a newspaper job."[15] Working as a cub reporter marked the first time that writing allowed Katherine to control her destiny. After some real-world journalistic experience, two years after she graduated from college she reapplied to Radcliffe with the intention of earning a master's degree in English. In her application, she explained that she had been working as a "newspaper reporter since graduation from Radcliffe," a profession that would continue to fascinate her when she later sought newspaper work in New York City. There would also be countless male reporters in Parrott's published stories and, though she would not yet have known it, journalism would be the chosen profession of the two most significant loves of her life.

As it turned out, Katherine attended Radcliffe for only one partial semester of graduate study, taking courses during the spring of 1922 but earning no grades. Instead of completing her master's degree, she exchanged vows with Lindesay Marc Parrott in the summer of 1922, a decision that would lead her to a life in the seat of American bohemia, Greenwich Village, New York City.[16]

THREE

First Husband, Lindesay Parrott

"STRANGE MOMENTS OF TENDERNESS
AND PRETTY CONSTANT DISLIKE"

The man who gave Katherine Ursula Towle the last name she would use, on and off, for the rest of her life was Lindesay Marc Parrott. The middle child of Ohio-born Dr. Thomas Marc Parrott and South-African-born Mary Adamson Parrott, Lindesay entered the world on July 26, 1901, in the city where his parents had married in 1895, Edinburgh, Scotland. The three Parrott children were raised abroad while Dr. Parrott conducted research before settling into a thirty-nine-year position as a professor of English literature at Princeton University. Members of the Princeton elite, the Parrotts raised their children to be worldly: after attending schools in England and Switzerland, Lindesay went to the private Lawrenceville School in New Jersey and then Princeton University, from which he graduated in 1921, not long after meeting his future bride.[1]

Katherine was at her first newspaper job when she decided to attend a Princeton prom and ended up meeting the man who became her first husband and the father of her only child (see figure 7).[2] Both college educated, their mutual interests in journalism and travel provided an initial sense of shared purpose and intellectual connection. Katherine, who would not be rechristened Ursula until her publishing reinvention in 1929, had long fantasized about the kind of passionate relationship she would later write about in her stories. When she met Lindesay, she believed that she was entering into a union that would allow for equality in all things, as was the modern way. This was a shared hope for many of her generation, inspired by what the *New York Times* described, in its 1922 coverage of the movement to remove the word *obey* from women's wedding vows, as an age of revised expectations that reflected "woman's new economic independence."[3]

Kitty and Lindesay's romance blossomed amidst the excitement of New

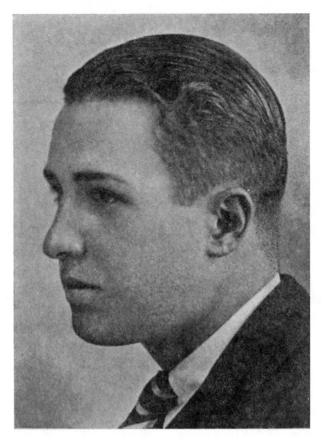

FIGURE 7. Lindesay Marc Parrott's 1921 Princeton yearbook photo. (Courtesy of Princeton University, Firestone Library, Department of Special Collections.)

York City, where the pair ventured from not-too-far-away New Jersey. While still attending Princeton, and then after he graduated and moved to the city, Lindesay took Kitty on dates in the legendary neighborhood of Greenwich Village. "One night," she recalled, "when it was getting dark…L. took me to dinner at the Pirates' Den," located on Christopher Street in a former stable renovated to feel like a ship's deck on each of its three floors. "I couldn't eat," Kitty recalled, so enthralled was she by the romance of the environs. "Everyone looked absolutely clever and beautiful and gay and young…as if they were going to pop out with a perfect sonnet instantly." As she fell in love, she became enchanted by the edgy, creative energy of the Village, which she had fantasized about as a teenage malcontent. Kitty was especially delighted that

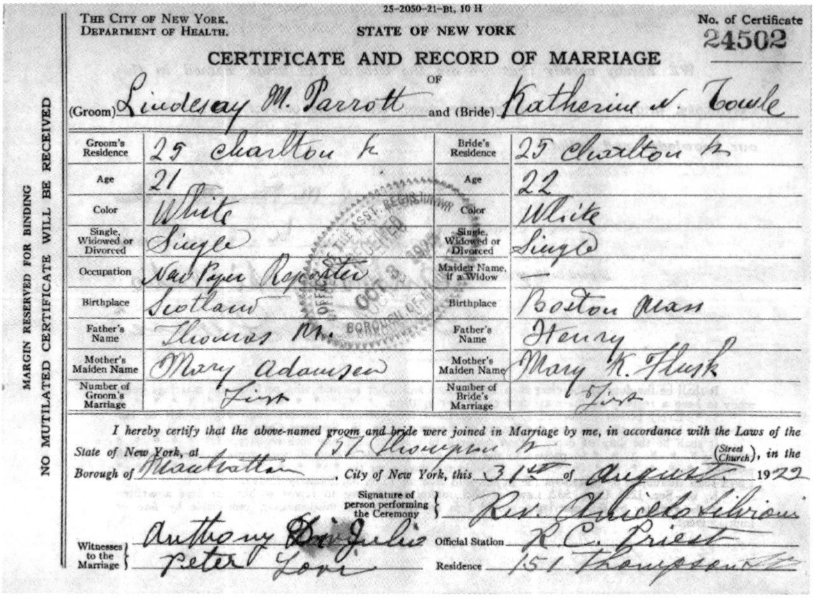

FIGURE 8. Lindesay M. Parrott and Katherine U. Towle Certificate and Record of Marriage issued by the State of New York, August 31, 1922. (Courtesy of the New York City Department of Health Archive.)

Lin, as she called him, wanted to "be adventurous in New York, not Boston"; he was her ticket to a new start in America's most exciting city.[4]

Lindesay and Kitty did not marry in a fashion befitting either of their upbringings, but rather in accord with their unconventional times. Instead of an extended courtship and formal ceremony surrounded by family and friends, the pair eloped. On August 31, 1922, just two years after her graduation from Radcliffe, a Roman Catholic priest performed their nuptials at the Church of St. Anthony at Padua in Greenwich Village. Lindesay was newly twenty-one, and she was twenty-three, although she shaved a year off her age on their marriage certificate. The groom listed his occupation as a newspaper reporter; there was no equivalent space for the bride to report a profession, only a "maiden name, if a widow" (see figure 8).[5]

Neither the bride's nor groom's families were present at the modest ceremony, nor did the family have advance notice that it was to take place. Precisely how Dr. Towle or Professor Parrott reacted to the news of their children's surreptitious marriage is unknown. But any displeasure that might have come from Dr. Towle's quarters was mitigated by Kitty's beloved childhood housekeeper Dado, who "did not permit [Kitty] to be scolded, saw that

[she] had a trousseau belatedly, and occasionally made a trip to New York to 'straighten out' a Greenwich Village apartment otherwise adventurous but disorderly."[6]

The kindly Italian landlady, Mrs. Donato, in Ursula Parrott's novel *Next Time We Live,* who aids Christopher and Cicely as they elope and make their way through difficult early years together, is likely based on a similarly disposed landlady from this period in the Parrotts' wedded life. This novel's portrait of a young marriage is also as close to a recounting of Lindesay and Kitty's romance as we are likely to find: "They had met at a Princeton house-party in spring of his senior year, the year previous. They'd fallen in love to the beat of the newly fashionable saxophones, with a desperateness rather unfashionable that year when the code was to be poised and nonchalant." Christopher works as a cub reporter for the *New York Morning Star,* and Cicely visits him by train in New York, drinking and dancing at the Pirates' Den and the Greenwich Village Inn. One weekend, they decide that she will not leave the city but rather stay in New York, marry him, and begin their ultimately tragic life together.[7]

Following their wedding, Lindesay and Kitty moved into a brownstone apartment at 25 Charlton Street, five blocks south of Washington Square Park. He had begun his career as a reporter with the *Newark Evening News* before moving into a variety of posts at newspapers in the city. As with all cub reporters, the pay was low and the hours long. In the 1920s, he was part of a cohort of wisecracking, booze-loving, and almost exclusively male reporters who made Manhattan and its boroughs their home, many of whom drifted between papers and crossed paths between pressrooms, speakeasies, and women. Kitty clipped out the newspaper stories Lindesay wrote to commemorate the fruits of his labors during the couple's honeymoon phase, which did not last long in either quasi fiction or reality. The couple apparently had a volatile relationship almost from the start. Sportswriter Lester Bromberg recalled Lindesay making late night drunken appearances in the newsroom, "swaggering, ribbing the early rewrite men and retelling his latest war with Ursula."[8] Theirs was not to be the kind of peaceful, lasting union one read about in the Victorian novels that Ursula recalled, with mixed feelings, when she was forging her philosophies of modern marriage and its discontents a few years later.

The Parrotts were, in fact, thrown an early curveball, which was neither inherently good nor bad: several months after their wedding, Lindesay was offered an assignment in London, which he accepted. In Ursula's stories, a distant job offer for a career-hungry male character always results in a difficult decision: to sacrifice success for love or to forgo love for career advancement. In this case Lindesay chose the career, but this was likely a mutual decision since his new bride followed not far behind him. Although she had herself been working at newspapers, Kitty eagerly plunged into an anticipated year of adventure and overseas travel. On her first passport application, she is described as five-foot-two with grey eyes, a high forehead, and black hair (see figure 9). Along with most of the other female passengers listed on the Cunard ledger for her overseas passage, Katherine Towle Parrott's "Profession, Occupation, or Calling" is listed merely as "H'wife."[9]

In London, the newlyweds rented a flat on Porchester Square, less than a mile north of Hyde Park. That spring, while Lindesay worked, Kitty wandered the city and went for long walks through Kew Gardens, admiring the bluebells. For reasons unknown, after only two-and-a-half months, Lindesay returned to New York, arriving on April 11, 1923.[10] Unbeknownst to him at the time of his departure, his bride was two months pregnant.

In late May, Kitty made the overseas return trip at what would have been the end of her first trimester.[11] It must have been a difficult passage, physically but also mentally, because Lindesay had made it abundantly clear from the start of their relationship that he had no interest in children at this point in their marriage and his career. What happened in the months following her homecoming is murky. Kitty and Lindesay both listed their respective family homes as their stateside destinations, perhaps because they had given up or sublet their New York apartment, or perhaps because they intended to soon return to London. But that does not explain why Lindesay's bride stayed in London more than a month after Lindesay returned to New York. Had he planned to come back until something intervened to make his return impossible, or did he in fact sail back and they essentially crossed paths during their respective journeys? The biggest and most important question of all, however, is whether Lindesay knew that Kitty was expecting a child. There are reasons to believe that, at least at the time, he did not.

At St. Elizabeth's Hospital in Boston on October 28, 1923, Kitty gave birth to Lindesay Marc Parrott II, whom she would call Marc. She sought the familiarity of her hometown to give birth rather than Princeton or New York City because she "wanted Dado," the Irish domestic who had raised her and still tended to her father, by her side.[12] Her mother long dead, her hus-

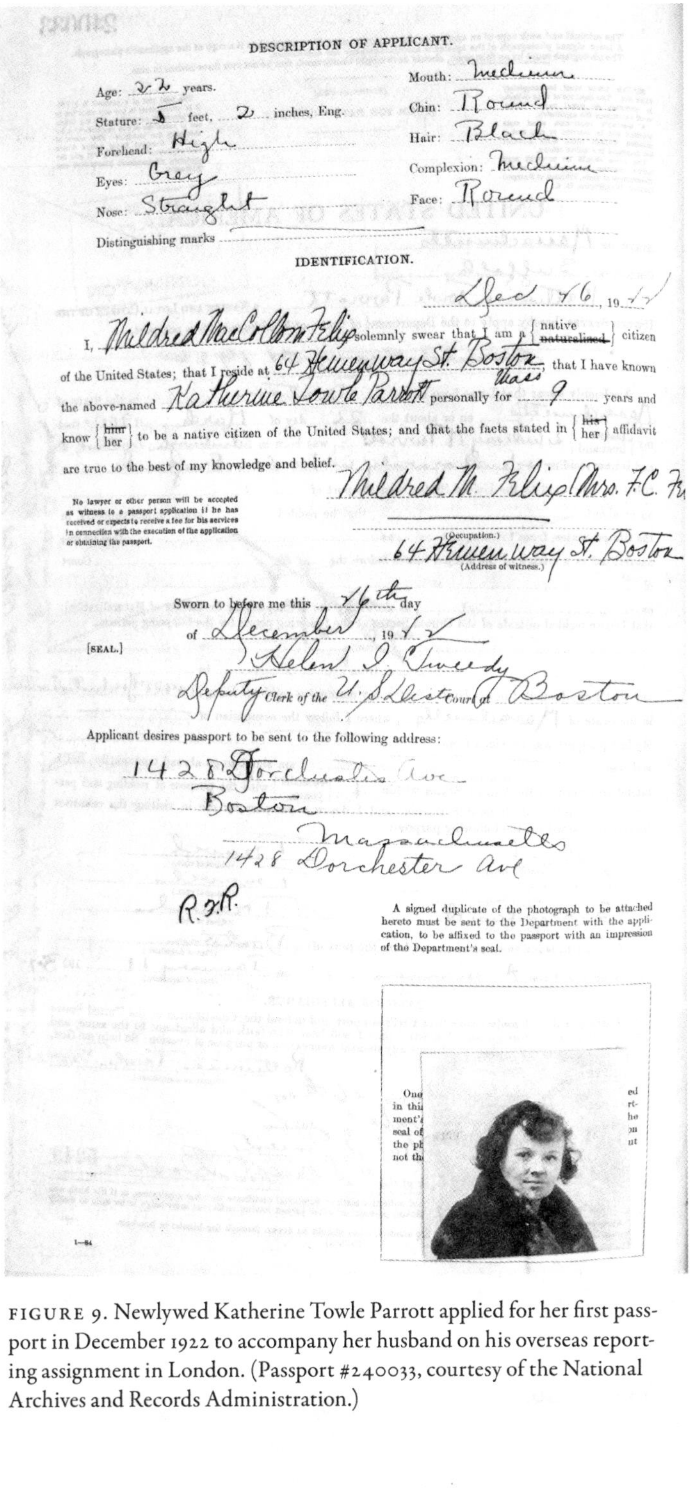

DESCRIPTION OF APPLICANT.

Age: *2 2* years.

Stature: *5* feet, *2* inches, Eng.

Forehead: *High*

Eyes: *Grey*

Nose: *Straight*

Mouth: *Medium*

Chin: *Round*

Hair: *Black*

Complexion: *Medium*

Face: *Round*

Distinguishing marks ....

IDENTIFICATION.

Dec 16 19 *__*

I, *Mildred MacCollom Felix* solemnly swear that I am a {native / naturalized} citizen of the United States; that I reside at *64 Hemenway St. Boston Mass* that I have known the above-named *Katherine Towle Parrott* personally for *9* years and know {him / her} to be a native citizen of the United States; and that the facts stated in {his / her} affidavit are true to the best of my knowledge and belief.

No lawyer or other person will be accepted as witness to a passport application if he has received or expects to receive a fee for his services in connection with the execution of the application or obtaining the passport.

Mildred M. Felix (Mrs. F.C. F...

.... (Occupation.)

64 Hemen Way St. Boston
(Address of witness.)

Sworn to before me this *16th* day of *December* 19 *__*

[SEAL.]

Helen I. Tweedy

Deputy Clerk of the *U.S. District* Court *at Boston*

Applicant desires passport to be sent to the following address:

1428 Dorchester Ave
Boston
Massachusetts
1428 Dorchester Ave

R.2.R.

A signed duplicate of the photograph to be attached hereto must be sent to the Department with the application, to be affixed to the passport with an impression of the Department's seal.

FIGURE 9. Newlywed Katherine Towle Parrott applied for her first passport in December 1922 to accompany her husband on his overseas reporting assignment in London. (Passport #240033, courtesy of the National Archives and Records Administration.)

band not playing the role of anticipatory father-to-be, Dado was as close to a caregiver as Kitty had.

It was not an easy labor. However difficult the delivery was, the greater challenge was convincing her husband that fatherhood would not derail his career or ruin their young lives together. Lindesay had been adamant about children handicapping new marriages and nascent careers. In fact, it seems likely that Kitty kept her pregnancy a secret until it was at least too late for her husband to compel her to do anything to terminate it, and it is certain that she spent her postpartum months trying to figure out how to bring her career-focused husband on board for the parenting project.[13]

After Marc's birth, the couple rented an "enormous six-room apartment" in a rundown area of Chelsea at 336 West 19th Street, complete with a "spare bedroom with rose-colored walls." The baby stayed for several months in Boston as Kitty conspired with Lindesay's mother "that spring after Marc was born, to be tactful, but get Lin interested in Marc, who was getting to be a quite big and pretty baby, and shortly move him in" to the apartment. Lindesay's mother, Kitty recalled, thought the rose-colored spare bedroom "would make a lovely nursery." However, it also ended up serving another function: "we used it to put to bed whomever passed out on parties…and they all said the pink walls were awful, when they woke up with hangovers."[14] The couple's life as freewheeling newlyweds was certainly complicated by the arrival of a child, but their adventures were not yet over.

"I just don't remember," Katherine recalled in 1928, looking back at this tumultuous time in her life, "what it felt like to be twenty three and married to L.…. Things happened too swiftly in the years afterward." When she later discussed her first marriage, as she was often asked to do after publishing *Ex-Wife*, she attributed its failure to "too youthful a marriage, too much responsibility, too little money to live on." These things were, no doubt, true. But the final rupture in the Parrotts' marriage came not from an unwanted child or inadequate resources but rather as a consequence of infidelities. As she eventually described in *Ex-Wife*, Lindesay perpetrated the first offense, an allegedly inconsequential encounter, which she—in the modern way— forgave, no matter how badly it stung. But he would not reciprocate the forgiveness after her own indiscretion with journalist Courtenay Terrett, nicknamed "Terry" or "Brick" (see figure 10). Part of the New York City newspaper boy's club, Terry was a charismatic fellow with a notorious but far

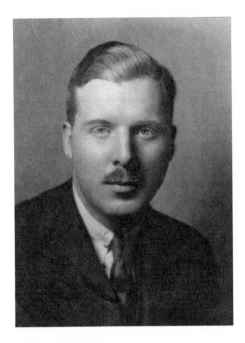

FIGURE 10. Although she remained friends with Courtenay "Terry" Terrett, identified on the back of this photo as a writer for the *New York Telegram*, he was the man with whom Katherine Parrott committed the act of infidelity that inspired both her divorce and the turning point in her first novel. (Newspaper Enterprises Association photo, author's collection.)

from unique penchant for liquor and women. Because of the close interconnections in their professional circles, Kitty refused to reveal Terry's identity to her husband—which certainly, as Terry would later rightly guess, "added to her difficulties."[15]

When she confessed her transgression to her husband, without naming names, "in fifteen minutes [she] knocked out all [Lindesay's] pleasant ideas, due to the simple British upbringing…faith that there were things 'one didn't do'…and more things one's wife didn't." He deemed her one-night stand an irreparable moral failing. The wounds she inflicted, he told her, would "never mend"; he could not trust her or, for that matter, any other woman again. "He will never understand until he's old," she later explained, that she "in telling him was living up to some ideal as funny and as young as his about a wife's impeccable honor."[16] This was supposed to be a marriage of equals in all things—honesty included. In the arc of a life, or of a marriage, this seemed to her to be a relatively meaningless trespass that could be righted and forgotten—blood under the bridge of modern living. Instead, it became the pivotal act of her young adult life, the final blow to an already strained relationship. Lindesay announced that he was moving out, leaving Kitty a "deserted wife."

In a short story Ursula wrote some years later, when a young woman leaves a boring marriage for a passionate affair, the narrator reflects that she "walked out of a doorway once, uncertain, confused" and "never found her way back…to tranquility and safety."[17] By the time Ursula wrote these words about a different kind of marital rupture, she knew the feeling well, though she could only have imagined what a peaceful marriage might have been like, given the amount of conflict and drama that had characterized her own.

When pressed to discuss her first marriage after she became famous, Ursula tried—out of respect for Lin—to offer only generalities, describing things like lessons learned and the traits she believed men and women required for "success of the matrimonial venture": a "sense of humor; the ability to see two sides of a question; patience, comprehension and gratitude; ability to make reasonable compromises; ability to have disagreements… without having a row." When she added that "men must have tolerance, and the ability to treat their wives as friends instead of possessions," she was, however, implicitly criticizing him, although nobody but they would likely have known it. Her first marriage taught her about the thorny ethics of the new morality and provided a significant lesson in the double standard. Lindesay gave his wife precisely what she needed to formulate her first lessons about the perils of modern living. Later in life she would recall her extramarital transgression when she "needed to think of something funny. It was so funny in its devastating consequences." She had, however, become "sort of grateful for the incident, because it precipitated all it did."[18] Ursula had to experience suffering before she could write about it.

On at least one occasion during their separation but prior to their divorce, Kitty tried to get her husband back, "partly because I wanted him, partly because weight of upbringing and so on made me quite sure that there lay my only chance of achieving for myself and Marc the normal stable sort of life I ached for, then." For the most part, however, Kitty soldiered on as a "separee" and tried to avoid seeing Lindesay around town. They rarely spoke, unless he rang her up after being emboldened at a speakeasy, which he did just prior to their divorce to discuss "his anguish over the [Ruth Brown] Snyder execution" (for the murder of her husband). Lindesay came to his soon-to-be-ex-wife to discuss his distress over the case and Snyder's sentence, telling her things that he could not share with readers on the printed page.[19]

After having spent a good portion of their less-than-six-year marriage apart, Kitty and Lindesay obtained a divorce in January 1928. Without any objection, Kitty was awarded sole custody of Marc by the courts. Ursula would later advise women whose marriages had failed that they "wouldn't be hurt nearly as much if she had been trained to believe that maybe it wouldn't last," urging realism, not resignation. "Do your best to make your marriage last forever," she counseled, "but don't feel that it is a catastrophe if it doesn't."[20] In *Ex-Wife*, however, published the year after the Parrotts' divorce, Pat's father uses that same word to discuss his regret for "the catastrophe of [her] marriage," urging her to "come home to live," which of course she does not do. Newly divorced, Katherine Ursula Parrott reacted similarly to her father's offer, although she did agree to move her son to the Boston family home since she could not manage his care on her own.

Years later, Ursula reflected that she and Lindesay still had "strange moments of tenderness and pretty constant dislike of each other because we spent a pretty trying post-adolescence together, and our experiment parental was just an added complication. We'd married and been parents and separated, before either of us grew up." Many of her stories would depict too-young married couples embarking on lives that they are not mature enough to successfully navigate. She and Lindesay were so young when they married, Ursula remarked, that "the S.P.C.C. should have sent us food baskets," humorously referring to the New York Society to prevent Cruelty to Children.[21]

Both moved on romantically well before their divorce. In 1927, Kitty began her affair with journalist Hugh O'Connor, and Lindesay declared himself "single" on a ship's manifest on a trip to Bermuda with Eleanor Pollock, nicknamed Polly. After their divorce, Kitty occasionally ran into Lindesay and Polly, recounting one such encounter at Alice McCollisters on West 8th Street, which the couple had frequented while they were married. Kitty tried to behave nonchalantly, acting like a good ex-wife navigating deeply interconnected stomping grounds. But as soon as Polly went away on vacation that summer, Lindesay began calling and asking to see her. "I refused," Kitty proclaimed, not for reasons of moral conscience but because she had concluded that they were "just not good for each other." Occasionally, however, she gave in: "apropos of a damn fool promise I made to him when I was twenty three or some such, I saw him."[22]

As their lives became unentwined, Lindesay ascended in the newspaper world, including a very brief stint as a "rewrite man" at the *Morning World*. Shortly after his arrival at that paper in early 1931, the employees were surprised to learn that it was one of three Joseph Pulitzer newspapers quietly auctioned off as part of a Depression-necessitated bankruptcy sale by his heirs, making the end of the "Park Row" era.[23] That storied newspaper publishing avenue, enlivened by a dozen churning presses during its heyday, had been reduced to a lone survivor, *The Sun*: "Some have merged, some expired painlessly and the others have built new plants throughout the city." A literary wake prepared for "The End of the World" listed numerous contributors, among them three notable names: Courtenay Terrett, Hugh O'Connor, and Lindesay Parrott.[24] If one needed evidence of the tricky interconnectedness of Ursula's social and romantic life, it could be found in just one newspaper's office on Park Row.

By the time Katherine Ursula Towle entered and exited her first one, the institution of marriage was in a widely recognized state of transformation and, as some alleged, crisis. In the past, marriages had not been transacted primarily for self-indulgent notions like unfettered choice, romantic love, or even compatibility. Marriage had been a largely social and economic arrangement influenced by parental will and assessments of a potential spouse's suitability based on practical criteria. As the pendulum swung to prioritize individual choice and romantic love, one prominent ethicist of the early twentieth century complained that "over-emphasizing the individual claim to happiness" had led to the notion that "nothing is now to be considered except the happiness of madame and monsieur." Women's ambitions became one scapegoat for the institution's perceived weakening, since the "college education of girls" and "emancipation of women" had erased "sex difference" by encouraging women to pursue life outside of the home.[25]

The function of marriage was also being seriously reconsidered. Not long after the finalizing of Kitty and Lindesay's divorce, Denver judge Benjamin Lindsey published a book about "companionate marriage," a marriage-like arrangement using legalized birth control to avoid bringing a child into the mix and dissolvable by mutual consent or by conversion, after an agreed-upon time, into a legal marriage. This was not, Judge Lindsey argued, to be confused with free love or a trial marriage colored by the "psychology of impermanence," but rather it was a sincere acknowledgment that some marriages, no matter how earnestly undertaken, were best served by an undramatic exit strategy. Companionate marriage was one of the water cooler topics of the late 1920s, and the now-former Mrs. Parrott considered Judge Lindsey's book "very very swell." She discerned the origins of his proposed arrangement in the "New Morality" of Greenwich Village, where the "Younger Generation," herself among them, had experienced something akin to an awakening.[26] Of course, companionate marriage was widely mocked and criticized, especially by the Catholic Church, under whose authority Kitty had been raised.

Judge Lindsey's idea for companionate marriage was just one of many attempts to address the increased number of failed marriages in the United States. The 1920 Federal Census showed an over twenty percent increase in divorces since 1916. This surge was happening not just in big cities or on the coasts, either. In one study of a Midwest city of about 30,000 people, which was referred to as Middletown (actually Muncie, Indiana), Robert and Helen Lynd observed an uptick in divorces from 9 for each 100 marriage licenses in 1895 to 42 for each 100 in 1924. The Lynds concluded that "with the spread of the habit of married women's working, women are less willing to continue an unsatisfactory marriage arrangement." But divorce did not simply escalate as women became more self-sufficient; after a dramatic surge in the 1920s, divorce rates dipped in the early 1930s, before rising to new heights at the end of the decade.[27]

Divorce was getting harder to ignore. One 1930 study found that 92.5 percent of young women surveyed "believed that divorce should be the solution for unhappy marriages, and fifty-four percent approved of divorce even if there were children." "Marriage," this study concluded, "is no longer considered an endurance test that must at all costs be won for the good of society." First lady Eleanor Roosevelt got in on the national conversation by decreeing in the pages of *Ladies' Home Journal* that divorce was both "necessary and right...when two people find it impossible to live happily together, after every effort has honestly been made to come to an understanding."[28]

Katherine had, she fully believed, tried her best to come to an understanding with Lindesay before conceding to their divorce. It was neither her wish nor her idea. Years later, when she could reflect on their marriage with detachment, she admitted that it took her "two or three years to get over Lin." After feeling utterly lost at first, during their separation, she started learning how to move on as an ex-wife, including by working to support herself. "I thought mine an unusual case," she explained, "but I discovered, when I found a job, that there were hundreds just like me. It seemed to me that the divorcée is one of the modern phenomena, one of the new products of the age. She is so new that she doesn't quite know what to do about herself yet, nor do people know what to make of her."[29]

Katherine began to look at the mistakes she had made in her first matrimonial venture and imagine them as a story she might tell others about the experience. Years later, she recalled with a mix of sadness and nostalgia

> a memory much clearer than, when I'm away from here, any memory of this room in which I sit, of [Lindesay] and me standing in that funny livingroom [sic] of the last apartment we had—the color of the walls, the way that the sunlight had faded an oblong on the green sofa, the pattern on the rug, and he and I so very young and bewildered, on the day he left. We had a banjo clock that belonged to his family, so that, afterward I sent it back to them. It had an odd sort of tick. I can remember the sound of it. I'll remember the sound of it ticking when I'm seventy if I live so long.

She once confessed, "If you asked me what I wanted most in the world, and I could bear to expose my heart face to face (which I probably could not, I'd probably say something flippant) I should tell you, to have Lindesay back again." She added, "He is the other half of me, and he knows it too. Once very recently we talked about it, soberly. But it's almost hopeless. Almost, not quite." She held on to a sliver of hope, however, because Lindesay had indicated a possible willingness to give their marriage another shot, on one condition: "if I would be willing to live on his salary in New York, and spend my money only on Lucy and the child."[30] In Ursula's stories, a version of this condition is presented by numerous male characters, who are possessed of a traditional need to support their wives and to make them dependent. It never works.

FOUR

Modern Parenting

The Parrotts' newborn spent the first months of his life in Boston before Katherine tried to integrate him into the couple's New York City life, which required plenty of logistical support from Lindesay's mother. On top of her daunting paternal relations mission, Katherine fretted that her maternal impulses were woefully inadequate. She knitted sweaters for Marc, a skill she learned as a teenager when "all the women in the world began to knit" socks and mufflers to keep American soldiers warm during the cold European winters. However, "with my usual impatience about a child's slow growth (I want him to be all grown-up you know day after tomorrow) I made them all huge, hoping he would grow into them in a month or so. So finally my sister wrote me that she preferred to buy ones that fitted." Using humor to camouflage any hurt feelings, Katherine editorialized, "No one ever encouraged my maternal instincts, at all!" Her beloved housekeeper Dado affirmed Lucy's criticism: "Whatever the Lord made you for, you'll be. But it won't be anything connecting with sewing or knitting. I promise you."[1]

That the request for fitted sweaters came from Katherine's sister is significant: Lucy functioned as a second and often primary caregiver for Marc, overseeing his day-to-day life. Following the untying of the Parrotts' marital knot in early 1928, Katherine resided in New York City while her son lived in the family home in Boston, tended to by Lucy, Dr. Towle, and the two Marys who helped with the house. Lindesay paid child support, and Katherine relied upon her ex-husband's money for Marc's care; but he did not otherwise have a significant presence in their son's life. When Parrott later wrote a story about a character whose ex-husband leaves the United States to work abroad and only saw his son "twice since his infancy" though he had "made most fair financial arrangements for his support," she was drawing on something very close to home.[2]

The summer after their divorce, Katherine "reluctantly" met with her ex: "Lucy had wanted me to get if possible a slight increase in Marc's support, for some special French lessons we're planning to have him take this Fall" when he turned five. She often acted as a go-between, negotiating resources from her ex that would undergird the wishes of her sister regarding the child's upbringing. It must have been complicated having three strong-headed caregivers (Katherine, Lucy, and Dr. Towle) and three secondary ones (Lindesay, in whatever limited capacity, and his parents, who appear to have been more involved). Modern parenting of this collaborative variety—including extended family, servants, and exes—involved negotiations and battles of will. On one occasion, Katherine took the train from Manhattan to Boston to weigh in on which elementary school Marc should attend. He was "beginning his second year at this Hill and Field school," "An Experimental Joint" with a cutting-edge educational philosophy that inspired a family feud over an issue she described, in headline form, as "Whether or Not the Child Shall Read." Dr. Towle had taught Marc "his alphabet before he was three and a half, and to read a few words." However, "at this school they wave their hands about and say 'He must not read before he's seven,'" the result of which was that Marc had forgotten his alphabet, upsetting Dr. Towle "because they won't let his grandchild be a prodigy."[3]

Henry wanted to send his grandson to a Jesuit school, but Aunt Lucy was all in for the latest methods. Although Katherine believed Marc could handle the rigor of a traditional education, she thought children should be raised "to be 'modern' according to the lights of their generation, and there is no doubt that the Shady Oak is one of the three most 'modern' schools in the country." However, she shared some of her father's concerns, referring to certain of the school's methods as "applesauce." "For instance, they transport a child to the atmosphere of medieval Merrie England. I mean exactly that," she explained. "They believe that this complex mechanical age is too difficult for a child to comprehend," so his class was observing "tadpoles turn into frogs" (the older kids were watching "guinea pigs being born"), making "wooden broadswords in the carpenter shop," and learning Morris (English folk) dancing. Dr. Towle was appalled by the school's disregard for the fundamentals. Instead of learning Greek, he complained to his daughter, Marc "learns to milk a goat, and watch a chicken come out of an egg (father hasn't heard about the guinea pigs yet, thank God) and do you want him to become a poultry farmer?" "And you spend five hundred a year," Dr. Towle added, "so that he shall not learn to read."

Since Katherine was "committed to modernity," Shady Oak won out, although she admitted that she "shall feel he's a moron if he doesn't read at seven," adding cheekily, "He'll undoubtedly be a swell Morris dancer though." She especially admired one aspect of this experiential education, which she witnessed during her visit to the campus: "the calm acceptance by the ones over six of divorce as the normal way of life for parents." As she saw it, divorce had become commonplace, at least if you judged by the number of her contemporaries who had at least one under their belts. As divorce rates rose, some observers noticed children adjusting surprisingly well to the realities of divided households, despite countervailing arguments about the devastating disintegration of American families. In 1928, *Children: The Magazine for Parents* shared a New York City private school teacher's experience with a group of under-eight-year-olds, out of which only one child had married parents: "these children were happy—and—they were actively aware of the drama of being children of divorce."[4] Problem solving, self-reliance, and emotional intelligence were useful—perhaps even necessary—skills for young people dealing with the new family structures their parents were forging.

In the early decades of the twentieth century, doctors, psychologists, social workers, and reformers were lavishing attention on child-rearing and education, as well as on mothering. "What Is to Become of Your Baby?" asked G. Stanley Hall, author of several books on the subject, in *Cosmopolitan* magazine. "Will children reared under the new, scientific methods be superior mentally and physically to those reared in the old-fashioned way of our mothers?"[5] Like everything else about life, parenting was undergoing modernization, in no small part because shifts in women's work outside of the home and an increase in divorce were complicating the logistics of traditional child-rearing.

Not long after the Parrotts' divorce in 1928, Marc visited his mother in New York "for an hour or two" on his way to camp. "He's been at the shore all July, and [camp] was the solution Lucy and I chose, for August," she reported, casually remarking on coparenting with her sister. On this occasion, she found Marc overwhelming. "He disconcerted me," she explained, because he had "grown about four inches this Spring" and was "anything but a pathetic child"—almost too grown up since she saw him last, several months before.[6]

She took him to lunch and then to the train station "to meet one of his play-school teachers, who's counsellor at the camp." "He doesn't fuss about these journeys any more," she was relieved to find. "But I don't know…there he was, a very properly dressed child, in dark blue linen shorts and blouse for travelling, and sensible correct ugly shoes, and the doublebreasted navy coat and beret they all wear, being turned over to this woman with two other well-dressed calm young children to go to camp for six weeks. Going along in a very matter-of-fact way with a porter carrying his suitcase, and he isn't five years old." Shady Oak had done its job, perhaps too well.

To commemorate his send off, she bought him a "huge cake of Park and Tilford's milk chocolate, which is supposed to be very pure," though she suspected that "the counsellor'll take it away from him, no doubt." "I know this is a better system," she asserted about sending him away. "I was a very spoiled child and he won't be.… But such a philosophical sullen-eyed little boy, trotting off to live some more under ideal psychological conditions. (It says so in the prospectus.)" She had now had her "semi-annual half day as a parent."

Though this was a quippy underestimation of their time together, her flippancy concealed real anxieties. Her own mother had been absent for long periods during her childhood because of her ailing health, but the sense of distance she now felt from her son, in tandem with his jarringly precocious autonomy, rattled her. Around this time, the general secretary of the Bureau of Social Hygiene in New York City observed, in an article on "Divorce and the Child," that "the impulse toward individualism is the tempo of the age," a necessary outgrowth of women's "mental and economic freedom" that was making itself evident in children of divorce.[7]

Parrott embraced many modern and scientific ideas about parenting, especially those regarding children's autonomy. Of course, this was a convenient philosophy for someone who had no intention of being a traditional, full-time mother. Juggling work and a child was extremely difficult, but especially so for unmarried women, and like many things in her life there was no clear way to manage the undertaking, so she did the best she could. This became even more complicated following her father's death in 1930, after which Parrott purchased "Twin Elms," her first country estate, which replaced the Dorchester family house as home base for Marc and Lucy—as well as Dado (see figure 11). Located in Wilton, Connecticut, an easy sixty-mile train ride from New York City, this began a new era for Marc, whom she "wasn't going to bring up in the city." At Twin Elms, mother and son spent "lots of time together, and we read history together. I want him to like it." She fostered

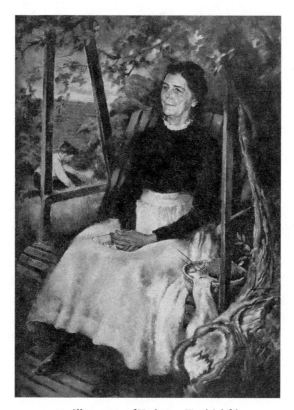

FIGURE 11. Illustration of Katherine Towle's lifelong domestic caregiver, Mary Donahue, with her son Marc playing in the background, from Parrott's nonfiction reminiscences of her childhood, "Dado." (*Woman's Day*, November 1946.)

his intellect and interests, taking him "to every museum in this part of the country where there are dinosaurs. He drags me everywhere that he thinks he will find one."[8]

Parrott realized that one of her greatest challenges was that she had "to be father and mother." Lindesay's absence was a constant concern, and she felt pressure to overcompensate for his disinterest. "Children of the divorced," as she described this group, were part of the reorganization of society in an age of marital impermanence. She tried to fill the holes created by Lindesay's absence, usually—after she began making it—with what money could buy. While discussing things she had purchased or was planning to purchase for Marc's benefit—the house in Connecticut, a horse, a swimming pool—she explained that she was "delighted to do all these things. I'm trying desperately to make up for Marc not having a father. He misses that. The other boys at school talk of their fathers, and I can see it hurts him. What's the answer to that?" As she worked through the unresolved threads from the fraying fabric of family life, she observed the downstream costs of divorce. "Marriage may be finished in this age—but what of children?"[9]

In some ways, however, hers was not a new or even unusual way of parenting. Parents of means had long relied on nannies and nurses, boarding schools and summer camps, spending time with their children when it was convenient to do so during holidays and vacations. This was especially common with affluent Boston families, who founded some of the nation's first boarding schools, many of which were in the Northeast.[10] What was different about this arrangement was that she was undertaking this as a divorced single mother, eventually with a career that underwrote most of the arrangements, not as one of a pair of globetrotting parents behaving according to the customs of their class. In Parrott's story *Forever, Perhaps!*, the widower Muriel only spent Sundays with her son, "who lived for the rest of the week in a small boys' school that was much more tranquil and orderly than any life his mother might have evolved with him." This was a rationalization. But it was also a practical solution in an age that made allowances for decreased maternal sentiment, experiments with modern educational methods, and even psychological validation for altered parental relations.

Since she spent so much time away from him, some of Katherine's friends questioned why she bothered to keep her son at all. One offered his unsolicited recommendation that she would "be better off if you gave that child to the Parrotts, once for all." Lindesay's parents had, more than once, offered to assume her son's care. Her response was a one-word "no." She did, however, maintain a relationship with Marc's paternal grandparents, going to a periodic "long drinking dinner with my ex-paper in law." At one of these, she and Professor Parrott "met for a long talk about Marc's future—the tenth millionth long talk"—during which he "went on about what he had expected his children to turn out like—and took hours of highballs to get Reconciled to realities (his phrase)," deriving from his disappointment over Lindesay and Katherine's divorce and its consequences for his grandchild.[11]

Her initial reliance on Lindesay for economic support made it hard for her to make and execute decisions about her son's upbringing. This all changed after she became both wealthy and famous, seemingly overnight, at the end of 1929, just as Marc was turning six. When she burst into the public eye, Ursula spoke openly about her son. *Screenland* magazine made a gentle

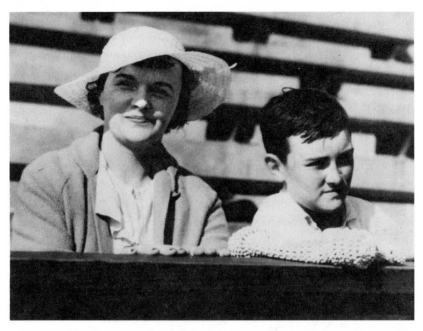

FIGURE 12. March 1935 press photo of Ursula Parrott and her son Marc watching a tennis tournament at the Hamilton, Bermuda, tennis stadium. Parrott never missed an opportunity to discuss how she was raising her son. (ACME Newspictures, author's collection.)

joke about her unabashed dedication to Marc, "whose picture we must all admire." "Hollywood is having a hard time understanding Miss Parrott," *Chicago Sunday Tribune* columnist Rosalind Shaffer reported, explaining that she "is the mother of a 7 year old child to whom she is devoted." Ursula was not reluctant to claim her son as part of her life. Speaking about how she was raising him was an important assertion about being an unmarried mother, made at a time in which there were few outspoken models for this role. A press photo of Ursula with Marc during a trip to Bermuda shows the two of them watching a match at the Hamilton Tennis Stadium (see figure 12). Ursula smiles directly at the camera, looking pleased to be alongside her son.[12] She was proud of being a parent, married or not. In this modern age, why should her marital status have any bearing on her fitness as a mother?

Many, in fact, admired Ursula's parenting. Journalist Helen Welshimer anointed her a "very modern mother" who was raising her son commendably during an unprecedented era for parenting. Columnist Charles Driscoll observed that "she devoted much thought and money on the education of her son, Marc, hiring special private coaches for him in tennis and other games." In an interview in which she discussed child-rearing methods, Ursula described plans to take her son out of school so that he could "spend the winter in France" since making him worldly was one of her priorities. "I won't have an over-developed little prodigy for a son," she insisted, "who is ready for college at 16. He's going to be going on 18 before he is a freshman." True to her word, nine-year-old Marc had his European winter and spring.[13] She did not just talk about modern parenting; she put her resources and will into seeing her philosophy through.

Sometimes their adventures had undesired consequences. Ursula had fond remembrances of road trips she took as a child with her parents through the New England countryside, and she wanted to offer analogous experiences for her son. So in 1937, when he was thirteen, she rented a car and drove Marc from Tucson to Florence, Arizona, stopping in small towns along the way. As they were departing Nogales, a young man whom she later described as "nice mannered, wearing a brown suit and an olive drab hat, and about five feet ten inches tall" asked for a ride. "I told him that I did not want to take him because my car was loaded with luggage," she defensively explained to the press, adding, "If I had been in the east I would never have taken him but he seemed a nice man and I relented." Once on the road, the man's demeanor changed. He drew a gun to enact "a typical western holdup," forcing Ursula and Marc out of the car. The man drove off with her purse and their luggage in the rental car, leaving mother and son to walk the highway until a passing motorist eventually picked them up.[14]

The perpetrator of this carjacking was Johnny Quantrell, a convicted first-degree murderer serving a life sentence. Quantrell had just pulled off his fourth prison escape and was eventually captured and rejailed. The punchline to the story came when Ursula was sued for $1,600 by the rental car agency "because she could not return the automobile." Despite newspaper headline proof of what happened, the agency charged that "Mrs. Parrott had refused to pay."[15] This was evidence—if any was needed—that trouble followed Ursula wherever she went.

Despite Parrott's outspoken commitment to providing a stimulating childhood for Marc—travel, a country estate, boarding school, summer camps—she was not as confident about her methods or their outcomes as she seemed. She did not, however, discuss her insecurities in interviews, for which she always put on a good face; rather, Parrott used her stories to air her parenting anxieties. "Appointment with Tomorrow" includes the reflections of a forty-year-old man who has raised a daughter on his own: "He had believed that he was devoted to her. Yet he was invariably busy. The time they shared in the intervals between her schools and summer camps he spent conscientiously in the way he thought he would entertain her. He took her to theatres, to concerts occasionally, for brief journeys by car or train to places supposed to be of interest, historic or otherwise, to a growing girl. But—there hadn't been time to know her well, and their relationship had grown increasingly formal." Although Parrott was not at all sentimental, she had precisely these concerns about parenting performed largely from a distance.

In "First Love," she imagined how children in divorced families yearn for their absent father's affections. Neither Stephen nor Martha lack anything material; they are clothed, fed, and housed. But their first Christmas at boarding school unites them through a shared sadness when their mothers forget to send them presents allegedly from their absent fathers (who would never remember to do so themselves), an ongoing charade. Stephen and Martha are ashamed when surrounded by the patter of "my father gave me this" and "my father gave me that." They bond over their shared sorrow, backing each other's fictions about caring, attentive fathers for the benefit of the other children, who, in possession of complete families, tease the pair about what they are missing.

In "Peter Keeps Memorial Day," Peter, age nine, lives with his childless Aunt Janet and Uncle Roger. The child recalls the last time he saw his "much-married" mother, when she brought her latest fiancé to Janet and Roger's home. During this visit Eleanor asked her sister—who is, like Lucy Towle, ten years her senior—to keep Peter permanently because "he's better off" in a quiet, stable home. Janet pleaded with Eleanor to break her engagement, "Live in Boston with Roger and me. Acquire some dignity." Eleanor's answer was cowardly but honest: "Thanks just the same, and have Boston make allowances for the rest of my life? It's much too late. I should go mad." Peter, overhearing all of this, watched his mother drive off. He "never knew which of her husbands that one was."

Parrott's most difficult and personal observations about parenting were nestled in her tales about unmarried mothers. In her serialized story, "Breadwinner," the widow Linda's young daughter is being raised in Ohio by her family: "Though she chose for it French frocks from the smartest Avenue shops, her own motherhood seemed a little unreal." Linda, who lives in New York, only sees her daughter a couple times a year because she wants her to be raised in a secure, stable environment and knows that her career requires all her energy and time. When Linda starts making enough money to move her daughter east, along with an aunt, who (again like Lucy) cares for her child, she buys a home in nearby Connecticut where she can see her daughter more often. But as in "Appointment with Tomorrow," the young girl is indifferent to her mother's affections. Linda realizes, "It's absurd to be disappointed that the child doesn't love me. How could she? She has seen so little of me." Four years later, Linda looks "at the little girl who was her own" and "felt a wrench at her heart." "She had managed so far to give her daughter a secure childhood, even if she had not managed to give her much of herself." This unintended consequence of women's ambitions was not quite a lesson, for Parrott offered no solutions; but it was an acknowledgment of just how difficult it was to feel good about modern parenting.

The recurrence of inattentive mothers in Parrott's stories did not go unnoticed. One letter to the editor of *Redbook*, from Mrs. O.G. of Indiana, complains about too many Ursula Parrott stories in which mothers are possessed of "pint-sized intelligence," spend "time and money on gin rummy and bridge," and are "spoiled and hysterical" or "silly." Mrs. O.G. accusatorily asks, "Where does Ursula Parrott find the pattern for her mother characters?" "I am sure that I would never survive the shock if I found a down-to-earth, real mother" in a Parrott story.[16] Mrs. O.G. might have been even more shocked by the answer to her question, as well as by the notion that many women saw reflections of their mothering dilemmas in the same stories she found so impossible to believe.

FIVE

Greenwich Village

THE PATH TO BECOMING A "SELF-SUFFICIENT, INDEPENDENT, SUCCESSFUL MANAGER OF HER OWN LIFE"

Many young women of Katherine's generation, who came of age in the first decades of the twentieth century, were rethinking what was possible for their lives. Women could now get college educations, pursue careers (which made it easier to stay intentionally single, should one wish), and even enter politics. Divorce rates and skirt lengths rose, seemingly in tandem. When young women began bobbing their hair to lengths unthinkably short—"of course Greenwich Village lassies wear short locks but society's doing it too" declared the *New York Times* in 1920—many fretted that through this act alone women were descending into immorality and "radicalism."[1] The idea of gender equality, at least in some arenas, was on the table in a meaningful way for the first time. Advocates for the status quo, however, argued that women's desire for education, the right to vote, jobs outside the home, unaccompanied travel, and pleasure seeking foretold a domino-like instability in every aspect of life. Those who wrung their hands about this were not incorrect: new patterns of behavior for women were changing the character of American life.

By the 1920s, the United States had become a nation of cities, in which more people lived than on farms or in small towns. New York City, a mere 322 square miles in size, had a population of 7.5 million in 1938. Some saw this "cityward trend" as marching in tandem with "religious and moral decline" because the "city environment is inherently inconsistent with a sound religious and moral life and sentiment." Urbanization, one 1927 study argued, was a "threat to the welfare of society."[2] In no place was this more evident than in New York City, and in no neighborhood within it more so than Greenwich Village.

When Kitty first arrived with Lindesay in the early 1920s, Greenwich Village had long been considered "a symbol of the repudiation of traditional values," as the writer Malcolm Cowley put it in his remembrances of Village life. Cowley, in fact, brought a recent Radcliffe graduate to a Liberal Club fundraiser in the legendary bohemian neighborhood not long after the end of the Great War. "I noticed people gathering about the Radcliffe young lady admiringly," until she began "biting them in the arm and shrieking." "We never saw her after that night. She had met a copy-desk man and later I heard that he was asking the address of an abortionist; still later she wrote that she was married and had a baby." Although it is implausible that this young woman described by Cowley could actually have been Kitty, his description is a reminder that an attractive, educated, thrill-seeking young woman descending on the city and embracing its hedonisms was not at all unique. "There were many people like that," Cowley noted; "they appeared in the Village, made themselves the center of a dance or a crowd...then suddenly they were gone." Young men also arrived "from week to week, as colleges held commencement exercises or troops were demobilized," a mass migration of young people drawn to the "idea of living for the moment." Cowley characterized the Village as "the home of lasting impermanence," filled with people living by the notion that "it is stupid to pile up treasures that we can enjoy only in old age, when we have lost capacity for enjoyment. Better to seize the moment as it comes, to dwell in it intensely, even at the cost of future suffering."[3]

Earlier denizens of Greenwich Village had mixed their pleasures with a commitment to making art and literature that bucked convention, engaging with radical politics, pushing for liberalizations on numerous fronts, and laying the intellectual and creative groundwork that helped to make New York into the United States' cultural capitol. These impulses still existed, but Parrott was onto something when she characterized the years she spent there as "the war's over—have a good time" era. As one of her later story characters declares, "I don't think I'm capable of taking anything with desperate seriousness, after the war," and so one did as one pleased and dealt with the consequences at a later date. F. Scott Fitzgerald similarly characterized his generation of pleasure seekers as people desperately looking for outlets for "all the nervous energy stored up and unexpended in the War." New Yorkers of the era were, the writer Ben Hecht observed, "devoted to pleasure, particularly to the pleasure of not giving a damn."[4]

The Village—which was both a literal place and what the historian Christine Stansell calls "a selective vision of city life"—had long been a haven for writers; artists whose low-rent studios doubled as staging grounds for all-through-the-night parties; culture changers like birth control advocate Margaret Sanger and anarchist, feminist Emma Goldman; and wealthy patrons like Mabel Dodge who hosted fabled salons where the aforementioned types mingled after listening to lectures on cutting-edge topics of the day. Nicknamed the "American Montparnasse," a reference to the fashionably shabby Paris neighborhood inhabited by artists who practiced "free love, free verse, and all the isms, social and esthetic," the Village was also renowned for being a magnet for liberal thinkers, especially of the feminist variety.[5]

One contemporary study of the neighborhood concluded that people who were "drawn to the Village came to seek escape from their community, their families, or themselves," or "to reconcile new conditions with whatever remained of their traditional ways"—precisely the aims that drew people like Katherine as they sought to buck convention. Most Villagers felt that unmarried couples should be able to live together, that even married women should work, and that divorces should be easier to get. In this environment, it was presumed that women should have equal pay and "the same opportunity for drinking, smoking, taking or dismissing lovers." As one of Ursula Parrott's narrators explained, "The New York in which they moved was a liberal city: If she married Keith, no one would care very much about the precise details."[6] The city allowed people to evade the kind of judgment they might experience in a small town or a more conservative city like Boston, which also meant that those who fretted about its corrupting influence on the wider culture were right.

Parrott's generation saw the emergence of the first significant female professional class and a near doubling of the number of married women who worked, either out of necessity or a desire for stimulation outside the home. During the Great War, many jobs and careers (Parrott always differentiated between the two, one being a matter of wages and the other a more intrinsically satisfying pursuit) were made available to women for the first time. After the war, however, men returned en masse with the expectation that they would be taking back their positions, resulting in significant reversals in women's progress in the workforce. In one postwar study, Dr. Elizabeth Kemper Adams saw that "women who worked shoulder to shoulder with men are discovering that the masculine shoulder may again be coldly turned" as workplace competition was drawn across gender lines for the first time in US history. Dr. Adams offered no opinion about how women's professions might impact the institution of marriage, however, since this "is a topic in too unsettled and transitional a state to admit of more than brief consideration."[7]

This question was, however, in the air. "Scores of eager girls just step-ping out of college, scores even of already happily married women, are ask-ing themselves the question: How shall they have the heritage of happiness implied in a husband and children and still retain the mental activity and stimulus of interesting work," another study observed. New York City adver-tising executive Helen Woodward described a related problem: "A man is expected to do better than a woman. He is trained to feel ashamed when he doesn't." In a marriage, this could be disastrous—as many an Ursula Parrott plot would detail.[8]

The norms of Village life did not resonate, or even make sense, outside of it. There is a stark contrast, for example, between encouraging women to obtain educations but not to use them in the same way as men, as was often the case at women's colleges, and what was happening in a place like Green-wich Village, where it was presumed that women wanted and should have the same things from life as men.[9] This included sex, and part of learning to be a woman of this time and in this place meant learning how to navigate sex in the city. When Parrott discussed what it was like to be an unattached woman, she did not always paint a pretty picture. The men she met were sexu-ally aggressive, and alcohol made them more insistent.

At the tail end of a long night on the speakeasy circuit with two of her reg-ular male companions, Katherine observed that "we're an ill-mannered gen-eration, and all that, but people should not get so drunk they announce their secret ambitions to each-other across a speak-easy table," advances she man-aged to deflect on this occasion. In her circle at least, sex was not taboo—to talk about or to have. Still, she wondered, "We weren't any of us brought up the Pride of the Brothel, why must we always act it?" Women like her wanted to be perceived as women of their time. The fact that they had sex before, dur-ing, and outside of marriage, however, often complicated their lives. This was the era of Sigmund Freud, who "provided a philosophical justification and made it unfashionable to be repressed" and was understood as giving a "sci-entific imprimatur...to self-indulgence."[10] In the absence of rules governing courtship that guided earlier generations, women like Katherine had to fig-ure out how to have, negotiate, and survive affairs.

After her separation from Lindesay, one of Katherine's most significant affairs was with Nickolas Muray, a Hungarian-born photographer and com-mercial illustrator. In 1927, she met Muray in the Village, where she spent time at cafes and densely packed apartment parties where drinking, smoking, and sexual antics often abounded. At the time, Muray was developing a reputation as "*the* Village photographer and *a* Village character whose Wednesday-night studio parties were invariably a cross section of celebrities from both uptown and downtown." His MacDougal Street studio was frequented by Edna St. Vincent Millay, Sinclair Lewis, Eugene O'Neill, and Heywood Broun, not to mention curious young women like Katherine.[11]

When their affair was coming to an end, Katherine penned a meditation on his decision to terminate it, written largely in a distancing third person voice she used throughout her life when tackling difficult matters: "She had told him that sooner or later she would shed some tears over him, and apparently the moment had arrived."[12] Her newly adopted New Yorker wit saved her from mawkishness: "Not very many tears—just three blocks north and two blocks east, of tears." She was "so afraid of sounding sentimental about things" and tried to shed the creaky moral baggage of the Victorian Age; her relationship with Muray was part of her education on being a woman of her time, to which she wanted to pay tribute.

Muray "had been completely honest with her,—had never pretended" that theirs would be more than a brief affair, which "left her quite self-respecting." She knew the deal when she entered it, even if she would have preferred different terms—a lesson she carried forward with great difficulty. Muray "had treated her always as a person, and not as a female thing to be fed cocktails or kissed into a state of acquiescence. And because of that…he had made sex, again, to her, a very beautiful thing. So that she would not any more let it become a tawdry business, mixed up with permitting one's self to be mauled in a taxi-cab, and that sort of thing." Such humiliating rites of passage were avoided by women of her grandmother's generation through early, long-lasting marriages.

She credited Muray with making her, "for the first time in her life probably, genuinely anxious to be [a] self-sufficient, independent, successful manager of her own life." He had encouraged her to take up one of his favorite pastimes, fencing, "so that she felt better, physically, than in years." Now she wanted "to find a job in which she could do decent work. And then work hard at it a long time." Careers and independence were, in the recent past, male domains; now they were rightfully hers as well. In her farewell missive, she did not anticipate her next romance. In this moment, before fame and prior to three other failed marriages, what Katherine Ursula Parrott most wanted was self-sufficiency.

Parrott would eventually write novels that affirmed that some sexual relationships—and even marriages—were simply not meant to last. "Some people have criticized me severely," she told an interviewer, "for writing so plainly about sex. But that is the one thing in which most of us are interested—if we are honest." She went on to say, "Many more people have criticized me for refusing to make my heroines sweet young things. But that I don't care to do. I don't write about sweet young things because I feel women today are more experienced than they were twenty years ago. And since I write about typical modern girls, I insist that they be typical!"[13]

Liberated ideas about female sexuality were emanating out from the big cities like New York and into the provinces through magazines, books, and movies, leading people like the Right Rev. William Hall Moreland to blame novels and short stories for being "tainted with an insidious form of free love presented in literary form," encouraging people to accept promiscuity as a normal way of life. Another way to look at it, as one 1930 study did, was to admire the "realistic modern novel" and its calm acceptance of women who loved more than one man over the course of their lives, and to acknowledge that "these relationships are matters of sex attraction . . . and not the result of a pre-destined coming together for two individuals who could not have found happiness with any one else."[14]

Speakeasies, clubs, and restaurants—and the attire required to look up-to-the-minute in them—came at a significant expense, even if one sang for one's supper every now and then. After her divorce, Katherine had to support herself and so undertook a series of part-time jobs, largely at advertising agencies and in department stores. One of her surviving letters to Muray, typed on Bloomingdale Bros., Inc. letterhead, describes "walking up Madison avenue" on the way "to a morning at the advertising business," one of her several "jobs-but-not-careers" with which she supported herself after her marriage ended.[15]

According to her neighbor at the time, the writer Alice Hughes, Kitty was "a little Boston-Irish girl five feet tall and full of ginger" who lived beside her in a "dingy brownstone" where they were both "recovering from first marriages" and struggling to make ends meet. "I am living on milk," Kitty complained when she was out of work in 1928, had run up debt through several charge accounts, and had only one work prospect: an offer to "wear a grey taffeta frock like a maid in a show." The dress was a tiny size thirteen, leading her to declare that she "shan't dare eat more than three glasses of milk a day all week." She was determined to get a "newspaper job," but after being turned down by every city editor in town Kitty jested that she was "just a girl that newspaper men like, but city editors don't appreciate," referring to her relationships with both her ex and her present, an up-and-coming journalist named Hugh O'Connor, whom she had recently begun seeing. When she finally took a position for $90 a week, writing for a department store advertising department, she lamented that it was likely she would "ache to work on a paper" all her life.[16]

Katherine also realized that reporting "work in New York has some particular disadvantages." She described a meeting with a city desk editor of the New York *Sun*: "[He] went on about how disillusioned I'd get about newspaper work, and how it would break my heart to find out how little of the story got in the paper finally. To which I just kept saying that I knew all that.... I had been with newspaper people all my life," and since "he wanted details on that...I mentioned Lin in one sentence." O'Connor's name came up next, to which the editor replied, "Well, I never heard that Hugh O'Connor was a specifically good judge of women reporters, but he is an excellent judge of women, all right." In what she described as "a nice cold Boston voice," Katherine responded, "Really, Mr. Barrett. I can't quite see the relation of that interesting observation to our conversation." The chastened editor reconsidered his stance, replying that unfortunately he had "nothing doing on a woman's angle in politics this week." He would think it over and "may give you a shot at it."[17] Katherine did not get the shot, but she did recognize the maddening sexism of the newspaper world, and on more than one occasion.

She went from one editorial office to the next in 1928 and was turned away each time. She inquired with the managing editor at the *New York World* so frequently that he eventually told her, "You're a nice girl, but I doubt if you can write at all," hoping to put a stop to her visits. She eventually learned why. One night at a party, after a steady stream of highballs, Terry, her partner in infidelity during her marriage to Lindesay, whisked her into a closed-door room in his apartment to tell her something "that you won't like to hear." "I knew a month ago that you wanted a newspaper job, Kitty," he continued, because "Lin called me up to tell me so." "He said, 'Terry, I had lunch...with Kitty yesterday, and she's trying to get a job on a paper. I won't have her on a paper in this town if I can help it.... It might complicate things for me sometime, somewhere."[18]

Man to man, Lindesay told Terry, "You can see that it would be a damn nuisance to me to have [a] wife I left turning up on a paper." Terry surmised, "It will drive him simply crazy if you get a job on a paper, and meet all his friends and they like you." Terry defiantly declared that he would introduce Katherine to everyone he could in the newspaper world: "I owe you a debt, for silence long ago. I sometimes think that silence must have added to your difficulties." Her decision not to name Terry to Lindesay as her partner in one-night-stand crime had at least afforded her some understanding of why a career as a reporter in New York City would never come to pass.

Reconciled to realities, as she might have put it, Katherine applied to Kresge's "enormous new store" in Newark for a full-time job as a fashion copywriter and stylist. She decamped from Manhattan to make the ten-mile trek to New Jersey, where—much to her surprise—she "was offered the job for seventy five" a week but "held out for ninety." Parrott had little love for the work, complaining that "writing about Summer furs and the latest in hosiery got on her nerves."[19] She soon realized that "the only way one gets out is to get out, and if one waits for an excellent time, one stays in," and so a few months later she quit her job: "It's just what I don't want to do."

As it turned out, however, she was good at advertising and—having been barred from the New York newspaper world—bad at identifying an alternative career. "I'm a brilliant copywriter," she proclaimed sarcastically, but "the routine drives me simply crazy." She also acknowledged a personal weakness, which had been evident during her student days at Radcliffe and would plague her future writing career: "I'm always late." The desire for a regular paycheck eventually won out and she accepted another full-time job in the summer of 1928, this time in the advertising department at Arnold Constable & Company on Fifth Avenue. At least this job had a shorter commute and a better address.

After months of writing copy at Arnold Constable, she applied for a long-shot publicity director position at Bedell's department stores. Much to her surprise, she landed it and was offered her first ever salary of $5,000 a year, roughly the equivalent of $80,000 today.[20] This was a real job, the kind that could be a first step in a career. Katherine celebrated the way she liked best, by purchasing "a couple of expensive black dresses, long-skirted, the Lord & Taylor type." Never a saver, she justified her impulse to spend—often on credit, as the stores now allowed—to reward herself for her achievements: "It's a good deal of kudos, for my age, as those things go in retail advertising." She needed a decent salary, too, since she had so many expenses, for "Marc's clothes, and my creditors, and the things I've got used to having." "That last is pretty much what does for all of us. Or makes Successes of all of us, depending on viewpoint." At least she could pay off some bills and start saving for a hoped-for trip to Paris. She was pleased to be "running [her] own department," although she had no love for the work. She joked: "Someday, God, when I have saved money, and lived down my reputation for being temperamental…I shall go find something I'll be crazy about doing, and do it for eighteen a week. Probably do it on crutches, by then."[21]

At Bedell's she learned "how to be an advertising manager": budgeting, ordering paper, doing layouts and typography. She was pleased that "there'll be pages in Vogue and Harper's to play with," high-profile magazine outlets for her work. Since her boss "has just heard something about modernistic art," she saw an opportunity to "out Saks Saks" by hiring photographer Ben Pinchot and model Marion Morehouse, the future wife of e.e. cummings: "Pinchot's got some new lighting effects that go [Edward] Steichen one better." Parrott was getting ambitious and refining her aesthetic sensibilities. Her newfound zest for life compelled her to Tammany Hall in the summer of 1928 to join her ward block because she was proud to be "a Dummocrat, a Cath'lic, and Irish."[22] She may not have agitated for the vote, but since she had the ability to cast one, she would.

Parrott later described her three years of intermittent advertising work as a valuable experience in "an amazing field." At the time, women often held copywriter positions in New York City department stores, generating content—by women for women—for ads, direct-by-mail flyers, and package inserts. The job went beyond the limits of secretarial or behind-the-counter sales work and provided writing experience on quick deadlines, albeit within the confines of what was required to sell hats, dresses, and lingerie. One 1921 women's vocational manual advised that those interested in the profession should be possessed of "few nerves, for many times work must be done under pressure and copy written 'while the presses wait,'" although it also counseled against considering "advertising as literature," with one experienced woman copy editor explaining that "it is really salesmanship clearly expressed." Some female advertising copy editors explicitly warned "that this field is not the place for those whose ambition is to 'write.'"[23]

Parrott, in fact, later wrote about department store advertising in several of her stories and novels, including *Ex-Wife*, in which the female protagonist enters the spring season, dives into writing Easter apparel ads, and produces fashion pages after frantic buyers' conferences: "Rush the art work; rush the cuts; rush copy to the typographer; tell him to rush proofs."[24] Indeed, Parrott found the frenzied pace of the job exhausting; she once complained about having to write "thirty-four ads, which is three full pages, today. Each one dumber than its predecessor, and the first one outstandingly dumb." She worried about getting stuck in an uninspiring career, fretting once that "there are no jobs in the world you know, except in department stores." When she came home one night, tipsy from drinks with her newspaper pals, to find that her friend Alice Hughes had just been published—with a byline no less—in the *Evening Telegram*, she was "completely utterly overcome with jealousy...by gosh if she can get herself...well, anyways, eyes absolutely green with envy."[25] Jealousy was a good reminder of the work she actually wanted to do.

Writing was already Kitty Parrott's trade, but not in the way she hoped. When pressed by her lover, Hugh O'Connor, about why she was not trying her hand at more ambitious writing, she said that it was because she was simply unable to "write pieces" for newspapers or magazines, to which he responded, "You mean you won't." His answer rattled her. "I was startled," she recalled, "but put it away to take up later. I mean I can't. What the hell could I write pieces about, and who the hell would buy them?" She went on, "Only the tabloids buy pieces about the GREAT Facts," by which she meant of women's lives, "and only then if one has gone to [prison in] Sing Sing because of difficulties with them," alluding to the commercial appeal of sensational true crime tales about husband-murdering women. Referring to a Cockney copywriter she worked with at one of her department store jobs who regaled her with tawdry stories about her life, Parrott half jested that perhaps she could write them up and title them "Places from Which I Have Walked Home." "I can think of title you see," she reasoned, "but not pieces to sell."[26] As it turned out, such stories were salable. In fact, Parrott had already experienced enough of life to populate many of them; she just needed encouragement to write them down.

SIX

Hugh O'Connor

HIGH FELICITY ON THE "ROAD OF NO RULES"

After her separation from Lindesay but before her January 1928 divorce, Katherine Ursula Parrott entered into a relationship with a charismatic and intractable, red-headed newspaper reporter named Hugh O'Connor (see figure 13). Parrott and O'Connor had an on-again, off-again affair that began in 1927 and lasted until around 1933. She began her writing career because of his encouragement. She developed her ideas about modern relations between men and women through their debates, which vacillated between the Socratic and the sadistic, in the process learning the limits of her tolerance for the new morality. She experienced the felicities, as she called them, of an intensely pleasurable sexual relationship with him, even as she underwent multiple abortions because he did not want to have children with her. When things were good between them, she wanted nothing more from life; when things were bad, she felt that she would rather die than endure the emotional pain he put her through. O'Connor loomed over Parrott's career, appeared in many guises in her published fiction, and was, by her own estimation, the most wonderful and most awful thing that ever happened to her.

Born on February 16, 1894, in New York City, Hugh O'Connor and his three siblings were raised on 21st Street in Manhattan. In the 1890s, Chelsea was a working-class and poor immigrant neighborhood, populated by newcomers from Europe and Russia. Hugh's father, a saloon keeper and later a brush salesman, and mother, who supplemented the family's income by doing domestic work, were—like the Towles—Irish immigrants. Hugh attended La Salle Academy and Columbia University and eventually earned a civil engineering degree from Cooper Union. Along with many young men of his generation, he heeded the call during World War I, in which he served as a first lieutenant of field artillery with the 304th. Starting in August 1918,

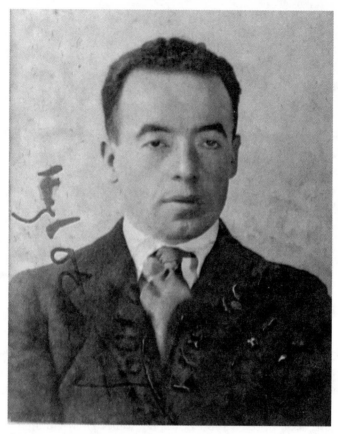

FIGURE 13. The man who nudged Parrott to write her first book, Hugh O'Connor, as he appeared in his January 17, 1920, passport application. (Passport #166098, courtesy of the National Archives and Records Administration.)

the twenty-four-year-old saw action on the perilous western front, including the battles at Aisne-Marne, Champagne-Marne, Saint-Mihiel, and Meuse-Argonne, bloody campaigns that helped bring the long war to its close. Parrott often remarked that men of her generation who fought in the war felt they were owed the hedonism in which they indulged on their return, shaping the new morality through their pursuit of life's pleasures in an effort to forget their horrific experiences, as turned out to be the case with O'Connor. Following an honorable discharge, he enrolled at the Sorbonne and then returned stateside, where he got his first reporting job at the *New York Herald* followed by a string of publications that would eventually include the

New York Evening Sun, *New York World*, *New York Herald Tribune*, *New York Times*, as well as the *American Magazine* and the *New Yorker*.[1]

In 1920, O'Connor married Dorothy Brenner, nicknamed Dot. Unintimidated by the new breed of career women about whom much handwringing was taking place, he married a woman who was bright and ambitious, with a job working for the Rockefeller Foundation's *Journal of General Physiology*. Theirs was not a conventional marriage. They lived apart for much of it, having on and off encounters with each other during what seemed, from the outside at least, like an open marriage.[2]

When Parrott began her affair with O'Connor in 1927, he was married to Dot, and she to Lindesay. They likely met at one of the many parties or speakeasies where New York reporters mixed. Parrott found the five-foot-eight O'Connor handsome, athletic, and worldly—and he was equally drawn to her. She was a recently separated, cash-poor occasional model and freelance writer, and he was an up-and-coming reporter and notorious ladies' man. "I was fully sorry you were a newspaperman when I first met you," she told O'Connor in one of the hundreds of letters she wrote to him. After running such a rocky course and coming to such a bad end with her first reporter, Lindesay, she "felt that life just didn't owe [her] any more newspapermen." Wives and girlfriends of reporters, she halfheartedly jested, lived in a state of constant disappointment, with deadlines always winning out. After the premature death of one of Parrott's friends, she reminded O'Connor that the deceased, "Poor John [Regan]," was the one who urged her "so strenuously" not to involve herself with him, a warning that she did not heed.[3] Although Parrott would later claim that she did not regret getting involved with O'Connor no matter how unhappy he made her, she must certainly have wondered what her life would have been like had she more seriously considered Regan's warning.

In the beginning, though, it was wonderful. During the couple's honeymoon phase, O'Connor told Parrott that in her he had found "the one woman" whom he believed his "equal." Writing to him while he was traveling on assignment about a night on the town involving countless "Tom Collinses" at speakeasies and dinner at Sardi's, Parrott reassured O'Connor that "one doesn't kiss anyone else, or want to"—she was head over heels for him. They often stayed up all night debating local, national, and global politics. In addition to their thrilling intellectual exchanges, they had a ferocious physical attraction to each other. Parrott believed that she was "the most fortunate of women, for [she] had found not just a lover, a gay friend, but comprehension." She struggled for a word that would adequately define their relationship, referring to it as "a friendship, affair, or whatever inadequate label one chooses to affix to the emotions you and I share."[4]

But there was a wrinkle. For reasons she could not understand, O'Connor would not pull the plug on his marriage. Out of deference to his still-wife and to protect his ascending career, O'Connor insisted on certain restraints when they were in public, which Parrott began to feel shameful about maintaining. But if their relationship was supposed to be beneath the radar, theirs seemed to be the secret that everyone knew about, including her ex-husband's parents. She told O'Connor that over lunch one day with her ex-in-laws that they asked her if she was planning on marrying him, to which she replied, "No, I did not plan to I just hope to."[5]

About a year into their affair, O'Connor went on assignment to cover President Calvin Coolidge's summer retreat in Wisconsin and subsequent return to Washington, DC, resulting in months of separation. When he traveled for work, reunions occurred on O'Connor's schedule, for which Parrott rearranged her life, taking trains to meet him as far away as the Midwest and as close as Albany. At O'Connor's invitation, Parrott took a train to Brule, Wisconsin, in the middle of the hot summer of 1928. She was thrilled about taking a long train trip, never having traveled by rail farther than between Boston and New York City. Coolidge's retreat to Cedar Island had been the cause of great fanfare in this otherwise sleepy town, for which a new railroad line had been built to make it easier to import the president, his wife Grace, over sixty soldiers, fourteen house servants, ten secret service agents, and a bevy of reporters, O'Connor among them.[6]

Parrott and O'Connor spent several blissful weeks together before she returned by train to New York City. A heatwave struck the Midwest as Parrott made her way home: it was 94 degrees in Chicago, and the soot streamed through the open windows to mix with the humid air in the train. O'Connor had given her a bottle of White Rock Scotch for her journey, which she looked forward to drinking "surreptitiously" since she did not want to be caught with illegal liquor. She learned from fellow travelers that customs agents had, just before she boarded, seized "a truckload or so worth of Scotch from the baggage car—besides getting just about everything passengers had." With a mix of relief, pride, and humor, she bragged, "Me, I'm probably the only one onboard with beautiful Scotch."[7]

During the journey, "four fat middleaged Northwesterners who began to talk to me about weather, as is their innocent wont," hatched a plan to escort Parrott—who, as a measure of protection, had told them that she was married to a newspaperman—in a yellow cab to the Stevens Hotel ("the largest hotel in the world," they told her) in Chicago on the shore of the lake for lunch and then to the station where she had only "two minutes to spare" before heading to Washington, DC, her final stop before New York. "By the time I got to Washington," she declared, "I wouldn't have gone to see fifteen White Houses, crated. I just wanted to get the dust out of my hair." She opted for a "languid breakfast-lunch, and a highball," and described the weather as "one of those 'Heat Wave Kills Twelve' interludes." But it was all worth it for the time she had spent with her lover.[8] Parrott paid homage to this trip in *Ex-Wife* when Pat, now a divorcée, and her lover, Noel, cannot bear their physical estrangement during his reporting assignment in Wisconsin, so she travels to spend a month with him. In the novel, this visit has a significant outcome: "Noel sat down, the night I left Wisconsin for New York, and wrote to his wife, asking her if she would not be just as happy, if she divorced him. His wife did not want a divorce, however." O'Connor had, in fact, reassured Parrott that he was in the process of divorcing Dot during much of 1928; but there was always a reason that the final break could not yet come to pass.

While she was away from him during that long summer, Parrott began to do something important: she started developing her philosophies of modernity in her letters to him, trying to understand what exactly had changed for women of her generation. She began with a thesis, of sorts: "My grandmother would have mourned you—I mean your grandfather—in tears over her embroidery, in his absence. I bet I mourn your absence more violently, in a cab with the wrong person, or in a speakeasy over a drink I'm not having with you." No longer confined to carefully supervised courtships or marriages, or to illusions about women's asexual purity, women had to develop their own rules about dating, sex, and unattached life. She explained her behavior to O'Connor matter-of-factly: "One goes to dinner... and one's nice, and entertaining as one knows how to be... sings for one's supper, why not?... I don't row if I get kissed once in the course of an evening or so. I don't invite it, either, and I make it obvious to a moron that I'm damn well not reciprocating in the least."

This almost-divorcée believed that it was incumbent on her to prove that she could be in the world on her own, accepting the rewards as well as the risks. Parrott eventually used the language she began crafting in this letter, almost word for word, in *Ex-Wife*, in which she also includes a response from Noel that fills in the other side of their conversation: "Patricia—I miss you steadily. I have not taken to wenching. I have sat around talking politics with the old men or listening to young men (the photographers) talk of their probably fictitious dealings with the local virgins. I have a memory of you that seems undiminished in warmth, with which I go tranquilly to sleep, alone. This summer will end. And, darling, darling (as you say in your 'cello' voice) I am closer to you at two thousand miles distance, than I could be to any other woman in my arms." These are the devoted, poetic words from O'Connor that Parrott clung to in the years to come; by publishing them in *Ex-Wife* she was preserving those cherished sentiments, which he was already in the process of disavowing.

None of O'Connor's letters to Parrott survive. It is hard not to think of a scene in Parrott's *Marry Me Before You Go*, in which the doting and successful Audrey ceremoniously burns every letter written to her by her unfaithful husband Theodore in an attempt to cleanse herself of him. Or of Phyllis in Parrott's final book, *Even in a Hundred Years*, who burns every letter written by the man she loves after he marries someone else, sparing only one five-year-old postscript, a reminder of his final lie: "I shan't change in my love for you in a year. I would come back to you if I had to walk the width of the world, even if the journey took a hundred years."

It is certain that O'Connor was not much of a correspondent. Parrott described her usually "one-sided correspondence" with him as akin to "posting letters into a dream." But writing these letters served a practical purpose as she nudged herself toward a writing career she did not yet know she would have: she was working out her thoughts and feelings about the contemporary situations in which they, and so many others, found themselves. Parrott optimistically forecast, "When you are eightyseven and I am eighty—I see no reason we shouldn't be sitting about in front of a fire with high-balls, having a swell time talking about books or politics or airplaning or people." Theirs was not a marriage; but she imagined their relationship enduring because they had "become such extraordinarily intimate friends."[10]

There were signs, however, that this imagined future was not to be. O'Connor made her feel that being too public about their affair could cause trouble for him at the *Herald Tribune*, where he had recently become a bylined correspondent. "You are a well-known newspaperman," she once told him after agreeing not to visit him while he was away on assignment, "the ramifications to which my visit might lead might be damn boring—the world being what it is." Parrott initially accepted O'Connor's unconditional rejection of marriage as a denunciation of the institution; but as their relationship devolved into sporadic one-night encounters, fights, and—on Parrott's end—deep suffering, it became clear that O'Connor was in fact rejecting marriage *to her*. If she wanted to be a part of his life then she would have to accept his terms: "It will just be the same thing over, every time he and Dot get as far as mentioning the word 'divorce,' he'll assure her he does not want one. And every time I get pregnant he'll say, 'No.' And every time he thinks he must be masculine and go sleeping around, I shall go through unmitigated hell."[11]

Parrott wished she could walk away from such lopsided terms. But she found herself stuck—having waded in too deep, she could not extricate herself from the unfavorable arrangement. Instead, she bowed out of parties that she knew Dot would be at, even if they were big, with a "couple of hundred people there," to avoid a confrontation. "It might annoy Dot to have me turn up," she wrote to O'Connor about skipping one such event as she was trying to figure out the etiquette for such tricky social relations, for which there was, as with so many things in her life, no playbook.[12]

Parrott and O'Connor were united in more than just romance. When their affair was flourishing, she agreed to conduct research on his behalf for a book he had contracted to Dial Press about the colorful history of Greenwich Village. While he was covering presidential vacations and political trials, Parrott read old copies of the socialist magazine, *The Masses*, which she fell in love with. ("It's like a New Yorker with the guts left in. Amazing.") She researched the "Little Theater" movement and the Provincetown Players (among them Eugene O'Neill, Djuna Barnes, and Edna St. Vincent Millay) and spent time "in the history room at the library." But she did more than just research, taking extensive notes and even drafting chapters. "I'll do you a lot of pieces myself," she wrote O'Connor, "on Village speakeasies and tea rooms and characters...so that you can select from them what, if anything, is useful."[13]

Parrott was pleased to undertake this work. The subject was of interest, and it got her "in the habit of writing," which she correctly believed might serve her at some future date. Even after she took a full-time department store job, she continued to dedicate up to four hours a day doing this work for O'Connor. While Parrott was reading up on "historical background" and writing summaries, he was supposed to be outlining and drafting the book. Flush with enthusiasm for their joint literary venture, Parrott volunteered to "write as much of the thing as you like . . . with the definite understanding that what I write is designed to serve you as a shortcut simply—if you are busy with assignments, as you will be—you can tell me to do the chapter on this and that." Later, she jested—perhaps only partly—"You know if this book works out you'll become the first Newspaper Man to have a Ghost-Writer."[14]

Parrott had long imagined a writer's life in Greenwich Village. It was a "symbol of the dreams a girl dreams when she's twenty, in the provinces"— or, as was the case with her, two hundred miles north in Boston. Now she was living and loving there as she studied the storied neighborhood's past. What Parrott was most intrigued by was not "the historical side, nor even the account of those who survived the Village . . . to go on to fame and family life," but "the Village that cradled . . . the cigarette-smoking female intelligenzia." For someone who at times declared herself antifeminist, she took a surprising interest in the Village's female pioneers. There were many such figures, such as Henrietta Rodman, one of the leaders of the Greenwich Village Feminist Alliance, who in 1915 observed that childcare was the greatest obstacle to women's career pursuits. She proposed building a cohousing apartment complex on Washington Square for professional women, with needs such as childcare, laundry, cooking, teaching, and housework built into the apartment's infrastructure.[15] These are the kinds of women Parrott encountered during her research hours, and their ideas seeped into her emerging philosophies of modernity.

Parrott's pleasure in aiding O'Connor's book writing, however, transformed into resentment when it became clear that he was neither committed to her nor to the book she had been pouring her efforts into, both of which he was in the process of trying to abandon. Adding insult to injury, O'Connor told Parrott that he was giving up writing the Greenwich Village book for an utterly shallow reason: because he "felt it would not make much money."[16]

Although O'Connor had told Parrott when he met her that his marriage was over, except in the legal sense, she was often reminded that it was "as legally binding as ever." O'Connor supported Dot financially, which Parrott believed would end in 1929, "now that you've decided to do something about it."[17] But he did not follow through, and Dot remained in O'Connor's life until well into 1930, which served as a constant reminder to Parrott that her status was precarious. A case in point occurred after O'Connor underwent an emergency tonsillectomy operation. When Dot arrived soon after Parrott settled in beside her lover's hospital bed, the result was a scene—Parrott was shamed out of the hospital. When Dot showed up, "the legal owner had returned." "Yet," Parrott mourned, "the women outside the walls," such as she, "can love, and despair, and suffer. They can be wounded as badly."[18] After being discharged, O'Connor convalesced at Dot's parent's home, making it impossible to communicate with him—another lesson about what was lost for the "other woman" in this arrangement. As she was wont to do, Parrott studied this painful incident to reflect on the larger picture of men and women, marriage and whatever moderns were doing. Confronted with the benefits of the traditional framework of a marriage, Parrott was reminded of the terms that her grandmother would have sensibly demanded. In her stories and novels, Parrott would always be sympathetic to the women "outside the walls" because she knew how awful it was to be relegated there.

After the hospital debacle, Parrott spent an evening with her friend Pete Borden, another reporter who knew both her ex and her present. Parrott, for a change, did not partake of the cocktails, part of a temporary reform enacted as she sought clarity about her life. They ended the evening by throwing "ten cent store glasses" into the back of her fireplace, where they broke in the flickering light. "They were," she wrote in a letter to O'Connor, "all her fragile gleaming illusions about this world," though Pete "didn't know they were symbols." Parrott was learning the hard way that affairs provided no protection for women who abandoned the proprieties that had once protected them. The days of chivalry and security were over, and Parrott now understood that she had been party to her own entrapment in this disadvantageous arrangement.

Parrott diagnosed the essence of their problems as deriving from the irreconcilable differences between men (like O'Connor) and women (like her): "You have the instinct to wander,—I have the instinct to cling. Men have built civilizations out of their instinct to wander—women have built races, out of their instinct to cling." "There is no blame anywhere," she generously declared. O'Connor had, like Nickolas Muray before him, warned her that he was not interested in a new wife, nor even an exclusive relationship; this was his nature, which she tried her best to accept. When she couldn't muster the intellectual power to reason through her situation as an unfortunate consequence of the modern world, Parrott wished she "had morphine," fantasizing of "a drug invented that would take away feeling, and leave the mind washed clear."[19] Alcohol was the closest thing to it, and she regularly availed herself of its fleeting comforts.

Sorrow overwhelmed her when O'Connor rejected her attempts to sway their relationship into conventional territory and then began pushing her away, leading Parrott to realize how "unfashionable" she actually was. She now understood "completely about the Victorian women who were faithful to a memory forty years or somesuch." She loathed feeling so 1880s about O'Connor, but perhaps not as much as she hated him acting so 1920s. Trying to reconcile her intellectual understanding of their situation with her emotional reaction to being in it, she was left with "this awful taste of complete frustration and defeat." "It tastes like dust. It makes everything taste of dust."[20]

By agreeing to his terms and, in the process, sacrificing "the orderly and constructive life [she] wanted and believe in," she had been inexplicably weak. She regretted not doing a better job of asserting her own wishes: "I went along your road of no rules but of your making and those changed at your pleasure." She began to understand that in "waiving" her "code" for his that she had, in essence, spent years "trying to comprehend a masculine code as flexible, as alterable by mood, as the wind. There was nothing to understand." "You did as you pleased, and I had to like or leave it." She tried to "remember what I used to believe in when, working in a department store, I was a person in my own right, before I let a man so color my life."[21] These were painful realizations, which came not long after the similarly agonizing takeaways from her divorce—a one-two punch. But they were not just personal lessons; they were the underpinnings of Parrott's thinking about women's place in the changing landscape of American life. Now she needed to figure out something productive to do with her observations. From the ashes of her unhappiness, her first novel was born.

SEVEN

New Freedoms in the "Era of the One-Night Stand"

THE EX-WIFE IS BORN

In the summer of 1929, nearly two years after her divorce from Lindesay, thirty-year-old Ursula Parrott went to "a trick fortune teller" who told her that she "was going to have great financial success, and a Great Sorrow," two predictions that came true. The financial success arrived following the publication of her first novel, *Ex-Wife*, in July; the sorrow in the form of her protracted breakup with Hugh O'Connor, to whom she dedicated the anonymous first edition of *Ex-Wife* with a discreet "H." Even before Parrott's name was attached to later reprintings of the first edition, the book's dedicatee was expanded to "Hugh O'Connor," who makes a thinly veiled appearance in the novel as Noel, loved and lost in *Ex-Wife* as in Parrott's life. Parrott later claimed that she wrote *Ex-Wife* while she was in love with "a distinguished, important figure, but his line of work brought him no fame." "It was the notoriety that I received from my books, my career, that separated us."[1] However, success-envy was the magazine-friendly version of the couple's breakup story, which Parrott tailored to fit into a narrative about career women in which she now had a significant stake. What really happened between Parrott and O'Connor was significantly more complicated.

Ex-Wife would prove to be inseparable from Parrott's ill-fated love affair. At a New Year's Eve party on December 31, 1928, thrown by the pioneer of modern public relations Eddie Bernays, O'Connor dared Parrott to begin writing what became her first book. At the party, O'Connor "told everyone [she] was going to write a book," and on New Year's Day he reminded her that now she had better do it since he'd "mentioned it to so many people." So on January 1, 1929, Parrott "just began to write." Drawing on notes she had collected during the past two years, she produced a first draft in seven weeks.[2]

Parrott would always credit her writing career to the urging that issued from O'Connor. While she was drafting the book, she called him "the fire underneath [her] felicity." He read chapters and offered feedback, letting her stay in his apartment because he knew she'd "do better work if [she] were happy." However, as things deteriorated between them at the very moment that her writing career was taking off, O'Connor would remind Parrott of these favors by tallying debts he felt were owed to him. Pressed in the early 1930s to pay what amounted to bills from her lover, Parrott made it clear what O'Connor did and did not do for *Ex-Wife*: "You made me take out things, and change the order of words and sentences." However, she was adamant that he "did not add a line."[3]

At her first department store advertising job, Parrott had "noticed that of the twenty women there, nearly all were divorced, separated, or actively or phlegmatically unhappy in the marital relationship. We were all in the same boat!" She was surprised to find that she was not alone but rather that she was part of a new phenomenon, along with many other women "going through the difficult period of readjustment" following their transformation into ex-wives, which had quietly become a shared condition for young women of her generation. She jotted down stories, hers and theirs, which she drew from when she began drafting her novel in the evenings, often after ten-hour working days.[4]

Frustrated by this piecemeal method of writing, she quit her day job and borrowed enough money to dedicate herself to the task.[5] Her benefactor was Richard Beller, a fellow traveler on the speakeasy circuit whose wealth derived from his father's successful clothing manufacturing business, A. Beller, Ltd. All told, Parrott tallied the substantial debt of $4,500 (around $75,000 in today's money) from Richard. A woman working an especially well-paid job as a stenographer, typist, or bookkeeper in New York City at this time might make $1,800 a year, so this was no small loan.[6] Parrott was also a born spender and had amassed significant debts for new dresses, shoes, and hats even when she could not afford them. Although O'Connor had dared her to become a writer, it was the exigency of debt to Richard that she would later claim pushed her to finish her book—how else could she repay such a significant balance? Richard, she reflected, was a true friend and a gentlemen who "remains in my life the only man who believed in a woman, backed her with money and advice, and never asked a quid pro quo."[7]

After finishing several chapters, Parrott shared them with some of her writer friends, including Clare Ogden Davis, who was in the process of selling her own recently completed book, *The Woman of It*. "This is salable stuff," Davis told her after reading the chapters. "Come with me and we'll see what we can do with it."[8] Davis introduced her to one of the principals at the new trans-Atlantic publishing firm Jonathan Cape & Harrison Smith, and Parrott inked a deal for a book that she had titled "Confessions of an Ex-Wife." Smith shortened the title to the catchy phrase that would make Parrott famous and follow her for the rest of her life.[9] While she waited for page proofs and her first paycheck, Parrott complained that she could not go anywhere because all of her "money went for a hat, two dresses, shoes and six pairs of stockings." She was spending her book money even before it arrived.[10]

The decision to publish *Ex-Wife* anonymously was also made by Smith. By 1929, anonymity was a well-tested gimmick used to build curiosity with the implicit promise of illicit material. Anonymous publication signaled that a book's scandalous contents were based on real life—why else would the author's identity need to be protected? Harper had published anonymous best sellers in 1904, 1905, 1909, and 1910—many years before *Ex-Wife*. Most of the popular tell-all monthly magazine the *Smart Set*, which billed itself in the late 1920s as containing "True Stories from Real Life," consisted of anonymous articles bearing titles like "I Long for a Wife and Home...But Who Would Have Me Now?" and "Can a Good Wife Be a Good Sport? My Husband Urged Me to Become a Petter." Those who found this method distasteful blamed *Ex-Wife* for reenergizing "this peeking-through-the-key-hole clan of 'now, by gosh, it must be told' thumpers upon many clattering typewriters."[11]

Smith's decision, however, paid off in prepublication anticipation and advance sales. Even before *Ex-Wife* came out, rumors circulated about the author's identity. At lunch one day at the fashionable, heavy-on-the-red-lacquer, Park Avenue restaurant The Crillon, with Ben from her publisher's office, "two unknown females (very nice looking) stopped Ben and asked him if I was the author of 'Ex-Wife' because I answered the description they'd had of me," leading her to quip, "So much for anonymity." After *Ex-Wife* hit the shelves in July, the widely read gossip columnist Walter Winchell cheekily leaked that "Ursula Parrott, the 'anonymous' author of the sensational 'Ex-Wife' tome, is not permitted to admit that she is." "They say that the authoress of 'Ex-Wife,'" whispered another columnist, is "Ursula 'Kitty' Parrott, an advertising woman." This otherwise successful marketing stunt also came with some awkward moments. "Oh Lord," Parrott practically groaned one afternoon, "Winchell just called me: am I standing by the autobiography or am I not…I shouldn't have answered the telephone." She was unnerved by his "prying into the autobiographical elements of the thing" for good reason: her first novel would be fixed as autobiography from the moment her identity was revealed, despite her protestations that this was not, at least entirely, the case.[12]

A tale from the trenches of marriage, infidelity, divorce, dating, and remarriage in boozy, dissipated Manhattan, *Ex-Wife* is filled with spousal conflict, casual sex with veritable strangers and outright creeps, awkward courtships, and conversations between women about the logistics of postmarital life. Parrott's debut novel made unnerving observations about the formerly venerable institution. One of the novel's central divorcées, Lucia, sums up the state of marriage for women of her generation witnessing its decline from within: "Brought up under the tattered banners of 'Love Everlasting' and 'All for Purity' we have to adapt ourselves to life in the era of the one-night-stand." Parrott described what it was like for women to navigate an emerging hookup culture, including the often overwhelming task of navigating life without the rules that guided past interactions between the sexes.

The novel begins with a stripped down, unsentimental declaration: "My husband left me four years ago. Why—I don't precisely understand, and never did. Nor, I suspect, does he." *Ex-Wife* is a confessional, tweaking a Catholic tradition beyond recognition, told in a first-person voice to a reader one can imagine leaning into the page, eager to find out what happens next. *Ex-Wife*'s story of Patricia and Peter's breakup is filled with affairs, endless financial juggling, late night dinners (many of the liquid variety), and unbearable hangovers. Parrott peeled back the glimmering surfaces of that often romanticized idea of effervescent New York youth to reveal deep misunderstanding, emptiness, and sadness.

Early in the story, happy newlyweds Peter and Pat have a baby boy, Patrick, who is not welcomed by Peter because of their precarious financial situation. At three months of age Patrick dies, relieving the young couple of the financial burden his existence created and giving Pat her first gut-wrenching loss, about which she puts on a good face. *Ex-Wife* is a tale of shattered expectations, especially for Pat, who believes, along with Peter, that her marriage is based on a mutually agreed upon notion of equality. "He and I were definitely committed to the honesty policy," she declares with confidence, after the second gut-punch arrives when Peter confesses to having sex with another woman while she is "at the shore for the weekend." Stung but committed to her marriage, Pat forgives Peter and moves on.

When Pat is subsequently left alone and goes out on the town with Peter's oldest friend, Rickey, she at first rejects his sexual advances. "But in that moment I had lost the wish to do much about it. Curiosity? Desire? The feeling that Peter experimented and why should not I?" So Pat goes down the primrose path of sexual equality, 1920s style. After agonizing over what to do, she confesses her one-night stand to Peter without naming names. Crestfallen, Peter sobs. He had believed Patricia was "the cleanest person in the world." In a fleeting moment of culpability, he blames his encouragement of her drinking for her bad behavior. But despite his professed love for her and his own transgression, Peter cannot live with his wife's infidelity. Resentment festers. An old Boston friend, Hilda, comes to stay with them, and Peter begins an affair with her while Patricia works freelance jobs in the evenings to pay the bills.

Parrott probed the hypocrisy of the double standard by describing the abuses Pat endures as she tries to win back Peter's affections before resigning herself to a divorce she does not want. At one point Peter calls Pat a "complete slut" and then has drunken sex with her, refusing to speak to her the next day. He stops giving her money to pay rent and strikes her "across the mouth" when she displeases him. During one argument, he twists her wrist until she fears it is broken, leaving her "crying, raging, pleading." When Patricia discovers that she is pregnant again, Peter disparagingly asks her if she knows who the father is and, in a subsequent fight, throws her "through the glass door of the breakfast room," leaving her bleeding on the floor. This is the charred earth, world-weary landscape of modern marriage, laid out in language stripped down like a battlefield report. Parrott leaves no room for Pat to have emotional responses—just a drink of Scotch, a salve Peter introduced her to—before heading to a Greenwich Village doctor to get stitched up. While many contemporary reviewers of the novel criticized its sensationalism, none expressed concern over the violence Patricia endures. That reviewers compared *Ex-Wife* to novels ranging from Daniel Defoe's 1724 *Roxana: The Fortunate Mistress* to Anita Loos's 1925 *Gentlemen Prefer Blondes* suggests a certain blindness to the real atrocity in the novel, which has to do with the way men repeatedly, forcefully, and viciously take liberties with women's bodies. Was this violence so ordinary, or seemingly justifiable, that it went unnoticed?

After getting her arm stitched by a "polite blond young" doctor, he offers to take Pat to an abortionist and tactlessly propositions her *en route* on the appointed day (a pickup that eventually pays off). Patricia ponders the risk of "turning up a corpse before sunset" because of the abortion but puts on a good face as she thinks to herself, "I just feel dead." Numbness and detachment were the only way a woman had a chance of surviving in the merciless world Parrott describes. Later in the novel, Pat is raped by a hulking Russian whose access to her sleeping body is facilitated by another man with whom she's had a one-night stand. She struggles at first but realizes it is futile. Parrott, in fact, experienced a real-life version of this incident, observing that the men who did it thought their attack "ever so funny." After it, Parrott felt she "couldn't go on any more, not another day." She was ashamed and, not for the last time in her life, suicidal.[13] In *Ex-Wife,* Parrott depicts a world no woman would wish to inhabit, showing her reader the ugliest sides of modern life. The novel does not advocate for hedonism, though it was often misunderstood in this way; rather it offers a strong case for the protections of marriage and the dangers of being an unattached woman.

Patricia's divorce occurs in a courtroom scene two-thirds of the way through the book; she describes it as "just an incident in the career of a Modern Woman." As was often the case in New York, where adultery was the only legal grounds for divorce, the transgression that earns this couple theirs is staged for the sake of the courts. Pete paid a "poor little unwashed wench" fifty dollars to pretend to be his lover, which Pat helps him orchestrate. After she is granted the divorce, Pat rushes home to change clothes before heading into the office—truly just another day in the life of a modern woman.

Their divorce seems like it should be the end of the story since Patricia has become what she did not set out to be and in so doing is set adrift with the many other leftover ladies of Manhattan. But the novel goes on for another seventy pages, pursuing a subplot featuring Noel, a very thinly disguised O'Connor, a red-haired, broad shouldered, dimple-chinned reporter, whom Pat loves but gives up for the sake of his wife. The final act of the novel involves Pat's friend, Nathaniel, about whom she has no romantic feelings, who proposes a practical marriage. They are wed in the same municipal building in which she married Peter, where she echoes the vows "to cleave to him only, forsaking all others, as long as you both shall live." "Well this time, it might be true," thinks Patricia, as they set sail around the world. Her wedding gift from Nathaniel is an ermine wrap, the ultimate status symbol in an Ursula Parrott story. The newlyweds sail off on a world cruise, where, Pat confesses, she hopes "that in some far city" she shall find her love again.

Was this a happy ending? It certainly had the architecture of it: marriage, wealth, status, travel. But the final sentiment expressed as readers closed the book's covers is that Pat pines for Noel. The prevailing feelings of disappointment and disillusionment undermine the marital finale. *Ex-Wife* was written with grief in mind.

After *Ex-Wife* sold out multiple printings, Ursula Parrott's name—which was chosen by her publishers "on the ground that [her middle name] Ursula was a far more picturesque signature" than her birth name, Katherine, and her married name catchier than her maiden name, Towle—was affixed to future editions. Newspapers as far away as China published notices bearing headlines like "Anonymous Author Can't Stay That Way," as if the public's curiosity was simply too much for the publisher to resist. Once outed, Parrott went on a public relations mission to explain that the incidents contained within *Ex-Wife* combined her own experiences with that of her female coworkers and friends. "Imagine my embarrassment," she would say, "when everybody thought it was my word-for-word life story!" She even claimed that her "former husband," Lindesay Parrott—who gave her the last name that she would retain, at least between marriages and on book spines—"read the manuscript before it was published," proof positive that there was "no autobiography in it."[14]

It is impossible to imagine that Parrott's devout Catholic physician father, Dr. Towle, felt anything but mortification about the incidents that take place in *Ex-Wife*. Even if they had no autobiographical basis (which they did), the characters' behavior would have been disgraceful to think, let alone write down and circulate. After doing a radio interview about *Ex-Wife*, which gossip columnist Walter Winchell described to his listeners as "the sensational book about husbands and sex," Winchell mocked Parrott when she "stamped out" her cigarette before news photographers took her picture. "My father is so strict, you know," she explained, "I wouldn't want him to see a picture of me smoking." Winchell titled his item about this incident, "I thought I'd die!"—of laughter, given the relative sin of a woman smoking alongside the misadventures about which Parrott had written.[15]

The first-time author did enjoy at least some of her newfound notoriety. A rebel at heart, Parrott gleefully reported "a rumor" that she was "being banned in Boston," her hometown. Though *Ex-Wife* never actually earned a spot on the banned book list, it certainly would have been warranted given the criteria that led to other novels of the time making the dubious grade. It was, in fact, in Parrott's childhood neighborhood of Dorchester that the first enforcement of the book ban took place, when two drugstore clerks were arrested for selling Percy Marks's *The Plastic Age*, a fictional novel about the misadventures of college-age boys and their escapades involving bootleggers, prostitutes, petting, profanity, and going all the way, racy but relatively tame fare in comparison to *Ex-Wife*.[16]

Ex-Wife was marketed to readers as a "sociological document" and, somewhat implausibly, a book of marital advice, which "should be read by women before and after marriage" as a warning that "a wrecked home may mean a ruined life." It is true that Parrott's novel explores her generation's failings, showing what one reviewer calls the "hopeless despair of wrecked ideals" lurking under the "alluring glamour" of women's freedom. (Perhaps not surprisingly, this reviewer neglects the male freedom that inspires Pat's reciprocal behavior.)[17] In the end, Patricia wants something conventional: to restore her marriage, have children, and make a home. The "his and hers" liquor-induced bad behavior has nothing to do with what anyone wants; it is a nightmare born of the age in which they live.

Ex-Wife was a publishing phenomenon. In the fall of 1929, it was featured prominently in the display window of Brentano's on Fifth Avenue in Manhattan alongside an enlarged photograph of its author. Parrott heard rumors that publishing mogul William Randolph Hearst forbade his tabloid *New York Daily Mirror* from running it—but they did, starting their one-page-per-issue serialization on October 3rd, which ensured that Parrott's story reached even the non-book-buying public.[18] Billing it as "the most talked of novel of the day," *Ex-Wife* was still being meted out in daily doses on October 25, when the *Daily Mirror* headline read "Morgan Halts Stock Panic!" Four days later, on October 29, a reader of the *Daily Mirror* would have first seen the all-caps headline "9 Billions Lost! Morgan Deserts Market" at the top of page one, and "'Ex-Wife' Is Thrown Out in Storm" at the bottom of the page, as Parrott's tale continued to unfold at the start of the greatest financial catastrophe in US history (see figure 14).

Toward the end of 1929, a parodic riposte, *Ex-Husband*, was published, also anonymously and presumably written in great haste. It, too, became a best seller and earned its place on a shelf next to its literary predecessor at Lee Chumley's speakeasy on Bedford Street in Greenwich Village, one of Par-

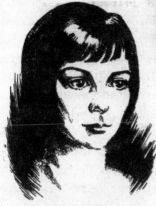
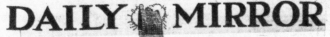

FIGURE 14. The *New York Daily Mirror*'s publication of *Ex-Wife* in short daily installments starting on October 3, 1929, coincided with the stock market crash and the start of the Great Depression. The paper promoted "the most talked of story of the day" by teasing readers with the question of its status as "fiction or confession." (*New York Daily Mirror*, October 2, 1929.)

rott's neighborhood haunts. Two other anonymously published "ex-" books also materialized in 1930: *Ex-Mistress* and *Ex-'It'*, the latter boasting twenty-one chapters with titles such as "I Am Taken In" and "I Am Thrown Out." The most absurd entrée into the field was Aben Kandel's *Ex-Baby*, which begins with the mock mournful declaration, "I had a wonderful time while it lasted."[19]

Parrott's first check from her publisher, which she had anticipated would be "goodsized," arrived in October 1929, the month of the stock market crash. It was for $16,000, roughly a quarter of a million in today's dollars.[20] *Ex-Wife* provided Parrott with a salary of over $350 a day, one newspaper reported, a staggering sum, especially given the economic state of the nation.[21] After a long period of financial precarity, Parrott was awed by the instantaneous resuscitation. "I don't mind admitting that the acute economic harassment of this last year has almost driven me crazy," she declared in August 1929, two months before her first check materialized. "No money coming in for maid or food or shoes or rent. Borrow it here or there, and wonder how the hell it can be paid, if ever."[22] Now, at least, Parrott knew how she would repay her debts and indulge her penchant for nice things, leaving one practical exigency solved and the rest of her messy personal life to fix.

Indeed, O'Connor's rejection was the dark cloud hanging over Parrott's otherwise sunny situation. She was bombarded with congratulations, except from the person who mattered most. In the midst of being celebrated as New York's newest literary celebrity, she described "the most dreadful moment of my life, of my whole life." She ran into theater critic Burton Davis, who whisked her into a cab to show her something she *had* to see. The cab pulled up in front of Brentano's bookstore on Fifth Avenue where "there was a windowfull of the book, and my picture." Davis said to her, "It's too bad that Hugh isn't here to see it with you. He would be so proud." Crushed by their devastating breakup, about which Davis had no idea, Parrott held back the tears like the good, detached modern that she was trying to be as she thought to herself, "God is a devil and he mocks people."

Sinking into depression, Parrott wished she did not "have to go on living and talking about the art of writing" in publicity interview after publicity interview. The best that she could do was hope that she might eventually get over moods she described as "suicidal," "desperate," and "hopeless" and "be a successful author whose [sic] of no damn importance to anyone," expressing the either/or of having a successful relationship or a career, a dilemma she would grapple with in dozens of her plots. In this moment, Parrott—like so many of her future female characters—found little comfort from professional success. Her instant celebrity felt unwarranted, even undignified. "It's cheap," she reflected uncomfortably, "to have any reaction when twenty heads turn round in a lobby because a man says in a loud voice, I want you to meet the author of Ex-Wife." "Sure I can write books," Parrott quipped after a few cocktails. "Too many people write books—too many words to describe life, anyways."[23]

She did, however, anxiously await reviews. Over lunch at the Algonquin, Ben from Jonathan Cape & Harrison Smith shared the good news that *Ex-Wife* "had leading space in every book section in town"—and many of these were laudatory appraisals. *The Nation* credited the novel with possessing an "intangible quality of truth," describing it as "an interesting portrait of a particular type of post-war woman." In the *Herald Tribune*, Florence Haxton praised Parrott's book for capturing "a growing tendency among young women to scrutinize with sceptic eye 'this freedom' which their mothers fought for and stubbornly won with exultation" by questioning the value of choosing a "job instead of marrying it." Although the *New York Times* called her writing "often sloppy," their reviewer had to admit the avidity with which the novel was being read: he left his copy of *Ex-Wife* "idle on the couch for only a few minutes before his wife was flipping over the pages, with another wife reading over her shoulder." Parrott's debut novel, he conceded, successfully channeled the zeitgeist of contemporary marital relations and contributed a "new descriptive tag to the American language," *ex-wife*.[24]

The idea of ex-wives as a category was in its infancy in the 1920s. Although the word had been used for some time in newspaper articles about high-profile divorce settlements, evaded alimony payments, property and name-use disputes, remarriages, and even an occasional murder, Parrott had named and described the life of a type of woman who had seemingly just arrived on the scene en masse.[25] Divorce rates had been steadily rising during the 1920s, despite fault-based divorce laws that required varying degrees of proof—adultery, intolerable cruelty, abandonment—before a marriage could be legally dissolved, with acceptable reasons varying from state to state. In the eyes of critics, this was the pernicious cost of allowing personal choice to determine the course of a marriage, eroding the institution to the point of meaningless impermanence. Behavioral psychiatrist Dr. John B. Watson predicted in 1930 that there would, in fact, be no marriages by 1980, at which point "every woman will train herself for economic independence."[26] Who was benefiting from increased female self-sufficiency? In *Ex-Wife*, Patricia offers a cynical take: "Ex-wives…young and handsome ex-wives like us, illustrate how this freedom for women turned out to be God's greatest gift to men."

Not everyone admired Parrott's novel and its of-the-moment observations. It was accused of being sensationalistic "Greenwich Village 'art'… shot through with literary pretense." "I can't help it if they think a fantastic amount happens to Patricia in so short a time," Parrott complained defensively after reading one negative review. "Maybe not so much ever happened to them. Maybe they were fortunate it did not." Parrott would not have known that her book was, on at least one occasion, deemed unfit for description. When Lewis Gannett of the New York *Herald Tribune* attempted to summarize the story of *Ex-Wife* in his review, he so shocked the newspaper's veteran copyeditor that this "was the only time that [his] copy was ever censored."[27] Given the book's controversial content, it was unsurprising that there were attempts, however futile, to dampen the public's enthusiasm for ringside tickets.

In the fall of 1929, *Ex-Wife* shared space with Ernest Hemingway's *A Farewell to Arms* on both Brentano's and Baker & Taylor's lists of best-selling fiction, and in December it became one of the most frequently sold books in Hollywood. Macy's placed *Ex-Wife* fourth on their best-seller list, just behind Erich Maria Remarque's devastating World War I novel, *All Quiet on the Western Front*, Ellen Glasgow's *They Stooped to Folly* (a post–World War I "comedy of morals" that brokered in kindred themes of marriage and infidelity), and Warwick Deeping's *Roper's Row*. *Publisher's Weekly* reported that 100,000 copies of *Ex-Wife* were sold during its initial publication run.[28]

In 1930, Parrott's book was featured in a cutting-edge sociological study of recent novels that represented divorce as "typical of modern life" rather than as "a tragedy for the woman because of the social stigma involved."[29] *Ex-Wife* provided "an excellent picture of the young woman's difficulty in making over her life. The heroine of this book easily solves the problem of self-support, but her emotional readjustments are far more complicated. She seeks to forget her attachment to her husband by plunging into promiscuity, but does not find again any real contentment until she falls in love again." The social scientists who conducted this study—both women themselves—praised *Ex-Wife*'s frankness about the difficulties of divorce and remarriage, and its representation of female characters as "human beings, with all the inconsistencies that human flesh is heir to."

The fate of other female characters described in this study might have been plucked from any number of Parrott's future novels and stories: "If they do not have to face the bearing of illegitimate children or complete social ostracism as the result of extramarital sex experiences, they still have the capacity to be tortured with longing for the lover from whom they have been separated, nor is their present grief any the less real because the future holds out the hope that they may be permitted to love again. If the unhappy wife no longer has to suffer silently to the end of the story, she is still tormented by the question of whether she has the right to deprive her children of a father's affection." As Parrott understood from experience, and as novels like hers were exploring, certain mechanisms of female entrapment were dissolving, but others were far from resolved. *Ex-Wife* was not a celebration of the new woman; it was a warning about and for her written by a someone who had, during her first thirty years, witnessed and experienced a dramatic recalibration of gender expectations and a complete upending of domestic life.

EIGHT

Ursula Goes to Hollywood

Just after *Ex-Wife* was published, Metro-Goldwyn-Mayer (MGM) purchased the film rights for the impressive sum of $20,000, more than doubling Parrott's initial payday. Parrott watched from the sidelines as MGM struggled to get her novel on screen. The studio's notoriously finicky star, Greta Garbo, refused the lead role. Norma Shearer, who had been playing characters cut from more modest and moral fabric, plotted to land the juicy part, hiring a portrait photographer who was just beginning to make his name in Hollywood—George Hurrell—to take pictures of her in "a luxurious and revealing negligee" procured for the occasion and leaving the photographs on her husband, producer Irving Thalberg's desk. The scheme worked; Shearer got the role.[1]

Next there were the censors. Hollywood's immorality was in the spotlight in the early 1930s, just as one of the nation's newly anointed immoralists and her parade of sinful stories arrived in town. The movie studios had been trying—with varying degrees of seriousness and success—to appease religious groups, social reformers, and federal, state, and local politicians who accused the dream factory of dragging down the moral compass of the nation. In 1930, the major Hollywood studios agreed to a Motion Picture Production Code, which prescribed ways to make "morally good" movies and was overseen by former postmaster general Will Hays, now head of the Motion Picture Producers and Distributors of America. Although it was a rather slippery gentleman's agreement with no real mechanism to compel compliance until 1934, it presented producers with hoops through which they had to jump.[2]

In early 1930, the Hollywood trade press reported that MGM was being forced to abandon the adaptation of *Ex-Wife* by the "Hays organization" due to the story's "vastly censorable" nature. Will Hays, whose name was synonymous with enforcement of the code, had even "ordained that 'Ex-Wife' could not be used as a title for a talkie, nor could the theme be employed," effectively nullifying MGM's purchase. Not willing to abandon their investment, MGM classed up the film's title to the seemingly more elegant *The Divorcee* and retooled the story. The shell game worked. The Hays office gave their cautious blessing, advising MGM not to mention the original title in their advertising because to do so "would be shortchanging the public by leading it to believe that the screen version was a faithful adaptation." MGM threaded this needle carefully, always mentioning Parrott—though not her book's too-crass-for-Tinseltown title—in their promotional campaigns and using a titillating tagline to set the audience up for their encounter with the story's faithful-to-the-book focus on the double standard: "HER SIN WAS NO GREATER THAN HIS...but SHE WAS A WOMAN": "If the world permits the husband to philander—why not the wife? Here is a frank, outspoken and daring drama that exposes the hypocrisy of modern marriage."[3]

Promoting the film at the time of its release, Norma Shearer assured reporters that *The Divorcee* was more "discreet than the book," commending the movie for daring "to do what other films have been afraid of. It handles the question of infidelity openly, but delicately." Parrott played nice with the motion picture sausage factory, explaining in a *Screenland* interview titled "Sex and the Talkies," "Naturally, the picture companies must change my stories to meet the demand of the censors, as was the case in 'The Divorcée,' made from 'Ex-Wife.' I like the film and thought Norma Shearer gave a remarkable characterization, even though it was *not* 'Ex-Wife.'"[4] (See figure 15.)

Released as the country was descending into the Great Depression, *The Divorcee* became a much-needed "smash" for MGM and for the cash-starved theaters who booked it. There were lines around the block at the Criterion Theater in Los Angeles to see the film during its opening week. In New York, *The Divorcee* was held over after bringing in $84,000 during its first week at the Capitol theater, an impressive sum in comparison to the prior months' dwindling box office tallies. At the Penn theater in Pittsburgh, it "shot house back into real dough after several lean weeks and at $34,000 something to get excited over," giving the theater its "best figure in months."[5] Although she would be nominated five times during her career, *The Divorcee* earned Norma Shearer her only Academy Award (see figure 16).

The Divorcee was not the last on-screen encounter between Ursula Parrott and Norma Shearer. In July 1930, the Hollywood press announced that Parrott's as-yet-unpublished second novel, *Strangers May Kiss*, had been pur-

SEX *and the* TALKIES

In which Ursula Parrott, of
"Ex-Wife" fame, explains how
an honest treatment of sex on
the screen can help reduce the
ratio of unhappy marriages

By Gray Strider

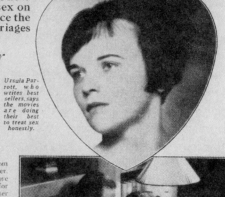

*Ursula Par-
rott, who
writes best
sellers, says
the movies
are doing
their best
to treat sex
honestly.*

"NOTHING is so important as sex
in the life of the American
woman today," declares Ursula Parrott.

Ursula, as you all probably know, is
the much-talked-about young author of
the best seller, "Ex-Wife," and of the
later book, "Strangers May Kiss."
Miss Parrott also wrote the original
talkie scenario, "Gentleman's Fate,"
for John Gilbert, and adapted "The
Divorcee" and "Strangers May Kiss," from
her two famous novels, for Norma Shearer.

"There is hardly anything in life more
difficult," continued Miss Parrott, "than for
the average woman to solve perfectly her
marital relationship with her husband. The
movies can help. But have they the courage
to do it?

"Some people have criticized me severely,"
Ursula Parrott went on, "for writing so
plainly about sex. But that is the one thing
in which most of us are interested—if we're
honest. Many more people have criticized
me for refusing to make my heroines sweet
young things. But that I don't care to do.

"I don't write about sweet young things
because I feel women today are more experienced than they were twenty years ago. And
since I write about typical modern girls, I insist that they be typical! Besides, a sweet
young thing has no history. For that reason
I confine my literary attention to women who

*Norma Shearer and Chester
Morris in "The Divorcee," a
sophisticated film from Ursula
Parrott's first novel, "Ex-Wife."*

understand the meaning of life.

"And, by the way, this, I
think, is the most difficult age

FIGURE 15. Parrott dishes out marital, literary, and movie-making advice in Gray Strider's
"Sex and the Talkies," in which she makes a case for films depicting sex "honestly." Her
heart-shaped glamour shot appears above a still of Norma Shearer and Chester Morris in
The Divorcee, MGM's adaptation of *Ex-Wife*. (*Screenland*, February 1931, courtesy of the
Media History Digital Library.)

chased, again by MGM. Joan Crawford was rumored to have landed "the
star role," but Norma Shearer ultimately performed it, thereby repeating
a proven formula that was used as one of the film's selling points: "If you
enjoyed Norma Shearer in 'The Divorcee'—don't miss her in this dramatic
picture based on Ursula Parrott's sensational novel."[6]

Aware that they had acquired another "extremely censorable story"—
including "discussion of abortions" and "the agonies of giving birth"—
MGM repeatedly met with the Hays Office and submitted script revisions

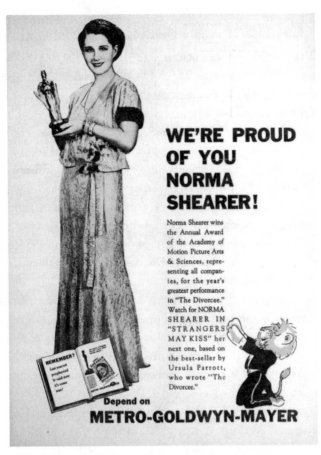

FIGURE 16. MGM took out full-page advertisements to congratulate Norma Shearer on her Best Actress Academy Award for *The Divorcee* and to build anticipation for Shearer's upcoming appearance in the adaptation of Parrott's latest best seller, *Strangers May Kiss.* (*Exhibitor's Daily Review* and *Motion Pictures Today*, November 12, 1930, courtesy of the Media History Digital Library.)

for approval.[7] On January 13, 1931, Irving Thalberg received a congratulatory letter praising him for so adroitly cleaning up the script. The Hays office had a few additional requests: to remove the adultery aspect of the story (which the film ultimately retained) along with two remaining "hells," four "Lords," and one "nurts" from the dialogue (concessions MGM was apparently willing to make since the offending words are not in the final film).[8] *Strangers May Kiss* premiered in Los Angeles in March 1931 to a crowd described as a "throng" who had turned out to see this "smart, clever, and of the minute" film.[9]

For millions of viewers, Norma Shearer had become the embodiment of an Ursula Parrott protagonist. Whether they knew it or not, audiences watched a version of Ursula's marriage to Lindesay Parrott disintegrate in *The Divorcee* and her affair with Hugh O'Connor play out in *Strangers May Kiss*. By virtue of their need to appease the censors, MGM's presentation of these two relationships vastly improved upon the experiences of her female protagonists as well as of their author: after Shearer's characters in both films descend into debauchery, they get a shot at marital reconciliation at the end of *The Divorcee* and an opportunity for marital legitimacy at the end of *Strangers May Kiss*. Ursula must have marveled while watching these plots play out on the screen, especially as her cinematic stand-ins are handed escape routes from regret, emptiness, and exhaustion in the final act of each film, at which points these unhappy women are offered a second chance by a pair of hypocritical men who fail to adhere to their own allegedly modern values until just before the curtain falls.

Although the Hays Office had given MGM their blessing for *Strangers May Kiss*, not everyone was pleased. Lupton A. Wilkerson, who worked for the major studios' trade organization, expressed "revulsion at this picture" and a "sense of horror that our present setup is permitting product of this type to go through." His panicked, almost hysterical memorandum claimed that *Strangers May Kiss* "is a reflection of the initiatory stages of the degeneration of a people. It embodies and personifies the warped moral sense which has disintegrated every previously civilized nation"—a nod to everyone's favorite fallen empire, Rome. Not only is this film "disgusting," he warned, but even "a few recurrences of its type will result in destruction of what freedom the screen now possesses." The Hays Office, the memo suggested, would be wise to tighten the noose around the neck of future pictures possessed of such immorality, which they did with their 1934 administrative restructuring. When one of the original coauthors of the Production Code, Martin Quigley, published a 1937 book on *Decency in Motion Pictures*, he singled out *Strangers May Kiss* as an example of the way films encouraged an aberration of "moral standards," deeming it "infectious to the mind and morals of impressionable people."[10]

While *The Divorcee* was being filmed on the west coast, the motion picture agent Leland Hayward brokered Parrott's first movie writing deal in 1930 with Paramount's "Eastern film plant," where she was hired as a staff writer assigned to actress Claudette Colbert's unit. At Paramount, Parrott joined a writing team that included Donald Ogden Stewart, who went on to write *The Philadelphia Story*, and Herman Mankiewicz, who would author *Citizen Kane* (see figure 17). Although drawing a salary from Paramount, Parrott was not under exclusive contract so could work for other film producers as well as on stories and novels. She enjoyed the experience and found screenwriting agreeable, telling her literary agent, George Bye, "All I have to do for Paramount between now and Friday is do all over my original Colbert story, with the new character built-in,—bring him [producer Walter Wanger] one outline for Clara Bow and an outline of an idea for Ina Claire." She believed that Wanger was on the verge of purchasing this new story "for Ina Claire (for whom they are crazy to get something of course)" and began speculating about what she might fetch for such a sale, "Forty thousand, maybe? or am I getting impressive ideas?"[11]

She was, but she had reason to since so many deals were on the table as her literary stardom was on the rise. The head of Fox Film's story department was excited about a plot she was developing for what became her 1931 gangster novel *Gentlemen's Fate*—published for reasons unknown under the name K.U.P. (Katherine Ursula Parrott's initials), although the book's dust jacket bills it as "an exciting novel of love and racketeering by one of America's most popular writers" and its serialized publication in the *Household Magazine* credited Ursula Parrott (see figure 18). Parrott dashed off a ten-page scenario of the mobster tale for Fox, describing the method she was instructed to use: "you write it all in present tense for one thing because present tense is moving tense and gives magnates the sense of action." The deal with Fox fell through, but MGM stepped in to purchase both silent and sound rights— as was often the case during this period of transition to talkies—for $5,000. Not known for their work in the gangster genre, MGM borrowed director Mervyn LeRoy from Warner Bros. and cast John Gilbert in the starring role, described unfavorably by one reviewer of the film as an actor who "battles the cruel microphone more successfully than usual in his latest attempt to overcome the handicap that the talking pictures have placed upon him." Although this review criticized Parrott for not being "as expert at gangster melodrama as she is at high-powered sex tales," LeRoy shared the blame for the film's lack of "vigorous credibility" despite being fresh off Warner Bros.'s smash gangster hit *Little Caesar*.[12]

As Parrott's "spicy works" were in the process of being "eagerly gobbled up by the producers," she realized that she had to learn how to write for the

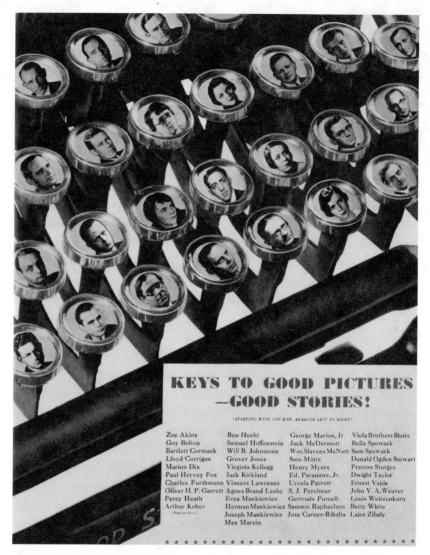

KEYS TO GOOD PICTURES —GOOD STORIES!

(STARTING WITH TOP ROW, READING LEFT TO RIGHT)

Zoe Akins	Ben Hecht	George Marion, Jr.	Viola Brothers Shore
Guy Bolton	Samuel Hoffenstein	Jack McDermott	Bella Spewack
Bartlett Cormack	Will B. Johnstone	Wm. Slavens McNutt	Sam Spewack
Lloyd Corrigan	Grover Jones	Sam Mintz	Donald Ogden Stewart
Marion Dix	Virginia Kellogg	Henry Myers	Preston Sturges
Paul Hervey Fox	Jack Kirkland	Ed. Paramore, Jr.	Dwight Taylor
Charles Furthmann	Vincent Lawrence	Ursula Parrott	Ernest Vajda
Oliver H. P. Garrett	Agnes Brand Leahy	S. J. Perelman	John V. A. Weaver
Percy Heath	Erna Mankiewicz	Gertrude Purcell	Louis Weitzenkorn
Arthur Kober	Herman Mankiewicz	Samson Raphaelson	Betty White
(Plus not shown)	Joseph Mankiewicz	Jose Carner-Ribalta	Lajos Zilahy
	Max Marcin		

FIGURE 17. Parrott earned a place on a typewriter key for Paramount's 20th Birthday Jubilee campaign in 1931. Some of the notable writers appearing alongside her are Donald Ogden Stewart, who went on to write *The Philadelphia Story*; future director Preston Sturges; journalist and playwright Ben Hecht; and Herman Mankiewicz, who would author *Citizen Kane*. (Courtesy of the Media History Digital Library.)

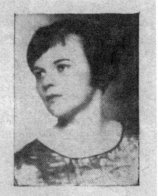

No reader can fail to be moved as well as thrilled by this tale of the strange life of Giacomo Tomasulo. Not only is it an extraordinary story by Ursula Parrott, the brilliant young author of Ex-Wife *and* Strangers May Kiss, *but it is a startling revelation of life among the gangsters of today—a subject of which no one interested in the welfare of the United States can afford to be ignorant.—The Editors.*

Ursula Parrott

FIGURE 18. When *Gentleman's Fate* ran as a serial in the *Household Magazine*, Parrott's name and "brilliant young author" status were touted even though the book was published, for reasons unknown, under "K.U.P." (*Household Magazine*, March 1931, author's collection.)

movies. Her book of choice was the hot-off-the-presses *The Art of Sound Pictures* from 1930, written by Walter B. Pitkin and William Moulton Marston, the eccentric psychologist who went on to create Wonder Woman and was at the time working for Universal Studios. According to Marston, eastern writers who had cut their teeth in journalism or fiction had no concept of how to write for "sound pictures," "for the difference between the public that reads and the public that patronizes movie houses is vast."[13] Studio executives would have heartily agreed with this assessment, which caused famously bad feelings between eastern writers and movie producers.

Marston also interwove his kinky philosophies about domination and submission into the book. I have no doubt that Parrott would have scoffed at some of these, most of all that "passion must be thought of as a preponderantly male emotion." However, if Parrott's personal copy of *The Art of Sound Pictures* had survived, there might have been some special annotations made in the "Feelings and Emotions" chapter. In it, the authors warn that the "screen heroine who merely makes a success of her career will never attract a large number of box-office patrons." Writers should make female characters "conquer the world, or at least enough of it to give them a good living. Then show how their economic conquest enables the girls to captivate the men of their choice."[14] For these male psychologists, women could have it all—at least in the movies.

The Art of Sound Pictures must have given Parrott enough guidance to get going with some degree of competency since her movie writing deals kept coming. Walter Wanger at Paramount asked for a two-page outline of a story set in a West Indian location, one of Parrott's favored vacation-and-research destinations. Universal hired her to write "a five hundred word synopsis called 'She Owed Him Everything'," followed by an original story intended for actress Mary Nolan.[15] Paramount signed her to work on two different films in development, "Hurricane" and "Only Once in Life," for Clara Bow and Mary Brian respectively.[16] Parrott was in the East Coast movie industry swim now—literally, at times. She was asked to spend "Sunday at Adolf Zukor's place in Nyack," New York—not by the Paramount cofounder himself but by the wife of a director who lived next door. "I thought it would be fun," Parrott exclaimed, "to see the more than Pompeiian multi-colored marble swimming pool." But Parrott ended up skipping the party (due to illness or, perhaps, pregnancy?) after she realized that she "would have felt so bunned, starting—without a single drink. I should have passed out on the first cocktail, no doubt." One of the Warner brothers invited her to their New York office for a meeting, after which they sent her story, "But Not in Budapest," out to the West Coast for evaluation by the studio's script department. At Universal, "Carl Laemmle Jr. was turning flip-flops about the 'Gambling Mothers' type" of story, which she had been asked to consider writing for him. Parrott joked with her agent that "this week I am so broke that for $4,000 I would write a story called gambling goats, but I would want to be sure that the check was forthcoming on delivery, and they're so funny up at Universal."[17]

At this point Parrott had not yet set foot in Hollywood. When her April 1931 trip west was announced, she appeared poised to take the town by storm. "Of all the writers brought to Hollywood," Mollie Merrick wrote in her column, "Ursula Parrott is perhaps coining the most money at the moment. That girl writes 'em rapidly. They're sold before she has had so much as a chance to jot the idea out sketchily on paper." She accepted an invitation to a writers' luncheon covered by the *Boston Globe*'s Hollywood correspondent Mayme Ober Peak. Peak celebrated New England's latest arrival, crediting Parrott with being the "creator of the modern woman." Peak described Parrott as "smart" and "dashing," painting a picture that sounded straight from central casting of a scintillating, young authoress just in from the East: "Her face is round with a few friendly freckles, her eyes are blue and quite earnest; hair very black and worn in a straight bob. She wore black wool crepe, with white pique vest and cuffs, and carried under one arm the inevitable publisher's package of manuscript, which, no doubt, she was correcting on the jump between appointments."[18]

Parrott checked into the Beverly-Wilshire Hotel where she "collected the most preposterous apartment. It looks like a gilded love nest. Everywhere you don't look at brocade you look at rosebuds on the lamp shade." Despite its gaudiness, the accommodations were comfortable and the room adequately cool for the warm LA spring. The hotel was also "fairly central as these things go," though Parrott added the very New Yorker aside that she "can't find what is central here." After learning that she was overpaying for her accommodations, she and her dog, "Ex-Wife," moved to 6750 Wedgewood Place in the Hollywood Hills into "a house very pleasantly furnished with a little garden, balconies to have breakfast on, big living room with piano, radio and phonograph, dining room, kitchen, two bedrooms, maid's room, two baths for about half" of what the Beverly-Wilshire cost (see figure 19).[19]

Even with improved accommodations, however, Parrott did not enjoy Hollywood. "I do have hours a day in which I think I will die dead of homesickness," she wrote to her agent, "a few that I have died and waked up in a sort of gaudy hell—what with California sunlight." Parrott reluctantly concluded that "nevertheless the sunlight is probably damn good for me," even as she complained that she liked "snowdrifts now and then. Human being need to combat things, to struggle," mocking Southern California's endless sunshine. Even her banker got a serving of complaints—"I don't like Hollywood any more than I thought I should"—between financial directives.[20] Parrott later made the case for the city's inferiority in "The Second Mink Coat," in which the main character "ached vaguely for narrow Manhattan streets, for crowds of passers-by looking in New York more self-sufficient always than street crowds anywhere else."

It wasn't just the sunshine that bothered Parrott; it was the culture. She felt out of her element. "This place and its intrigues is pretty terrible," she bemoaned. "I just want to go home!" The gossip was overwhelming. "This place is so full of rumors," she declared, "that they should be discounted 50%." Her anti-Semitism flared up in a town and industry run by Jews, who were easy scapegoats for her unhappiness. "I hate this place worse than any town of any size I ever saw," she complained. "The instant I land, I begin to feel as if I had a rope about my chest, and was tied to a tree with it." She summed up her feelings about the town and its denizens with a perfectly New Yorker quip: "The best clothes, and the worst conversations in the world."[21]

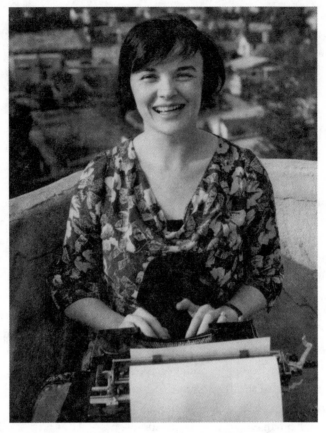

FIGURE 19. Parrott "banging a typewriter" in May 1931 at her temporary California residence during her first trip to Hollywood. (Associated Press photo, author's collection.)

She was, however, quite comfortable with the spending habits of the preposterously wealthy denizens of the movie colony. Actress Laura Hope Crewes, whom Parrott described as "terribly sweet," loaned the newly arrived author "her second best car—a Pierce Arrow—with a definitely old world atmosphere about it." All she had "to do is hire a driver for it," and then she could be ferried about the city like an important studio employee. A month later, Parrott telegrammed east: "Have bought magnificent car worth at least twenty five hundred in New York" for the greatly discounted price, she bragged, of $1,500. She instructed her agent to wire the necessary funds to screenwriter Edward Dean Sullivan at the Hollywood Knickerbocker Hotel. Anticipating his disapproval of her latest extravagance, Parrott added, "Am not crazy it is Cadillac

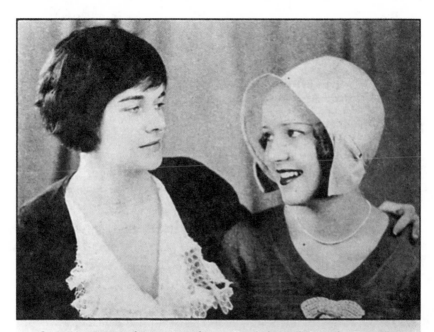

One Winner Looks at Another. Dark-haired Ursula Parrott, who wrote "Ex-Wife" and "Strangers May Kiss," likes blonde Frances Dean's name. And why not since she gave it to her herself? The little Dean girl's real name is Betty Grable and she was chosen from a thousand girls by Samuel Goldwyn to be groomed for stardom

FIGURE 20. Although she professed no love for being in Hollywood, Parrott got in on the celebrity author act when she renamed Kansas City–born Betty Grable "Frances Dean." The name didn't stick, but Grable's career under her birth name did. (*Silver Screen,* August 1931, courtesy of the Media History Digital Library.)

will last five years."[22] Spending was one of her lifelong weaknesses—the more money she had, the more ways she figured out how to expend it.

Though they referred to her as "the best box-office writer in the country today," the press also reported that Parrott was "not looking forward to a long career in motion pictures. She's really looking forward to a job finished in Hollywood and a chance to get back to a home in Connecticut," which she had just purchased. Her displeasure would have been difficult to believe since she appeared to be getting in on the celebrity author act in every way, from renaming an actress to being spotted with actors Robert Montgomery and Reginald Denny "actually kneeling at her feet in the studio restaurant out at M.G.M."[23] (See figure 20). Parrott, however, was unimpressed: as soon as she arrived she was already counting the days until she could embark on a homeward bound train.

Her East Coast contract with Paramount had been suspended during her West Coast trip, so Parrott could act as a free agent. This was a dizzying liberation, as she made clear when she summed up her multistudio entanglements during her Hollywood stay: "[Irving] Thalberg gave me a lecture on working for so many other companies besides Metro. Eddie [Montaigne] also gave me a lecture on working for everybody but Paramount. Sammy [Goldwyn] maintains if I would just hang around with United Artists I would be much better off in the long run." Parrott had "nine to five duties" working on a script for *Gentleman's Fate* for MGM, on which "there is nothing but trouble." Pathé was ready to buy one of her stories for $15,000, "Women Need Love," which was slated to go into production in the fall, starring Ann Harding. There was a feeding frenzy for a book she was just starting to write, *The Tumult and the Shouting*: "William Randolph Hearst himself demands a synopsis for Marion Davies. Howard Hughes screams for a story for Billie Dove." In the meantime, she could not pass up doing a Pathé original, she said, which "is just too good to let go considering Connecticut [where she had significant expenses for her new estate] and family responsibilities."[24]

Although she had initially told her agent that she was "strongly against selling anything to Columbia [Pictures] at any price.... They just want name will give cheap production that will hurt me badly," she caved and sold them the short story "Love Affair," which she had published in *College Humor* in 1930. Parrott had been right in her prediction. Starring Dorothy Mackaill and Humphrey Bogart in one of his first leading roles, the film shares little beyond its name with Parrott's story, which was about serious matters of class and sexual exploitation, pregnancy, abortion, and single motherhood. The film rated a one-star write-up in *Liberty* magazine, where the reviewer accused it of having "more plots than a suburban real-estate development."[25]

Parrott's frenzied studio juggling act occurred partly due to a no-fault-of-her-own hiccup in an initial agreement with United Artists. Samuel Goldwyn had brought Parrott west to write a screenplay for her yet-to-be-published novel *Love Goes Past* for Gloria Swanson, who was under contract to make one film per year with the studio. Almost as soon as Parrott arrived in Los Angeles, Swanson had a widely publicized falling out with Goldwyn that led the "runaway star" to decamp for New York City, leaving Goldwyn with a writer but no actress. Parrott was in limbo while "Sammy," as she chummily referred to her "amusing" new friend, tried to lure Swanson back to town. Swanson "is supposed to have gone East to try to get capital from Joe Kennedy," her beau "who backed her before. Of course they assure me that she likes my story and I believe that is true. Not because they tell me so at United Artists but because E.B. Derr at Howard Hughes said quite casually that he discussed the book and she was crazy about it."[26] Parrott was name dropping as if she had been a Hollywood lifer, though she had arrived for the first time just two weeks prior.

She wanted to start work on *Love Goes Past* as quickly as possible because she wanted to complete the script as quickly as possible and return east. She pleaded with Goldwyn to "okay this situation so I can go ahead" and complete work on the screenplay, arguing that there is "no purpose in staying here the full term of my contract for no reason, since the whole situation is as nebulous as it is." Sammy threw the anxious author a bone, authorizing Parrott to write what she described as a skit, around seventy-five pages of "the major scenes built up and the minor scenes synopsized." Rumor had it that Parrott was being put through her paces, Hollywood style, with rewrites demanded every night. She was frustrated, complaining that if Goldwyn "refuses to okay this script for development—it's my third, I did two short treatments incorporating everybody else's ideas and then went back to my own—I don't see what to do next. I'm certainly not going to sit down and start it all over again. What I want to do is to develop and polish this thing, compromise my contract and go home and let him worry about Miss Swanson."[27]

In May 1931, with eighty-two days remaining of her contract with United Artists, Parrott packed her bags, left her home in the hills, and decamped without saying goodbye to anyone, baffling everyone in an industry accustomed to writers hanging on as long as they possibly could. When Gloria Swanson returned later that summer, she began work on a film called *Tonight or Never*. The papers reported that *Love Goes Past* was being "shelved" until Swanson's new project was finished.[28]

Parrott described her time in Hollywood by saying that she had "lived like a dead woman, in a sort of daze, where everyone made a great fuss of me, and seemed to think I was a very grand person."[29] Her landlady in the Hollywood Hills was not, however, one of her admirers. At the end of May, Geraldine G. Lackey sent Parrott a telegram: "Just discovered your departure. Have conferred with Paramount and United Artists and other people who knew you and all report unlike you to leave in this fashion. Please return at once my keys and the months rent now past due. Feel there must be some explanation. Am unable to get in the house as yet. But see six windows left open. I shall hold you responsible if there is any damage from rain we had over weekend. Please answer at once." A few days later, California Bank sent Parrott a notice that she was overdrawn by $224—a relatively insignificant overdraft in the arc of what became a lifetime of inadequate funds, no matter how much money she was making.[30]

Geraldine Lackey's communique went unanswered, so she sent a second one a week later complaining about Parrott's lack of response: "If none comes by tomorrow shall place the affair in attorney's hands who will take up matter with studios. Unpleasant publicity will not help you. Cannot believe you intentionally mean to be dishonest. Mr. Lehr and Miss [Laura Hope] Crews say you will do right thing and pay money due on lease."[31] In typical Ursula Parrott fashion, spine straight and hackles up, she threatened to countersue.

The highlight of Parrott's otherwise unpleasant California experience derived from time spent with Sylvia of Hollywood, masseuse and diet guru to the stars whom she anointed "the only interesting personality I have met in Hollywood." Parrott had always maintained an exercise regimen, taking long walks (before work, after work, at lunch, while unemployed), going to the gymnasium when she could afford membership dues, and doing home calisthenics. She once described her daily regimen of going to Elizabeth Arden's gym as "an investment in fitness."[32]

Sylvia had a national reputation. She did regular radio broadcasts and published health and fitness advice in *Photoplay* magazine. Within twenty-four hours of arriving in Hollywood, Parrott was singing the praises of "Sylvia, a lady what makes moving picture actresses what they are. She admits to being fifty, is 4'10" and has a figure like a dancer. She gives you elaborate calisthenics, massage, and so forth, accompanied by the most preposterous combination of gossip and profanity." Sylvia "makes you live on tomato juice chiefly and it seems to agree with me": Parrott had lost "five pounds in four days, two inches around my waist and some more." She wittily announced, "I may be done with high romance, but it is better I recover my figure in case I want to start a revival at a different address.... After all, a broken-hearted little fat girl just ain't romantic at all." Sylvia counted among her clients Gloria Swanson, Bebe Daniels, Constance Bennett, and Norma Shearer, whose autographs bedecked her office walls. Parrott's photograph bore the inscription, "To Sylvia, who gives you a future instead of a past."[33]

Parrott would have agreed with Sylvia's advice to women who were foolish enough to think that they "do enough for their husband if they keep his house, bear and bring up his children, cook his favorite dishes, and see that his toes are not sticking out of his socks."[34] Sylvia told them sternly that they could not expect "to be loved for these domestic virtues alone": "You are only as fine as you look—plus your usefulness." This was not a frivolous concern. Women who opted for wifely dependency were, in fact, reliant on husbands to feed, clothe, and shelter them. Sylvia asked such women to confront the possible consequences of letting themselves go: "Do you ever wonder what you would be able to do if you had to make a living for yourself and family if suddenly the provider you now have could no longer provide?" By staying "attractive and charming," "you will increase your earning power, which may come in handy some day."

In addition to diet and exercise, Sylvia advised her acolytes to "read as light and amusing literature as possible. Don't go to see hectic, melodramatic shows"; her preferred movie "tonic was Laurel and Hardy, or something like that." Parrott would certainly have drawn a line here since Sylvia's prohibition sliced into her bread and butter, which she could skip at the dinner table but not at the bank. Her feelings about Sylvia dimmed when the masseuse began "telling all" in a serialized memoir published in *Liberty* magazine, sharing confidential gossip gained on the massage table. Parrott, who was spared by Sylvia's airing of personal secrets, rechristened her "a simple-hearted dynamic savage."[35]

A decade later, Parrott shared her own diet advice in the pages of *Ladies' Home Journal*. "Nice People Don't Eat" detailed the author's weight-loss regimen, drawing liberally upon Sylvia's dietary recommendations sans exercise (see figure 21). At the time of its publication Parrott was in her fourth decade of life and confessed to having "found, in good rich food a minor sedative for disappointments, nerve strain or boredom" adding that "No one's life comes out quite as one expects." Despite her lifelong practice of it, she confessed that her "special hate in this world is calisthenics. Nothing I've ever known is so boring as to touch one's toes with one's hands when one's not putting on stockings." She was surprisingly honest about having gained, and then lost, forty pounds by excising "sweets, bread, potatoes or butter" along with riding an electric horse—a 1930s exercise fad—twice a day. Although she did not share this method with her *Ladies' Home Journal* readers, she once wrote

Nice People Don't Eat

BY URSULA PARROTT

Ninety-five per cent of us can be as slim as we want, if we really want. And the author isn't kidding! She's proved it. She shed forty-three pounds in three months.

AT THE end of my teens, I weighed a hundred and twelve pounds. In the midst of my thirties, I weigh a hundred and ten. There was a time between when I weighed a hundred and fifty-three and a half.

On a passport, I fill in the question about height: "Five feet one inch." That's in my stockings. The question, "Any other distinguishing characteristics?" I might well have answered truthfully: "I love food."

One of the pleasantest memories of my sixteenth year is my Saturday luncheons with my best school friend. We always had the same thing: chicken patties, peas, a fantastic dessert called chocolate ice-cream cake—a compound of cake, chocolate ice cream, a pint or so of fudge sauce, and two or three dozen pecans floating about in the sauce, with some whipped cream splashed over everything.

En route to a matinee, after this luncheon, we provided ourselves with a two-pound box of mixed chocolates and bonbons. We were always finished with these before the curtain went down on the third act, and, invariably, had a double chocolate ice-cream soda on our way home to an adequate Saturday dinner.

We weren't fat because we played five sets of tennis and went swimming for a couple of hours, most summer days, or skated from luncheon until dark on winter afternoons.

One's adult life doesn't generally permit of devoting half one's waking hours to exercise. Therefore the lady, size forty-two, panting between bites of pastry at tea, who became an old stock joke with her "My dears, it runs in my family. When I married I only weighed a hundred pounds."

My personal opinion is that most people have found, as I have found, in good rich food a minor sedative for disappointments, nerve strain or boredom. No one's life comes out quite as he expects, even if it's a very fortunate life, and it's undoubtedly true that the contract one didn't negotiate, the salary raise one didn't get, the children one has who don't win all the prizes at school, or the story one wrote that no one liked but oneself, ceases to seem so catastrophic after a four-course dinner with plenty of starches therein. However, months and years of taking potatoes creamed au gratin, as solace for the imperfections of the world, do in most cases have the fatal effect of turning one into a cartoon of oneself when very young, and don't improve life in any way to compensate. In fact, they make a woman's life much duller.

As to men, I wouldn't presume to judge. One of the ultimate proofs that man conquered the world because he was the most optimistic of the vertebrates is, in my opinion, the sight of a male, height five-seven, weight two-twelve, being consciously charming to three girls aged nineteen on a country-club porch.

Which is beside the point that you—95 per cent of you—can be as thin as you want, if you really want. *(Continued on Page 58)*

(Continued on Page 58)

Editor's Note: The reducing regimen Miss Parrott followed so successfully was laid out for her by her own physician, after a thorough physical examination, including metabolism test. No one should undertake a reducing regimen under any other circumstances. And, as Miss Parrott says: "Once you've got your reducing regimen from your doctor, don't debate it with anyone. A diet must be based on a patient's own blood pressure and metabolism."

Ursula Parrott when she weighed 153. She was only 31, but at a party someone said to her, "Nice to see the young people enjoying themselves, isn't it?" And that did it!

She went on a diet that made her look like this—slim, svelte and ten years younger. Honest, it's the same girl—but size 12, weight 110! It takes grim determination. But it can be done!

FIGURE 21. Parrott drew on some of her lessons learned from Sylvia of Hollywood in her surprisingly frank account of her own weight gain and loss in "Nice People Don't Eat," in which she also described, with humor, the lamentable sight of "a male, height five-seven, weight two-twelve, being consciously charming to three girls aged nineteen on a country-club porch" as "evidence that man conquered the world because he was the most optimistic of the vertebrates." (*Ladies' Home Journal*, March 1941.)

that heartbreak had its "very small compensations": "Without doing a thing about it, I have lost eight pounds. Another week's grief will make me a thin young woman. And if one has to break one's heart to recover one's figure, one exchanges a liability for an asset, doesn't one?"[36]

Despite Parrott's displeasure about her time in Hollywood, she had warmed up to the fact that movies gave her a way to reach millions of people with her ideas while earning staggering sums of money, which she had developed a propensity for spending. She believed that movies could reeducate people about the modern woman, telling *Screenland* magazine, "There is hardly anything in life more difficult than for the average woman to solve perfectly her marital relationship with her husband. The movies can help. But have they the courage to do it?"[37] Parrott loathed "fairy-tale romances" and believed there should be more movies about "human, compassionate relationships." But she was equally aware of the tension between an informational movie campaign that might benefit women and the pressure for commercial success. "Since all of us want to make as much money as we decently can," she admitted, "it is perhaps asking a lot of the producers to take this risk."

So many movies of this era end in marriage: a church scene, a ring on the finger, rice in the air, a "Just Married" sign hanging from the back of a car, a woman carried over a threshold, the wedding march playing as the camera holds on a kiss. This is the fulfillment of countless plots, the easy way for a movie, especially of a certain age, to achieve a "happy ending." Parrott argued that motion picture producers should reject this story arc and instead begin "their stories at the altar instead of ending them there," thereby "giving the unsophisticated, inexperienced feminine theater-goer some idea of just what she is up against when she slips on the good old marital bonds." What awaits the modern newlywed and what Hollywood should be representing, Parrott argued, was "terrific economic pressure, terrific female competition," and "a condition twice as threatening as these two—the old marital specter, familiarity!"

Parrott told the press that she accepted one of her motion picture contracts "on the condition that I would not have to white-wash my heroines or life in general. They agreed. And in my scenarios," she said proudly, "I present life as it is and sex as it is, not trying to pretty things up." She was so sure that movies could help women understand what life was really like that she predicted that "as women see more and more sophisticated films, and more and more begin to look on marriage logically instead of hysterically" that divorce rates "will be lowered." If movie producers would let her have her way, and pay her handsomely of course, they could work together to solve America's pesky marriage problem.

NINE

Second Husband, Charles Greenwood

"THE STUPIDEST THING I EVER DID IN MY LIFE"

Parrott referred to 1931 as the year in which she "did not do a single thing [she] meant to do." From the outside she appeared to be flourishing, with book, story, and movie deals abounding. Parrott's agent, George Bye, to whom she dedicated her latest book, sent his client an ebullient telegram expressing his congratulations and esteem: "Affectionate congratulations from the happy and grateful dedicatee to you on a debut of *Love Goes Past* which is beautiful writing art."[1] Her words graced the pages of many a newspaper and magazine—not yet because of any scandal but because she had become a highly sought after authority on the modern woman.

Despite mounting evidence that all was well, Parrott was feeling unusually pessimistic. Ever since her first big paycheck arrived in late 1929, she managed to spend everything that came in and more besides. It did not take long for her to establish a rhythm that prevailed over the rest of her career: scrambling to meet writing deadlines in order to earn enough money to pay for the often extravagant things that she—and her son and sister, and anyone else in her orbit—enjoyed. This included the purchase of her first Connecticut estate. At the end of 1930, she paid $26,000 for the property and spent another $25,000 improving it—roughly a million dollars in today's money. Parrott associated Manhattan with thrilling but wearying days and nights: long hours of solitary writing in rented hotel apartments followed by into-the-wee-hours nightlife, part of a pattern that was difficult to break. Connecticut is where she planned to slow down, tend a garden, raise chickens and ducks, and spend time with her son. After completing her purchase, the philanthropist Otto H. Kahn congratulated Parrott on "happily rusticating far from the madding crowd."[2]

But there was always more work to be done on the estate, and more money

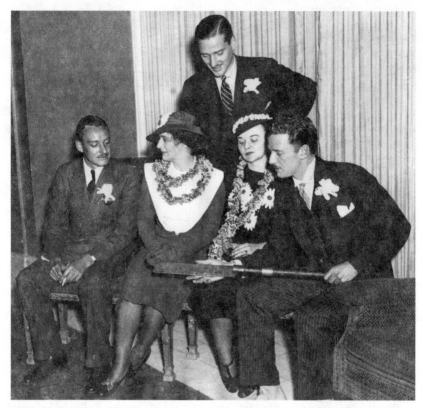

FIGURE 22. Although she found going to such events increasingly unappealing, Parrott (second from right) is pictured here surrounded by "socialite sportsmen" Morton Clark (standing), Henry Whitney (seated left), and Phillip Carr (with the Samoan knife), and the actress Joan Lowell, at a May 1935 literary tea, the likes of which authors were expected to attend to keep in the celebrity swim. (ACME Newspictures, author's collection.)

to be spent. Country homes came with country problems—rats, rain (too much or not enough), leaky roofs, weekend visitors, gardens, and much more—which were both distracting and costly. She told *Photoplay* magazine that her son "loves to ride," so she "bought him a saddle horse." "Perhaps had I never written 'Ex-wife,'" she added, "he would have had only a pair of skates—but the idea is the same. Now they're telling me how cheaply a swimming pool can be built. They'll have the swimming pool, I'm sure." Indeed, they did. Parrott found herself unable to get off the hamster wheel. She became so bad with her finances that her agent, who was fully aware of his client's flaws and foibles, agreed to directly supervise every expenditure she made in an effort to staunch the fiscal hemorrhaging. Parrott instructed her banks to only accept checks that were countersigned by George Bye. However, she soon resented the oversight even though she had asked for it and so terminated the arrangement, letting the chips fall where they may.[3]

After almost two years of being the most famous ex-wife in America, Parrott found herself deriving little pleasure from going to the smart places or being around the set that frequented them. She started skipping big parties and openings, only going "once in a hell of a long time to a literary tea to watch the critics getting tight with the authors' wives" because "it's not in the least soul-filling" (see figure 22). Each on-again/off-again encounter she had with Hugh O'Connor—by typewriter, telephone, and in the flesh— reopened the scabs on her emotional wounds. She had so little to show for having heavily invested in him and wanted to stop squandering her affections, although she seemed unable to walk away. As she pondered what might lay ahead, however, she expressed optimism about second marriages. "The one fact which cheers me up most of all about the future of matrimony," she announced, "is that statistics show that while one of out every five marriages—that is twenty percent—ends in the court of domestic relations either in separation or divorce, in second marriages only three out of every hundred do, which is only three percent."[4] The odds were in Ursula Parrott's favor.

Manhattan banker Charles Terry Greenwood had romantic intentions when he arrived at Parrott's temporary doorstep in Hollywood in the spring of 1931. Born in Brooklyn on April 22, 1890, Greenwood was from a "well known borough family." His father, Joseph William Greenwood, was a lawyer; his mother, Lola de la Mesa Greenwood, raised Charlie and his sister in a brownstone on the edge of Prospect Heights. After attending Polytechnic Preparatory Country Day School, he graduated from Brooklyn Polytechnic Institute, the second oldest private science and engineering educational institution in the nation. Described in the local paper as a "popular young Brooklynite" sought after by "Brooklyn girldom," Greenwood was an active member of the glee club at Yale University, from which he graduated in 1912.[5]

Greenwood served his country during the Great War in a fashion befitting his social class. He joined the Officer Reserve Corp in 1917, training at the Plattsburgh barracks in upstate New York, where he became a lieutenant before deploying as an adjutant with the Army. There would be no years-long trench warfare for Greenwood, who shipped overseas on April 6, 1918, and earned a promotion to captain that fall while in France. He was overseas during the war's final, difficult months on the French front before being honorably discharged in the late summer of 1919. In an outlandish coincidence, on his return voyage to New York, a few weeks after the Versailles Treaty was signed, Greenwood's name appears on the ship's passenger list next to another returning veteran, a first lieutenant from the 103rd named Hugh O'Connor.[6]

After the war, Greenwood accepted a job as an assistant cashier at the oldest chartered bank in the country, the Bank of Manhattan Company, which counted among its founding members Aaron Burr and Alexander Hamilton. In 1931, Greenwood became an official with the Manufacturer's Trust Company of New York and could consider himself fortunate to have such a position in the midst of the greatest financial crisis in US history. He and Parrott had known each other in the years following her separation from Lindesay, during which they spent many nights together on the speakeasy circuit. She occasionally weekended with Charlie and his friends in their rented Westport, Connecticut, summer homes, and in the late 1920s a mutual friend had even encouraged her to have a casual romance with him—"leaving out the beds of course." But since she had no romantic interest, she took a hard pass on the recommendation.[7]

The passage of time had not changed Parrott's feelings. When he got to California, she dismissed outright any possibility of romance. "Of course, nothing will come of this trip of Charles'," she told her agent, "other than the Pathé deal," which he was trying to broker on her behalf. "If I had any illusion that anything might, I'd have changed my mind before his arrival. A thoroughly nice person—but, if the person is not the person one wants." Despite Parrott's certainty that Charlie was not a romantic prospect, as she reconsidered her options during the summer and early fall, she changed her mind: five months after she described him as "not the person one wants," Ursula Parrott married Charles Greenwood in the chapel of the Manhattan marriage license bureau. At their wedding ceremony, on October 14, 1931, which was as sparsely populated as her elopement with Lindesay, George Bye and his wife were the sole witnesses to the couple's nuptials.[8]

Reporting on their wedding, which was Greenwood's first, the newspapers had some gentle fun. The *Los Angeles Times* explained that Ursula Parrott, "the small, black-haired, gray-eyed writer, deserted the ranks of ex-wives." The bride sent telegrams to friends and family to announce the good news: "Married Charles Greenwood at eleven o'clock. Very happy. See you soon." But the newlyweds' contentment was fleeting. A little over a month after the wedding, Ursula began describing her marriage to Charlie as "the stupidest thing I ever did in my life." She told Bye, "I knew I was wrong in a day. I stuck it a month. I stayed until I could not stand it another minute." "I would not go back, no matter what was said to me. So, darling, as my agent, be discreet if he comes to you with any long sad stories or advice as to my investments. I'm not telling any long and sad stories, but—he never cared a scrap more than I cared, and even if he did, I can't go on."[9]

Before the end of the year, Parrott got on a boat to the West Indies to escape the sticky situation she had gotten herself into, explaining, "When I do come home I'll have to go to Reno or some damn place and get out of this stupid mess I got in." As Walter Winchell liked to put it in his column, Parrott was already hatching plans to get Reno-vated. She said that she went to the Caribbean "on a physician's advice" to recover from a marriage-induced nervous breakdown. The recommendation did, in some ways, work—Parrott experienced a burst of writing energy, sending stories couriered by ship to her agent in New York. Rallied by this bout of productivity, she reported from the islands that she was "having a lovely time, working hard, and feeling better, more ambitious and more [herself] than in endless years."[10]

From the West Indies, Parrott asked her agent to make arrangements with her lawyer, Wilder Goodwin, to rush through a divorce. The "thought of that person," as she now referred to Greenwood, "hanging about with some legal claim on me is the only thing nowadays that disturbs my serenity." She feared that Charlie would "undoubtedly be vindictive," and she wanted to get her "status cleared up." Puzzling through the legal complexities of divorce law, Parrott wished that "he'd give me New York grounds," by which she meant that she wanted him to pretend to have committed adultery for the sake of the courts. "He should, and I'll have him approached on it, but if he won't,— I want to find out the exact status of these Mexican divorces. I know they only take a week, and are more or less all right. Reno is too expensive and too horrible a place." She deeply regretted that "I shan't have the two years' Connecticut residence that's necessary [to get a divorce there] until December and I want to be six months over this thing by then."[11] It was easier to enter into a marriage than to exit one, especially in the state of New York.

Liberty magazine dedicated its entire January 24, 1931, issue to the subject of divorce, taking special aim at New York state's "outworn and absurd" laws, which allowed only one legal ground: adultery. This rigid requirement necessitated countless acts of spousal collusion in which affairs were staged by adulterers-for-hire for the benefit of a witness who would then testify in court. This method, which Parrott described in *Ex-Wife* and hoped to use with Greenwood, forced the husband to look bad even if the divorce was initiated by the wife or was mutually desired. The couple had to become perjurers, not to mention criminals since adultery was also a crime in New York. For those who could afford it, going to Reno for three months to establish residency—another lie, not to mention an expenditure of time and money—at least enabled divorce on an array of uncontested grounds. "Wouldn't it be better," *Liberty* asked, "to permit divorce when there is definite desire on both sides to separate"?[12]

The point of making divorce difficult was to disincentivize it, thereby keeping more people married—no matter how miserably. "I cannot understand why it is so easy to get married and so hard to be divorced," complained the actress and six-time divorcée Peggy Hopkins Joyce in her breezy, comic 1930 memoir *Men, Marriage, and Me*. Indeed, divorce in the United States was an uneven and bizarre enterprise, with laws varying significantly from state to state. One fifty-cent pamphlet that tried to simplify information about the erratic nature of divorce laws reads like a bizarre compendium of behavior: a state like New York had only one "ground for divorce, adultery, while in Nevada there are eight, impotency at the time of the marriage, adultery, conviction of a felony, desertion, extreme cruelty, habitual drunkenness, insanity for a period of two years, and non-support by the husband for a period of one year." Parrott surely encountered this pamphlet or something like it as she studied the strange ways of marital undoing. "I read an article," one of her divorce-seeking characters says, "Nevada, six weeks; Arkansas, ninety days; Mexico only a minute, but only medium thorough. Florida, ninety."[13]

Making divorce complicated was also not a very effective method of saving marriages. First lady Eleanor Roosevelt argued in the pages of *Ladies' Home Journal* that a good marriage required shared interests and enjoyment, agreed upon standards of conduct, principles, and ethics, not to mention a sense of mutual respect, without which a not-too-difficult divorce remedy was needed. In the big, sophisticated cities, at least, divorce was no longer seen as a tragic event damning the female party to a life of loneliness and shame. In fact, magazine publisher Bernarr Macfadden, for whom Parrott freelanced during her early working life, argued that being a divorcée had become an asset. Not only was it "no longer a stigma," Macfadden wrote in a 1935 article, but "socially such people are often viewed with added interest because of their dramatic experiences." In New York, people began throwing divorce parties to commemorate the occasion. Referring to one such champagne-laden fête, Parrott declared that "I don't think a divorce is anything to celebrate nor yet to mourn, should just be acquired en passant."[14] Divorce was, in other words, becoming a fact of life that might best be handled without legal acrobatics or histrionics, marking a new chapter instead of a tragic end of the story.

Parrott reluctantly returned from her island getaway to New York City in early 1932, believing that she would feel better as soon as she finalized her divorce from Greenwood. She was anxious about coming back and confided in her agent, "I still wake up in cold perspiration in the night with the feeling that he might be around being arbitrary about something. Actually I have been terrified of him, which is silly I suppose, but those things are unaccountable." Although she hedged about Greenwood seeking retribution against her, Parrott's feelings were such that she made the decision not to move into a prospective apartment because it lacked a doorman: "I would never sleep there at nights because every time I heard a footstep on the stairs I would be sure it was C.G. coming to murder me. Of course I know that's silly but I would have felt that way."[15]

Why on earth had she married him in the first place? She was motivated by a desire to do something to move past the wreckage of her breakup with Hugh. "I tried," she explained regarding these concerted efforts, "with Charlie last year." "Whether you know it or not," Ursula's sister Lucy inveighed against Hugh in the only letter she ever wrote to him, "the principal reason in my opinion that she left Charles Greenwood as quickly as she did is that he presumed to make jeering speeches about you." Lucy blamed Hugh "for the whole catastrophe of that marriage, and its consequences in expense and ruined nerves for her."[16] Charlie was, it seems, a spectacularly bad attempt at object replacement. Ursula's effort to get out of one bad situation had put her smack dab into another.

Theirs would not be an amicable disentanglement either. When she wrote to her agent about her increasingly complicated financial troubles, she included a plea: "Don't let that bastard I married find out I'm hard up. It would please him too much." Parrott ended up able to take her divorce case to Civil Superior Court in Bridgeport, Connecticut, sparing herself the inconveniences of Nevada or Mexico, and the adultery grounds of New York. She quietly filed suit—using the name Katherine Greenwood in a failed attempt to dodge the press—on May 20, 1932. A state-appointed referee was employed to make a recommendation to the judge in another effort, also failed, to avoid "unfavorable publicity."[17]

Parrott was increasingly wary of the gossip columns, which were both a blessing and a curse for people whose livelihoods depended on their reputations and ongoing relevance. Press agents scrambled to get their clients into the columns for doing some things, and to keep them out for others. Walter Winchell's column, along with a host of others of varying reach and longevity by Leonard Lyons, Dorothy Thompson, Sidney Skolsky, Louella Parsons, Ed Sullivan, Dorothy Kilgallen, Hedda Hopper, and others, fueled an industry that revolved around published bits of praise and condemnation, rumors and half-truths, predictions and proclamations. Readers devoured the columns to gain "insider" access to the lives of the rich and famous. The writer Ben Hecht described the columnists as "café Prousts," "a new species of writers and reporters" for whom "a full-blown 'scoop' consisted of a line or two of trivia."[18]

New York columnist Walter Winchell exemplified the way that gossip, once contained to tabloid magazines, had seeped into mainstream news. "In 1925," historian Neal Gabler observes, "at a time when the editors of most newspapers were reluctant to publish even something as inoffensive as the notice of an impending birth for fear of crossing the boundaries of good taste, Winchell introduced a revolutionary column that reported who was romancing whom, who was cavorting with gangsters, who was ill or dying, who was suffering financial difficulties, which spouses were having affairs, which couples were about to divorce, and dozens of other secrets, peccadilloes, and imbroglios that had previously been canceled from public view." Winchell's radio broadcast and daily column, which was published in over two thousand newspapers in the 1930s, reached around fifty million people in the United States every week.[19] Columnists could easily ruin someone's day, not to mention destroy careers and lives. In Parrott's "Brilliant Marriage," the narrator compared publicity to a virus: "unwanted newspaper publicity resembles an attack of influenza, in that if one weathers the first shock to the system, one is likely to recover."

In this gossip-hungry climate, the circumstances of Ursula Parrott and Charles Greenwood's undoing generated significant attention, finding space in the columns and in stories covering leaked details of the divorce proceedings. In early October 1932, Judge John A. Cornell took testimony "at a secret hearing in New Haven," during which Parrott's counsel, Max Spelke, argued that her marriage to Greenwood had lasted under six weeks, from October

13 to November 24, 1931, and that the couple had begun quarreling "the day after they were wed." "Both," Parrott explained in court, "suffered nervous breakdowns" because of their incompatibility. She "attributed their marital difficulties to constant bickering, which, she said, was caused by Mr. Greenwood's objections to the presence in their household of Lucy Towle, sister of Miss Parrott, who acted as a nurse" for eight-year-old Marc.[20]

Parrott's testimony aired some of the complexities of modern family structures, especially the presence of a child from a previous marriage who required a live-in caregiver. Charlie reportedly asked Lucy to leave "their" Wilton home, which Ursula—who had bought and paid for said home—refused. Greenwood also "insisted" on "rearing her son as he 'saw fit,'" a stunning allegation, if true, from a woman who valued her independence and had unflappable beliefs about childrearing. Parrott testified that Greenwood objected to the "unlimited freedom" that she allowed Marc, "trying to enforce a strait-laced regimen upon him."[21]

Why Greenwood would have taken such a heavy hand with her son is unknowable; it is not out of the question that the need for cause in a Connecticut divorce suit might have necessitated that Parrott amplify some complaints to justify the marriage's termination. Under oath, however, Parrott alleged that Greenwood "drank, used unpleasant language and pinched her." During one of their "heated verbal arguments," Parrott said that Greenwood also "struck her." When the press asked Greenwood about these accusations, he claimed "he knew nothing of Miss Parrott's action." But after reporters dug up Greenwood's "answer…denying all charges," proving that he was, in fact, well aware of the suit, he replied, "'There will be no comment.'" The press reported that Greenwood "at first intended to contest his wife's divorce suit in open court, but changed his mind" after his lawyer conferred with his wife's counsel.[22]

Alleging intolerable cruelty, drinking, and abusive language, Parrott was granted a divorce on October 13, 1932, exactly a year from the day she married Greenwood, an episode she described as a "brief absurdity" during a year of well-intentioned mistakes. Her hometown paper, the *Boston Globe*, reported that "Miss Parrott, seen frequently at literary teas in dusky red ensembles, was given permission to discard the name of Greenwood." It added an important detail: "She asked no alimony." Perhaps this was the negotiation that inspired Greenwood to take the beating he did in the press over her accusations. The *Los Angeles Times* summed matters up: "The second attempt of Ursula Parrott to achieve the domestic felicity denied the heroine of her best-selling novel, 'Ex-Wife,' has ended in failure" (see figure 23).[23]

Parrott was now unburdened of her second husband but had, in the process, accrued significant expenses related to her divorce, in addition to "going through the publicity of it, and always being worried and never feeling well." The columns had been relentless and embarrassing. On top of that, she suffered serious injuries after she was thrown off of a horse and "broke half a dozen bones" and was "an invalid for six months." In an effort to get her act together, Parrott gave up drinking, asking her agent to do her a favor, if he ever saw her having a drink again: "You might come over quietly and remind me that I married a man [Charles Greenwood], falling for the stupidest line in the world, just because I had consoled myself so long and so thoroughly for the alleged tragedy of Hugh, with brandy and soda and Scotch and soda."[24]

Indeed, alcohol had become a significant problem in the author's life—as it was for many of her generation. In 1927, one observer described New York as a city that "swarms with speakeasies." New York City's police commissioner estimated that there were 32,000 of them in the city in 1929, double the number of drinking establishments prior to the start of Prohibition in 1920. Women had not been allowed in many New York watering holes during the wet years, especially in male-only saloons or clubs; nor was public drinking considered a decent pastime for the fairer sex. But in the speakeasy years, public drinking became both fashionable and a sign of women's new freedom.[25]

Marc recalled that when he visited his mother in New York, "a third of the grown-ups were fairly tight, or drunk—one did learn the gradations—by dinnertime, especially on the weekends." Parrott's own letters describe frequent trips to the city's plentiful speakeasies, with cocktails preceding and following. "I am a little drunk," she began one, "not badly,—just enough to have the edge of feeling blur." When her pride was wounded, "it took four and a half Scotch and sodas" until "nothing hurt a bit." She drafted a nonfiction essay "On the Use of Alcohol as an Anaesthetic," about boozing to cope with the indignities of modern living, affirming the motto, "It is better to drink than to weep." Having finished off a bottle of cognac ("all gone in my tum"), Parrott penned a "burlesque moral lecture" titled "If You Must Drink…": "If you are one and twenty—and the YOUNG Men You Admire never look upon forbidden fermentations, turn the page read only elsewhere." "But,—if your life goes otherwise, if the transient, or recurrent or intermittent, or permanent Men In Your Life count the evenings of the week by their

Capt. Greenwood, War Veteran, Dies

Native of Brooklyn Was Former Husband Of Ursula Parrott

Funeral services will be held at 8 o'clock tonight in Grace Episcopal Church, Grace Court and Hicks St., for Capt. Charles Terry Greenwood, 49, World War veteran and banker, who died Tuesday in the Garfield Hospital, Washington, D. C. The Rev. Dr. Frank E. Townley, rector of St. Bartholomew's Church, will officiate.

Captain Greenwood was born in Brooklyn, the son of Lola de la Mesa Greenwood and the late J. William Greenwood, and was graduated from Brooklyn Polytechnic Institute in 1908 and from Yale College in 1912.

Attending the first Plattsburg Camp he won a lieutenancy, and in France served on the staff of Gen. Evan M. Johnson. Subsequently he was promoted to captain of Company G, 308th Inf. of the 77th Division.

After the war, he was for some years an assistant cashier of the Bank of the Manhattan Company. His marriage in 1931 to Ursula Parrott, the novelist, ended in a divorce a year later.

Surviving besides his mother, is a sister, Mrs. John Van Pelt Lassoe, of 2 Grace Court. Burial will be at Salisbury, Conn.

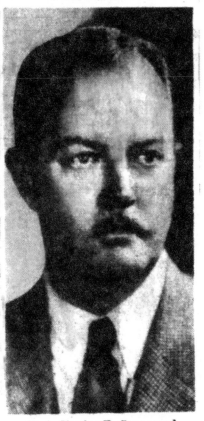

Mourned Here

Capt. Charles T. Greenwood
Member of well known borough family, Capt. Greenwood died Tuesday in Washington

FIGURE 23. Seven years after their divorce, Charles Greenwood's obituary describes him as the "former husband of Ursula Parrott." ("Capt. Greenwood, War Veteran, Dies," *Brooklyn Daily Eagle*, December 28, 1939.)

favorite speakeasies, learn when and what and why to drink,—and when to stop most firmly."[26]

Moderation and abstention, however, were easier said than done. It is therefore not surprising that Parrott's stories are riddled with alcoholics who drink heavily, get "cock-eyed" or "bunned," and then behave in self-destructive ways. Cocktails allowed characters to cushion themselves from the disappointments of life: "Don't feel—don't dare to feel. Be hard, be contemptuous of what you were....If you feel you will suffer—again."[27] In *Ex-Wife*, Peter provides Pat with a prophetic credo: "Good Scotch...it'll stand by you, Pat, in the days you have great sorrows." "Men used to bring me violets," Pat later reports after putting Peter's recommendation into practice, "and now they bring me Scotch." Pat could not survive another "Great Romance," but luckily "one gets the same feeling, or near enough, on four Manhattans if they're good; and that failing, one can see what five will do. The hangover from Manhattan's shorter'n that from Romances." And that was just in her first book.

In *Love Goes Past*, when a successful woman is hurt by the man she loves, she doesn't cry, "She just asked for a highball." In *Strangers May Kiss*, Steve drinks constantly to cope with a broken heart, downing cocktails and suffering hangovers, day after day. When he eventually proposes to Lisbeth, Steve says that she might reform him, after all, and "ship [him] off for a Keeley cure," referring to the institute that pioneered the treatment of alcoholism as a disease. The Keeley cure offered at least some hope for those who sought relief in an age of rampant alcohol abuse. Peter, from Parrott's 1933 "In Heaven Surely," dies of acute alcoholism. In "No Answer Ever," Parrott described an appropriately "modern still life": "a highball glass by the fireside, and a revolver to shoot oneself if the highball did not make the world endurable."

As she did when she was trying to recover from her marriage to Charlie, Ursula often tried to steer clear of the bottle—but she always returned to its temporarily numbing comforts. She once proudly reported, "I haven't been tight—not even a little bit—since the time I said I wasn't going to be any more for a long while." Admiring the beauty of Bermuda during a working vacation in the mid-1930s, she explained, "I always get poignant when I give up cocktails, and I've only had three in ten days." On another occasion, she swore off the bottle "because it's simply no use to diet and drink," using weight loss to motivate her dry spell as she channeled fitness guru Sylvia from Hollywood, who prescribed "not one cocktail, not one highball, not even a glass of wine now. You're all on the wagon with Sylvia, remember!"[28] Although her commitment to sobriety never stuck, the persistence of Parrott's commentary on drinking suggests how difficult the habit was to give up.

At the end of 1932, her second divorce not yet two months behind her, as New Year's Eve approached, she was met with another significant disappointment when Hugh O'Connor would not ring in the occasion with her, considering, as she wrote to him, that it was "as much of an anniversary as you and I, who were never married have." She did not "have many friends," she told him, partly because she considered herself "not a very social person" and partly because she had not developed deep friendships during the years she lived according to his irregular hours and erratic demands while she held on to a sliver of hope that things might work out between them. "There is you, and acquaintances."[29]

Parrott was despondent. She had botched her second foray into matrimony, which defied those rosy statistics on second marriages. She acknowledged that there were "many happy marriages, which we don't hear about because only the unhappy ones publicize their dissatisfaction" and steal the headlines, as she now knew from personal experience. One of these belonged to her agent, who married his wife, Arlene Victoria Coyle, in 1912 (they remained married until his death in 1957). In a wistful letter to Bye, Parrott pondered "the almost insurmountable difference between people who live within the norm and outside it." She envied what George and Arlene had created together, feeling "a sort of ache that comes when one sees people together who have married a long time before, and been steady, and built things, built with each other a beautiful security against all the sorrows and disappointments."[30]

Those who lived in such a state of contentedness existed in a world entirely different from hers, as if they occupied some vestigial space from the prior century that she could only observe from the outside—the way successful career woman, Alice, literally does in Parrott's "There's Always Tomorrow" as she looks through a window at the seemingly wonderful family life her ex-lover has created with his wife and children. Given her track record thus far, Parrott was embarrassed to say that what she really wanted was to be—and to stay—married: "I want to belong to one man, forever, all the world knowing it and to be good to him, always, helpful to him in his work, [and to] work,—alongside him." She had tried "to pose as disbelieving in marriage, in permanence, in monogamy," but if she was honest about it, she wanted a lasting marriage and all that came with it, including "a happy ending like an old-fashioned novel."[31]

Despite all the arguments she had been making, in her interviews and stories, about how important it was for women to have careers *if* they wanted them, Parrott never gave up the dream of also having a happy marriage. She told *Screenland* magazine, "A woman may achieve a business career—she may travel, flirt, gossip, write, paint, be a concert artist and all that. But, in my opinion, the woman who wins first prize in the grab bag of life is the woman who marries the man she loves—and holds on to him!" In the 1930s, some alternative imaginations were circulating for intentionally unmarried women—for example, in Marjorie Hillis's best-selling advice book, *Live Alone and Like It: A Guide for the Extra Woman*. Parrott was personally unconvinced, and she was not unaccompanied in her beliefs. One study of US women concluded that, "Working has lost the glamour which surrounded it in the days when women had to struggle against odds for this means of self-expression. It is no longer the ultimate aim of life, but has taken a subsidiary place." Once the ability to pursue a career had been gained by women, the "crusading spirit attached to holding a job" dissipated. Now the "first choice of sixty percent of the girls as to the position in life which would bring greatest satisfaction was for making a home for husband and children."[32]

We often associate the romanticizing of housewifery with the 1950s and with that other postwar generation, but it had roots in the 1930s when women's professional opportunities first took hold. Parrott's stories of this period often revolved around men who only wanted wives if they did not have careers, as in "You Ride Success Alone," about an unsuccessful and untalented painter, Carew, who leaves his adoring wife, Alison, because her accomplishments so quickly outpace his. In Carew's eyes, Alison chooses her writing career over him. Years after their divorce, when the exes meet again, Carew arrogantly declares, "You didn't love me as much as your name in print." This is untrue; but there is no convincing him otherwise. His prideful insecurity deprives him of her devotion, not to mention the notable material benefits of her success.

In Parrott's "Grounds for Divorce: Nonsupport," a college professor comes to resent his vastly more successful wife, disparaging her as an "American phenomenon." As they negotiate the terms of their divorce, Hilary chides Ariel that "she doesn't take her equality for granted, she takes her superiority" and laments that "all you career women...flourish in an era that's extremely hard on career men." Could women really be blamed for being successful, or for men struggling to keep up? The answer in these stories is yes. Ariel comes to the realization that her success is hollow without a happy marriage to go with it and decides to give up her career to avoid divorce. But it is too late: Hilary plans to marry his secretary, a woman with a nonthreatening job who adores him and shares his interest in biology. The story metes out "suitable" mates at its melancholy conclusion, but not love or happiness, at least not for the career woman.

Although Parrott's success was hardly the most significant problem in her failed marriage to Greenwood, she began to consider the possibility that career women might be better off with no marriages to wreck, like Marjorie Hillis's "live-aloners." That did not mean that she enjoyed the experience of being a successful single woman: "I find, after dinner, a handsome and expensive coffee service that I bought for myself. I'd prefer a cheaper and less beautiful one had it been given me by someone who loved me." A career woman would have a busy and full life, but was she missing something that could only be found in "the companionship of a loving husband"? "Perhaps middle-aged wives are as unhappy as middle-aged professional women," Parrott concluded. "I don't know."[33]

TEN

"Extravagant Hell"

Parrott considered 1931 to be a year of disappointment and failure, and 1932 turned out to be its equal. After struggling with her health, with depression, and with writing, she ended up anointing it her "year of jitters."[1] She had made every effort to be flippant and tough, but her tank of mental and emotional resilience was on empty. She accepted that O'Connor had wasted her time and affections but could not, as she frequently bemoaned, help the way that she still felt about him. So she studied her experiences with him "as case-history, as illumination on the ways of the world," considering "them good material for a book,—but in that book, I'll disguise the characters very carefully."[2] From *Ex-Wife* on, in fact, iterations of O'Connor appeared in numerous Parrott plots as she returned to him in her fiction with adoration and with wrath, using versions of their story to work through the larger question of how women were struggling to navigate a modified world.

Parrott's best-selling *Strangers May Kiss*, for example, is an extremely pessimistic book about extramarital sex, pregnancy, and abortion.[3] After enduring a ten-year occasional affair with Alan, the novel's Hugh O'Connor stand-in, enacted entirely on his terms, Lisbeth accepts a belated marriage proposal in the book's final act. She has earned her stripes as a modern woman by working and supporting herself, and by enduring alone the painful, stillborn death of what is likely Alan's child. When she accepts his late-in-the-game proposal, Lisbeth knows that she "should feel happy. She was to have everything that she had wanted, since she was seventeen years old. But she was too tired to believe it." Parrott might have given her reader something to enjoy at the end of this grim novel by writing the wedding scene that she wished for herself. But she does not indulge this fantasy even in fiction: Lisbeth dies of pneumonia before getting the thing she waited for her entire adult life.

The Nation used their review of *Strangers May Kiss* to snub a reading public they described as "avid for intimate description of illicit relations, obstetrics, disillusion, drunken or sober, and true love not quite conquering all." Perhaps they were right, although they failed to understand why this might have mattered. Parrott was pulling back the curtain on women's debased circumstances in a permissive age. "If we are shocked by some of the literary presentation of the new freedom in sex behavior for women," posited a 1930 study about young women's changing morality, "we cannot but admire the self-reliance and the ability to struggle against odds with which the modern authors endow so many of their feminine characters."[4] Female characters like Lisbeth were strong and self-reliant; but they were miserable, too.

Not long after *Strangers May Kiss* was published, Parrott made O'Connor an extraordinary proposition: a year of his life. She offered him $6,000, the equivalent of his annual salary at the *New York Times* but less than what Parrott typically earned for a single magazine story. With these funds he could "go round the world, stay in New York and decide where you want to go. Write a play. Write nothing. Stay away from women, or take your casual beds as you find them." The check, however, came with one condition. O'Connor's offers always did; why not hers? Parrott wanted one year as O'Connor's wife in exchange. "If I happen to get pregnant" during this period, "let me go through with it." "As your wife," she continued, "I can go live in Connecticut, with dignity, and peacefully with my sister and son" and "carry the comfort that I had been your wife,—to the end of my life."[5]

Had Parrott written this scenario into one of her novels, which she never did, it would have seemed a ludicrous plot twist. But it is proof positive that she was radically rethinking male-female relationships in ways that defied tradition beyond recognition. If society was evolving to allow women more economic, social, and political power, then why shouldn't the institutions that had developed at a time of male domination evolve along with them?

O'Connor did not take Parrott up on her offer.

By the end of 1932, Parrott had identified the root cause for much of her grief—the children she might have had with O'Connor. "You made me live years without anything to make life worth living, not child, nor status . . . to count on," she unleashed in an angry, end-of-year missive. "If I went mad in the end, what of it?" When O'Connor took his ex-wife, instead of her, out for New Year's Eve 1932—"you must know that most people don't believe you are divorced even—she never mentions it either"—Parrott had finally had enough. Two days later, from a rented room at the Barbizon Hotel, which catered to "young women engaged in the study or practice of the arts," Parrott trotted out a double-edged accusation: "You made a talent that might have grown, sterile forever."[6]

Sterility was an especially apt metaphor not just for her present writing difficulties but also for reproductive matters that disproportionately impacted women in this age of relaxed morality. "I've tried to understand your ideas about non marriage, and no children," she wrote to him. But "whenever I'm alone, I ached for a child of ours to live for. I wish that I could have persuaded you of that." Parrott had been willing to bear O'Connor's child *on her own*— she had, after all, been raising her son without a father and was comfortable with the idea of independent motherhood. She blamed O'Connor for allowing her neither this route nor the sanctity of marriage. "You wouldn't marry me," she began in one of her epistolary eviscerations, and "you made me kill the children we might have had." "If you had been willing to build a normal life," she argued as she aligned herself with tradition, then matters would have been different.[7]

Parrott was peeling the skin off problems caused by a rule-averse culture while she grappled with the mechanics, as she would have called it, of an inequitable relationship, which she characterized as an "extravagant hell." "Such an old Victorian plot this is, after all," Parrott concluded, as she reckoned with the dreadful irony of her situation. "It makes me a little sick to recognize it. The woman 'gives her all' to a man without marriage, and he 'spurns' her, finally. Oh well, the new twist is this matter of female economic independence."[8]

But the most consequential twist in modern love involved reproductive issues. Years before, when she conducted research for O'Connor's never completed history of Greenwich Village, Parrott had drafted "a few pieces bearing on Feminism...and the campaign they waged for birth-control—in re Mrs. Sanger's first difficulties with Comstock," referring to the birth control advocate's 1914 arrest for obscenity. Sanger was initially targeted by authorities for publishing the *Woman Rebel* magazine, which contained discussions of birth control in violation of the 1873 Comstock Law. A subsequent Congressional Act prohibited printed communications about or the provision of tools intended for contraception or abortion, which were deemed equal offenses described as "obscene," "lewd," "lascivious," and "filthy," and punishable by imprisonment for up to five years and fines up to $5,000.[9]

Sanger opened the first US birth control clinic with Ethel Byrne and Fania Mindell in Brooklyn on October 16, 1916, after which all three founders were arrested and prosecuted. Sanger's New York Court of Appeals judgment in 1918 conferred legality on contraceptive advice only in the service of "disease prevention" and "the protection of health." The law made no provisions for women to choose to have children or not. By 1927, the number of contraceptive clinics in the country had grown from Sanger's lone outpost in New York to twenty-one across the country, and by the fall of 1931, nearly 25,000 women had received birth control advice at the clinic's original New York location, although state law still forbade giving information to patients about birth control unless motherhood posed a danger to the health of the mother.[10]

Without safe or reliable birth control options, women like Parrott had to take their chances and deal with the consequences. Her monied, city-dwelling contemporaries easily found ways to "have it done," "be put straight," "get fixed up," "get rid of it," or "be relieved" when necessary. In letters to her female friends, Parrott casually mentions "morningsickness" or being in "another difficulty," which would be "resolved in a couple of days." Disclosures about pregnancy or its termination did not phase her. Women had long ended pregnancies before laws and medicine made it easier in some ways, and harder in others, to do so, for example by "taking the trade," which involved ingesting compounds to induce abortion. As debates intensified over the morality and medicalization of "induced miscarriage," such matters were shifting from the domain of midwives into the hands of largely male doctors with increased governmental oversight. The medicalization and criminalization of abortion intensified in the early twentieth century, just as women were entering medical schools in significant numbers for the first time, making inroads into what been the male-dominated obstetric profession.[11]

Historians of women's medical history in the early twentieth century have described abortion as "an open secret." It was illegal but widely available, performed by individuals with a range of expertise and experience. Abortion was policed erratically, usually entering the legal system only when patients died after botched procedures or infections. Although statistics about how many abortions were performed in this era are impossible to accurately ascertain, one medical book from 1928 claims that around one third of New York City women had undergone abortions, many of them self-induced.[12]

The most common procedure involved the dilation and emptying of the uterus, "either manually or with the aid of instruments." Another, often "employed by quacks or the women themselves," injected soap solutions, paraffin, or Lysol into the uterus, often resulting in injuries and hemorrhaging, a condition Parrott dealt with over the course of her life. There was a new "Heiser" method that had recently been developed in Europe, which involved injecting a paste of iodine and essential oils into the uterus, which promised fewer side effects and a decreased risk of infection. Orally administered drugs and compounds were often used but were generally frowned upon as ineffective or dangerous. As one gynecological researcher put it in 1931, all abortions were serious matters for women; the best method was a matter of "choosing the lesser evil."[13]

Getting an abortion was a risky undertaking. But many women, Parrott among them, considered the procedure an acceptable hazard of modern sexual life. When a woman found herself pregnant and decided to take "matters into her own hands" she had, as one 1930 study put it, several choices: "she may visit the abortionist, secretly, and with good or bad results; she may have the child and keep and care for it; or she may seek official or unofficial aid in producing an adoptive home for an illegitimate infant, without ever letting her love know that he has been a father. Whatever may be thought of feminine ethics in such cases, at least it must be admitted that girls are not shirking responsibility for their own conduct."[14] As Parrott bemoaned, the responsibility for such matters fell squarely on women's shoulders. Women had to covertly seek out birth control—sometimes outmoded or ineffective—often through midwives, resulting in a kind of contraceptive bootlegging culture. When those methods failed, they might return to these same midwives for an abortion.

One study of 1920s Greenwich Village described a doctor advising a female medical student to specialize in obstetrics: "there will be plenty of work because the midwives often do a bad job in performing an abortion and a doctor has to be called in," resulting in the ability to "collect a high fee."[15] No wonder Dr. Towle had been so adamantly opposed to his daughter's fleeting aspirations in the gynecological arena.

In *Ex-Wife*, Lucia says to Patricia, "I think chastity, really, went out when birth control came in. If there is no 'consequence'—it just isn't important." There is, however, a consequence in the novel when Pat finds herself pregnant as her marriage to Peter unravels. He refuses to take responsibility for the child or for the termination of the pregnancy, and so Pat heads to a physician's office where she matter-of-factly inquires: "By the way, I have to have an abortion. Will you do it for me? And how much does it cost?" The doctor is not shocked, though the reader might have been. Pat discusses her need for an abortion with the same emotion as if she were going to the dentist, which was in fact Parrott's preferred euphemism when she wrote letters about seeing the abortionist herself.

On the appointed day, Pat enters a "dingy waiting room" with "no magazines" and "a desiccated potted palm." As she is about to undergo the abortion, her thoughts are offered in parentheses, where Parrott always relegated hard-to-reckon-with emotions: "(Be a corpse by then, maybe? Oh, don't lose your nerve, Patricia. A thousand a day in the city of Chicago, they say.)" Pat's lost children—one dead not long after childbirth, this one terminated—are the only things about which she ever expresses grief. Although Parrott often discussed her own abortions casually, her literary imaginations of the procedure provide more anguished reactions.

The first fiction story that Ursula Parrott ever published had, in fact, been about abortion. "Love Affair" was billed as the "sort of daring love story most editors are shy of—but a tender tragedy of a remarkably good girl." Twenty-year-old, up-and-coming dancer and singer Millicent finds herself in female trouble courtesy of affluent, handsome Richard, who tells the stage novice that she is the "prettiest girl he'd ever laid eyes on," seductive lines delivered at the start of a two-year affair that ends when Richard marries a woman of his class. After Millicent experiences "mad, bewildering hours in Richard's apartment," her friend Eloise comforts the "unhappy and ashamed" young lady by reassuring her that "outside New York it might be called going wrong, but inside, it was just making the grade." Thus educated about sex in the city, Millicent embarks on a proper New York City love affair.

After she confirms with a doctor that she is pregnant—"(of course, she did not tell the doctor she was not married—he might have been shocked)"—she decides to tell Richard; but his engagement, reported in the papers, stuns Millicent into silence. Eloise explains the ways of rich city men: "Richard was the son of a very important banker," and "sons of very important bankers did not usually mean that they wanted to marry a girl in a show, when they said they loved her." Millicent, a beauty contest winner from Iowa who now performs on the fringes of the New York stage, asks Eloise if they "can go see this man you know." "This man" is an abortionist—not stated directly, but clear enough that any nominally savvy reader would understand. Halfway through the story, Parrott makes Millicent's pregnancy explicit when she considers smoking a cigarette, despite her doctor's warning, and reasons that she could because "she wasn't going to have a baby."

Eloise advises Millicent to take "four or five days off" from the theater and not worry herself about it because "everybody gets in some kind of trouble, once in a while," assuring her that the procedure was "nothing." Eloise tells her to "remember it all goes past" but adds one troubling exception: "every time in your life you see a kid that looks something like him—like Richard—you'll remember it and wonder what your kid would have looked like." "Then," Eloise counsels, "you'll order yourself another drink," that modern cure-all for sorrow, pain, or regret.

Left to ponder the road ahead, Millicent calculates what she could get selling the gifts Richard gave her during their affair plus what she might make working as a secretary and then concludes that she is not going to the abortionist, after all. She leaves Eloise a note telling her that she "would rather have the kid than another boyfriend" before decamping for the deep cover of the Bronx to have her baby on her own. The final lines of the story convey Eloise's reaction to Millicent's note: "I don't believe Millicent's crazy. I don't even believe she's dumb, any more."

Parrott experienced at least three pregnancies during her affair with O'Connor. She often wrote in the third person—just as she might in a magazine story—when she wanted to communicate difficult things, as she did when composing "Just a Full Day," a story within a letter to O'Connor. "I'm writing this instead of telling it to you," she began, "so that, if your first reaction is 'God how unfortunate' you won't feel restrained by a sense of politeness or the thought that you might hurt me by some such comment, as you might feel if I were there."[16] In the story, she wakes up on this "full day" with a "curious dizziness," which is "an unmistakable indication, to anyone who's ever been in what the Church so subtly describes as 'delicate health and condition'" that she "could be" again. She makes an appointment with "the doctor who'd announced to her that that would probably never happen to her," who informs her that he had "thought the possibility remote," but "it undoubtedly has happened": she was pregnant. It is unclear if the pregnancy was a surprise because she had been practicing birth control or because of prior gynecological problems.

Parrott shifted gears to address O'Connor directly: "If you would like to have a child...the stalwart son to be a great delight to your fifties...I am entirely willing. I should be very glad in fact, to have the child." She continued: "If, however, you think (my favorite phrase) the world being what it is, the managing of the project would be too complicated, that's that.... I find myself entirely willing to defer to your judgment." She assured him that, as with Marc and Lindesay, if she had this child Hugh would be under no obligation to her. She was an assiduously modern woman, after all, perfectly capable of raising a child without a father. She would not involve him more than he wanted and would never "let it circumscribe [his] life." Rather, she would "go right on working [at her department store advertising job], diet and take care of one's self...save one's money...arrange some well-thought-out lies, and take a couple of months off in the late Fall." She had friends who lived out of town who already considered her "eccentric," with whom she could stay after she started showing. "With good luck," she continued, "I can go back to work in six weeks. Bad luck, figure eight or ten. Then, obviously, your responsibility for me ends." "The responsibility for the child," Parrott added, "we'd share equally." It would all be handled with discretion, laid out on the page just like the plot of a very modern novel.

"And what would one do with the child after?" Parrott asked in anticipation of objections to the outcome that she clearly preferred. She knew "dozens of women in Boston who board infants for from four to twelve dollars a week," noting that the same kind of women must surely exist in New York. Alternately, her sister Lucy was "baby mad" and would "jump at the chance to bring another up, and would believe, or pretend to, that it was the child of a friend," if Parrott told her so. Parrott described a kind of "Companionate Parenthood," as she put it, invoking Judge Ben Lindsey's "Companionate Marriage." It is, she argued, "not preposterous for two grown up and civilized people to decide to share responsibility for a child." Of course, it surely would have seemed so at the time; Parrott was reasoning in terms that remain, nearly one hundred years later, far from universally accepted.

Parrott was cavalier, more so on the page than in reality, about what would happen if O'Connor decided "it can't be managed." If that's the case, then "I'll go have it fixed up sometime in the next couple of weeks." The thought of having an abortion "disturbs me just about as much as the thought of a brief visit to the dentist." "I don't want to have my hand held metaphorically, in any sense at all. Just one of a couple of things about which I'm thoroughly feminist." In the three years since she and Lindesay separated, this was the first time that she had found herself pregnant. Deploying her wit, she added, "Well, what's a half hour in three years? Fault of the system."

Sandwiched in an otherwise trivial letter between discussions of her new sporty haircut, going to work on the Hudson Tubes (as the railway line between Manhattan and New Jersey was called), and O'Connor's latest article about Secretary of State Florence Knapp's census fraud trial in Albany, she revisited the unresolved matter: "this is my last comment on the progeny project. Can do gayly and nonchalantly and happily. But if you feel it would develop into a curtailment of your freedom of action, sooner or later, the answer is absolutely 'No.'"[17]

O'Connor opted for Parrott to undergo the abortion. As promised, she put on a good face. Of the doctor, Parrott wrote, "She is putting me through a very strange procedure that I never heard about, but assures me that all will indubitably be well forthwith." She soon reported, "Been to see dentist. Exercise verboten for three or four days....I feel simply gala," adding "it will be simply lovely to see you and have no concern with delicate this or that."[18] Parrott saved her suffering for her stories.

This was not Parrott's first abortion. When she was a twenty-three-year-old newlywed, in 1922, she terminated a pregnancy. The doctor she saw in 1928 remembered her from six years before: "You were a funny child with a string of amber beads and an expression of complete bewilderment about everything." Parrott wittily volleyed that she had "lost the amber beads and the bewildered expression both." She now saw abortion as a rite of passage for women, irreverently suggesting that "someone certainly ought to write a Book of Etiquette about" it; "it would be very useful....Write it myself when I'm seventy."[19] Like many of her social set, Parrott used flippancy to mask the things that troubled her most.

This was also not Parrott's last abortion. While O'Connor was filing articles from the field, Parrott made another "announcement." "What shall I do?" she asked rhetorically, "Nothing, except visit dentist at end of September, if your decision is as before." Parrott again did her best to be cavalier, giving O'Connor "a month to consider" what she referred to as his decision, relegating her wishes to the back burner.[20]

The doctor she consulted for this abortion was Dr. Mary Halton, a Stanford-educated "surgeon, obstetrician and pathologist" whom the *New York Times* described as "a champion of women's rights." Parrott described Halton as "someone very good" when she at first held out hope that her obstetric experience might involve bringing a child into the world. At O'Connor's urging, however, Parrott underwent another abortion, which she described in some detail because of its novelty. Dr. Halton "persuaded me last Monday to wait another fortnight (from then) before...having the tooth extracted," she explained, using her favored euphemism. "This system of treatment which she has evolved (it originated in Vienna) is ninety percent effective, has the advantages of avoiding the least shock, necessitating no modification of one's freedom of action whatever, and produces a return to normalcy with not even an hour or two's discomfort." Parrott saw Dr. Halton twice a week while undergoing the treatment, of which she said, "Objectively, I find it very interesting." Recall Parrott's youthful gynecological ambitions, which contributed to her ability to study this matter somewhat at a remove. This was "a very interesting truth about so many things," she explained. "Keep them detached, examine them as curious phenomena, and they are interesting, illuminating,—even entertaining. But let them lose their objectivity, get subjective about them, and oh God." This is a "swell system about things like the dentist," she added.[21] She had become a first-class compartmentalizer.

Parrott got pregnant again in 1931, the same year as her disastrous marriage to Charles Greenwood. This time she did not ask O'Connor for anything, including permission to proceed. Instead, she announced that she had decided "to have a bastard," using a term of derision that she certainly did not mean. She was rethinking her life, she told O'Connor, sounding an awful lot like a feminist freeing herself from the patriarchy: "I shall live now, and work, and be free of men forever," move "to Connecticut, permanently," "work as hard as I can, and take care of myself," and not "drink again for a year." The child would be "something of my own to work for. Not a child with whom I have the choice of taking him away from my sister, or letting him alone with her, and stirring up a conflict," referring to ongoing parenting tensions with Lucy.[22]

Despite her certainty in this moment, Parrott eventually agreed to undergo another abortion. This one was grueling. Despite the fact that she "did the best [she] could for this situation not to come about," presumably referring to some form of birth control, she "tried to be brave about it when it did." The "physical pain and weakness" that followed the procedure were awful, as was the "mental anguish" she underwent when O'Connor left her alone to recover from the surgery. Her "year of jitters" had become unbearable. Parrott began a letter to O'Connor that she said would begin and end with clichés, which she could not help, given the circumstances: "By the time you get this,—I shall be at least an hour beyond ever receiving its answer. Yes, dear, I shall be dead."[23] Intimating James Cain–worthy plotting about her impending "odd accident," Parrott expressed hope that her "family will collect double indemnity under the accident clause." There should "be enough left to educate Marc…and I can do no more for him, for there is not enough of me left to do anything for anyone now."

O'Connor had, at last, driven her to this low point. He had "cast enough illumination on modern life" that she could "bear no more." "I went with you," she told him in her suicide note, "as far along the road of modernity as I could, farther than many women would have gone. But, now I take the only dignified exit that remains." She would have welcomed the traditional path with him, marriage and child-rearing, and could not help but think about the traumas of her abortions as she contemplated an end to her suffering. "I tried to live by your terms. They weren't bearable. I fought hard for bearable ones. I was fighting (this is the cliché at the end or near it) for life." "And so goodbye," she signed off, "Kit."

Reading this downtrodden letter, it is hard not to think of the scene in *Ex-Wife* in which Patricia "experimented with argument, rage, anguish, hysteria and threats of suicide" when her husband leaves her. As he packs his things, she considers slashing her wrists so that he would have to call the doctor and stay until she recovered. Pat decides against it when she realizes that "he might just walk out and leave me to die of the slashes." In Parrott's "Life Sentence," the narrator describes a character named Kitty—yes, Kitty—who "tried to kill herself once" after a "battle of the century" with her lover, who publicly put her "in her place" by telling her what a "stupid, tiresome, exigent gal she was." Kitty slashes her wrists with an "old razor-blade," hitting "a good-sized artery." She survives only because a concerned friend gets the janitor from her building to let him into her apartment and whisks her off to St. Vincent's Hospital in time to save her life, while also managing to keep it out of the papers. Her savior later explains that Kitty's attempt was "all over a heel that made speeches about women! But Kitty thought she couldn't live without him."

Parrott, too, survived. In the spring of 1933, when she was admitted to French Hospital on West 30th Street under the name Mrs. Katherine Peters to avoid publicity after experiencing what she described as multiple uterine hemorrhages in three weeks, she told her agent that this stress-induced emergency was to blame for her recent spate of missed writing deadlines. She had been "all alone working on that new outline of *The Tumult [and the Shouting]*" when she "had one so awful" that she "just ended up on the floor." Had she not been able to phone a friend to take her to the hospital, "no fooling" she "would have been thoroughly dead by morning." She was "all fixed up now except so weak," anticipating discharge soon and expressing hope that she might be able to get back to work.[24] Was the story she told her agent on this occasion a cleaned up version of what happened in "Life Sentence" or simply a better outcome than befalls the passionate, modern, appropriately flippant woman in Parrott's "Though You Be Far," who has an unspecified "hemorrhage" that leads her to Switzerland to seek treatment, where she dies?

Parrott struggled with problems of a gynecological nature for the rest of her life and underwent multiple operations to try to resolve her condition, including one that she described as "a complete flop." "Noone on earth," she explained, "could estimate whether this is the conclusion inevitable from the time of my first abortions in my marriage, or for things that happened later." Parrott reflected philosophically, as always, on her situation, pondering an elective surgery that would solve the problem once and for all, which she described as a complete excision of her sexual life: "It is in a way a release, from any more disasters, or hopes that turn out badly, or misunderstandings inevitable for a woman like me dealing with the modern pattern, or that complete hell of sexual jealousy." Always searching for the bright side, Parrott described a silver lining: "My mind won't ever be obscured any more by my female emotions.... And I should be able to recollect enough of love to put in books."[25]

1933 marked the real end of Hugh and Ursula's six-year affair. It was a rough and punishing finale, so much so that it even inspired one indignant missive from her usually stoic sister. Lucy explained to Hugh that she had just been "summoned to New York," where she found her sister "on the point of collapse," the cause for which she laid at his feet.[26] "All I can get out of her," Lucy wrote, "is that you are so tired of her...and I'm not to worry...and something about a story she was supposed to write." Ursula had taken sedatives, thanks to which she was "sleeping completely exhausted." No wonder she had been struggling with her writing; she was in the depths of despair. Lucy blamed him for squandering her sister's talent "as ruthlessly as if it belonged to you," explaining that "you keep her so miserable she can scarcely ever write." Because Ursula felt herself forever in his debt "for encouraging her" to be a writer in the first place, she remained devoted to him despite his neglect and ill treatment.

Lucy wished that she had enough money of her own that her sister could "go completely away, and enjoy herself for a long time." But Parrott had to keep writing because she had "spent so lavishly on a tennis court and a beach club and liquor for her friends to have the best possible time at her home" in addition to supporting her, Marc, and "three people in Boston, whom father used to support." "I could cry," Lucy went on, about how dedicated her sister was to others' happiness and how much she spent on improving the quality of other peoples' lives. "Last week when she looked as miserable as possible," Lucy recounted, "she spent a whole afternoon taking me to Abercrombie's new dog department and to tea, my favorite place, and insisting that I have a new Spring coat." O'Connor would "never find anyone more generous or honest in important matters or more anxious to be fair to everyone." She begged him to be kind to her downtrodden sister to help her get back on her feet. Despite its moving portrait of a woman who had given until she had nothing left, there is no reason to believe that Lucy's letter made any impact.

Parrott eventually looked back on her relationship with O'Connor as a "long war," which she was "forgetting so fast" that it reminded her of what she'd heard men say of their time in the trenches, "that afterward it all blurred, and one didn't remember anything except isolated and inconsequential incidents and couldn't think any more why they had seemed so tremendously important at the time." "You don't know how often you talk about twenty four being the ideal age for women," Parrott wrote to O'Connor in a postmortem assessment of their relationship. "I was twenty four when you met me. Dot was twenty four when you married her, wasn't she? No, you find any woman a great nuisance when she graduates from the irresponsible age."[27]

On April 13, 1934, in Manhattan, forty-year-old Hugh O'Connor married twenty-four-year-old Hope Kelsey, a recent Radcliffe graduate with whom he would have two children and remain married until his death in 1967. Parrott knew about the wedding well before it happened, telling her agent, "I'm reminded by a couple of people that I always predicted Hugh would marry, faced by his fortieth birthday, a very young girl, any very young girl—which he did last week you know."[28] There was no comfort, however, in being right.

ELEVEN

The Business of Being a Writer

In the midst of one of their arguments, O'Connor told Parrott something that appalled her: "It should be some satisfaction to me that the things I've written down on paper, faint echoes of emotions we shared, will be remembered after me." Her book publisher, Hal Smith, was equally unfeeling when he tried to cajole her out of a period of writer's block by telling her, "Love may be an illusion but Royalties are a reality." Parrott was not amused by what she termed "the implications" of Smith's aphorism, which she interpreted as, "You may be broken hearted little girl, but I'll make you fifty thousand dollars and then you won't remember."[1]

Being an author was, however, Parrott's job, and her only means of supporting her family. Fortunately for her, during the booming 1920s, the United States' increasingly educated, urban middle class developed an enthusiasm for buying books and magazines. People displayed them in their living rooms and had animated discussions, over cocktails, about the latest novel reviewed in the *Times* or story from the *Saturday Evening Post*. In the 1920s, nineteen different US magazines hit a subscriber base of over one million, and six surpassed two million. Parrott's stories regularly appeared in the widely read pages of *Liberty*, the *American Magazine* (see figure 24), and *Cosmopolitan* (which was not associated with a female readership until much later), as well as in women's magazines like *Ladies' Home Journal* and *Good Housekeeping*, which *Vanity Fair* called "the most powerful group of periodicals in America, in the sense that they are the most far-reaching and claim the greatest degree of intimacy with the daily life of their [presumably female] readers."[2] The sheer number of eyes on these magazines convinced advertisers to invest in each issue, allowing the magazines, in turn, to generously compensate writers.

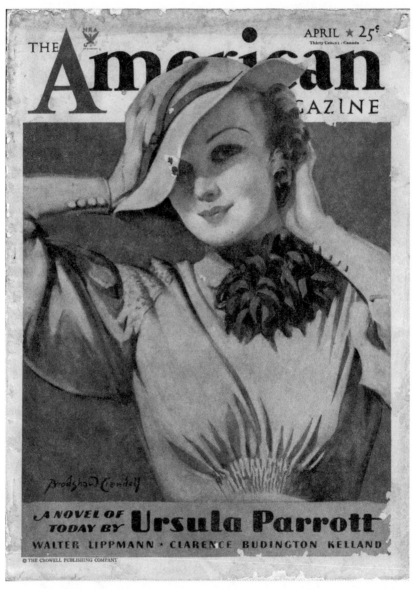

FIGURE 24. Parrott generated much of her income by publishing of-the-moment magazines stories, which also kept her name in circulation between books. Her "novel of a business woman," *Merchant Princess*, got top billing when it began its serialization in the *American Magazine*'s April 1934 issue. (Author's collection.)

It was not unusual for Parrott to earn $10,000 or more for a substantial short or multipart story in the 1930s—that's around $200,000 in today's money, adjusted for inflation. Such an impressive figure makes it obvious why so many authors would publish in popular magazines, even if some claimed that such placement served a purely economic purpose. The tension between being thought of as an artistic or a commercial writer was especially acute at time when American literature was experiencing a renaissance, along with the proliferation of literary taste- and culture-making from the "high" (prestigious literary magazines and literary prizes) to the "low" (like the mainstream subscription-based Book-of-the-Month Club, which began in 1926).[3]

Mass market magazines filled their pages with fiction by the best-known authors of the day, the likes of Edith Wharton, Sinclair Lewis, Edna Ferber, Dashiell Hammett, Dorothy Parker, Sherwood Anderson, F. Scott Fitzgerald, and many others whose names are all but forgotten now, including Ursula Parrott, Viña Delmar, Betty Smith, Faith Baldwin, Viola Brothers Shore, and dozens of others. Writers knew that prestige was meted out for "capital-L literature," deemed such when it was published in "genteel," intellectual, but modestly paying magazines like *Scribner's*, *Harper's Monthly*, and the *Atlantic Monthly*, along with books that garnered critical acclaim in the "right places." But the lines between these imagined markets was blurry in both the magazine and book worlds. When Jonathan Cape & Harrison Smith published *Ex-Wife*, it was advertised alongside their other first editions, like William Faulkner's *The Sound and the Fury*, Radclyffe Hall's *Adam's Breed*, and the collected poems of D. H. Lawrence. Stories that appeared in the more widely read magazines could also meet with critical recognition, winning literary prizes as Edna Ferber did for *So Big*, which was first serialized in *Woman's Home Companion* before the novel went on to win the recently created Pulitzer Prize.[4]

The magazines Parrott spent her career writing for were largely considered purveyors of "middlebrow" writing, which, as fellow author Margaret Widdemer observed in 1933 without any condescension intended, focused primarily on the challenges of contemporary life.[5] These stories spoke to readers about the issues they faced in the worlds in which they lived, which is precisely why *Vanity Fair* saw the fiction-laden women's magazines as achieving exceptional intimacy with readers. Widdemer argued that "highbrow" writers—she specifically names Hemingway and Faulkner—wrote about matters that were far removed from most readers' reality; they earned their elite status in part because their writing was neither relatable nor useful, which is precisely what made it seem more like art.

It was the so-called middlebrow writers, however, especially the women, who consistently engaged with the gender wars of early twentieth-century life. Although they often wrote about the same ideas—work and careers, marriages and divorces, motherhood and reproductive issues—their treatment of these subjects varied considerably. For example, Faith Baldwin's 1932 *Week-End Marriage*—first a novel, soon after a film of the same name—is one of many like-minded stories of the era about what happens when women move into traditionally male jobs (as lawyers, reporters, doctors, executives): they are blamed for undermining the male head of household.[6] *Week-End Marriage* cautioned its readers about female ambition, as did many of Parrott's stories. But Parrott's stories usually revolved around how successful women were unfairly scorned by less successful, or even unsuccessful, male characters. In Baldwin's novel, a female character plays outside of her league, becomes too much like a man, and suffers for it. In a Parrott story, there was no league women should not have access to; it was male attitudes that failed to accommodate the new woman.

These differences were not, however, always evident to the reading public or the critical establishment, which tended to lump mass market writers together—especially when they were female. In fact, *Cosmopolitan* once played a game with its readers when it published "A Little Love," which they billed as "a story written by guess who?" "This is a good story. Naturally. But who wrote it?" The magazine listed a dozen regular *Cosmopolitan* contributors—Faith Baldwin, Charles Bonner, Paul Gallico, Katharine Brush, and Ursula Parrott among them. Most readers guessed that the story had been penned by Parrott, but they were wrong. It was, in fact, Faith Baldwin's story.[7] Baldwin—who was one of Parrott's Connecticut neighbors—traversed similar thematic territory, though she was nowhere near as critical of the sexist problems women faced.

When she conducted a surveyed of women's magazines of this era, Helen Woodward deemed most of the fiction to be "sugary and noble and with the inevitable happy ending," following the "sentimental conventions of the period" and devoid of the "illusion of reality." Although writers like Parrott were stigmatized for catering to romantic tastes, her stories not only lacked sentimentality but were relentlessly cynical; they have plenty of romance in them but are rarely romantic. Could you be considered—and, as was also the case, dismissed—as a romance writer if the relationships you imagined were almost all failures and if you used your romances to address subjects like abortion, unmarried parenting, and the intense pressures on women in the workplace? *Time* magazine described readers turning to Parrott's "books to find many a lush passage written in…hot chocolate sauce."[8] Which is to say, the answer is yes.

When Parrott's "First Love" was republished in *The Best American Love Stories of the Year* for 1932, editor Margaret Widdemer—who published her assessment of middlebrow writing the following year—categorized Parrott's story with another that appeared alongside it in the collection, F. Scott Fitzgerald's "A New Leaf," about a love affair doomed by alcoholism. The stories were both "so deliberately aloof and ironic…that we are precipitated into complete acceptance of love's primary importance unaware."[9] Parrott's story was about how hard it was to be a child of divorced parents. But one could not be blamed, based on title alone, for thinking it was "just another love story," precisely the kind of misunderstanding that obscured many of the things that Parrott wrote about.

Looking back on fiction that appeared in *Good Housekeeping* between 1932 and 1950, the magazine's editor refuted the misconception that "large-circulation magazines will print only light fictional fare, with most emphasis on romance," observing that "this was never more than partly true." Parrott's stories insistently revealed cracks in the veneer of the upward trajectory of the "new woman." But she also had to make money and often bemoaned that she was developing a reputation for being a light writer of emotional stories. Her retort to that, however, was both clever and insightful: "melodramatic [is] just a word men use to describe any agony that might otherwise make them feel uncomfortable."[10]

Parrott wrote "all the time."[11] Staring at a blank wall to reduce distractions, she typed her own stories, which were then retyped by a secretary before her agent took a light editorial pass. If she did not have time to have a manuscript typed and corrected prior to handing it off, Bye would have to navigate her "typing at its worst." On such occasions she might recommend that he scrutinize a manuscript with extra caution if, for example, a story was especially "subtle in its implications" and "only needs three or four dumb typist mistakes here and there to ruin it."[12] She considered writing a craft, something she had to work at every day of the week. When she was not frantic to meet a deadline, Parrott was a perfectionist: she preferred producing anywhere from two to seven drafts of a manuscript before handing it over to a publisher. She once boasted that she never turned in a manuscript until it was polished to her satisfaction, at minimum three drafts in; however, this was a professional practice that she was not be able to sustain.

Parrott was a heavy researcher, taking notes during her travels, using her set of Encyclopedia Britannica to mine details, and spending hours at the library, as she did when she wrote *Next Time We Live*, which required four full days at the library before she could accurately describe the details of a Manchurian railroad station for a single scene. Her narrators and female characters are always smart and literate, quoting William Butler Yeats, Robert Browning, and Lewis Carroll; discussing John Galsworthy, H. G. Wells, or *Vanity Fair* ("Thackeray's not Condé Nast's"). In her correspondence she casually drops lines from John Gay, discusses her thoughts about recently published books (the new biography of Mussolini, the latest sociological study of marriage and divorce), and quotes from published literary letters (for example, George Bernard Shaw).[13] Parrott kept up with culture and events both to be literate herself and to make her female characters smart, expert conversationalists.

But despite her seriousness about the sophistication of her characters and the craft of writing, Parrott struggled with procrastination and a tendency to get distracted, problems that had been in evidence since her student days at Boston Girls' Latin School and Radcliffe. Parrott's Connecticut estate was supposed to provide an escape from her hectic life in the city and a quiet place for her to write, but when she was there, she often felt that she could only get writing done in town, which meant bills incurred at hotels like the New Weston, Barbizon Plaza, Algonquin, and Lombardy. She struggled to balance her time and her finances, running (and writing) here and there, in the process realizing that it was impossible to do everything well. In the spring of 1933, her agent pleaded with her to "try staying out in the country for three months without coming in to see if you would not feel a lot better." Parrott took his advice and moved "up to the country permanently."[14] But permanence was never Parrott's strong suit; within days she was drawn back to Manhattan.

The fault did not just lie with the distractions of the city, either. "I had to scrub floors," she complained to Bye from her country estate when she was short on help and in the middle of a string of back luck. "A lady ran into the little car and smashed it up. I had to order groceries. I had one of my three days attacks of insomnia which makes me unable to distinguish between the names of my own characters, in other words, I shall be 100% late on everything this week." Her literary to-do list was formidable:

A. Red Book. Mr. Balmer will get his missing pages Tuesday.
B. Cosmopolitan. (I am but sick about this as a new contract.). Tell Burton copy dependably Wednesday.
C. Good Housekeeping. (No need of bothering him until Tomorrow at least.). The new copy Thursday.

   [*Author's note: there is no D in Parrott's list, a sure sign of its author's frantic state.*]

E. McCall's. I owe them a short story before the serial. The short story called "A Princess Goes Home" (Russian). The first installment of serial is due today. Copy from then in progress of work. Pages will come on Friday.

In classic Parrott style, she signed off humorously. "When you have comforted all those people you should get a medal and you will get my appreciation for a miracle. Love, wearily, Ursula."[15]

Time management had been a known weakness, but money management was her Achilles heel. Around the time he encouraged her to stay out in the country, Bye also tried to help Parrott stabilize her finances, urging her to reduce her "expenses to $200 a month for everything" (see figure 25). He observed that she had "little idea of the value of money" and might "sharply be faced by a painful catastrophe."[16] She had developed extravagant spending habits, perhaps understandable given her astronomical paychecks and the way acquisition soothed, however superficially, the disappointments she experienced. Although her female characters were almost always responsible spenders and even diligent savers, Parrott "evidently went in for living on a what the hell, here today and gone tomorrow, basis," she told her agent as she tried to modify her behavior. "Living for the moment," Malcolm Cowley recalled of this era in New York, "meant buying an automobile, radio or house, using it now and paying for it tomorrow."[17]

Parrott's son characterized his mother as "a spender," remembering her being "totally tapped out" as "an almost annual event" requiring a mad scramble "in the atmosphere of black coffee, cigarette stubs, and the clacking upright on a card table, and sleepless nights."[18] Parrott would overspend, borrow money or sell stock to pay debts, prioritize the most consequential creditor, and then beg for advances to keep the financial machine moving until her next story, book, or movie payment came in. As with so many aspects of her

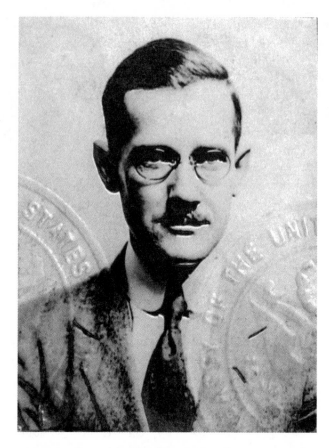

FIGURE 25. Parrott's longtime literary agent, Connecticut neighbor, fixer, and friend, George T. Bye, as he appeared in his March 5, 1920, passport application. (Passport #181630, courtesy of the National Archives and Records Administration.)

life, Parrott increasingly relied on her agent to see her through these matters. Bye was her frontline fixer—with editors and publishers when manuscripts were overdue and with banks, mortgage companies, and debt collectors when she bungled her expenditures. He also repeatedly loaned her money, sometimes deferring his percentage on a sale or giving her cash outright, putting a significant stress on their relationship as she entangled him in her formidable financial puzzle.

In a single letter, she might instruct Bye to "sell twenty shares of Long Island at the [stock] market" and cash out "over twelve hundred"; write a $300 check for Lucy's expenses; send $500 to pay her lawyers; compensate

Bye's agency for whatever debt she owed from an earlier loan; and pray, for her sake, that a magazine check would arrive on Friday to get her through the weekend. In late summer 1933, Parrott itemized $1,789 in outstanding bills:

$356 taxes due May first

$310 payment on note promised for August fifteenth

$230 Barbizon-Plaza, who write threatening notes daily

$100 Holden-McLaughlin—same thing

$100 Saks—same thing

$350 balance Artesian well—same thing only worse

$250 Five accounts here on which fifty dollars a piece at least should be payment (gasoline, grocer, Packard repair etc.)

Asking Bye if he could hold off taking his percentage of a payment until she paid off these debts, Parrott assured him that she was living "very economically at the moment, and not incurring any new debts at all." She was especially anxious to pay off her Barbizon-Plaza Hotel bill because they were holding hostage, until she settled her debt, her new Encyclopaedia Britannica set, with which she filled out the textures of her stories.[19]

Bye urged Parrott to "think twice before spending money for even telephone calls, taxi cabs, any little casual expenses. He cautioned that "there will be daily temptations to buy this and that. You cannot be free with even small sums of money without breaking the back of your credit, already badly wrenched." He was concerned "that the chief sources of income of writers— magazine and motion pictures—are going to have to reduce their prices considerably" as the Depression continued to take its toll. "This, combined with small issues, is going to mean a hardship that has not yet touched you."[20]

In this, Bye was right. William Randolph Hearst's *Cosmopolitan* saw their advertising revenue drop 39 percent between 1929 and 1932, the year New York City claimed one million unemployed adults, and smaller cities, like Cleveland, Akron, and Toledo in Ohio, hit 50–80 percent unemployment. Magazines lowered advertising rates at the same time they were losing subscribers, with revenue dropping proportionately. *Cosmopolitan*, in whose pages Parrott frequently published, was fortunate, having spent much of the 1920s building up affluent, urban-dwelling subscribers with a taste for sophisticated products and stories.[21] Bye's point was that earnings would not always be what she was used to, so she should tighten her belt and keep her nose to the grindstone.

At the middle of the decade, Bye advised her to be proactive and pay the remaining $14,000 mortgage on her Connecticut house to avoid any future catastrophes. She agreed that it was the prudent thing to do: "My particular source of income being entirely dependent on keeping up my earning capacity and supporting two absolute dependents," Lucy and Marc, "would make it so much safer if we owned the place free and clear." At the moment, however, she was overdrawn and so announced austerity measures. She fired her assistant and typist, Louis Florey, because he "has gone in for little expense accounts" (she could "save money keeping an opera singer in the long run"). This is "in line with my new policy of trying to make slightly more sense" by saving around $80 per week using a local typist instead. She also vowed to send "Lucy to secretarial school to type my stuff," pressing her sister into unpaid administrative service.[22]

Despite these efforts, she found herself "in a worse jam" than ever before until she could scare up "a check or two." "I am the worst person about money I know," she humbly told Bye, acknowledging that she still owed him $1,100 in addition to being "overdrawn five times in the last eight days" at her bank. She was proceeding with reforms: "Lucy is off to secretarial school Monday morning. Marc is made to help Danny [the groundskeeper] round the place, hours and hours a day, to save Mamma the money for extra labor." "It'll be fine for his muscles," Parrott proclaimed with her characteristic positivity. There were always reasons to think that relief was, as the saying went, just around the corner. However, as anxious, unproductive, check-free days dragged on she grew increasingly pessimistic. "If in a week I haven't produced anything," she plotted, "I will take the Packard out and manage an accident, so at least [Marc and Lucy] won't be broke, as they will be if I can't write any more."[23] Given the number of fatal car wrecks that occur in Parrott's stories, and her occasional bouts with depression, was this just gallows humor?

Parrott often described writing as a mix of misery and gratification. After "fumbling around for days and days and days" on a story, Parrott was elated when "suddenly it flows like mad," allowing her to experience writing as "a pleasure." When she was in a bind, she would vow to "write [her] way out of it," and usually she did. But she bore such responsibility for her family's support that she never had the luxury of writing only what she wanted when she wanted. "Oh if I could only get this book written," she once proclaimed with desperation, "I would be free for a year,—and establish Lucy and Marc somewhere, and go around the world by myself. I keep saying to myself, 'Ten pages a day, thirty days, and then I could go.'" She fantasized about a different kind of literary life, one free of deadlines and pressure, and pined for "a day off from my word factory": "All the writing ladies, Miss [Edna] Ferber, Miss [Fannie] Hurst and so on, by the half-dozens have taken a shot at it, so why not me?" She loathed "being locked up in a room like a condemned criminal to wait for genius to burn. I like to see things going by. That's why I take so many trips—so I'll have new scenes."[24]

When her writing was at its best, she knew it. She usually offered assessments of her stories as she turned them in—as serious, ambitious, modern, or light reading. She described one story as "nice, though of no enormous cosmic significance" and another as "so full of cosmic significance I have a fear the plot gets lost here and there in the cosmos."[25] When she was struggling, Parrott welcomed guidance during the drafting process, from Bye or the magazine editors with whom she dealt. After she pitched a story idea to her agent, who usually sold it before or while it was being written, she might work with a magazine editor to agree on the length, setting, and even the story arc. These were certainly middlebrow negotiations for stories crafted to satisfy a given magazine's imagined readership. Usually this made for smooth and expeditious sailing, but not always.

In early 1935, for example, Parrott began writing a serialized story, "Country Club," for Sumner Blossom at the *American Magazine*, for which she was paid a substantial $8,000 advance. When Blossom was disappointed with the first two installments she submitted, Parrott conceded that her writing thus far was "not so hot." They discussed how she might fix the story, exchanging ideas about a scaled-down structure and modified plot. Parrott volunteered "to rewrite the first two parts" with the aim of making the characters more sympathetic to readers as well as tightening the story. After months of revision, however, she was "extremely disturbed" when Blossom rejected the serial. Parrott undertook further revisions only "to have it rejected again." "Mr. Blossom seemed anxious," Parrott reported to her agent, "lest Country Club be dated or unmodern. In my revision, I was unable with that story, to modernize it successfully, and as you know, I do not turn in bad work when I know it's bad. So I wrote him a brand new story ['Red Peonies'], spending just as much time on it as I usually spend on a serial, except for the ending, which I hurried."[26]

Mr. Blossom did not like "Red Peonies" either and proposed that Parrott's agent should sell it to another magazine. He also accused Parrott of not being "any good at revisions," about which she took great offense. She cited Edwin Balmer and William Bigelow, of *Redbook* and *Good Housekeeping* respectively, who both said they "don't know anyone who is able to add to the value of a story so much with a few revisions." Parrott had now "written nearly two hundred thousand words for Mr. Blossom for that eight thousand dollars," which she would have to return if they did not accept some version of the story. In addition to the unpaid labor, Blossom's rejection demeaned her writing abilities in a way she had not experienced before. Motivated by financial need and professional pride, Parrott kept revising "Red Peonies" through the end of the year, documenting her revisions installment by installment: she rearranged the story, shortened sentences, strengthened character motivations, rewrote entire episodes, and explained her motivations for each change.[27] This was her first writing catastrophe, and she was doing everything she could to fix it.

The *American Magazine* published only one story by Parrott after this debacle, which bore neither the title "Country Club" nor "Red Peonies" but rather the appropriately named "Second Choice." Of the over one hundred stories and serials she published during her career, this is one of only a handful that reads like a pure romance, complete with a happy ending.

Parrott never had the luxury of ignoring the marketplace. Since the magazines worked on shorter turnarounds than book publishers—despite their significant word count requirements for novels-in-one or serials—and paid quickly, she often wrote for them. She also took advantage of her literary cache when she participated in one "all-star serial," "The Woman Accused," published by *Liberty* magazine in 1933 in partnership with Paramount, who produced a film version. She was one of ten authors to contribute a chapter, along with Zane Gray, Irvin S. Cobb, Vicki Baum, and six others, which meant that this was well-paid, low-word-count, quickly produced work. The collaboration was a total Hollywood gimmick: "Script for Story Was Sent 19,800 Miles to Publishers," read the headlines. Despite the charming Nancy Carroll and Cary Grant in the starring roles, the film was "just fair entertainment."[28] However, it splashed Ursula Parrott's name across advertisements and reviews for months, as the serial and film were promoted by one of the foremost magazines and movie studios—not a bad dividend. Best of all, *The Woman Accused* includes a few seconds of celebrity-author footage in its opening sequence, the only moving image footage of Parrott that survives (see figure 26).

Parrott knew that authors who did not regularly produce "consequen-

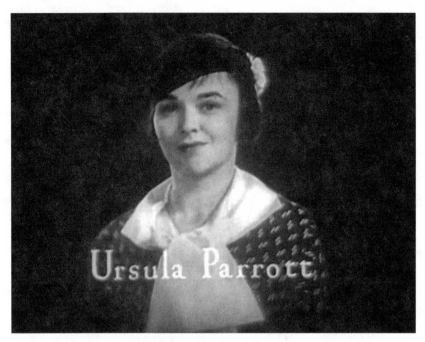

FIGURE 26. The only surviving moving image footage of Ursula Parrott appears in the opening credit sequence of the Paramount film *The Woman Accused*, which Parrott cowrote with ten other writers, including J. P. McEvoy, Gertrude Atherton, Rupert Hughes, and Viña Delmar (1933). (Frame enlargement.)

tial novels" were not taken seriously. Although she was often driven by a word-by-word and dollar-by-dollar work ethic, which she often struggled to maintain as her health, relationships, financial status, and emotional states ebbed and flowed, she also cared deeply about her literary reputation. She was stung when people like columnist Charles Driscoll dismissed her as "a 'money' writer," deeming "the quality of her writing" to be "not high, from a literary standpoint," which he attributed to her "tremendous rate" of publication. Her son Marc remembered her working "like a galley slave" with "the chaos and tension of making those eternal deadlines," at times producing up to 8,000 words in a single day to meet a deadline. Mass-market fiction writers have been defined by "speed, volume, and predictability, none of which aids in composing great literature." But this was the pace required of a writer whose financial exigencies never waned. Not surprisingly, Parrott had a clever refutation for this particular disparagement: "Well, the Victorians and the Russians all did their best work on a deadline, usually for a newspaper."[29]

At several points in her career, Parrott embarked very deliberately on what she considered a weighty literary undertaking, as she did with what became her 1933 novel, *The Tumult and the Shouting*. When she first conceived of it in 1931, she asked O'Connor if he would coauthor the book with her, promising half the proceeds in return. After he declined, Parrott struggled to draft it on her own. If only she could write fifteen pages a day, after twenty days of that she would have a draft and then could "take myself the hell out, sit somewhere in the sunshine and recover something to go on with." "I've got a psychosis about the Tumult and the Shouting," she explained to her agent as her writer's block dragged on. "It's been around my life so long, and tangled up with so many things, that I just stare at it instead of getting rid of it." The book was steeped in Parrott's family history, its seriousness about life over the course of generations meant to elevate her literary status: "Through it or never I get distinction as a novelist." She hoped it would "be the mechanics of setting [her] free"—financially, but also of the middlebrow reputation she feared she had developed.[30]

As she struggled to complete it, the novel came to epitomize "the sense of failure that for years now colored everything so much so greatly.... I am strongly conscious that I don't believe this or anything good for me can last, and sort of look for the disaster I've really expected for myself for so long." However, as she revised the manuscript in late summer 1933, she decided that it was "better than any book [she'd] ever done." Buckling under debts to creditors ranging from Saks to Uncle Sam, and in the midst of a push to finish revisions, she ended up in the hospital with her "old trouble—under the name of Pitman, because with the recent scandalous rumors broadcast about [her], to have Ursula Parrott turn up in a hospital with elaborate uterine hemorrhages would be just too much." From her hospital bed, Parrott worried: *Tumult* "may not be as perfect as once I hoped" but perhaps would be "good enough to be my chance for a comeback." As she finished work on the book, she encouraged her agent to "swagger just a little and not be thinking about troubles and debts as much as possibilities."[31] It must have been difficult to avoid being seduced by Parrott's optimism, which she managed to muster from the depths of increasingly dire situations.

After defecting from her long-time publisher, Hal Smith, over disagreements about advances and deadlines, Parrott published *The Tumult and the Shouting* with Longmans in November 1933. She dedicated the tale, which revolved around three generations of a Boston family through shifts in morality, social standing, and economic fortunes, to her sister, Lucy, and her son,

Lindesay Marc Parrott II. Although it is heavily plotted at times, including a rather dizzying cast of characters with numerous loves found and lost, secrets and betrayals, scandals and deaths, it has touching insights about the way one generation feels they suffer because of the time in which they live, knowing that a generation or two later they might have been able to manage different careers or marriages that are impossible in their day. This is especially the case for women who "get into trouble" and must deal with the consequences of their affairs. Halfway through the book, one character declares how strange it is "to see the generations coming along one after the other, all starting in so brave and sure, and all growing old and timid-like and uncertain. Until at the end there's nothing." In *Tumult*, Parrott was equal parts realist and nihilist.

Parrott, who was disappointed in how much she had done and how little she had to show for it, sharply critiques her generation throughout the novel. Parrott wasn't blaming others for her unfortunate situation exactly, but she used the book to take aim at some of her own worst impulses. As an older character observes, "They are all so busy now. Still, they get no more from life, they get less, than we do. It is as if they're afraid to stop." Another adds, "It is a kind of permanent hysteria, a hypnosis of motion, which keeps them going." Late in the novel, two characters around Parrott's age reflect, "We wanted to be free when we were young. Free for what, I don't remember." "Just to experiment," answers another. "Only we've got tired, too, if we'd embarked on the substantial life—marriage eternal and children frequent and troublesome.... The tacit choice was variety or permanency."

There is, the novel suggests, no easy path—only curiosity about the road not taken. Although Parrott came to regret almost everything about the process of writing of *The Tumult and the Shouting* and the difficult time in her life that it represented, the novel was warmly received, described in the *New York Times* as so "far beyond anything which Miss Parrott has previously written" that the reviewer felt "justified in demanding something more ambitious in the future." When another reviewer asked Parrott about the source of the novel's "measured tempo of maturity," she replied, "in explanation of the metamorphosis," that "one grows up as a writer."[32]

TWELVE

Third Husband, John Wildberg

THE FAINT RESEMBLANCE OF STABILITY

In the summer of 1933, Parrott arrived at her Connecticut home with the intention of hunkering down to put the finishing touches on *The Tumult and the Shouting*. Within weeks of her arrival, however, she abruptly decamped to Quebec for a romantic liaison with a writer named Robert Carse, with whom she took up temporary residence at the Hotel Bellevue in the Rivière-du-Loup. She reported being blissfully happy, despite the fact "the top of Canada is cold as hell" and she wished she had a "winter coat" with her.[1] Had she the requisite item it most certainly would have been a fur coat, the likes of which her up-and-coming female characters often received as gifts from men and her successful female characters bought for themselves.

With varying degrees of seriousness, Parrott entertained the possibility of several marriages in addition to the ones she executed. Bob Carse was one of these spousal contenders. Parrott casually informed her agent that she would "probably marry Bob. For various complicated reasons." For one, "he really loves me. Of course he's full of ambitions to reform me, and adores ordering me about, but all that doesn't matter. He makes me feel old, because I know underneath that I'm stronger than he, only I'll never let him know about it." In fact, Parrott was older, although Carse was unlikely to have known it given her expert concealment in this arena: he was born in July 1902, three years after Parrott, enough of a gap to upset someone exceedingly apprehensive about the disadvantages of time.[2]

She knew a few things about herself at this juncture in her life. "I'm difficult—that, also, I'm my age, have what is known as a flamboyant past (I'm perfectly indifferent about that now, I wanted to find out what this and that was like, I was restless, I was lonely, well I did what I did and it's done). To be vulgar about it, I'm no prize package. And I'm grateful to him for thinking

I'm so wonderful." She expressed little in the way of romantic feeling about Bob, though she felt that she was "fairly good for him, very stimulating and all that" despite the fact that "he doesn't stimulate my mind much, but he tries very touchingly to be good to me, and is often amusing and sweet.... He's companionable. Why should I expect more?" Parrott had downgraded her expectations as she sought a way to get back on her feet. With cheery optimism, she assured her long-married agent that her relationship with Bob would be as "permanent as your own marriage, my sweet."[3]

After returning from Canada, Bob moved into Ursula's country house. He didn't particularly "want to live in my house much, but I don't see where else is very practical for us to live, and be comfortable and do the amount of work we've got to do the next two months," referring to their respective writing deadlines. It was "nice living with a writer"—she had never had someone by her side with whom she could discuss the craft. However, their close working conditions had some peculiar consequences, for example when their stories had similar titles and plots. This became a problem when Parrott submitted "Country Club" to the *American Magazine*, because it bore an "unfortunate similarity to the short story 'Disenchanted,'" which they had just purchased by none other than Bob Carse. Parrott was forced to undertake those substantial revisions during her disastrous dealings with the magazine's editor in part due to the similarity.[4]

There was one other significant problem: Carse had a wife, whom he left to have his affair with Parrott. This was not an undisclosed marriage that Parrott might have professed ignorance about, either. Bob Carse had been married to Janet Carse, formerly Janet Wood, since the fall of 1925 and Parrott frequently had "the Carses" to dinner at Twin Elms.[5] Later in life Parrott would express regret about having broken up a marriage, and theirs was certainly a candidate for such remorse—not because she felt badly about having an affair with a married man but because she was blackmailed by Mrs. Carse.

This was, in fact, the second time Parrott had been blackmailed. The first was by "a maid, easily scared off," a relatively minor hiccup. This time, however, she "was the victim of quite an elaborate scam, the other parties being a cheap writer and the man's allegedly complaisant wife." Parrott disclosed very little about "this awful blackmail business" to her agent, only enough to get his advice about how best to keep her name out the papers and avoid another expensive legal incident. "I've always laughed off publicity as unimportant. I never shall again. Since that stupid woman proved herself able with her stupid lawyer—to make me so humiliated—so hat-in-hand and shabby and unsuccessful—I want the comfort, the reassurance of being Ursula Parrott much more than I ever wanted it before."[6]

There was nothing more characteristically Ursula Parrott than to write a thinly veiled version of her experience, turning her mistakes into income. Published from the safe distance of 1942, Parrott's "One More Such Victory" is about a successful woman writer, Susan, who meets Gregory at a cocktail party. He flatters her, holds her hand in a taxicab, and escorts her to "night clubs and smart dining places." Susan is halfway through a six-part serial for "*Women's Work*, the most conservative of the women's magazines," for which she would earn $24,000, money she desperately needs. One night at the theater, Gregory casually mentions to Susan that he had "been married—not happily. (She assumed that he had been divorced for many years.)." Since Gregory lives in New Jersey, Susan allows him to stay in her country house one evening "in the empty guest wing"; on another occasion, during a blizzard, she makes the same accommodation in her "six-room New York apartment." The story presents these sleepovers chastely, complete with locked doors and an emphasis on physical separation, which makes it even more shocking when Gregory's wife's lawyer names Susan as a respondent in her divorce suit. The lawyer threatens that once the papers are filed with the courts, "they will be public property." "Naturally," the lawyer adds, "you might like to see me" to avoid the bad publicity. Although Susan initially rejects giving in to blackmail, she realizes that no respectable magazine would ever publish her if the accusation got into the columns. So Susan hands over her precious income to the blackmailing wife, paying "a small fortune for her carelessness."

Unlike Susan, Ursula knew Bob was married. She was also certain that paying to keep her behavior out of the papers was worth it; she could swallow her pride for that and move on. "Because I begin to discover, in this my final effort to become a reasonable person in the sense that's usually used,—to be like everyone else, and know what I have in the bank, what I owe, and read my morning letters, how one feels inside is a matter of no importance."[7] Parrott was, in her own flawed way, trying to do the right things.

When Parrott looked back at the past several years of her life at the end of the 1930s, she wrote to the man she always thought of around New Year's Eve—Hugh O'Connor. Everything she had done "for at least three years" after their breakup was "a reaction from" him. Using parentheses to broach an uncomfortable subject, she added, "(yes, including my marriage—I was will-

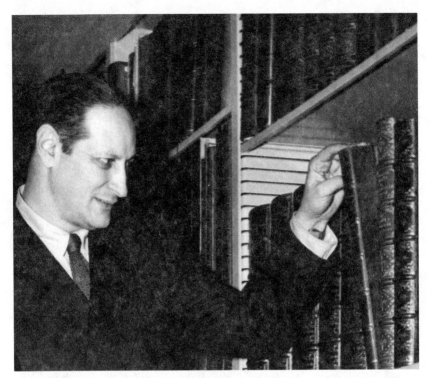

FIGURE 27. Parrott's third husband, John J. Wildberg, after giving a talk at Harvard University in 1947. (Unidentified photo, author's collection.)

ing to sell out for anything that faintly resembled stability)."[8] The marriage that Parrott was referring to on this occasion, which was the second that she blamed on O'Connor, was to the man who became her third husband, John Wildberg, whom she hoped might save her from a rash of passion-inspired mistakes (see figure 27).

Born in 1902 to Jacob and Joan Schwartz Wildberg, John Jacob Wildberg—nicknamed Jack—and his brother George were raised in a modern apartment building in a predominantly Jewish enclave on Eighty-Sixth Street on the Upper West Side, three blocks from Central Park. Jack graduated from Columbia College in 1921 and Columbia Law School in 1923, with a specialty in copyright law. He married his neighborhood sweetheart May Untermeyer in front of Rabbi Nathan Krass in the Crystal Room at the Ritz-Carlton in 1928. After honeymooning in Havana, the Wildbergs settled into a brownstone on the east side of Central Park. Five years after they tied the knot, in 1933, the Wildberg-Untermeyer marriage ended in a Reno divorce.[9]

Ursula met Jack under strange circumstances, when she went to him for legal assistance during "that shabby and dreadful business" of the black-mailing Carses. After their first meeting about the situation, Parrott offered Wildberg his "usual retaining fee," which he refused. He first wanted to see if he could do anything for her before accepting a retainer. Wildberg's generosity in this matter prompted Parrott to editorialize that "not all Jews are like Spelke and Herwitz," other lawyers with whom she had worked; the former had handled her divorce from Charles Greenwood. Whenever the occasion arose, Parrott did not miss the chance to be casually anti-Semitic, making disparaging jokes and comments, in this case en route to a compliment. She once remarked that she was "the only one not of the Chosen People" living in her apartment building on the West Side, a situation that she "simply hated."[10] But there were, as Wildberg would prove, exceptions to Parrott's alleged distaste for "Semitics."

What started as a client relationship quickly evolved into something more. Wildberg "began to take me places, to meet his family, and to dinner and places and we began to talk to each other."[11] He told her that he "did not plan to marry again, until he was forty or so," many years in the future. After meeting her, however, "he changed his mind." Just months after her humiliating Carse debacle, Parrott had reason to be jubilant about this out-of-left-field romance. She'd "never understand why he fell in love with [her]...but he did, sort of between a Friday and a Monday," despite the fact that she "told him about the saga of O'Connor to Greenwood to Carse," a full confession about her recent exes. Wildberg's outlook inspired hope in the weary author: "He said in substance that he'd spent his twenties about as foolishly too, and that it didn't matter if I cared about him enough to make a new start with him, and be old fashioned and permanent about marriage. He said all the things, quite simply and honestly, that I'd stopped believing men ever said, and every time I met him I liked better a solidness and calm about him." Solidness and calm were precisely the qualities that Parrott had begun imagining as positive attributes for male characters in her stories as the 1930s progressed. Such men did not have traits that would dazzle a twenty-one-year-old looking for adventure; but thirty-somethings knew better than to follow only their passions down the aisle.

Parrott pleaded with her agent not to make a joke about "gefeulte fisch" when she made her announcement: "I want to marry John Wildberg and he wants to marry me, with an if." Disagreements about finances had contributed to the demise of Jack's first marriage and made him cautious when considering a second. During their expeditious courtship, the two discussed the matter frankly, which is why Parrott presented Wildberg's wish to marry her as having a proviso. Jack told her, "I don't want ever to touch a cent you earn, I want to support you, I couldn't marry and not support a wife. I mean by that, I'll provide you with an apartment, food, a servant, a car. But you've got to live on my income. You can spend your money on your child, your sister and your clothes, because. Because I can't afford to take over your responsibilities."

Versions of this arrangement appear in many an Ursula Parrott story. But such demands involving financial dependence were usually inspired by male pride, meant to bring a successful woman down a few notches to make a less competent man feel better about himself. The situation with Jack was different. He was offering her security without asking her to give up her career. Jack told Ursula that they would have $100 a week for expenses, or around $2,000 a week today, hardly a pittance.[12] He reasoned that, "because having lost all he'd made in the Depression, and started a year or so ago to make it again, he was determined to live on less than he made." Parrott had never experienced this kind of fiscal responsibility before.

Although he had been practicing law for many years, with offices in Midtown on Fifth Avenue, Wildberg's passion was the theater. He had just begun producing plays, and his first successes took place alongside his budding romance with Ursula.[13] Jack pledged, "I'll see you never starve while I'm alive, and have insurance when I'm dead, only I want to save enough before I'm fifty [so that] we can retire."[14] Here was someone promising to care for her who fully accepted her right to a career of her own. But Wildberg had one significant "if" that accompanied his proposal. He could not marry her "with seven thousand dollars worth of debt round [her] neck," which is what she had at the moment. She had to figure out what she owed and what she made, pay her bills, "and promise to spend just so much a month" for herself, Marc, and Lucy. This was to be done *before* they got married. Jack's demand was controlling but not unwarranted. As Parrott's agent could attest, she could not handle her own finances without running them into the ground.

Ursula was untroubled by Jack's conditions. Bye had just sold a story to *McCall's* and she was expecting to "be solvent" right away. The letters she penned the year prior to Jack's proposal had been frantic, brimming with desperation, missed writing deadlines, and anxiety. Parrott now beamed with pride over the fact that Wildberg said "all the things," she supposed, "responsible men had said to women they wanted to marry, forever." "Only no one ever said them to me before." She was especially pleased with their discussions about Marc, who was part of the package for anyone marrying this ex-wife. Wildberg told her, "If I said I'd be a father to your child, it would be a silly lie. He's too old, and you've brought him up according to your ideas of your own with which I should have neither the right nor the desire to interfere. You have him live with us always, of course, and I'll try to be a friend to him." He was saying all the right things.

But as with so many things in her life, the *McCall's* story, which would have made her solvent, fell through after she missed one too many deadlines. Parrott told Wildberg about the hiccup, and he said he would work it out with her agent by paying off her debts to expedite the marriage and to meet his conditions for her debt-free status. It was a shell game, or perhaps a calculated investment. Wildberg told his fiancé that he wanted them "to be married forever not for a month or two," and Parrott hoped for the same. "I'm in an awful daze," she explained. "I just can't believe that there is anyone in the world who wants to take care of me, actually." It had never happened before.

Two weeks after Parrott accepted Wildberg's proposal, the *Boston Herald* ran the headline "Ursula Parrott Weds Third Time." The couple exchanged vows in Parrott's long-term apartment at the Hotel Lombardy on March 29, 1934. The rabbi who performed Wildberg's first wedding ceremony was replaced by a secular officiant, New York Supreme Court Justice Aaron Steuer. Around fifty "persons important in the literary and theatrical worlds witnessed the ceremony," along with Parrott's ten-year-old son. The orchestra leader John Green, who had recently written the music for the hit "Body and Soul," and "a friend of the bride" from Weston, Connecticut, Mrs. Burton Davis, acted as witnesses.[15]

After the wedding, "Mr. and Mrs. Wildberg sailed on the steamer 'Haiti' for a West Indies cruise," after which, the papers announced, they would live in Parrott's home in Wilton. On the passenger list, "Ursula Wildberg" shaved four years off her of age to make herself a respectable five months younger than her new husband. Parrott had selected the West Indies for their honeymoon for a practical reason, of which Wildberg surely approved: she was writing a story for *Redbook* and needed to study local color.[16] The pragmatism of their honeymoon destination, to which she had been with other husbands and lovers before, does not reflect how wonderfully Parrott felt about Wildberg at this moment. After he insisted that they have guests at their wedding, Ursula made an emotional confession: "Nobody else ever wanted to marry me in front of people as if they were proud of me. Or take me on a honeymoon either, as if it were that important." She had moved fast on this marriage, she told Bye, because "if I postponed marrying him, we'd both stay in chaos and if this turned into a New York love affair I'd want to drown myself." This is as clear a statement of Parrott's urgent desire to attain equilibrium as she ever made.

Parrott was trying to steer herself away from the kinds of bad decisions she had made in the past. But she was also sincerely warming up to Wildberg: "The first time I saw him I wasn't much impressed, and every single time since I've liked him better." Although this is about as far away from the intense felicities she had shared with O'Connor as one could get, this mature criteria for marriage actually "made sense." Her stories categorized such unions as "formal marriages," lacking passion but endowed with purpose and security. These marriages usually ended badly, with affairs and divorces because either husband or wife is ultimately unable to live a passionless, dull life, however much they wish it were otherwise. In one such story, Parrott declared unambiguously that a character "had been wrong to marry without love"—something she knew from experience.[17]

There may have been another reason behind Parrott's haste. Two weeks after she exchanged vows with Jack Wildberg, O'Connor married his second wife, Hope Kelsey.[18] Ursula had known that her ex-lover's nuptials were impending and managed to beat Hugh to the marital punch.

During their honeymoon Ursula made a $50 bet with Jack that he could not "spend a month with her in New York without a single penny in his pocketbook or even a check book on which to rely. Just credit!" This was a test of Wildberg's status, which his new bride bet against. But Wildberg was a lifelong New Yorker with a deep social network. "We lived at the Algonquin and I used to have the taxicabs put on my bill. I ate in the smart places where I was known, I had drug store supplies sent up from the hotel store and I managed to do very well." His first challenge came when he threw a party for the actor Phillip Holmes at the Ritz. "I didn't have an account there and the manager looked askance when I didn't pay for the party. Just then I saw an old friend who did have an account—I asked him to sign for me." What almost lost the bet for Wildberg was a minor expense with a significant logistical challenge, "the early morning papers." The hotel newsstand closed at midnight, so Wildberg's only option for reading theatrical reviews was the corner newsstand, a business not accustomed to the idea of credit. Wildberg's solution was to wait for the newsman to "cross the street" for food, which gave him a chance to steal a paper and smuggle it back to his room. "He never saw me once," he boasted of his skilled thievery. When the month was over, "I left all the money I owed him in an envelope with the explanation."[19] Sportsmanship was one thing, shoplifting another.

When the Wildbergs came to the city, they rented long-term rooms at hotels like the Algonquin. They threw parties. But theirs was a passionless marriage, albeit one that made Parrott appear and feel legitimate. Of Wildberg, Parrott said, "This is a pleasant man I've married. We'll never be in the slightest intimate—but will go to a lot of theaters and what not, which is better than nothing, and a great saver of face."[20] And go to the theater they did, since it was Wildberg's new avocation. On May 8, 1934, not long after they were married, they attended the opening of one of his productions, *Milky Way*, at the Court Theater.[21] After the performance, Jack casually promised his bride a financial piece of the play, "talked about giving it to [her] in front of so many of his friends." Revealing cracks in the freshly set veneer of the newlyweds' contentedness, Parrott soon complained, "The joke of course is that as soon as it started looking good, Jack forgot to give me my piece, said even when reminded jestingly, 'What do you want to get mixed up in show business for with all you have on your mind?'" Was this sincere care or intractable self-interest?

This was not the only tension to arise between the newlyweds. In what must have been a first for her, Wildberg gave Parrott a monthly "house hold allowance." She grumbled that he then used it to do things like "paying the Long shore club dues, which I never pay until June, having only a beach membership, but which he paid wanting to play golf there. The amount equaled the allowance, but the gasoline man and the grocer would not know that." Unaccustomed to financial oversight, Parrott at least had a sense of humor about her new life of frugality and semidependence, calling the entire situation "pretty comic." Ever the soothsayer, she acknowledged that Jack will "have lots of annuities when he's old, but I doubt he has Ursula."

Just six months after her marriage to Wildberg, on September 11, 1934, Ursula and her son set sail to London. She went on alone to Russia on September

22, where she stayed for over a month. Early in October she ventured into what she described as "back of beyond Ukraine" for five days before returning to Moscow. While she was there, she instructed her agent to address any correspondence to her care of the *New York Times* Moscow bureau. Ursula was working on a series of Russian stories and completed the first one for *McCall's* before she set sail for her return trip.[22] Her 1935 short story collection, *Dream without Ending*, contains two of these, both of which incorporate the textures of Soviet life that she observed as she furnished herself with another story locale to expand upon her arsenal of New York, New England, Los Angeles, and the West Indies.

While Ursula was in Russia, she certainly saw her remarried ex-husband, Lindesay, who was stationed in Moscow at the International News Service Bureau. If Ursula and Lindesay had a tryst, it would have been consistent with her acknowledgment that he would always mean something to her. Six weeks after her departure from New York, Ursula returned home on October 24, 1934, aboard the SS *Berengaria*. The widely published photograph of her disembarkation in New York shows the authoress looking smart in a leopard-fur coat (see figure 28). By the end of the year she was back in Connecticut with Jack, completing the rest of her Russian stories. Was Lindesay, perhaps, thinking of his recent encounter with Ursula when, two months later, he published a story, "Reds Urged to Wed Legally," in which he discussed Russian efforts to warn "against hasty marriage and rash divorces"?[23]

There were early signs that Parrott was not at ease with her latest marriage. Although her journalism days were well behind her, at the end of January 1935, she sought an opportunity to dip back into the pressroom, trying to finagle a way to cover the Lindbergh trial. Dubbed the "crime of the century," in March 1932, aviator Charles Lindbergh's baby was kidnapped from his home; the child's body was discovered over two months later. Parrott asked her agent to try to arrange for her to write a story about the trial, with an "if" of her own: "If you should have what [author] Damon Runyon would call my ever-loving husband on the telephone don't tell him anything about this project." The reason for the secrecy, Ursula said, was that Jack "has been at me for days and weeks to do a story and get two tickets for the trial so he could go too." The thought of having to go with her husband was mortifying. "I was once a newspaper woman myself and Jack would expect me to lean on

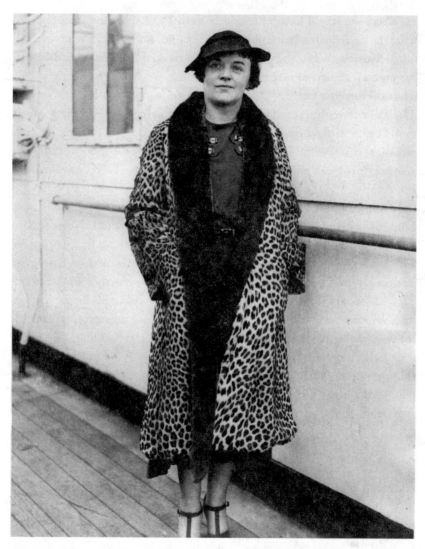

FIGURE 28. On October 24, 1934, Parrott sported a leopard-fur coat for her disembarkation from the SS *Berengaria* following a four-month trip to Europe and Russia. Always a devoted researcher and traveler, she took the trip in part to gather local color for a series of stories set in Russia. (ACME Newspictures, author's collection.)

his arm, gaze at him tenderly, muttering 'Jack darling' at appropriate intervals which I wouldn't disappoint him in and which I would die if I were compelled to do in front of an assortment of newspapermen who knew me when and when—."[24] There is little doubt that she was dreading the perfect storm of exes who would also have been in attendance.

Despite Jack's best efforts, Ursula continued to dig financial holes for herself, which she tried to conceal from him. As she juggled her finances in early 1935, she often asked her agent not to discuss "these arrangements with Jack." Given his rules about debt and spending, there were things it would be better for her husband not to know. Of course, it would have been surprising if Ursula could have gone from unrestrained spender to dependent wife without some bumps—not to mention shoes, furs, and jewelry—along the way. A year into her marriage she admitted that she could count on Jack "to some slight degree" but had for him "neither time, energy, nor any emotion." "I don't even seem to have the slightest confidence in him."[25] Parrott had hoped she was embarking on one of those dull but comforting marriages; but it was not the tedious parts of this marriage that she would blame for its undoing.

Walter Winchell broke the news in the lead line of his December 30, 1937, column: "Ursula Parrott, the novelist, and her groom, Attorney John Wildberg, have parted. No decision yet about a complete division." Under the headline "Marriage Fails," the *Los Angeles Times* reported that Parrott had filed suit for divorce, charging Wildberg with intolerable cruelty. Jack received news about Ursula's filing when he was in Hollywood on a trip to recruit actress Lupe Velez to take a role in a new play. The columnist Louella Parsons wrote that Wildberg was "surprised" by the court filing and had "told intimate friends he didn't think his novelist mate would go through with the separation." Parrott's longtime friend, Alice Hughes, commented on the separation by describing the author's chronic "husband trouble": "Kitty makes pots of money from her novels, magazine serials and the movie rights. This, I suppose, must be some compensation—but it is not what a woman wants, as I'm sure I needn't tell you."[26]

In a Bridgeport, Connecticut, court on June 17, 1938, "Petite and chic appearing in a blue ensemble, the dark-banged author of 'Strangers May Kiss,' 'Ex-Wife' and other best sellers spoke in a barely audible voice." Parrott alleged that less than a year after they were married, Wildberg "began being cruel to her on March 1, 1935." She described a combative marriage, characterizing Wildberg as mean and violent. Parrott "testified that her husband, during a quarrel once struck her and knocked her across the room into a chair." They "were constantly wrangling and arguing over Wildberg's treatment of her son," whom he called a "feeble-minded brat." Wildberg would "wake the boy at night without reason; yelled and shouted at him, and often used profane language." She blamed her ill health on her husband, saying that because of their "constant quarreling," she "was unable to follow her profession of writing" and for months "would sit at a typewriter and try in vain to write." Parrott's claims were substantiated by her secretary, "red-haired Michelin Keating, and Sam Bakos," whose role in the household was not described, who "testified as to many quarrels they overheard."[27]

The most shocking accusation against Wildberg was that he "once approached her with a pistol and said, 'I could shoot you with this.'" Parrott softened this horrific claim by adding, "I didn't think he would really do it." However, "I was afraid it would go off and the noise would wake up my son." Jack did not appear in court to defend his behavior or contest the divorce, and the reasons Ursula gave were enough to satisfy the state of Connecticut: her third divorce, and his second, was granted on June 17, 1938. "Mrs. Katherine Ursula Towle Parrott Greenwood Wildberg" was "granted the right to resume the name of Parrott." The *New York Times* headline simply read, "Ursula Parrott Freed."[28]

Parrott's divorce from Wildberg was, as she put it with deliberate understatement, "not a friendly matter." After making excuses for missing a writing deadline, she complained to her agent that she "had a dreadful time with lawyers over things he wanted in property rights." Parrott was in another tailspin. She begrudged an "outrageous bill" from her new lawyer, Morrie Ernst, who represented her in the divorce. Ernst was a cofounder of Greenbaum, Wolff & Ernst, who represented the American Civil Liberties Union, defended Random House in the 1933 obscenity case over James Joyce's *Ulysses*, and was counsel for the American Newspaper Guild in their victorious Supreme Court case upholding the right of the press to organize labor unions. Jack made her agree to pay him $5,000 as part of the divorce proceeding—likely a repayment of Ursula's debt that he had paid off prior to their marriage. She was completely overwhelmed by financial obligations. "I wanted to pay the government," she wrote to Bye about her back taxes, "and you and to get myself in good shape first." "Truly," Ursula added, "I have no moral scruples about keeping Jack waiting because I think to hold me up for five thousand dollars to get my divorce was awful."[29]

She wrote to Ernst about her overdue legal bills in November 1938. "I haven't paid Jack and I haven't paid you," she acknowledged. "After my divorce, I collapsed more or less for the summer. I wrote odds and ends for my current expenses, and that was all." Jack, however, had been "pressing me more than you" to get paid so got paid first. Ursula outlined an installment plan to her lawyer for December and January. "I assure you it hasn't been unwillingness on my part," she wrote, "but incapacity."[30]

Given how contentious their divorce had been, how awfully she described Wildberg's behavior, and how much their breakup set her back, it comes as a tremendous surprise that Jack Wildberg is the ex-husband with whom Parrott kept most in touch during the years to come. As early as the spring of 1939, just a year after their divorce, there were reports that Wildberg had plans to dramatize one of Parrott's novels, *For All of Our Lives*. That fall, Wildberg announced that Parrott was working on the script and that Worthington Miner would direct a film version for Knickerbocker Pictures. Lawrence Langner, of New York's Theatre Guild, wrote to Parrott asking to have a look at the play with the possibility of the guild staging it.[31] Whether the play and movie did not come to pass because of personal disagreements, an inability to complete the work, or some other factor, this was a missed opportunity for a lucrative, cross-platform deal.

After Wildberg moved to London in the 1940s, he frequently traveled to New York and Hollywood, where he brokered theatrical and film deals and visited his second ex-wife. In the fall of 1940, under the banner of what "New Yorkers Are Talking About," Walter Winchell hinted that Parrott and Wildberg might be reuniting. In December 1945, columnist Dorothy Kilgallen dropped that Wildberg was producing a play "based on a story by his ex-wife, Ursula Parrott." And in early 1948, Winchell announced that Parrott was "using her former groom's home," adding—with implications intended—that Wildberg's "recent wife filed in Montana." Soon after, Danton Walker reported that "Ursula Parrott rumored about to remarry John Wildberg, whom she once divorced, as soon as the current Mrs. W. gets her freedom in Montana."[32] The current Mrs. W. did get her freedom in Montana, but Ursula Parrott did not become the next Mrs. W.

That the two kept in contact, perhaps including romantic reentanglements, is especially fascinating given the fact that Jack outdid Ursula in remarriages and matched her in theatrics. His *New York Times* obituary—after a fatal heart attack suffered while driving home from a London theater in 1959—notes that he was survived by the former Norah Medina Martin, "his sixth wife." Wildberg's 1943 marriage to Wauhillau La Hay, motion picture critic for the *Chicago Sun*, lasted five months before she was granted an uncontested divorce on the grounds of cruelty. His marriage to Ellen Moe Leeds, a "beautiful blond" who was his production assistant for *Anna Lucasta*, ended in 1948. Wildberg's marriage to twenty-five-year-old Constance Bennett of Atlanta, Georgia, ended in 1950 with her suicide by sleeping pills in their Beverly Hills Hotel suite while Wildberg was asleep in the twin bed beside her.[33] With all the turmoil in Wildberg's life, perhaps rivaled only by that of his second ex-wife's, little could anyone have suspected that he would return to Parrott's orbit almost two decades after their divorce to help her at what turned out to be her darkest hour, when all other friends had forsaken her.

THIRTEEN

"The Monotony and Weariness of Living"

When Margaret Santry interviewed Ursula Parrott on her radio program in January 1936, she told the author that she had noticed a change in her female characters. Was she, perhaps, tired of frustrated women? No, it wasn't that but rather that women had "tired of being frustrated." They were accustomed to disappointment and had become "more adult" since the late 1920s, when she began publishing. Women were more poised and confident, Parrott went on, no longer needing to make "scenes" or rush "off to Reno" if things didn't go precisely as hoped. This "new woman has found that you can't always have the people you want on your own terms. You've got to compromise on the terms."[1]

In her mid-to-late 1930s stories, Parrott had started handicapping passionate, impractical marriages with inescapable poverty or low social status. When career women appear in these stories, they are usually tragic outsiders doomed to lonely lives, not bothering to fight for more. There are fewer ambitious women struggling to balance careers and relationships and more conventional romances and long-lasting marriages in which women worked only if they had to. Just a few years before, Parrott had been advising women to never let her "interest dwindle down to the apartment" after getting married, nor "marry anyone who will interfere with her career."[2] Were editors or audiences tiring of ambitious, career-oriented women, or was Parrott the one who was over it?

When the New York *Herald Tribune* published Parrott's "There's Always Tomorrow" in the fall of 1934, they assured its readers that it was a "triangle story that ends with all three people happy." Parrott tells the story of Joseph and Sophie White, a middle-aged, middle-class couple with five kids, on the eve of their twenty-fourth wedding anniversary. Theirs was a stable, long-lasting marriage. But Joseph is tired, irritated, and generally disappointed. "Life had dwindled, that had once been a glamorous journey" to a bore of having to "scramble for money"—it was "an endless stupid rush, with no time left to draw breath and be a person." Everyone in his orbit seems shallow and depleted: "Sophie's a machine and I'm a machine whose purpose is to make the wherewithal for electric light and telephone and gasoline and food. The children are young, hungry machines, who have to be stoked with amusement and excitement."

Sophie forgets their wedding anniversary, leaving Joseph alone when his old flame Alice appears at their door. A flashback explains their summer of youthful love many years prior, after which Alice's aunt sent her away to Europe to divert their plans to marry. Alice stays in France and begins a successful career in fashion; Joseph marries the girl next door. As she turns forty, however, Alice finds that "marriage, children, the commonplace sheltered life were things lost to her irrevocably," and so her thoughts turn to her former love of over twenty years ago. On at least a half dozen occasions, Alice watches Joseph, his wife, and his children go about their lives—imagining that this might have been her house, her children, her life—until she finally gets the courage to knock on his door.

Joseph is instantly at ease with Alice, explaining his diminished feelings about his marriage and complaining about the way his wife "has grown entirely absorbed" by the children. He exists to them only as an "inadequate family check book." Although he chastises himself for wanting to keep seeing Alice, she "made him feel so alive," and so Joseph pretends to go to weekly fraternal organization meetings but heads instead to her apartment for fireside chats, sandwiches, and coffee, after which they would, the story assures its readers, "shake hands" before he went home. Parrott sets a perfect scenario for an affair, which she does not allow her characters to have. One snowy night, Joseph's children see him with Alice and confront her (not him) with their discovery, thus diverting the fashion designer from her plot to "use him for defense against the fear of growing old alone." Soon after, Alice tells Joseph that she is not the marrying type, kisses "him once, warmly," and announces that she is leaving town.

Remember that happy ending promised in the tagline to the story? Here it is: "Joseph White would find remembrance of her ardent voice, her kiss, solace against all the monotony and weariness of living, believing that he was fortunate, because somewhere in the world one person loved him, not from duty or habit or for anything he would do in return for love, but just for himself." This conclusion was neither joyous nor romantic. And what of Alice?

The story doesn't say. Presumably she would yearn for Joseph, continue being successful, and remain very much alone.

This was Parrott's new beat. The modern woman had undertaken her big adventures and had to live with the consequences. Her story's chaste moral arc was ready-made for the cleaned-up conditions in Hollywood, so it is not surprising that it made the leap to the silver screen. The Universal film, starring Frank Morgan, Lois Wilson, and Binnie Barnes, takes place in a world that feels more quaintly turn of the century than of the moment, but otherwise it hews closely to Parrott's story, including the downbeat ending, which seems even more pathetic on screen than on the page. Alice—who does not have "even a divorce to [her] credit"—tells Joseph's children, after they discover the suspected affair, that she's a "businesswoman" through and through, and that she only decided to "make a fuss over" their father and "make him important" because he did not get these things at home. "Watch your love," she cautions Joseph's eldest's son's fiancé. "Keep some of your love for him when the babies come," and "never forget that he's a lover." If *Ex-Wife* offered cautionary advice for newlyweds, Parrott's latest story, on the page and on the screen, offered guidance for long-married survivors of the divorce age.

As in Parrott's story, the movie version of Alice sacrifices her chance at happiness to keep Joseph's family intact. This was a morally unimpeachable plot, something the Production Code Administration rewarded by being "impressed...very favorably" after screening the film, which chief censor Joseph I. Breen liked "immensely." *There's Always Tomorrow* was "keenly modulated for family trade"; it was Ursula Parrott on her best behavior, dangling temptation before her characters but pulling it back for the sake of the institution of marriage.[3] It was also a dramatic brand shift away from Parrott's too-risqué-to-film tales of modern life, although she was not entirely done with those either.

When Parrott saw her name in lights at the local "village movie house" where *There's Always Tomorrow* was playing, she walked up to the ticket window and told the girl in the booth who she was, saying that she wanted to "look in on her own picture." As Margaret Santry put it on her radio program when she told this story on the air, "The girl looked at her coldly—and said—'The tickets are 35¢.'"[4]

By the mid-1930s, Parrott was regularly endowing her characters with maturity, which mirrored her own attempts at behaving responsibly. This made for

Ursula Parrott Approves Change In "Next Time We Love" Title

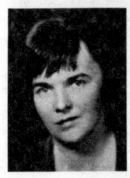

Ursula Parrott, author of "Next Time We Love," one of the most personable of all the authors. Yet this is the only portrait that Longmans-Green, her publishers, have.

ferring a story from one metier to another, while working adaptations at various studios in the film colony, I realized that the men who make pictures have put as much sincere effort and study into them, as the creators of stories put into the writing of their books. I am not one who pooh-poohs the poor producer. I find the average studio executive, instead of an ogre who bites the hand that feeds him, a level-headed business man who has something to sell and makes a comprehensive study of his market. My Hollywood experience has taught me that generally he knows fairly definitely what he is about,— and why,—and though I've had my share of heated arguments in fighting for my convictions, I've come around to understanding the reasons for certain changes in boiling down a story of 100,000 words, or more, to an hour and a half of visual entertainment which necessarily must be

We Live," to "Next Time We Love," frankly, I was quite distressed. The word love has been dragged into so many titles as a box-office lure. Then Carl Laemmle proceeded to explain to me why he held out for the 'o' in place of the 'i'. He maintained that the film audiences, on the whole, do not react favorably to pictures which deals with flights of fancy into spiritual realms or the hereafter. In this stark age of realism, he insisted, people are chiefly concerned with what happens here and now and they like their screen fare to reflect situations, emotions and aspirations, if not necessarily within their own experiences, at least within their own understanding.

"As my book is not a tale of reincarnation but deals with contemporary life, Mr. Laemmle feared the former title might mislead audiences into expecting—or suspecting—something quite apart from a domestic

FIGURE 29. Publicity from Universal, about Ursula Parrott approving the title change of her novel *Next Time We Live* to ensure that audiences did not erroneously think it was a movie about reincarnation, describes her as "one of the most personable of all the authors." In turn, she describes "the average studio executive" as "level-headed," not at all the "ogre who bites the hand that feeds him." (*Universal Weekly*, January 25, 1936, courtesy of the Media History Digital Library.)

increasingly somber stories, with characters that tended more toward self-sacrifice, as in 1935's *Next Time We Live*, which Parrott wrote at a time when she was hoping to settle down by settling for less. The story of two career-hungry characters begins with Cicely out-earning Christopher and ends with both of them achieving top places in their respective fields. But work has necessitated that they live on different continents, with Cicely raising their child essentially alone. Twelve years into their only occasionally in-person marriage, Christopher asks his wife and child to meet him in Italy. He does not tell them that, at thirty-five, he will die in a few months' time. He has tuberculosis, that disease chosen by so many authors to dispense with their female heroines, usually signaled by a violent cough and a spot of blood on a handkerchief. As Cicely and Kit head back to the States, she delivers the final line: "Next time we live, Christopher, we'll have time for each other." There is no blame; only an acknowledgment of what has been lost for this man and wife possessed of unrelenting professional ambition. *Next Time We Live* is a about how little, in the end, careers and success matter. It is a novel of futility.

SPRECKELS GAGS "LOVE" IN LOBBY

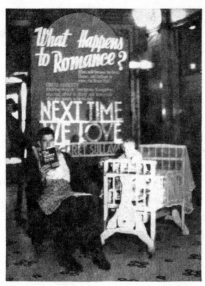

Realistic Display
Kids Marriage Problem

THIS inexpensive, unique lobby stunt, engineered by Manager Al Sobler and Publicity Manager Marian Gronaw, for "Next Time We Love" at the Spreckels Theatre, San Diego, drew much attention and thought from patrons. The young man, wearing the apron tended the life-like doll in the baby crib and at the same time read "The Modern Parent." The sign read: What Happens To Romance—When the Wife Becomes the Breadwinner and the Husband Becomes the House-Maid? Copy then ran into details of the Ursula Parrott story on which "Next Time We Love" is based.

Sobler's comprehensive campaign also included a substantial boost in the newspaper advertising space, posting of 24-sheets, distribution of bookmarks through the public and circulating libraries, and house to house distribution of accessory roto heralds.

FIGURE 30. A San Diego theater's marketing gimmick for *Next Time We Love* features a man in an apron reading a copy of *The Modern Parent* while rocking a "life-like doll." (*Universal Weekly*, Showmanship Section, March 21, 1936, courtesy of the Media History Digital Library.)

Next Time We Live was also made into a movie, which was retitled *Next Time We Love* because the studio feared that audiences might mistakenly think the film was about reincarnation (see figure 29). In preparation for its release in 1936, Universal suggested a marketing gimmick for movie theaters to drive interest to the film: hire a young man wearing an apron to sit in the theater's front alcove holding a copy of a book called *The Modern Parent* while rocking a "life-like doll" in a cradle in front a sign that reads "What Happens To Romance—When the Wife Becomes the Breadwinner and the Husband Becomes the House Maid?" (see figure 30). The schtick was cornier than the movie it was selling, which was reviewed as "brilliant" and "gripping." When the film was released in Boston, it filled Parrott's hometown RKO theater with "capacity audiences" at showings that took place "throughout the day." This did not surprise the *Boston Globe* reviewer who admired the "superb performance of a young newcomer" in the film, whom he said was worth watching out for in the years to come: a young James Stewart in his first starring role.[5]

Although she had initially expressed disdain for Hollywood, by the middle of the decade Parrott was reassessing. At her urging, George Bye tried to broker a number of movie deals on her behalf, though few made it all the way to theaters. Economically speaking, the outcome didn't much matter since Parrott got paid on the front end. In the mid-1930s, Bye sold her stories to MGM and her screenwriting services to United Artists.[6] She had become conciliatory, even generous, about Hollywood, a veritable one-eighty from when she fled the city after her first trip. "I believe that the cinema magnate who signs a fat check for an author's work," she told an interviewer in 1936, "and then risks hundreds of thousands of dollars in converting that story into a film has a right to add or subtract anything in an attempt to find its common denominator of audience appeal."[7] Parrott was playing nice and accepting the terms on offer as she reckoned with her need for money. "There are worse destinies than to be an almost first-rate hack writer here," says the failed playwright Neil about life in Hollywood, in Parrott's story "No Answer Ever." "In New York a failure is more noticeable. So many failures are congregated here that there's a bond of silence among us."

In 1936, low-budget Invincible Pictures produced the last original Parrott story made into a film during her lifetime, *Brilliant Marriage*, about high-society marriages and affairs. Featuring second-rate performers, it played short runs primarily in small town markets. Although one reviewer of the film described Parrott as "one of the keenest and most penetrating of modern writers," another dismissed *Brilliant Marriage* as a "light romantic yarn in popular vein for the not too finicky neighborhood trade." This was not big city sophistication with major studio and star backing; this was Poverty Row, where low-budget films were cranked out to fill the second half of double bills. Twenty years later, in 1956, Douglas Sirk directed a remake of *There's Always Tomorrow* with Barbara Stanwyck and Fred MacMurray in the lead roles. Parrott's story of "the dullness that frequently goes along with married life" took on new meaning in the postwar, suburban United States, even though the story remained the same.[8]

The movie studios didn't exactly stop knocking, but the offers dwindled along with the decade. However, there was to be one more especially intriguing chapter in Parrott's high-stakes Hollywood dealings. In 1938, MGM hired F. Scott Fitzgerald, the Jazz Age's most celebrated storyteller, to write a screenplay based on Parrott's recently published short story "Grounds for Divorce: Infidelity." By this time, Fitzgerald would surely have already encountered the story's colorful author one way or another—if not over a typewriter in Tinseltown then certainly a martini in Manhattan. MGM paid Fitzgerald the handsome sum of $1,250 a week for his services, which makes it all the more curious that when MGM began promoting "Infidelity" as their next big Joan Crawford film, Ursula Parrott's name was *always* mentioned alongside Crawford's but there was nary a mention of Fitzgerald.[9] This is a testament to Parrott's still-formidable marketability, as well as to her market: the ticket-buying women whom Hollywood assiduously courted.

"Infidelity" was the first of four stories Parrott published in Hearst's *Cosmopolitan* magazine under the banner of "Grounds for Divorce," a series of fictional tales revolving around different legal grounds: infidelity, nonsupport, incompatibility, and desertion. "Another 'case history,'" teased *Cosmopolitan* for the nonsupport-themed tale, "in this great series of modern divorce stories—the emotional problem of a woman whose career was more successful than her marriage." "Infidelity" is about eight-years-married Nicholas Gilbert and Althea Chilton, parents to twins, who care deeply for each other but lack passion—theirs is a dull but functional marriage on course to end up like Joseph and Alice's in "There's Always Tomorrow." Althea surprises Nicholas by returning home early from a trip to Paris to find him eating lunch with another woman—in robes and lingerie. Her trust and pride shattered, Althea goes to New York's top divorce lawyer to start proceedings. As the story progresses, however, it turns out that Nicholas's brief reunion affair with a woman who had once been his great passion is not so different from Althea's near affair with a man who had once been hers. After some soul searching, Althea proposes that they forget what happened and focus on their future together. (This is one of the most mature endings of any Ursula Parrott story, a rejection of the narrative with which Parrott had begun her writing career and marital life. "Infidelity" affirms the institution of marriage, despite its imperfections.)

F. Scott Fitzgerald considered the initial work he did on the script for "Infidelity" as a "labor of love" for a project in which he had great faith.[10] As he outlined the script, Fitzgerald screened Joan Crawford's recent films and made notes about her performance style. After completing a first draft, he enthused that it could be a prestigious "Three Star Picture," material worthy of MGM casting *three* big names in the leading roles. Fitzgerald believed, "We have fulfilled the original contract—and with a deep bow to the censors. We have shown how, when faced with a situation parallel to the one with which her husband was faced, [Althea] might have yielded too."[11] However, Fitzgerald's anticipated placation of the censors was naïve and misguided. After the Hays Office rejected the screenplay's original title, which was deemed too immoral, MGM producer Hunt Stromberg half-heartedly conceded to calling the film "Fidelity." This shell game, unlike the one they had successfully played in 1930 with *Ex-Wife*'s retitling to *The Divorcee*, was a bust. The censors "could not approve a story of this kind" despite its "considerable compensating moral values."[12] Whether it bore the original title or not, "Infidelity" was a complicated, ultimately nonjudgmental story about adultery. Perhaps worst of all, the story ended, as Stromberg had pitched with misguided enthusiasm, not "tragically" but "happily," with forgiveness and reconciliation.

After being rejected by the Production Code Administration just before the film was scheduled to go into production, MGM abandoned "Infidelity." The story could not be scrubbed enough to overcome its essence, nor infused with adequate "proper compensating moral values," one of the stated objectives of the Code. Writing to his daughter, Fitzgerald described the scrapping of "Infidelity" as an "infinite disappointment." However, MGM was "setting it aside awhile till we think of a way of halfwitting halfwit Hays and his Legion of Decency. Pictures needed cleaning up in 1932–1933 (remember I didn't like you to see them?) because they were suggestive and salacious. Of course the moralists now want to apply that to *all* strong themes—so the crop of the last two years is feeble and false, unless it deals with children."[13]

The "Infidelity" debacle was a last straw for Fitzgerald's notoriously difficult Hollywood career. Writing a postmortem to his agent, he reported that Stromberg had "so intensely" liked "Infidelity" that "when the whole thing flopped I think he held it against me that I had aroused his hope so much and then had not been able to finish it. It may have been my fault—it may have been the fault of the story but the damage is done now." Parrott never felt as burned by Hollywood as did Fitzgerald and many other writers like him, perhaps because she saw her movie deals, at this point in her career, in largely economic terms. Gone were her activist ambitions of using the movies to teach people lessons about successful women who could also make good wives or how to avoid the traps of the double standard. As she asked her agent, with some delightful swagger in her voice but with exigencies on her mind, "Now that you are back in the picture business baby, why not sell the

Ladies' Home Journal serial for large sums next week?" She concluded, with characteristic humor, "I'll give all the money to the government, if you do."[14]

Parrott had always felt like an outsider—in Dorchester during her youth, at Radcliffe in her late teens, and as an adult in the smart circles of Manhattan and the superficial ones in Hollywood. As the 1930s wore on, she tried to settle down and fit in, choosing Connecticut as the place to do so. Her agent did everything he could to facilitate her stabilization endeavor, not only because he had an investment in her productivity but also because he genuinely cared for her as a friend. In the fall of 1935, Bye urged her to take a break from fiction to publish an article for the new *Arts and Decoration* magazine—not about her career or her latest thoughts on marriage but about her landscaping methods. In a series of photos that appeared in the story—as well as in her essay about her formal, naturalistic, cut-flower, and vegetable gardens; the benefits of buying local trees; and the merits of tulips and peonies—this new Ursula seemed a far cry from the speakeasy Ursula of the early 1930s, though only a few years separated them. She was trying to put down roots, in every sense of the word.

Although Parrott's country life was certainly more favorable to teas and tennis matches than speakeasies till dawn, it was possessed of its own distractions. Her agent and his wife were nearby neighbors, as were numerous other weekending Manhattanites including the entertainers and writers Heywood Broun, John Erskine, Faith Baldwin, Gene Tunney, and Westbrook Pegler. Parrott signed on as the only female member of a group of nine coeditors and co-owners, led by Bye and Broun, of a "bucolic weekly put out around the cracker barrel." Debuting on May 26, 1938, and bearing the charming moniker *Connecticut Nutmeg*, this "rural organ of opinion" was infused with the literary shrewdness you'd expect from a group of worldly friends exercising their wit for the pleasure of their neighbors as well as subscribers from afar (see figure 31). Touting their annual four-dollar subscription in an advertisement that ran, audaciously enough, in a Hollywood trade magazine, the publishers gently ribbed, "We warn you that there are no pictures in the *Nutmeg*, so if you are illiterate (unable to read, that is) do not bother subscribing. That is, unless you keep canaries. We find that the *Nutmeg* just covers the bottom of a bird cage."[15]

In her first contribution to the *Nutmeg*'s pages, Parrott's "This and That"

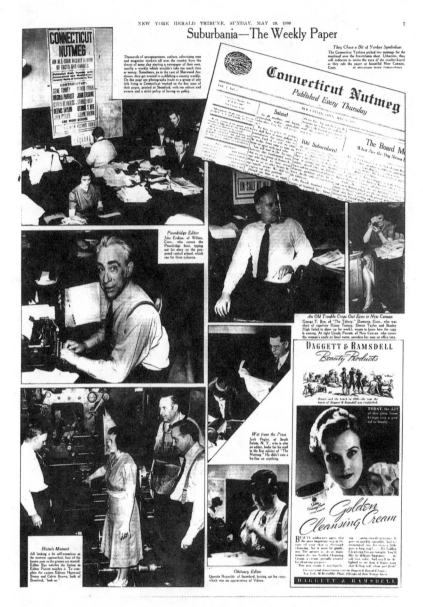

FIGURE 31. Parrott undertook her role as a cofounder and regular contributor to the weekly *Connecticut Nutmeg* in the spirit of community with her neighbors and colleagues in literary wit. This pictorial spread includes Parrott, pictured in the lower left corner, poised to push the button and start the presses for the *Nutmeg*'s debut issue. (*New York Herald Tribune*, May 29, 1938.)

column summed up her Connecticut experience. "People move to the country to live simply," after which they encounter unanticipated needs ranging from masonry reconstruction and insulation to rose sprays and arborists that make it both not so simple and awfully expensive. In a subsequent column, she regaled readers with a harrowing tale about the costly installation of an artesian well: "Every time I wrote a page I wondered if it would pay for another foot." She began "to be worried at [her] penniless state to which heat, plumbing, building of the ell, digging of the well and enlargement of the garden had already contributed—as well as more extensive entertaining than any city dweller ever expects to do, but which all city dwellers expect as due them for their trouble in travelling to see you in the country." Parrott's county house became just another part of the complicated life she created for herself, no matter how well intentioned. In this, at least, she was not alone. Her literary peer Faith Baldwin's contribution to the *Nutmeg's* inaugural issue itemized the "hornets' nest" of having a country home, concluding that "there is something to be said for hotels."[16]

The *Nutmeg* also gave Parrott her first brush with political controversy. Before cohosting a fundraiser at her home in support of the Friends of the Abraham Lincoln Battalion for funds to aid the American wounded fighting with Loyalists in Spain against General Franco in the Spanish Civil War (see figure 32), she penned a column describing overflowing Spanish hospitals, arguing that wounded American fighters needed better medical care, a way home, and possibly even long-term veterans' housing. Parrott's column inspired an outpouring of negative feedback, and so she spent her next column refuting accusations that she had become a radical. Promising to return to the inconsequential subjects of picnics and swimming pools after the fundraiser, Parrott defended her patriotism and the correctness of raising "funds to bring home American citizens." She was neither radical nor conservative, but rather "an American": "I don't believe in Communism, I don't believe in Fascism, I don't believe in Nazi-ism. I believe in American Democracy, no matter how self-conscious it makes me feel to say so, loudly."[17] Even her attempts at good deeds got her into jams.

Writing weekly unpaid columns for the *Connecticut Nutmeg* took time. It was also a conspicuous distraction. In the summer of 1938, two of her paying magazine editors, who were after long overdue stories, "expressed themselves at length as to their irritation at seeing [her] appear regularly" in the *Nutmeg* when she "owed them copy for which they would be pleased to pay." This tension, combined with some internal disagreements with her coeditors,

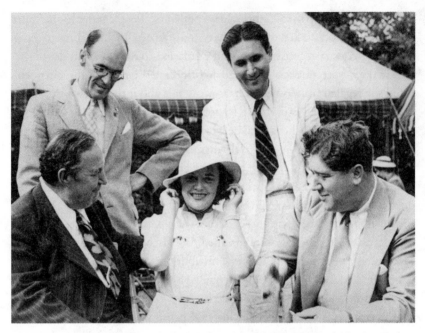

FIGURE 32. Parrott got a taste of political controversy after she cohosted a fundraiser on July 9, 1942, for the Friends of the Abraham Lincoln Brigade to bring home wounded volunteers from Spain. Pictured (sitting, left to right): Heywood Broun, Ursula Parrott, Quentin Reynolds; (standing, left to right) David McKelvy White and unidentified man. (Courtesy of New York University, Tamiment Library and Robert F. Wagner Labor Archives, Veterans of the Abraham Lincoln Brigade Photograph Collection, Box 7.)

resulted in an October 20, 1938, announcement in the paper: "Miss Parrott writes that she is behind schedule in her literary work, and that while NUT-MEG means a pleasant diversion she must give it up."[18]

Parrott parted ways as a co-owner and regular contributor, but she made one return appearance in the *Nutmeg*'s pages. In the Thanksgiving 1938 issue, the author expressed thanks that her doctor had recently put her on a successful diet, that she had finished her current serial, that Marc had grown taller than her, and that she "was born in a time and country where women have opportunities as wide as men's opportunities."[19] No matter how disillusioned, the matter of gender equality was never far from Parrott's mind.

FOURTEEN

Fourth Husband,
Alfred Coster Schermerhorn

"TWO CATASTROPHES SHOULD BE ENOUGH"

In the fall of 1938, Parrott announced that she wanted to publish "an important book badly"—but first she had to write it. She asked her agent to negotiate a contract with Dodd Mead for an "unserialized book to be called 'Until Sundown,'" asking for $1,000 in advance, $500 after the submission of two hundred pages in six weeks, and another $500 for the next two hundred pages. These were hardly astronomical sums, but they would be enough to get by. She promised to dedicate the winter to completing it.[1]

Parrott had spent several years primarily writing magazine stories, and believed it was time she did something at least as successful as *Ex-Wife* had been in 1929 and as serious as *The Tumult and the Shouting* had been in 1933. She wrote to Mr. Dodd directly to explain that "Until Sundown" was to be significant, "a six or seven hundred page novel, not to be serialized in any version." "I'm tired of saying, 'I want to write a book that seems to me important.'" "I've either got to write it or forget it by now."[2] Parrott said that she could finish a draft of the ambitious manuscript in less than four months. Mr. Dodd, however, did not agree to the advance, and Parrott does not appear to have written the book.

Just before New Year's Eve 1938, she found herself in what she described as "ghastly" financial trouble, with her taxes overdue and an immediate need for "about eight hundred dollars to get by." If she could get one more loan to appease her creditors, she told her agent, she could "certainly turn in a couple of short stories and be all right."[3]

On January 1, 1939, Parrott announced that she had entered into a new relationship with a "terrific beau" whom she had been seeing since her divorce from John Wildberg in June 1938.[4] Parrott and her new sweetheart had kept out of the gossip columns for the past six months because they "conscientiously appear occasionally with someone else." Despite their successful avoidance of publicity, the pair was frequenting New York hotspots like 21, the Sert room at the Waldorf, and La Rue's. Parrott was keeping company with someone who had, like her, already experienced his fair share of marital hard knocks. "We neither of us had much luck with the institution of matrimony," but "we're content with today and will see about tomorrow when it arrives." It's hard not to think of the many "tomorrow" stories Parrott published—"There's Always Tomorrow," "Tomorrow's Sun," "Appointment with Tomorrow," "Tomorrow We'll Be Free," "And Tomorrow to You"—which imply something good on the horizon but are in fact about hopes and expectations that are deferred or dashed.

The author had taken to her typewriter on this New Year's Day to offer a self-assessment, which she addressed to a recipient with whom she had not corresponded in some time, Hugh O'Connor. She described her New Year's Eve plans: Her lover "was coming in from the country where he spends a good deal of time with his child to meet me at seven, for a proper New Year's Eve. Dinner and Twenty One, *The Boys from Syracuse* [a Richard Rogers and Lorenz Hart musical] because we thought that would be gayest, the Colony party and our favorite La Rue's finally." As she waited for her date to arrive, Parrott sipped a martini prepared by her maid while wearing an extravagant "Argentinita dress, the white lace one," for which she had paid $225. She was surrounded by signs of her self-sufficiency and used these to demonstrate that she was OK. "The pearls 'round my neck were not very large pearls but I had earned them. My big diamond ring, and my diamond and ruby ring were mine, I had earned them.... They were comforting somehow, dress and jewels, even ermine coat in my bedroom with my purse and gloves." When her date arrived, he praised her. "What a heavenly, heavenly dress. You look nineteen but more distinguished somehow. I'll try to kiss you without crushing it." Parrott, who was, in fact, what she considered to be the significant age of thirty-nine "was happy to kiss him" because she loved him "very much."

This was vastly different from the New Year's Eve a decade prior, when she waited for Hugh O'Connor to take her to dinner and then to a party at which he would challenge her to write a book based upon her life. That night, she had worn "a narrow dress of gold brocade that [she] bought for seven dollars on a remnant counter, and had a village dressmaker make for five." "I had no jewels and did not miss them," Parrott recalled, adding "I was happy."

This evening was also a study in contrasts from the disastrous New Year's Eve in 1932 when she was at the end of her rope after O'Connor relegated her to a hotel room while he took out his ex-wife.

Parrott wrote her account of New Year's Eve 1938 as if it were a story, and perhaps it felt like one—or at least a new chapter. At 5:30 a.m., as the long night was drawing to a close, her date said to her, "Have an arm angel. You drink admirably, but you must be at least as cheerfully tight as I." "Thank you darling," she replied, "I could use an arm." The couple spent what remained of the night together. This was no chaste affair, despite the courtly sounding pleasantries with which it began. Waking up the next morning at the appropriately late hour of 11:00 a.m., he said, "Break the news to your maid.... Your reputation's gone, and she may as well serve breakfast in here. I'm damned if I'll eat mine in a stiff collar. I'll wear your red bathrobe." "I've told you a boring number of times," she replied, "I haven't had a reputation for years. It's odd how seldom I miss it." Thus began Parrott's tale of her latest romantic reincarnation. "In a way," she told her new paramour, "I feel as if I hadn't lived before you—as if all the things that happened happened to a different person."

Ursula was writing this story for Hugh's benefit as well as for her own. The New Year's Eve date that she described was with the man who would become her fourth and final husband three months later, on March 4, 1939, Alfred "Fred" Coster Schermerhorn, whom the *Radcliffe Quarterly* described in their announcement of the nuptials as Parrott's "literary agent." With amusement, Parrott told O'Connor, if "anyone had told me in my 'teens I would go on caring about my figure, my complexion, even the shade of my fingernails and seriously considering another marriage while my thirties dwindled I should have considered whomever told me mad." As she bemoaned in "Leftover Ladies" back in 1929, this was one of the curses afflicting women in the age of divorce. But here she was, "off the deep end in love," enjoying "having [her] hand held discreetly (but not surreptitiously) at the theater." She'd "been in love twice before," she told O'Connor, "and fought off caring much most of the summer and a bit of the Autumn because two catastrophes should be enough for the average female life." "To me the sentence never will be, 'They fell in love and they got married,' but always 'They fell in love and they came to a bad end.' There's no reason we should, particularly—aside from my odd destiny."[5]

Parrott's odd destiny had now delivered her into the arms of high society. Alfred "Fred" Coster Schermerhorn was born in New York on January 3,

1898, to "one of New York's oldest families." The only child of Alfred Egmont Schemerhorn, whose New York family descended from seventeenth-century Dutch settlers, the Schermerhorns were part of the economic and social bedrock of the state. Schermerhorn's father made his fortune in Southampton, Long Island, real estate, where he was one of the founders of the village's hospital, an establishing director of the bank, a vestryman of the church, and a "club" man, deemed so for his prominent role in many of the clubs that ruled New York social life.[6]

Fred Schermerhorn served as a lieutenant during World War I, graduated from Yale University in 1920, and followed his father's footsteps into the world of finance. Around the time he and Parrott got together, Fred broke with family tradition and "gave up his Wall Street activities to organize and head a firm [called Authors and Artists] of literary and radio agents," which perhaps explains how the couple's seemingly divergent paths crossed. He had two divorces under his belt when he married Parrott in the spring of 1939, by which time divorce had become routine, at least in their circles. In 1938, *Ladies' Home Journal* concluded that 69 percent of U.S. women—a notable majority—wanted more uniform access to divorce as a remedy for failed marriages.[7] Being an ex-wife in 1929, when Parrott first wrote about it, was noteworthy and risqué; a decade later it was often discussed as an accepted fact of modern life.

Schermerhorn's first marriage to Ruth Fahnestock in 1926 had been a high-society wedding between "members of old families," as the *New York Times* put it in their engagement announcement. The pair was driven to and from the Protestant Episcopal Church of St. Thomas on Fifth Avenue in the family's horse-driven carriage by the same coachman who had taken the bride's parents to their wedding. A decade after she walked down the aisle, Ruth went to Reno to procure an uncontested divorce on the grounds of cruelty. Hours later, Schermerhorn's newly minted ex-wife was remarried.[8]

Schermerhorn's short-lived second marriage, to Betty Buck of Beverly Hills, California, took place a little over a month after his first divorce. Buck, who acted using the name Julia Laird, had been married to the playwright John Kirkland for only three months when she got her March 1937 Reno divorce from him. The second Mrs. Schermerhorn walked down the aisle on January 3, 1938, before the Schermerhorns honeymooned in Havana. Four months later, in April 1938, the couple divorced in an Arkansas court.[9] The average duration of one of Betty Buck's marriages was, at this point, a mere three-and-a-half months.

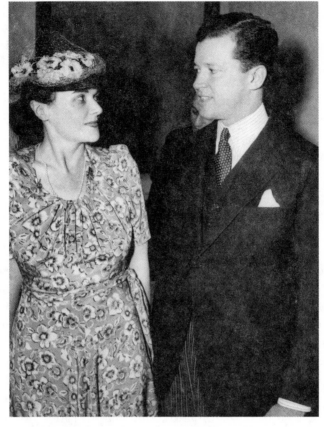

FIGURE 33. Ursula Parrott, "one of America's best-known novelists," and Fred Schermerhorn, "an ex-Wall Streeter," after their courthouse wedding on March 4, 1939. (International News photo, author's collection.)

Schermerhorn's third marriage was, perhaps appropriately, his least cere-monious: Ursula and Fred were wed by a New York municipal court judge on March 4, 1939 (see figure 33). The *New York Herald Tribune* reported that the author "said she was thirty-six years old" (Parrott's fortieth birthday, March 26, was less than two weeks away). When newspapers published the couple's wedding-day photos, they reminded readers that it was "the bride's fourth time," a detail that did not escape *any* reporting on the nuptials. Making the point by using her cluttered surname lineage, one newspaper described the union of the "ex-wife of three" and the "ex-husband of two" as transpiring between Mr. Schermerhorn and "Katherine Ursula Towle Parrott Greenwood Wildberg." At the ceremony, the bride declared, "This is the last"—rightly as it turns out, though not in the way she intended.[10] The couple decamped to one of Parrott's favorite destinations, Bermuda, for their honeymoon.

The Schermerhorns must have seemed a curious pair. He was described in the press as a "social registerite" and she as a "woman novelist," but Parrott would not have been considered high society by any standards. In what was surely a response to prevailing skepticism about their nuptials, Parrott's friend, the writer Alice Hughes, wrote in her column that "Kitty scorns the notion that she is marrying Schermerhorn for social position." Then why was she traipsing down the aisle again? "I am marrying Coster," Parrott stated with certainty, "because I think he is the nicest man in the world."[11]

The month after Parrott became Mrs. Schermerhorn, her agent began expressing concern. "Frankly," Bye wrote, "I am worried about you. I hate to call you for fear I sound like an accuser. You know that I am slightly clairvoyant, and I believe I know at all times what is going on around me." She had promised him that her wedding and honeymoon would not interfere with a now overdue deadline for a novel-length story for *McCall's*. Had she "recklessly dropped" work on the serialized novel at the start of her latest marital endeavor? Instead of begging or berating her, Bye proposed that they contact the magazine's editor, Otis Wiese, to "get started on a new idea," trying to pull Parrott out of a suspected tailspin. Thanking her "for a delightful lunch" in mid-April, Bye said that *McCall's* editor would give Parrott five more days to complete the story. But Wiese "is pretty brisk about expecting copy for his August issue."[12]

At the end of April, Bye wrote Parrott again, this time to describe "a black day" marked by newly received telegrams from *McCall's* as well as *Ladies' Home Journal*, both inquiring about overdue manuscripts, plus a warning from Fifth Avenue Bank about Parrott's overdrawn account. Later that day he telegrammed to see if her submissions were forthcoming; Parrott was unresponsive. [13] She had developed a habit of disappearing—not returning notes, not answering phones—when she felt unable to confront her literary debtors. With editors breathing down his neck and Parrott in a state of radio silence, her situation seemed irremediable.

In May, Otis Wiese wrote Bye about the $2,500 advance *McCall's* had paid Parrott almost a year prior. "All efforts to get information about the novel have proven futile. Nothing in her past record indicates that Ursula would play doggo on a job of this kind. In fact, the one reason why you have invariably been successful in seeking advances for her had been because editors were aware that she would always produce a satisfactory story in the nick of time."[14] Despite Parrott's long track record as a professional writer, Bye had seen inside the sausage factory for years. It is a testament to his skill as an agent that magazine editors seemed blissfully unaware of the cajoling she often required behind the scenes.

Wiese warned that "if a novel is not forthcoming in the near future I shall have to press you for a return of the $2500 advance." Horrified into action, Parrott turned in a draft at the start of August, staving off an impossible repayment. She seemed as surprised as her agent that she had pulled it off and sent Bye a blow-by-blow update "because you might get as confused as myself with all this sudden burst of effort." She had also just completed a second installment of "Road Leading Somewhere" for *Ladies' Home Journal*; an 18,000 word novelette, "You Love But Once—or Twice," for *Cosmopolitan*; and a "long-overdue" story, "River to the Sea," for *Redbook*. Buoyed by her return to form, Parrott was back in the optimist's club and enthusiastically told Bye, "It is to be hoped this autumn will be like one of our famous years when we had so many balls juggling in the air that you, my angel, could not keep them straight."[15]

Radcliffe Quarterly's 1939 news from the Class of 1920 had only one marriage to report, that of Katherine Towle to Alfred Schermerhorn.[16] Almost twenty years after her class graduated, there were a few other updates from her classmates. Elizabeth Boody Schumpeter "was the only woman speaker at the Foreign Affairs School held at Radcliffe in January." Miriam Pettengill "has taken a position in Maine with the State Services for Crippled Children." Mildred Weeks was working on her PhD dissertation. The rest of the alumni reported mundane details about their domestic lives. Lucretia Churchill Jordan "is now the usual mother, chauffeuring and so forth." Dorothy Mason Fuller reported that "badminton two mornings a week and singing lessons add zest to life" and that "in odd minutes she sandwiches in a bit of writing" under the pen name Sterling Thorne. Kitty Brown Collier "is not doing anything besides her ordinary housewife's duties but wishes she were."

The former Katherine Towle was the only woman of her graduating class who was, at least maritally speaking, starting all over again. Radcliffe women, it seemed, were more immune to the loosening of marital ties than the rest of the population, but not so much to domestic doldrums.

Around the same time that the newly minted Mrs. Schermerhorn was introduced in the pages of the *Radcliffe Quarterly*, and just a little over two months after they tied the knot, Walter Winchell accused "the novelist, and her fourth mate, A. Coster Schermerhorn" of "being hasty." Lest his readers not understand the implication, the columnist threw in a pun: "Parrotting is such sweet sorrow." A week later Winchell printed a refutation that must have come directly from the newlyweds: "The A. Coster Schermerhorns (Ursula Parrott) are sorry if they've disappointed anybody, but they're not dividing." Because Winchell's column was so widely read, Parrott was highly embarrassed by this tidbit, even after the retraction. Even more humiliating, however, was a subsequent item that ran in her local *Bridgeport Sunday Herald*. Harry Neigher's gossip column expanded on Winchell's original accusation: "Ursula Parrott, the authoress, says it ain't so about her and her groom A. Coster Schermerhorn—but you'll find her living alone at the Hotel Lombardy in Manhattan."[17]

Parrott was furious. She cast about for people to blame for the story, suspecting that her neighbor and former co-owner at the *Connecticut Nutmeg*, Heywood Broun, had been the source. Bye came to Broun's defense, assuring her, "He not only denied vigorously having anything to do with the *Bridgeport Sunday Herald* piece but he denied also knowing anything whatever of your personal affairs." "As for the other columnists," Bye continued, with a subtle admonishment, "I am afraid that they regard anyone as their game who goes to the night clubs." Perhaps a mutual friend, Bye advised, could be useful "in spreading the word around that you don't like this notoriety (which many victims do)." But they would likely just "advise that the best procedure is retirement and silence," neither of which were Parrott's strong suits.[18]

Parrott was trying to focus on writing and salvage her career, get her financial house in order, and soothe her strained relationship with her agent. But catastrophe was imminent. In the summer of 1940, she hit a wall with a six-part serial for the prestigious, well-paying *Saturday Evening Post*, in whose pages she badly wanted to appear. Bye was "terribly disappointed" that she had not yet turned in the story and hoped that she was "working on the *Post* serial exclusively." A month later, he telegrammed about not being able to reach her by telephone, saying (yet again) that he was "terribly disappointed" but hoped "we can get back on the track tomorrow" when the *Post* editor, Stuart Rose, wanted to meet with her in person. Soon after, Bye announced that "we have reached the end of our string" and that the *Post* "will want the manuscript or the loan," as he now termed her substantial $7,500 "advance."

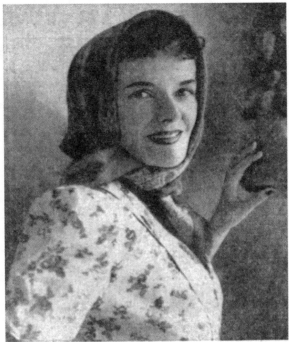

URSULA PARROTT, whose new book, "Heaven is Not Far Away," has just been released by Dodd, Mead & Co. The novel, which is the story of a woman in aviation, has a solid background of knowledge, as Miss Parrott is an experienced pilot. The photograph shows the writer in the Florida home where she spends some time each winter.

FIGURE 34. Never one to waste good story material drawn from her own life, Parrott used details learned from her recently acquired piloting experiences in her early 1940s stories. (*Miami Daily News*, October 11, 1942.)

He even offered to "try to find someone to finish the story" for her. "It seems such a devastating pity," he wrote with earnest sadness, "that on the threshold of a new up-turn in your career you should not have the strength to get over the door-sill." Parrott balked at the thought of a ghost writer. "Sorry. Never had one. Don't know what to do with one."[19]

As Bye struggled to get Parrott to meet her *Saturday Evening Post* deadline, he expressed incredulity over her latest adventure, "One wouldn't think you were in trouble when, with all your responsibilities, you take up flying, the most dangerous of all pastimes." It's true. Parrott was training to become a pilot with the Civilian Air Corps (see figure 34). F. Scott Fitzgerald could have been describing Parrott when he pondered Charles Lindberg's 1927 solo transatlantic flight to Paris: "maybe there was a way out by flying, maybe our restless blood could find frontiers in the illimitable air."[20] But George Bye was no doubt thinking less of Lindbergh and more of Amelia Earhart, who, after working for several years as the aviation editor of *Cosmopolitan*, where she encouraged women to take to the skies, disappeared and was presumed dead during an around-the-world trip in 1937.

The late 1930s were boom years for civilian aviation, and after the United States entered the war in 1941 the government actively recruited flyers of all sorts to help patrol the skies. "I stopped being an isolationist Sunday," Parrott told *Ladies' Home Journal* editor Bruce Gould after the Japanese attacked Pearl Harbor. "I'll be flying up and down the coast, reporting every plane I see. And don't think I'm going to be the only woman in the patrol. There'll be plenty of us in the air. You know, in time of war, they expect every woman to do her duty too."[21]

With regard to his client's take to the skies, Bye need not, for once, have had concern about anything other than lost time at the typewriter. Parrott had no mishaps related to her new hobby. Nor would she squander the experience, writing women pilots into stories and novels that were as immersed in aviation as *Ex-Wife* had been in the milieu of Greenwich Village divorcées and speakeasies.

On October 1, 1940, the *Saturday Evening Post* terminated Parrott's agreement and asked for repayment of her sizable advance. But just as the curtain was closing, there was a final act. "As usual, at fifty-five minutes past the eleventh hour, or maybe five minutes past the twelfth—I am not sure yet," Parrott wrote in December, she asked Bye for a final "great super-supermiracle" in the form of a last chance to turn in the manuscript. Parrott, who acknowledged that in their dozen years of working together Bye had "pulled an average of three miracles a year," was asking for "a last and final miracle."[22]

It would, in fact, be the last miracle request because George Bye had finally had enough. On November 25, 1940, he telegrammed Parrott his resignation, effective at the end of the year: "*Ladies Home Journal* informs me you again have failed to deliver story. Cannot understand your attitude unless reason is twelve years of emotional pyrotechnics and crises have left me wooden. Maybe you will be much better off without me." Mindful of Parrott's feelings, Bye concluded his telegram warmly: "I don't mean to let this break in our business relations interfere with our friendship." He sent out a notice to editors, "By mutual arrangement this office has retired as the agent for Miss Parrott."[23] *Retired* is a nicer word than *resigned*, but there is no question that this parting of ways came from a fed-up agent walking away from his troubled client. Parrott was now without a trusted advisor and advocate for the first time in her publishing career. She begged Bye to reconsider. "I think that what I decided," he responded, "is the best for both of us."[24]

After Bye's resignation, Parrott signed with Curtis Brown, Ltd., whose Madison Avenue offices were one block from Bye's agency. She still conferred with her ex-agent on occasion and sought his assistance a few years later when she was agent shopping again, for reasons she did not express beyond feeling "very disappointed." She wished for her new agent the same thing she hoped of each of her new romances: "Where I go I want to stay permanently." Bye, who remained a faithful counselor, responded with polite hedges and probable white lies about how Harold Ober "found there was too much competition with Faith Baldwin but he was very much tempted." He was more encouraging about the agent Elsie McKeogh but gave no indication of whether or not she was willing to take on Parrott and her headline-grabbing, missed-deadline baggage. In an ominous final letter of their archived correspondence, dated May 1944, Bye wrote to Parrott, "Elsie McKeogh is very worried because she has not been able to get in touch with you."[25] It was *déjà vu* all over again.

Parrott had always been topical: she took to the skies to help defend the United States during the war, and the war also became central to her stories. After all, World War II touched every aspect of American life, including Parrott's own. Against her wishes, her son took a leave of absence from college to enlist in the Marines, entering basic training in Miami before being deployed to the Pacific. Comparably disposed young men—usually economically privilege and college-aged—responded similarly to the patriotic impulse in Parrott's war-era stories. These young men possessed a sense of purpose that contrasted with their parents' self-interested, hedonistic, worn-out generation. In fact, they tried to right the messed-up world their parents bequeathed them. "We'll pay the check for the mistakes of our elders," says seventeen-year-old Dennis in "Until Some Other Year" from 1944, "and we needn't be sorry for ourselves either, because many generations before us have been obliged to do the same thing."

Parrott also began using some of her 1940s stories, including this one, to reclaim the idea of her generation's usefulness. "Until Some Other Year" begins as a stability-over-passion story, with poor, hard-working twenty-two-year-old Catherine marrying successful forty-year-old Alex Devirlake. Once married, she gives up all traces of her old life—the dingy Brooklyn flat, working day and night to support her family—and becomes a society wife, hosting parties, wearing expensive jewels, and feeling useless and isolated. Catherine gives birth to twins and begins to wonder if life was "to be forever a series of committee meetings, an increasing collection of jewelry (she understood now why dowagers were usually laden down—they'd had so many anniversaries), and the bringing-up of the twins—who were, in fact, brought up by the nanny and the nursemaid?"

After the Japanese attack Pearl Harbor, however, Catherine goes back to work at her husband's New York offices, where she had once been a secretary. At first she hates it—the early and rushed mornings, the commute, the long days. But as her coworkers begin to see her as "a smart businesswoman" and not just the boss's wife, the work becomes "absorbing." She realizes that the "business of finance was a weapon in war, because it provided so many other weapons." Work allows Catherine to contribute to the war effort while also fixing the problems created by being a wealthy, unproductive wife.

This is a story of a woman and a marriage saved by work. Alex delights in his wife's transformation—a far cry from the 1930s men who demanded that women play supporting roles—and Catherine easily deflects a proposal from an old flame because she realizes the value of her family and is committed to making a better world for the next generation. In the face of war, stability and monotony no longer seem like the compromises they did to a more naïve, self-centered pleasure seeker.

Parrott wrote most of her World War II stories, however, about the new generation of modern women, who could not be any more different from her own, which she had spent so much time considering in the 1930s. There were parallels between the two—most obviously the recurrence of a traumatic, life-altering overseas war—but also great divergences. These younger characters gave Parrott a chance to reimagine women's lives with purpose and meaning, taking her away from characters of her generation whose lives, for the most part and for understandable reasons, she could only seem to imagine as exhausting or irremediably dull.

In "The Years I'll Spend without You," Beatrix—whose husband Julian is killed in the South Pacific without having met his child, whom she gives birth to while he is overseas—finds purpose in factory work. In what other time, she wonders, "would she have been able to earn ninety-five dollars a week as a forewoman in the inspection department of a factory making precision instruments?" Such women could be good workers as well as wives, and they would also be fine on their own: they could support their children and knew that their sacrifices were for the greater good. Mrs. B.S. from Hendersonville, North Carolina, wrote to *Redbook* after reading this story, explaining that it "helped me find the strength and courage to face an uncertain future in the chaotic world of today. I hope other war wives will gain as much as I did from the tragic but tenderly beautiful love story of *Julian* and *Beatrix*." [26]

Younger female characters in Parrott's war-era stories had similarly strong senses of purpose. "A Far Off Music" uses the very recent Pearl Harbor invasion as the triggering event for a hot-off-the-presses story of male and female pilots in the war's early days. Angel Shore envies the men who get to go overseas; but she knows she can be "useful" doing what Parrott was doing, reporting plane sightings for the Civil Air Patrol. Single women in this story still think about marriage. However, they are equally concerned with having a "good useful job" to assist with the war effort; they want to "serve, to be patient and to be brave, to be unselfish and to be useful!" In "Postscript to a Love Affair," when a female character is asked why she wants to join the women's Navy reserves, a.k.a. the WAVES, her answer is a pithy "to be useful."

Unlike her young, up-and-coming characters, in the early 1940s Parrott was completely worn out. Her longtime agent had walked away, and she was drowning in debt. Her Connecticut house had become too much to maintain, so she decided she had to sell it. From January to October 1940, Parrott earned what seemed like a princely sum, $20,810.30, which included payments for stories and advances from *Redbook, McCall's, Ladies' Home Journal, Saturday Evening Post*, and Dodd, Mead & Co. But the IRS—to whom she was in arrears—and her debtors had first crack at those funds. Her banker's statement at the close of 1940 still showed her in the hole to George Bye, who had functioned for years as her payday lender, to the tune of $1,589.72. In 1941, the income she derived from her already-published work amounted to only $640.15. This was hardly enough for Parrott to live on for a year, let alone a month, or even a week. [27]

Things were only getting worse. As it turned out, the gossip columnists who had been whispering about the Schermerhorns not long after their marriage had been on to something. Though she would not file for divorce until

1943, when she did, Parrott claimed that she and Fred had, in fact, separated just six months after their wedding. From Miami, where she had been spending time with her son when he was training as a Marine cadet, Parrott charged Major Schermerhorn—who had enlisted in the Air Corps in 1942—with desertion. She asserted that she was a "true, loving and affectionate wife" and that her husband "deserted her without just cause." Ursula claimed that Fred never attempted a reconciliation with her, charges he denied. Nonetheless, she was granted a divorce by the Dade County circuit court on February 10, 1944.[28]

One columnist recommended that Parrott should bring *Ex-Wife* "out in a new and revised edition" and that Schermerhorn might also want to try his hand at "a book titled ex-something or other." Remarkably, these snarks had been made on the occasion of their marriage, before each had another divorce in their respective ledgers. In his column, Charles Driscoll took a public jab at Parrott's marital pattern, explaining to readers that each new husband was "presented to friends as the one permanent spouse." Some of these friends, Driscoll continued, "were faithful enough to believe that this time the marriage would last."[29]

This was the end of Ursula and Fred's story, as well as of her marital career. But their divorce was an anticlimax when considered alongside the series of events that preceded it, which supplied the press with almost two full months of front-page headlines involving Parrott's affair with a twenty-something soldier, drug deals, and a military stockade break in which Major Schermerhorn's wife was behind the steering wheel of the getaway car.

FIFTEEN

Saving Private Bryan

THE UNITED STATES VS. URSULA PARROTT

From the St. Regis Hotel in New York City in early 1943, Hollywood director George Cukor composed a handwritten note to gossip columnist Hedda Hopper. On hiatus from Hollywood to aid the war effort by making training films for the Signal Corps, Cukor had just read an item in Hopper's column about how he was barracking in "a suite of rooms at the St. Regis Hotel." Chiding her for revealing his high-class accommodations, Cukor made what he called, with gentle humor, a "final threat": "If you don't praise me from the skies—if you are not wildly flattering about me—if you don't write glowing reports of my bravery and stoic heroism, I will go A.W.O.L. and say you aided and abetted me—and look where Ursula Parrott is now. So have a care."[1]

Perpetrated a few days before New Year's Eve 1942, while still married to Fred Schermerhorn, Parrott's escapade—during which she liberated an army private from a Miami military stockade—was known not only to her former Hollywood associates like Cukor and Hopper but also to her New York circle, Connecticut neighbors, and anyone from San Francisco to Boston who followed the headlines of the day. Michael Neely Bryan, an army private hailing from Byhalia, Mississippi, had a long history of trouble before he got into significantly more with the famous author. Born more than seventeen years after her, by 1940 Bryan had been divorced once and was living at home with his family in Germantown, Tennessee, when he was not on the road performing as a traveling musician. He played guitar with many of the country's best bandleaders, including Artie Shaw, Bob Chester, Jan Savitt, and Benny Goodman. But he was itinerant in his affiliations, hinting at problems that had little to do with his musical abilities. For example, although Bryan claimed that he quit Benny Goodman's band before enlisting, the bandleader had a different story: that he fired Bryan for unspecified "constant gross misbehavior," the nature of which one might fairly guess based on the headlines Bryan would soon be making.[2]

When Bryan enlisted in the air force, six months after the Japanese attack on Pearl Harbor, he gave as his home address the Forrest Hotel on 49th Street in New York City. He was first stationed at the Santa Ana Air Base in California, where he performed in the Air Corps Radio band. After just three months, Bryan was dismissed from his post because of marijuana use and transferred to Williams Field in Chandler, Arizona, where he got in trouble again, this time for going AWOL to see a band perform at a local club. A pattern was emerging: music and marijuana were the Siren's songs that repeatedly lured the young private to trouble. From Arizona, Bryan was transferred in mid-November 1941 to the 655th squadron in Miami, where he was attached to the 17th Air Force Miami Beach Band.

It was in the Miami sunshine, where Marc Parrott was in training and Ursula had been keeping a winter home, that the two met. Bryan told the FBI that Parrott had invited him to several dinners at her home, after which they began seeing each other frequently. The FBI learned from an informant that Parrott and Bryan rented a room for a week starting on November 21 using the aliases Mrs. Lyle Thompson and Mr. Michael Browne and claiming that they were siblings. The informant "could hear them talking at nights, and they always had a quantity of liquor on hand in this room." She thought it odd that the two had no luggage or clothing, "except a man's rain coat part of the time," "a lady's girdle" (which she observed in the dresser for two days), and an empty "small tan bag."[3]

The unlikely pair's troubles began in New York City after Parrott bought an airplane ticket for Bryan to visit her there on November 28, 1942. Once in Manhattan, with Parrott by his side, Bryan bought marijuana from several "peddlers." After he returned solo to Miami, Bryan called Parrott in New York to request that she buy an additional $200 of marijuana on his behalf, telling her he would pay her back at their next liaison. Parrott told authorities that she did not fulfill Bryan's request. She also swore that Bryan "does not smoke marijuana, and has not smoked it since he volunteered for the Army," despite ample evidence to the contrary.[4]

About two weeks after their late November New York encounter, Parrott flew Bryan back to the city. The private had anticipated getting a three-day leave, which at the last minute did not come through. Not one to play by the rules, Bryan defied the command. He headed to the airport, picked up the ticket Parrott had purchased for him, and boarded the plane for New York City. Whether the motivation was Parrott, the pot, or a combination, Bryan stayed three nights in a suite at the Pennsylvania Hotel with Parrott by his side. It was later revealed that Parrott paid for the room and, at Bryan's suggestion, that they checked in under the names Mr. and Mrs. Lyle Thompson, the second of three aliases the couple would use during their brief affair.

During this trip, Parrott introduced Bryan to someone she called a friend, who went by the name Roy Anderson. Anderson turned out to be a federal agent who would subsequently witness what was described in the press as a "reefer rendezvous" Bryan had at the musician-friendly Forrest Hotel, where he resided when he enlisted. To arrange the rendezvous, Bryan called a musician friend, Rose Reynolds, who involved two additional men in the score. The crew—later described by the press as a more nefarious-sounding "ring"— sourced dope from an uptown dealer named Pork Chops who provided "half a pound of marijuana for $75, adequate for several hundred cigarettes." The deal went down in Reynolds's room at the Forrest.[5]

At the end of their three days together, Bryan stashed the reefer in a combination radio phonograph that Parrott purchased for him. Radio and drugs in tow, he boarded an Eastern Airlines plane back to Miami. When he stopped in Charleston for a layover, Bryan was met with a telegram from Parrott urging him to call her immediately. When he did, she instructed him to dump the reefer. No doubt a combination of perplexed, skeptical, and protective of his score, Bryan held on to it until he made his last layover in Jacksonville, at which point he reluctantly disposed of the marijuana. When Bryan arrived in Miami, sans drugs, he was arrested and placed in base prison for twenty days, not for possession but for being AWOL. Even though authorities had found no trace of the marijuana, the New York federal courts, with Agent Anderson's aid, prepared drug charges as Bryan began his confinement in the Miami prison stockade for leaving the base without permission.

Private Michael Neely Bryan spent the second holiday season since the United States entered World War II in military prison, where Parrott began regularly visiting him. She would arrive on base and surrender her car keys to the guard; the lovebirds were then allowed to visit for around twenty minutes at a time. On the afternoon of December 28, 1942, at approximately 5:00 p.m., Parrott—wearing a bright yellow hat and driving a green Ford sedan— drove off the base with Bryan concealed in the back seat of her car. Base commander Major Danuser sent out descriptions of the pair to the Miami Police Department, whose officers combed Miami for the fugitives. Danuser reported that "a vigilant search was made of all Airports, Railway stations, Bus depots, Night Clubs, to prevent, if possible their escape from Miami district." The police broadcast a description of the suspects along with the green Ford's license plate numbers.[6] Twenty-four hours later, Ursula Parrott and Private Bryan voluntarily surrendered themselves.

Because Bryan was a soldier and had a pending marijuana charge in New York City, Parrott earned herself a federal indictment alleging that she "aided a private of the United States Army to desert, and did harbor, conceal and protect him in said desertion" and that "she did interfere with the armed forces by influencing Subject, Bryan, to disregard orders and instructions of the United States Army." These were serious accusations. The *Los Angeles Times* headline was appropriately dramatic: "Ursula Parrott Seized by Federal Agents."[7]

The federal charges elevated the case from local scandal to national incident. This was an escape story tailor-made—sex and drugs!—for headlines. Private Bryan was twenty-six, five-foot-eleven and 155 pounds, described as both handsome and young, even "boyfaced." Like Parrott, Bryan was also currently married—to his second wife, Jean Cruse Bryan. The press called Parrott versions of a "four-times-married, thrice-divorced author" or the more efficient "much-married author." She was also described using such phrases as "aging." In fact, Parrott's age was always reported, usually in some version of "forty-year-old best-selling novelist and screenwriter."[8] If reporters had only known that Parrott was actually forty-three, they would, no doubt, have adjusted their mockery accordingly when it came to the age spread between the two suspected felons.

"It was just an impulse."

That's what Parrott told reporters at her arraignment on December 30, 1942. She was "trembling and biting her lip" as she spoke, "so nervous that she had to ask her attorney to open a package of mints for her." When asked by reporters about her marital status, Parrott replied "Let's skip that. This is embarrassing enough as it is."[9] She preferred to talk about how Bryan was "a first class swing musician" and "a very nice person" whom she had known "for a great while." The magnitude of their relationship, however, turned out to be pure fiction. In her FBI testimony, Parrott stated that she had known Private

Bryan for "approximately four months" at the time of the breakout, hardly "a great while." But even this was an exaggeration later amended to "about two months." (Bryan told the FBI that he had only met the author around November 20, a mere eight days before she flew him on his first trip to New York City.)[10] Parrott tried to take responsibility for both Bryan's AWOL and the stockade liberation incidents, telling reporters that she felt terribly about the trouble he was in. "Nothing of this was Priv. Bryan's fault," she firmly stated. "He persistently urged me to go back because I would get into a great deal of trouble." But when she got the car keys back from the supervising officer during that final stockade visit, "it was just an impulse" to abscond with her companion tucked in the back seat. Had this been a premeditated escape plot, the legal consequences would have been even more serious.[11]

Just after the start of 1943, Parrott was charged with a federal indictment on three counts. The most significant count alleged "subversive activities in undermining loyalty, discipline or morale of the armed forces." US district attorney Ernest Duhaime explained that, if she were convicted, this charge alone could warrant ten years' imprisonment and a fine up to $10,000. The second charge was that she enticed Private Bryan to desert from the United States Army. The third was that she subsequently harbored a deserter.[12]

Parrott's lead attorney, Bart Riley, argued that the indictment was "bad in substance" with charges so vague "that Mrs. Parrott might be in danger of further prosecution even if she is acquitted." Parrott's attorney especially objected to the subversion count, for which the prosecution relied on the War Act of June 1940, which was intended to thwart fifth columnists, as internal saboteurs were called, from undermining the government. According to her counsel, it was preposterous that this charge would be levied for such a minor infraction. Parrott's lawyer also deemed it "duplicitous" because the prosecution failed to show "what duty Mrs. Parrott interfered with by driving Bryan out of the Army stockade in her car" since he was a prisoner and not an active-duty soldier at the time—a clever bit of legal maneuvering. The defense's objections were overruled. During its two years on the books, no one had been charged with violating the War Act. Parrott thus became the first person in US history to be so accused, a fact noted by the prosecuting attorney during the proceedings.[13]

While most reporters playfully reported the twists and turns of this case, others found less to be amused about. There was, after all, a war being fought, with tens of thousands of men making the greatest sacrifice of all to defend the free world, while others like Bryan were shirking their duties in pursuit of dope and married women—and in uniform, no less. After accusing Parrott of being nothing more than a profitable hack, one anonymous commentator asked, "Are we to assume that civilians, just because they happen to be in the public eye, are to be given free run of our army camps and this to such an extent that they can walk in, take a prisoner from custody, conceal him in an automobile and spirit him away without anyone lifting a finger?" Calling for an investigation of the military base and the enforcement of military law, this critic argued that Parrott should "be made to pay the full penalty military law prescribes" in order to uphold the honor of the United States Army.[14] Impulse or not, the United States was at war; such behavior, the argument went, should have serious consequences.

January 23, 1943, was a rotten day for Private Bryan. First, he was sentenced to serve one year's imprisonment and hard labor for "breaking confinement." The *Los Angeles Times* didn't bother using his name; their headline read, "Ursula Parrott's Army Friend Sentenced at Court-Martial." That same day, in a New York federal courtroom, Bryan was indicted on the more serious charge of conspiring to violate the Marijuana Tax Act of 1937 through the act of "transporting narcotics." Assistant United States Attorney Clayton Hollinger charged that Bryan and three co-conspirators were operating a "marijuana rendezvous" at the Forrest Hotel in Midtown, which catered to soldiers from area army camps.[15]

By 1936, every state in the country had passed laws prohibiting the sale, possession, and use of marijuana. The Marijuana Tax Act, passed in 1937, was the first attempt to control the drug at the federal level. The act made not paying taxes on marijuana a federal crime, essentially outlawing the non-medicinal, untaxed possession, use, or sale of the drug. In tandem with a vigorous public information campaign by antidrug crusader and US commissioner of narcotics Harry J. Anslinger—the best-known downstream example of which is the 1936 film *Reefer Madness*, in which high school students introduced to the drug commit acts of depravity—the act played a significant role in solidifying antidrug attitudes in the United States. In the 1930s and 1940s, in no small part thanks to Anslinger's campaign, marijuana was firmly associated with socially marginalized groups, especially Mexican Americans and African Americans, artists, and jazz musicians. A story in the *American Magazine* authored by Anslinger proclaimed that marijuana was an "assassin of youth."[16]

In the early 1940s, there was no place youth was more valued than in the US military. The image of soldiers addicted to a drug widely considered to cause mental deviance and perverse behavior would have horrified most Americans. Roy Anderson, an undercover agent from the Bureau of Narcotics, had been posing as a Boston businessman to infiltrate the drug den, which Parrott helped facilitate through her introduction to Bryan. Without any knowledge that he was assisting in a federal investigation motivated by Anslinger's campaign to purge the nation of marijuana's influence, Bryan had introduced the undercover agent to the "other members of the ring and made arrangements for the agent to purchase supplies of the drug." In the process, Bryan personally sold the agent two ounces of marijuana. When Anderson arrived at "the rendezvous," "he saw many soldiers in uniform smoking the unlawful cigarettes."[17] The case against Bryan and his "drug ring" was meant to serve as an example, protecting the reputation of the United States military at a crucial time in its history.

On February 25, 1943, an all-male jury was selected for Parrott's federal trial in Miami. (In a feat of legal multitasking, Parrott had filed for divorce from Fred Schermerhorn eight days earlier, inexplicably alleging abandonment just as she was on the verge of testifying about her lover's military jailbreak.) The trial provided plenty of juicy details for reporters to spin into sensational copy (see figure 35). Major Danuser, the no-doubt highly embarrassed officer in charge at the time of Bryan's escape, testified that he had twice looked out the door of his office to see what Parrott and Bryan were doing as their backseat-of-the-car visit dragged on to around two hours. "What were they doing?" asked the D.A. Danuser replied, "They appeared to be making love."[18]

Investigators testified that Parrott took Bryan from the stockade to her home, located on "exclusive" 88th Street in Miami Beach, where the prisoner changed from his uniform into civilian attire. Parrott then did something she must have learned from the movies: she abandoned her rental car in a parking garage before she and Bryan walked to the bar at the Columbus Hotel for drinks and dinner. Fed and cocktailed, they tried to get a room at the Columbus for the night, but the hotel was fully occupied.[19] The pair checked into the nearby Miami Colonel Hotel for what we must hope, for Parrott's sake, was a night worthy of the crime it took to experience it.

This time Bryan used the jazzy alias Artie Baker to register at the hotel. The

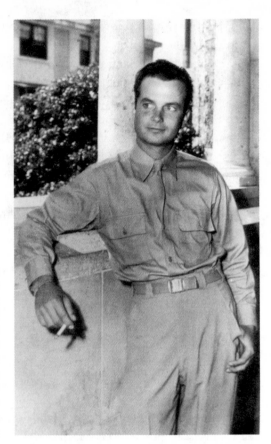

FIGURE 35. Parrott's "soldier friend," Private Michael Neely Bryan, having a smoke break during her trial "for aiding a deserter." The government's case against Bryan's "reefer rendezvous" was undertaken as part of a wider effort to protect the image of America's military during a time of war. (February 25, 1943, Associated Press Wirephoto, author's collection.)

"Bakers" had brandies and soda delivered to their room, and the next morning breakfast brought in. A waiter at the hotel told the FBI that when he delivered breakfast "there was a man out of the bed who let him into the room, and a woman in the bed with the cover pulled up closely under her chin." There was no doubt that the bed had been shared. Around ten o'clock that morning, Parrott went on a procurement errand at Burdines Department Store, where she purchased a pair of men's "tropical worsted trousers" and shoes, using the alias A. Baker to make the purchases. The salesmen who assisted her later told the FBI that Parrott "seemed very nervous" and "very excited." She told them "that she was buying this uniform for her brother, who was supposed to graduate from the Officers' Training School" and "had lost his uniform."

Prior to turning themselves in, Parrott and Bryan had a last hoorah: lunch at the Seven Seas Restaurant and more cocktails at the Columbus Hotel.

When Parrott, with what must have been a buzz, arrived with her paramour at federal officer A. L. Raithel's Federal Building offices around five o'clock that night, she took full responsibility for the escape. In his testimony, Raithel conveyed Parrott's version of what had happened at the base:

> "If you've got nerve enough to lie down in the back seat," she told Bryan, "I've got nerve enough to drive you out of here to get a good dinner."
> "You're crazy," the prisoner replied.
> "I'll show you," she declared, starting the car and speeding past the armed guard with a wave of her hand.
> "Look out, the guard will shoot," Bryan warned.
> "Let him shoot," she called.

Parrott was lucky that Bryan's warning did not come to pass. Gate guard Private Sanford Halmes testified that he asked the fleeing author to halt twice and only decided not to shoot "because there were too many soldiers about." During the trial Parrott explained that she had, in fact, been afraid the guard would shoot, using that fear as an excuse for why she "kept right on going." She also testified that the two "were only going out for dinner. We meant to get back sooner, but it was difficult."[20]

Parrott's defense attorney presented some shrewd legal arguments. Riley told the jury that Parrott "should never for such an escapade as occurred at Miami Beach be tried on so serious a charge" as impairing the loyalty and discipline of the armed forces—that was egregious overreaching on behalf of the prosecution.[21] Technically, Bryan had been sentenced to one-year imprisonment not for desertion but for breaking confinement, so Parrott could not be accused of assisting a deserter. Riley made the case that the author had, in fact, been helping the government break up a marijuana ring in New York, a twist no jury could have seen coming (see figure 36).

During the trial, local narcotics agent Raithel, testifying for the prosecution, affirmed the most seemingly outrageous of Parrott's claims about her supporting role in trapping the New York drug peddlers, which she had undertaken without Bryan's knowledge. In their report, the FBI described Parrott as a "voluntary, unpaid informant." Parrott's motivation for participating in this sting operation was never fully explained, though her Department of Justice records indicate that she had become "concerned over the possible ill effect of this activity upon her young friend and reported the matter to the Federal authorities in order to break up the narcotic trade." She told the US attorney "that she has a son in the Army," implying that she had a

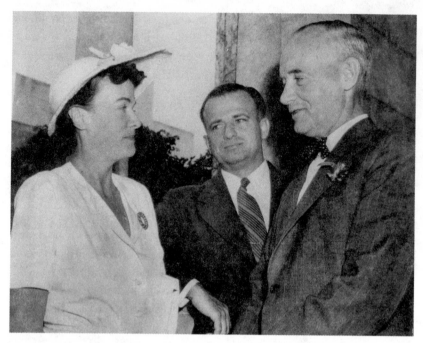

FIGURE 36. Parrott and her lawyers, A. C. Dressler (center) and Bart Riley, during a recess toward the end of the Bryan trial. Riley objected to a number of the prosecution's allegations, especially to the subversion count, and tried unsuccessfully to have the case dismissed for insufficient evidence. (February 1943, Associated Press Wirephoto, author's collection.)

stake in the military's reputation and did "not want to see this young man [Bryan] continue in his evil ways."[22] Parrott had, in fact, taken on the surprising role of undercover agent, making sense out of why she had so much latitude during her stockade visits. Her FBI file includes a significant note, which did not come up at the trial: that she was not considered "an addict herself."

Although she had been visiting Bryan in the stockade allegedly to talk him into turning "government witness," this could not explain the escape. As it turned out, Parrott had asked for permission to take Bryan off base and the request had been denied. Agent Raithel testified that Parrott called him from the stockade on the day of the jailbreak to inform him that Bryan had finally agreed to testify about the marijuana ring, but she had a "preposterous" favor to ask in exchange: four off-base hours alone with Bryan. Since she was soon returning to New York and "this was to be a fairly final goodbye," Parrott just decided to go for it. Claiming that she was trying "to make his life a little better," since "all of his troubles were my fault," Parrott told the FBI that when she got into the car with her keys on that fateful day and looked at Private Bryan and "knew how badly he wanted to go out to dinner" that she said to herself, "Everything is my fault; why not take a chance for him?"[23]

During closing arguments, the prosecution read the author's confession, which she made at the time of her arrest, to a "half-filled" courtroom "consisting of about 100 elderly women and a few men" who had showed up to witness the climax of this tawdry wartime melodrama. Parrott "sobbed and dabbed at her eyes with a dainty handkerchief" as she listened to her confession being read aloud: "I was entirely responsible for Bryan's AWOL sentence and it bothered my conscience." After fleeing the stockade, she and Bryan "spent the night 'walking around' in the vicinity of a Miami airport," a statement contradicted by all evidence about the night Parrott and Bryan spent at the hotel, but which sounded considerably more virtuous than the brandy-laden, shared-bed version that was undoubtedly the truth. Her attorney made a final request that the court dismiss the case for insufficient evidence; the motion was denied. As the court adjourned, Parrott "ran from the courtroom to Bryan, 26, who was standing in a corridor. She smiled as she clasped his hand and led him from the courthouse."[24]

Following closing arguments, United States Judge John Holland gave jurors specific instructions for their deliberations: they could not find Parrott guilty of aiding a deserter if they believed Private Bryan had not intended to desert the army when he left the stockade with Parrott, nor if they believed that Parrott had not intended to "undermine the morale and loyalty of all the troops stationed at Miami Beach." After a mere twelve minutes of deliberation, the jury handed Parrott her innocence. "Mrs. Parrott Freed on Army Charge," declared the *Los Angeles Times*, with a lead that stated the author was cleared of all "charges of impairing the loyalty and discipline of the armed forces...by driving a good-looking private concealed in the rear of her automobile." After the verdict was read, "spectators crowded around to congratulate the 40-year-old author," who smiled "happily" and "dabbed at her eyes a couple of times as if to wipe away a tear." Her "soldier-friend" was not there to congratulate her, since he had already been returned to the stockade to begin his one-year sentence. "Ursula Parrott's trial, like her books had a happy ending," wrote one reporter who must not have been an actual reader of Parrott's writing.[25]

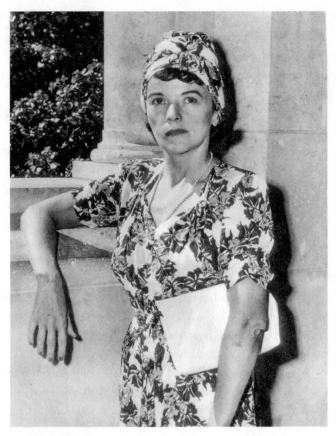

FIGURE 37. In their coverage of the case, *Time* magazine described Parrott as "aging" and "haggard." A coalition of women's magazine writers and editors took offense at *Time*'s reporting and announced that they would be asking *Time* to explain their inexcusable sexism on this occasion. (February 25, 1943, Associate Press Wirephoto, author's collection.)

In their coverage of the case, *Time* magazine described Parrott as "aging (40)" and "haggard, her impulsive uncombed head under a badly tied turban" (see figure 37). The magazine treated those who followed the story with equal condescension: "to many a *Hausfrau*, wrinkling into middle age, this saga of the popular author of slick, sleek magazine pap was a thrill beyond daily hopes."[26]

It was 1943. Women were working in war production plants, tending victory gardens, and raising children while their husbands were overseas. The hard-won battles of first wave feminism were yesterday's news, but women were hardly taken as equals on all fronts, and *Time*'s low linguistic blows did not go unnoticed. Bristling at the article's sexism, contributors and editors from the leading women's magazines announced plans "to even up *Time*'s recent description of Ursula Parrott [as] a middle-aged matron." They planned "to ask *Time* why Clare Luce, about the same age, isn't listed as a middle-aged matron and also why *Time* always describes a man in his 40s as 'a dynamic young executive?'"[27] Although Parrott had lost some of her publishing steam, she still had allies among the writers and editors who came to her defense on this occasion, sowing seeds that would grow into the next wave of feminism.

Never one to wallow in her disappointments, it was time for Parrott to get back to business. "Congratulated by spectators and the prosecuting attorney," wrote one newspaper, "Mrs. Parrott smiled happily, and said she would go back to work on a book." She told the press about "Sunlit," which she had started writing on New Year's Day. In the midst of the Bryan-related hullabaloo, Parrott claimed to have produced a miraculous 180-page draft of this "story of a man and woman who 'got in an awful jam.'" It's hard not to recall Parrott's letter to her agent, written more than a decade prior, about "those GREAT TRAGEDIES which seem to punctuate the lives of female authors (and may be traced in their plots, a couple of years after the event, for thus the young women turn life's losses into life's gains, which is damn sensible of them)." Parrott was wasting no time in trying to make something out of her latest misfortune. On the eve of her acquittal, Walter Winchell reported in his column that "Sunlit" "is about her current mess 'and it isn't.'" He said that the book was to be dedicated to Private Bryan, "the lad in the case," information Winchell must have gotten from the source.[28]

It's regrettable that Parrott never published "Sunlit." Her stories hewed so closely to her experiences that it would have been instructive to read her take on this dramatic episode and her brief stint as a volunteer undercover narcotics agent. All of the bumps in the rutted road Parrott traveled made for catchy headlines and first-rate story material, but the escapades were escalating in their erraticism and in the toll they were taking. Charles Driscoll hinted at darker forces swirling around the Bryan story. He concluded his column about the episode by noting that, "many of the friends of Miss Parrott explain the amazing incident on the ground that the author has been living in a mental world of wild fantasy so long that smuggling a soldier out of the guardhouse seemed to Miss Parrott only a mild form of relaxation."[29] It was no secret, then, that Parrott was in the process of being undone by her impulses.

SIXTEEN

Her "Breaks Went Bad"

In early 1942, the U.S. Department of the Treasury issued a Notice of Levy to Ursula Parrott for $8,674.74 in back taxes; that summer, they raised the figure to $10,149.36 in the form of a "Warrant for Distraint." She owed her agency, Curtis Brown, Ltd., almost $1,500 for unearned advances because of a story deadline she had failed to meet. Creditors headed to court to try to garnish Parrott's earnings, but to no avail. As her publisher's accounting office explained to the New York City Sheriff's Office, "there are no moneys due the author. As a matter of fact, it might be said that there exists an unearned advance."[1]

Toward the end of the following year, Dodd, Mead & Company accountants enumerated a list of debtors in order of judgments filed, starting with the Internal Revenue Service and running through eight other claimants, from Helena Rubenstein to Gimbel Brothers Department Store. The accounting department told one eager creditor, "As you can readily see, Uncle Sam is the most interested party of all and if the royalties on the sales of the books published by our company are to be the answer towards liquidating her liabilities, then my guess is that the indebtedness may never be earned." The only hope the accountant could offer was if Parrott could earn in magazine sales what she was not earning in book sales, "providing, of course, she continues to write for the pulp trade."[2]

Parrott published her last novel, *Even in a Hundred Years*, in 1944. It is a fitting closure to the author's novelistic career, which ran its course in fifteen years, starting with the fatalistic modern morality tale of *Ex-Wife* and ending with this introspective tale about generations, tradition, loss, and hope. The gist of the novel is that everything changes and repeats, with minor variations, over time: loves and wars come and go, as do fortunes; people are born and die, or are killed; time marches on. The novel is a far cry from the hedo-nistic, destructive freneticism of *Ex-Wife*, sharing more with the reflective, generational scope of *The Tumult and the Shouting*.

Parrott's last story, "Let's Just Marry," appeared in 1947, and her name would not grace the silver screen again until Douglas Sirk resuscitated *There's Always Tomorrow* for an exceptionally interesting remake in 1956, casting Barbara Stanwyck as the career woman who cannot find love in her busy life and Fred MacMurray as the husband who cannot find happiness with his family. Parrott did make two 1940s Hollywood sales—"A Far Off Music" to 20th Century-Fox for "the exceptionally high price" of $50,000 in 1942, and "The Conover Girl" to low-budget Republic Pictures in 1945—but it was the IRS, not Ursula, who benefited from these deals. When a headwaiter at the Ritz-Carlton was hesitant to accept a check from Parrott, whose reputation for writing bad ones now preceded her, she asked him to produce the news-paper, which showed her picture with the story about the $50,000 sale. This would be the last time Ursula Parrott would have such evidence of her suc-cess, and likely the last time the Ritz would take a check that was unlikely to clear, no matter the headline.[3]

It was the end of an era, and not just for Ursula Parrott. In 1952, colum-nist Robert Ruark characterized the 1920s as a dull time overshadowed by a group of unimportant writers who turned triviality "into what passed then for importance." Rereading some of these once-celebrated books twenty or so years after they were published, Ruark disparaged authors of the period for romanticizing "dull" and "shiftless" characters possessed of nothing but "shoddy problems" (see figure 38). From the perspective of post–World War II America, on the heels of another military conflict that did not spawn a generation of hedonism but instead families, home ownership, and subur-ban settling, Ruark criticized Jazz Agers for living in an "era of Wonderful Nonsense."[4]

Ursula Parrott had also been looking over her shoulder. In the later part of her writing career, her stories rethought rash behaviors of the past and imag-ined more adult ways of living. There was less drinking in her 1940s tales—some lacked even a single cocktail, where those from the 1930s rarely had less than one per page. Characters rejected materialism and avoided reckless spending. It now seemed appropriate to give up a fur coat that was being paid for in installments. Ostentatious displays of wealth had become déclassé, especially for the younger generation who knew better than their parents. "Don't wear that fur jacket when you are with me," says a recently returned,

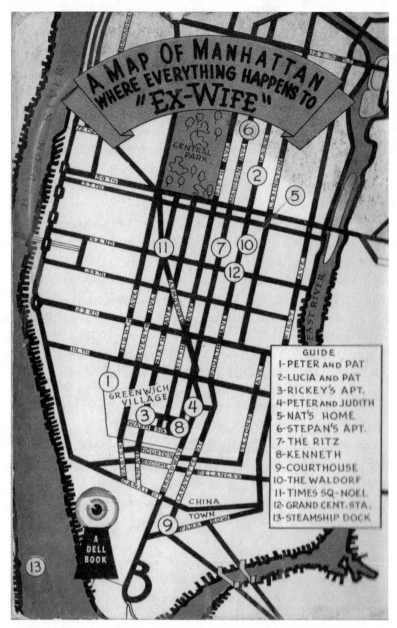

FIGURE 38. Dell's inexpensive 1949 mapback edition of *Ex-Wife*, which gave its readers a visual layout of the novel's key locations on the back cover, sold the novel as a story of "love and divorce in the turbulent twenties." Even though it was marketed as a story of yesteryear, Dell must have believed that Parrott's twenty-year-old novel would still generate sales. Given her outstanding debts, however, Parrott was unlikely to have seen a cent from its publication. (Author's collection.)

working-class war veteran to a high-society young woman living beyond her means. "It's too conspicuous."[5]

The war also provided new plot opportunities. In "And Then For Always," when Marcia is given a chance to join the Women's Army Auxiliary Corps while her fiancé is overseas (he is eventually declared lost in action), she jumps at the opportunity to contribute to the war effort, "delighted to be a corporal, and ambitious to be a sergeant"—suggesting a much-needed outlet for women's energies outside romance and family. Although these stories were always patriotic, Parrott didn't shy away from calling out the US military's gender-based exclusions many decades before this kind of criticism gained traction: "If women could go all the way, lie in the foxholes, stand watch on the ships, man the bombers' guns," her narrator ponders in "And Throw Away the Key," "maybe they would not value so much intangibles like being happy, loved, important."

But even if they spent World War II overseas or working as riveters, Parrott's postwar-era characters became daughters and wives again, or worked to pay the rent until they became wives with daughters of their own. Women who settled for domesticity had been shunned in Parrott's 1930s stories but became the norm in her 1940s tales. There were simply fewer successful career women in these postwar stories, so the need to cushion men from female success evaporated as well. In "Somewhere East of Sunrise," impoverished Mary spends her money training to get a commercial pilot's license so that she can support herself and her alcoholic father. At story's end, wealthy pilot Emory, who admires Mary's piloting skills, begins to question why she is so beset by "the desire to work like a man in a profession too hard for most men" and asks if she would like to "have a home of your own, a husband, children? Wouldn't you like to be like other women?" Within a page of this proposal, he goes from asking to telling: "You're going to be Mrs. Emory Thaddow, who flies as a hobby, same as her husband."

The occasional woman who possesses ambition in a 1940s Parrott story, like Audrey in "The Beauty of the Family," has good reasons for having a career rather than some self-indulgent drive for fame or wealth for wealth's sake. Helping her brother run the family farm—all that is left after they lose everything because of their father's bad Depression-era investments—Audrey aims to "be the best woman farmer in the whole country." That she ends up being a successful artists' model in New York City has nothing to do with hollow ambitions but rather the discovery that she can earn outlandish sums to send back to the farm for new machinery and to support her large, otherwise-incomeless family.

Parrott's 1940s characters worked through problems instead of escaping from them. In "Our Footsteps Echo," two married couples come to terms with a wartime affair between each other's spouses. After the wounding revelation and weeks of arguments and despair, the marrieds decide to stay their course and the adulterers agree not to carry on with their affair. In the marital conflict story, "Too Busy for Love," Natalie spends time thinking about her five years of largely unhappy married life before she decides to stay with her husband, who commits to trying to be the partner she wants him to be by working less and spending more time with her. There is no talk of Natalie having a career—she wants to be a good wife and mother, a realignment of values in an age of adjusted expectations. In a 1930s Ursula Parrott story, deception, drinks, and divorces would have ensued in both plots. But an older and wiser author gives her literary couples the more difficult path of building instead of destroying.

In "Let Go of Yesterday…," a mother character, of Parrott's generation, offers the perfect advice, in question form, to a young, unmarried woman whose great love died overseas during the war: "Don't you know all life consists of falling apart and putting yourself together again?"

Ursula Parrott's "breaks went bad." That's what Walter Winchell, the most powerful East Coast gossip columnist, had to say about her under the subhead "New York Melodrama" in his May 1, 1952 column. Parrott used to wear "mink and other finery," Winchell wrote. "Now, she says, her most intimate friends wouldn't recognize her." Parrott told the columnist that she had "always read such things about others" and "can't believe it happened to her." Winchell gave a shorthand explanation for Parrott's precipitous decline, without any hint of remorse for the way columnists like him had iced her path: "One unhappy front page story after the other sped her along the toboggan." "Her latest sleeping address, she adds, is in the subways."[6]

It's true. Ursula Parrott was homeless. According to Winchell, he was not reporting malicious gossip—Ursula herself had written to tell him about her situation. It is hard to imagine what would motivate her to so publicly advertise that she had sunk to this low point, especially given her prior aversions to embarrassing publicity. Perhaps this was a last-ditch cry for help, made with the hope that a former friend or associate might come to her rescue. The precise combination of illness, alcohol, petty crime, mental fog, and familial alienation that brought Ursula to this low point is unknown. At some point in her descent she found herself in such dire straits that she swallowed her pride to tell Hugh O'Connor that she had "fainted twice this morning from being hungry or nerves or something," asking if he could send her $5: "I have only three cents now and have had nothing to eat since twelve yesterday there is no coffee in the house and I tried to eat some stale bread but could not swallow it."[7] Ursula had, years before, imagined an oddly prescient version of the situation in which she now found herself in *Ex-Wife* when Patricia wonders, "What will become of me? A bad end no doubt—walking Sixth Avenue, and touching Peter on the arm begging for fifty cents."

It is certain that her mistakes and misfortunes were getting more difficult to overcome, and that years of financial juggling had finally caught up with her—Ursula had no more balls in the air. As a lawyer for her last book publisher, Dodd, Mead & Company, told a lawyer seeking to recover funds due his client, "none of the author's books are now in print, and as far as we are concerned there is no prospect of future royalties." Dodd had earned $500 total in 1948 "as a result of a cheap edition contract arrangement" from a Racine, Wisconsin, publisher for *Nothing Ever Ends*, but these funds would never make it beyond the Internal Revenue Service collector, whose claim against Parrott's income "supersedes all claims." The last time Parrott earned royalties over $1,000 through Dodd, Mead & Company was in 1944—and that was under $1,400. In 1945, she generated less than $50 through book sales. In November 1948, the Dodd, Mead & Company accounting department itemized Parrott's debts that had been attached to any future royalty earnings through the firm to the tune of over $11,000.[8]

In 1947, Parrott had begun working with literary agent Jacques Chambrun, still trying to do the only thing she knew how to do to fix her overwhelming problems: sell her writing. Chambrun had a reputable client list and was known as a debonair man about town. Despite his Fifth Avenue address, however, he also had what the *New Yorker* called a penchant for "stealing his clients' money," embezzling tens of thousands of dollars from writers such as W. Somerset Maugham, H. G. Wells, and Ben Hecht through a "kind of literary pyramid scheme" involving stolen manuscripts, illicit sales, and falsely promised paybacks.[9]

Ursula Parrott had been a debtor to all of her literary agents, so as it turned out, Chambrun actually got nothing out of her. It is, in fact, likely that this was the one time the shady agent got taken to the cleaners by a client instead of the other way around. Parrott allegedly gave Chambrun "a promissory note for $3,600 on October 29, 1947," and he loaned her an additional $300 on December 23. It is certain that she did not earn enough to repay these debts. Chambrun went to court to try to recover the funds, testifying that Parrott had repaid only a small portion of the borrowed money. In March 1949, a judge in the Manhattan Supreme Court gave Chambrun an uncontested $3,049 judgment against Parrott. Around the same time an additional $640 judgment was made against Parrott for funds owed to the Your Secretary agency for unpaid secretarial services. Chambrun and Your Secretary would never see repayment of this money, however, given what Ursula owed to her other debtors, especially the U.S. Department of the Treasury.[10]

Around the same time, Parrott was the subject of unwanted press for "smuggling herself out of her diggings" at the Henry Hudson Hotel, located on 58th Street, just south of Central Park, where she had run up a hefty $1,746 bill. When she fled the hotel, she left behind what was described as "a purely fictitious check for $1,500" and "six pieces of luggage—loaded with 'miscellaneous valueless items' including an old scale."

Though she dodged her bill, she did leave behind a note, dated August 26, 1949, which the hotel management described to the press as "rather incoherent." In it, she announced that she was "walking out of here tomorrow afternoon you understand for 24 hours with a suitcase, hatboxes, leaving behind all manuscripts, heaps of clothes and so on." She went on to explain, in incomprehensible terms, that she once "wrote a story about someone shut out of hotel and looked up things which seem to have troubled [her] the last half hour." She rambled on: "One really will live to laugh at but cannot have anything go wrong absurdly before I leave at half past three tomorrow and return late Saturday."

The hotel's assistant manager learned that Parrott had decamped to the Vanderbilt Hotel, located a couple of miles south at Park Avenue and 34th Street. By the time the Henry Hudson Hotel's attorneys could produce a summons for Parrott in an attempt to collect the funds owed to them, she had "checked out again." The hotel obtained a writ of attachment against Parrott in City Court, but they would have had to get in the back of the line for repayment. As the *Daily News* reported, the hotel was "at least temporarily at a loss for anything to attach." It is telling that the Henry Hudson Hotel management described the manuscripts Parrott left behind as "valueless."

The Henry Hudson debacle generated only local notice, but Parrott's next hotel kerfuffle landed her name and picture on the front pages of newspapers from California to Connecticut. Several months after her short stay at the Vanderbilt, the author headed south to Maryland, landing at the Washington House Hotel in rural Princess Anne, twenty-three miles south of the Delaware State Line. During her several-months stay there, she "was rumored to have been gathering material for a new novel" and became "a familiar sight in the town as she walked her brown and tan poodle, Coco, in the quiet streets."[11]

After paying her bills at the hotel for several months, with funds that must have been provided by a benefactor, Parrott skipped out on several weeks' debt of $255.20, decamping from the hotel around eight o'clock in the morning on May 30, 1950 in a car driven "by friends who were going to Dover." Mrs. Daisy Shrieves, proprietress of the hotel, went to the local police, fearing that Parrott was on the lam. Mrs. Shrieves had insisted that Parrott pay cash for her bill, which the author refused to do, offering her a no-doubt-bad check instead. The Princess Anne magistrate expeditiously charged the novelist with "failure to pay" and issued a warrant for her arrest. For the second time in her life, Parrott was a fugitive.

Once the car she was in crossed the Delaware state line into the town of Delmar, Parrott was dropped off at the train station. While waiting on the platform, she and her poodle were arrested by Delaware state trooper Homer Bramble, who took the pair to the police station at nearby Bridgeville. At the station, she told the police that the incident was "all a mistake." She gave her name as "Katherine U. Parrott" and, though she had not published anything in several years, listed her occupation as "writer."[12]

At an arraignment hearing in Georgetown, Delaware, the judge asked if "she would waive extradition." Parrott's one-word answer, "no," compelled him to hold her at the Sussex County Prison on $500 bail. She said little at the hearing beyond a brief explanation that she was waiting to hear from her lawyer. The *New York Herald Tribune*, read by so many of Parrott's former friends and associates, reported, "The only company the novelist had at the arraignment was her pet poodle, Coco" and that she "appeared tired after a night spent in a state police barracks cell in Bridgeville." At Parrott's urging, the warden of the Sussex County Prison spent "several hours making long-distance phone calls" to "New York, Philadelphia, Salisbury, and Hollywood, Cal., for Mrs. Parrott as she sought to reach friends to arrange for bond." He told the *Baltimore Sun* that "he had received a wire from New York saying the bond would be furnished" and that the novelist "refused to make any statement about the charges." As it turned out, Parrott's liberation funds originated not from the East Coast but from "an unidentified woman in Beverly Hills" who also paid off Parrott's Maryland hotel debts. Charges were dropped on June 1, and after thirty hours behind bars, Ursula Parrott was a free woman again.[13]

"As she left the modern brick jail…with her poodle Coco joyfully leaping about her feet," she "scoffed" at the notion that she had been trying to run out on her bill when she was arrested on the railway platform, offering an explanation that she must have cooked up behind bars: "Why, I left that State (Maryland) four or five times while I was staying there. When they arrested me I had $20 in my pocket and had been walking up and down the railroad station with my dog for four hours. I could have gotten much farther away if I had wanted to run." She commented on what she believed to be the more pressing matter at hand: "About the novel I was writing down there— there may be no novel now. I'll have to see my publisher. A writer isn't like an actress, you know. This sort of publicity is bad for a writer."[14]

After this incident, Parrott disappeared from the public eye for nearly two years. She published nothing, nor did she generate any headlines until March 1952, when she resurfaced again with headline variations of "Charge Ursula Robbed Brass of Some Silver." The "brass" was a pun, referring to retired brigadier general Donald B. Adams; the silver was literal, referring to seventy pieces, valued at $1,000, which the author had pawned from the Adams collection for $185. "Quite a few other things," which the general "refused to identify," were also discovered missing after General Adams and his wife, who had known Parrott for several years, allowed the author, who "was in financial difficulties" while "finishing a novel," to stay in their fifteen-room New Rochelle home on stately Beechmont Drive while they took a month-long vacation to Nassau.[15]

The Adamses told reporters that Parrott had visited them in their home several times prior to taking up temporary residence there. Mr. Adams said that his wife had assisted her "very considerably," no doubt helping Parrott out of some debt with the hope that she could finish the novel she had been promising, for several years now, to complete. Parrott moved into the Adams home on February 1, and a month later Mrs. Adams returned from Nassau in advance of her husband; "the next day Miss Parrott checked out without saying good by. In the next few days she sent telegrams from New York City, saying that she would come back." Instead of returning, Parrott mailed the

Adamses a pawn ticket from Paul Kaskel and Sons, Inc., on Columbus Avenue, allowing them to recover their silver for $206, "which included charges." That Parrott bothered to mail the ticket to her friends suggests how badly she must have felt about the depths to which she was sinking.

A warrant was issued for Parrott's arrest on the charge of grand larceny. After she fled the Adams home in early March, detectives tracked her down at the Sutton Hotel in New York. Parrott was, however, "a step ahead of police. The writer left her hotel by a service entrance as detectives bearing warrants charging her with stealing silverware worth $1,000 knocked on the doors of her suite."[16] There are no subsequent items in the newspapers covering Parrott's arrest or trial, making it likely that the Adamses, having recovered their silver, took mercy on their fallen friend and dropped the charges.

Back in Cambridge at Parrott's alma mater, Radcliffe, where librarians kept clipping files about alumni, someone added another item to Katherine Towle's file: a *Boston Herald* clipping with the headline, "Ursula Parrott Sought in Theft." At the top of the article is a handwritten note, penned by a librarian: "one of the items that doesn't get in the Alumn. Bullet.!" (see figure 39).[17]

Parrott's breaks had been going bad for some time, but they were irreversible by the time the summer of 1952 rolled around—even if she had yet to give up trying to put the pieces back together. In August, she moved into a Salvation Army shelter where she acquired "a slight ailment": "not venereal but I felt myself as if I had leprosy."[18] The shelter was a step up from the homelessness that Winchell had broadcast to his massive reading public—and it served its purpose as a bridge to a rented room in Brooklyn, where she lived with her dog and tried to get her act together.

Ursula was a fighter, and her weapon of choice was still a typewriter. So she armed herself with one by boldly showing up at her former literary agency's offices on Madison Avenue and asking for another chance. She had used her last ten cents to call her former agent, Alan Collins, at the Curtis Brown agency, promising a tell-all memoir that would sell like hotcakes, redeem her reputation, and put a roof back over her head: "The first quarter's how I got that way. The second what fun it was, the third intimations of catastrophe sort of, and the fourth what if anything is left for consolation on the park benches."[19]

In the summer of 1952, under the alias Sara March, Ursula rented a room

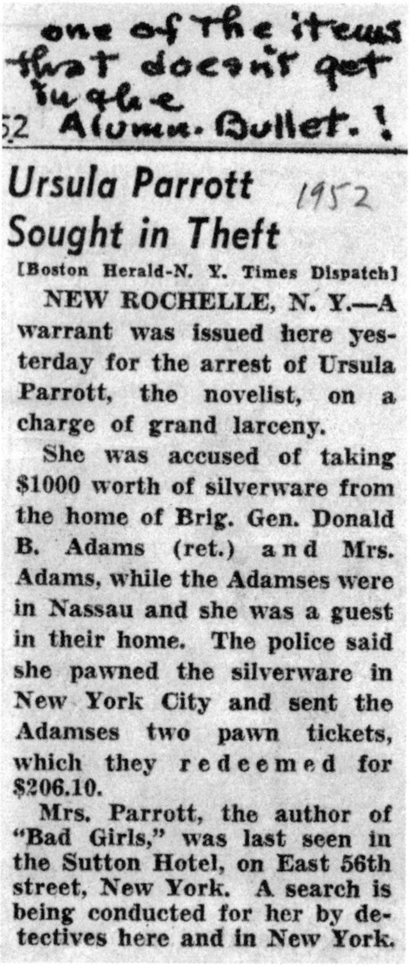

Ursula Parrott 1952
Sought in Theft

[Boston Herald-N. Y. Times Dispatch]

NEW ROCHELLE, N. Y.—A warrant was issued here yesterday for the arrest of Ursula Parrott, the novelist, on a charge of grand larceny.

She was accused of taking $1000 worth of silverware from the home of Brig. Gen. Donald B. Adams (ret.) and Mrs. Adams, while the Adamses were in Nassau and she was a guest in their home. The police said she pawned the silverware in New York City and sent the Adamses two pawn tickets, which they redeemed for $206.10.

Mrs. Parrott, the author of "Bad Girls," was last seen in the Sutton Hotel, on East 56th street, New York. A search is being conducted for her by detectives here and in New York.

FIGURE 39. As the years passed, Ursula Parrott's alumni clipping file at Radcliffe was subject to occasional editorialization about the nature of her exploits, which vastly differed from the experiences of her classmates (note, the novel "Bad Girls" was not, in fact, written by Parrott but is presumably *Bad Girl* by Viña Delmar).

(Class Collections of the Radcliffe Alumnae Association, 1890–1989, RG IX, Series 7, courtesy of Harvard University, Schlesinger Library, Radcliffe Institute).

at 173 Columbia Heights in Brooklyn. Her first month out of the shelter she "did nothing but sleep, read Plato, walk dog, scrub myself. Recovering from the streets." Parrott felt "better every month" and had regained enough of her sense of humor to sarcastically boast that "this is a wonderful fantastic neighborhood" although it was actually "one of the worst for muggings." "I wouldn't walk around here at three a.m. alone for my old short story price." "Behind the Victorian facades," she added, "what lives go on, however!"[20]

After a summer of "three flights up, no telephone, no maid service and two very weird characters recently moved in on the floor," Parrott moved to the nearby Standish Arms Hotel in mid-September. She had one demand of her agent: "No matter who, no matter what song and dance, you don't have my address. No exceptions for relatives or anyone." In 1940, Parrott had written a story about a penniless former debutante who pawns her last valuable, a mink coat, to pay her hotel bill before heading to Brooklyn to begin anew, creating an alias to cover her tracks.[21] Ursula was now following her own literary lead and was hiding from almost everyone. With her perennial optimism, she considered her situation temporary and believed that she could come out the other side with writing that would allow her to reenter the world of friends, family, and society.

Her agent agreed to pay $5.15 per month for the rental of a typewriter from July to August 1952, adding months as manuscript deadlines came and went. In July, Parrott promised Collins fifty to seventy pages a week. In August, she said that she had given around one hundred forty pages to a typist but did not yet have the pages to turn in. In September, Parrott responded to a nudge from Collins by asking him for two more weeks: the pages were being typed and she wanted him "to have as far as Miami episode complete," referring to the Private Bryan ordeal. Desperate for evidence, in early October Collins said he felt "like the guy in the old melodrama who wields the horse-whip," but he had to ask, "what goes on?"[22]

In almost every letter she sent to him, Parrott expressed gratitude to Collins for the typewriter. But by the end of October, he was done with being put off, asking her to set a time in the next week to return the machine. She thanked Collins profusely for the four-month loan and explained that she had "been awfully ill" with "some kind of virus flu," for which reason she "would love to have the typewriter until December" so that she could "turn this in finished or not at all." Having made the mistake of doing so before, she refused to "turn in short stories that I think are amateurish and strained" to make quick cash to buy more time to write her autobiography. "Probably," she concluded with a sense of unusual defeat, "I'll never be done." She recovered her wit before signing off: "I'll make no promises. Might break 'em."[23]

When she needed money, Ursula worked for a few hours at a nearby dry cleaners, where she earned $1.00 an hour—an unfathomable pittance for someone who had once made over $100,000 a year. While she was (allegedly) waiting for the typist to finish, Parrott did, in fact, begin a series of short stories titled "Brooklyn Heights," which she proposed to publish under the pseudonym Philip Oliver. "Written by an unknown," she explained to her agent, so "you'd have to have two or three complete to bother." Her vision for Oliver's stories, which took place in a universe far, far away from the Parrott tales of yore, was that "they're all supposed to be very very Brooklyn, masculine, a cross between Runyonesque and Betty Smith," referring to Damon Runyon, the journalist and short story chronicler of rough-and-tumble Prohibition-era New York, and the female author of the best seller *A Tree Grows in Brooklyn* from 1943. Ursula had "got a notion [she] could write like Thomas Wolfe now," she explained, and had the start of four stories already, though she was considering doubling the size of the collection.[24]

Parrott had always written about what she knew. The days of fur coats, cocktails, and Manhattan hotspots were over; now her stories, like her world, were gritty and hard-boiled. Her needs were so modified from those days, just a decade or so prior, of spontaneous car purchases, fine jewelry, and weeks in Bermuda that they would have shocked anyone who had known her. "My only life's problem at the moment," she told Collins, "is I've got to get a little coat to keep me warm." Not to end on a defeatist note, she added, "Well I will." In fact, she did. Asking Collins to thank someone named Edith for the black suit she had sent to her, Parrott reported, "I live in it. It's warm."[25]

As the end of the year approached and Parrott's prospects were dimming, an unlikely savior materialized: ex-husband number three, Jack Wildberg, who had tried and failed years before to get Parrott's financial house in order. London-based now, where he was producing plays, Wildberg took over the typewriter rental payments when Collins gave up. He became Ursula's long-distance writing coach, advising his ex-wife to "go completely objective, reportorial not emotional," assuring her, "and you won't lose your typewriter." Jack sent her a hundred dollars, despite having "his own US tax troubles," with which she went to the dentist—presumably a real one—to fix some abscessed teeth.[26]

"You don't realize that everyone in my old life except you treats me rather as if I smelled badly," she told Wildberg: "You alone, every time you are in town, meet me in front of a fashionable or very respectable address, kiss me tenderly, don't mind being seen across a restaurant table from me." Jack was, she told Collins, "the only man I ever was involved with in my life who gave a damn if I ate or not"; it was "thanks to him...I have eaten the last months." (It was likely he who had provided the modest monthly allowance to help her get back on her feet again.) "I never appreciated him....I took him for granted with emerald rings and ermine coats, and he's had three wives since, but the friend who sticketh closer than a brother, with nothing to be made out of it." Parrott promised "Jackie" that she'd have the book done by year's end.[27]

Behind the scenes, Wildberg was in conversation with Collins about the source of their mutual concern. In November, Collins warned, "I don't want to be hard-boiled but I am certainly put out with Ursula. She has made me so many promises on so many occasions that she would really get to work on her autobiography and give me enough copy so that I can get her a contract and so many times she has let me down (Each time a different excuse) that I have about come to the end of the rope." "In fact," Collins added, "I think I am at it." Wildberg's touching response, written just before Thanksgiving 1952, acknowledged how frustrating Ursula could be. "Nevertheless," he reasoned, "she is a human being and I think, as fellow human beings, we must try to help even if the cause appears hopeless." After appealing to Collins's heart and soul, Wildberg went for his pocketbook: "I honestly do feel that she has a highly commercial salable story and as long as you are in the business and have been a pal, why not let us see if we cannot drag it out of her for the sake of everybody concerned."[28]

The final letter Collins wrote to Wildberg promised to hold the typewriter reclaimers at bay until January 18, 1953, with the hope that Parrott would pull off one of the eleventh-hour miracles for which she had once been known. "I agree completely with you that Ursula has a saleable book in her memoirs," Collins wrote, "but the thing is will she write it."[29] This is the final note in her agency file, making it fairly certain that she did not.

In fact, Parrott had already written, sold, and published the "how I got that way" portion of her life story a decade earlier. "One More Such Victory" was the last story Parrott wrote in which the professional success of a woman destroys her prospects at happiness; it is also the most personal story she ever published. It was a return to form—one critic deemed it "an expert novel of New York life." When *Cosmopolitan* advertised its impending publication, they did so under a banner that could have been used for any number of Parrott's 1930s career women stories: "Do men ever love successful women?" "Here is a searching, emotional novel of love vs. success in modern life," they editorialized, "a new angle on the problems facing every girl who has a job."[30]

Susan Barr supports herself by doing secretarial work and writing sales copy until her novel, *Encounter*, becomes a sensation, allowing Barr to quit her job and dedicate herself to a writing career. As part of the whirlwind promotion for *Encounter*, it comes out that Susan's boyfriend (a term the narrator says "had just come up from unacceptable slang to be used by debutantes, divorcees, and business women alike"), Oliver, is still married to his wife. Susan's beau is shuttled to the margins as they embark on the invention of "Susan Barr, Author" through magazine interviews, literary teas, and cocktail parties.

Like *Ex-Wife, Encounter* sells: first a thousand copies, then four thousand, then ten thousand, and then one hundred thousand. Barr starts drawing money from her publisher against royalties, getting a taste for borrowing and spending. Having quickly blown her first hundred-dollar advance, she asks for another hundred dollars and finds that "no one had the least objection." She gets used to having "a maid bring a breakfast tray, run a bath for her, lay out the clothes she was going to wear," not to mention "taking taxis everywhere" and wearing "ninety-five dollar dinner dresses." "Once in a while," the narrator explains, "terror caught her at how easy it was to get used to all these things."

After Susan buys herself a mink coat and spends $5,000 furnishing her new Park Avenue duplex, she has officially arrived in New York literary high society by way of the hard-to-stop habit of overspending. Her new agent, Michael Nash, a quasi George Bye character, cautions her about getting distracted by the trappings of success, especially after he hands her an astonishing $28,000 check—her portion, less agent and publisher fees, from the sale of *Encounter* to Hollywood. Nash warns her not to lose sight of the big picture, urging her to walk away from her affair with the married Oliver for precisely the reasons that O'Connor proved to be so calamitous: it was risky to be "involved in an emotional situation that keeps you from working."

After Susan offers Oliver money from her Hollywood windfall to pay off his wife for a divorce, "nothing in the world would be as it had been between them again." For $10,000, Oliver's wife agrees to go to Reno. But Oliver stuns Susan by announcing that he is going to marry his boss's daughter, telling Susan that if he married her he would resent her wealth and "that beautiful apartment you arranged for a life I'll never live." And so Susan writes, has a child, buys and renovates a country house, and goes to parties and teas. A doctor advises that she "did too much working and running about," urging her to retire to the country where she can rest and write. There is hardly a note that Parrott strikes in the novel that she had not sung in her own life.

Susan becomes the word factory Ursula Parrott complained about having to be for much of her career. Although she makes fantastic sums of money, Susan is forever juggling debt: the plumber, the grocer, income tax, a summer wardrobe, the gardener. She starts missing deadlines, and because she is in arrears on magazine stories she cannot find the time to write "a serious novel on middle-class country life in America." Her life is reduced to "write, get checks, pay bills, run up new bills; write, get checks, pay bills, run up new bills." With the government at her heels for back taxes, Susan's long-time friend Clement approaches her with a marriage proposal, despite disapproving of how she has lived her life. He sees the "lovely person [she] used to be—lost, trapped in a mountain of nonsense"—and offers to save Susan by making her agree to stop spending money, live on his salary, and focus on writing "a good book." She weighs the benefits of stability and peace with the condition of "no adventure, risk, gamble" and refuses the proposal. Susan ends the story drinking a Scotch highball alone in her apartment. As someone from Susan's publisher's office advised early in her career, "Happy endings are so rare."

SEVENTEEN

"Black Coffee, Scotch, and Excitement"

One goes on somehow. Because one must.

Ursula Parrott, "Some Day You'll Find Him"

Moderns weren't supposed to ruminate on the past, but as the years went on Parrott found herself doing just that. She had spent most of her life moving ahead, starting over, trying one more time. "I never much liked this Ursula Parrott who was the creation of a smart publisher and a good agent, and never did feel very at ease in her clothes," she once said about her career, before adding the kind of relentlessly hopeful quip that was her specialty: "If she arises, next time she has any, they'll fit her." It is, in fact, astonishing how many comebacks Parrott successfully pulled off. In the depths of ill health, depression, and debt, Parrott would repeatedly, confidently, and accurately vow that she would "get better and make money again."[1] This worked, until it didn't. Parrott's publishing career ended in 1947, a full decade before her death.

When she was at the top of her game, Parrott had a vision for her future: "Every time I buy a new chair, it is to save me trouble thinking of chairs when I am forty and want to think only of the people in my books." Parrott never realized this vision of permanence and purpose, nor of a focused writing life; instead, she scrambled to buy that new chair during each of her many resurrections. The brightest dividend of her dogged resilience was that she lived to see her son get the education that she considered her principal gift to him. What could make a Boston-born Radcliffe alumna, who had worked so hard to make her son a capable young man of the world, happier than Harvard University? Parrott was as joyous as she'd ever been when Marc received news of his acceptance, proof that her parenting methods had been a success. She mailed Marc's Harvard admissions letter to her ex-agent, George Bye, beaming that "Marc was the only freshman in his class who went into Harvard with five highest honors in five college board examinations." Parrott took comfort in few things, but she delighted in her son's academic achievement. Later in life, Marc deemed his "very fancy education" to be his "chief share" of his mother's fortunes, which she had squandered by the time he graduated, but not before ensuring that her son had the benefit of the most prestigious education that money could buy.[2]

Parrott's next-to-last publication, the serialized "Of Course, She's Older," revolves around a female character who is older, wiser, and more nostalgic than her previous female protagonists. The story recounts the travails of thirty-nine-year-old Paula, a widow and successful fashion editor for *Right Appearance*, "one of the most successful of the fashion magazines," who has raised her eighteen-year-old daughter, Irene, on her own. Irene is on the verge of marrying, and Paula is being courted by a former WWII pilot, Carew, who is eight years her junior (much to her dismay) and significantly less successful than she (about which she could not care any less).

Paula's ability to support her child has been made possible by an act of feminist workplace advocacy: the woman editor of *Right Appearance* magazine, Ginny Launcell, gives her a job that eventually leads to her promotion to editor-in-chief. However, Ginny also cautions Paula, "No one guesses how lonely successful women can be, except other successful women." By the story's second installment, Ginny is headed to Reno because her dependent husband has grown so resentful of her success. Ginny explains the risks of "marrying someone younger and less prosperous than yourself": "If you want to marry Carew and be happy, put your marriage first, second and third, your job fourth or fifth or sixth."

Carew seems, at first, like the man that Parrott had always hoped to encounter in real life—indifferent about age, accepting of her child from a previous marriage, respectful of her career—but he retains that fatal flaw that men in Parrott's stories rarely transcend: male pride about money. Carew informs Paula that he could never live in her well-appointed and very expensive apartment, even if she agrees to marry him. Rather, she would have to live on his income in his tiny apartment, with his "adequate and commonplace" furniture.

Paula desperately wants to marry Carew, but cannot "change the name she used in business, no matter whom she married," or "share some Manhattan version of love-in-a-cottage in his establishment." Because of her as-yet-unspoken caveats to Carew's proposal, she feels little joy accepting it, despite the chance it gives her for "personal happiness." "It can't be fun," she tells him, "for you to love and want to marry a woman who lives three lives—maternal, professional and personal."

As they discuss the terms of their marriage, Carew lectures Paula that "a main difference circa 1946 between women and men who earn good livings in our time is that the women do 'take on' rather too much": "The three lives you personally are condemned to live, for instance, my darling! Who condemned you? Only you, Paula Ranbey." "Women executives," Carew continues, "take themselves too seriously. You're too nice to succumb to that ordinary occupational disease." He concludes his patronizing speech by telling Paula that after they marry, he expects her to leave her work at the office and come home at night—to his apartment—to dedicate herself to him. When Carew puts his arms around her, Paula feels a tempting comfort against "loneliness, fatigue, the nebulous fear of time's passing," despite the fact that she knows better.

The night before her daughter's wedding, Irene confronts her mother about Carew's outmoded stipulations. "You earned this place and everything in it, Mother....Also you love it." What was the point of the hard-earned career progress she—and so many women like her—made in the 1930s if she tosses it all away for a man in the 1940s? Irene blames Carew for not being able to "bear having his friends think you paid the rent." She elaborates, "Prewar, it mattered who earned what. Now plenty of nice responsible young men earn nothing but what they get under the Veterans Act, and their wives, some of them almost as young as I, think nothing of keeping jobs to help out while the men get the education they missed." Why should Carew diminish her mother's success just because he has not achieved his?

In the final pages of the story, Paula indulges in nostalgia the likes of which cannot be found in any other Parrott tale. She feels "the part of her that was modern, restless, habituated to hurrying from one mood to the next, one person to the next" gently mocking her. Parrott had spent a lifetime not looking into the rearview mirror long enough to reckon with what she had lost instead of finding ways—cars and furs, booze and men, trips and escapades—to forget. "We all want one more chapter of our own story," Paula says, "one more dream, one more scene in which to star." But she also acknowledges that this is something "we all want," not something "we all get."

Paula decides that she will not marry Carew because, at this stage in her life, she is unwilling to give up her career for romance. This is not a tragic realization. Paula gets the last word in the story: until sending her daughter off to live her own life, she had "never been content before." She has her work and her memories to sustain her for the rest of her life.

During the 1950s, many of the gains made by women of Parrott's genera-tion—in the workplace, education, politics—were erased in a postwar cul-ture that insisted women's place was in the home, her work limited to car-ing for her husband and children. Feminist critic Betty Friedan described a "strange stirring, a sense of dissatisfaction" plaguing suburban housewives who dared not ask the question staring them in the face: "Is this all?"[3] The United States had come full circle, with readers of 1950s magazine stories encouraged to "pity the neurotic, unfeminine, unhappy women who wanted to be poets or physicists or president."

In her study of 1930s women's magazine fiction, Friedan encountered career women who, instead of being housewives, which had become the norm in 1950s stories, were "happily, proudly, adventurously, attractively career women—who loved and were loved by men." Friedan erroneously claimed, however, that the post–World War II era was when "'career woman' became a dirty word in America"; Parrott had relentlessly explored this association over thirty years prior in story after story that did not fit the mold Freidan described. Parrott also took on the dilemma of women's postwar "is this all?" syndrome almost as soon as she realized it was happening. Her final foray into nonfiction was a series of articles for the *New York Journal-American* in late 1946, at the very end of her writing career (see figure 40). In these, Par-rott reclaimed the direct, accusatory voice that she used at the start of her publishing career in "Leftover Ladies" to take on the problems of a new gen-eration of young marrieds.

The first of these articles, "You call that work?" is illustrated with an image of a woman, toddler in one arm while cooking dinner with the other, opposite an angry young man, fist raised in the air and bearing the label "the never-helpful husband" (see figure 41). Parrott refutes complaints that the "recently soaring American divorce rate," especially "among those who married in haste in wartime" was the fault of young wives who had a "lack of common sense, flexibility, patience." Instead, she blames husbands who expect too much of their exhausted wives, who come home after work every day and start in about how the house or meal or child is not in perfect shape without understanding the extent of women's labor over the course of a day. This postwar variety of husband arrogantly "assures her that housework is

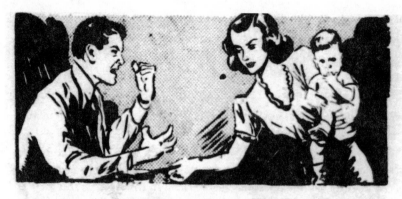

URSULA PARROTT'S NEW SERIES ON MEN AS MARRIAGE KILLERS

Beginning a revealing series on how blind, blundering men wreck many marriages.

FIGURE 40. After World War II, Ursula Parrott returned to the direct, accusatory nonfiction voice she first used in "Leftover Ladies" in 1929 for her "New Series on Men as Marriage Killers" in the *New York Journal-American*. (Advertisement, *Courier-News*, Bridgeport, New Jersey, December 13, 1946.)

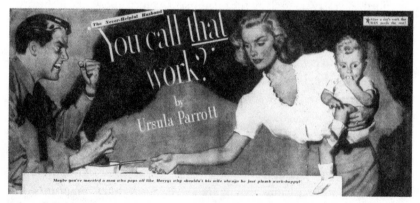

FIGURE 41. Parrott spoke to a new generation of modern women about the men who were failing them in her *New York Journal-American* series, presenting divorce as the only solution for marriages in which men have no appreciation for their wives: "Now he assures her that housework is no work. She ought to follow him through a day at the office!" ("You Call That Work?" *New York Journal-American*, December 14, 1946.)

no work." Parrott advises, in no uncertain terms, that "the sooner the wife…
gets a divorce and goes back to mother, job or both, the smarter she is." So
much for staying the course and overcoming marital difficulties; this was
about intractable ideological chains and the need for an emergency exit.

The second in the series, "Parked Wives," is about husbands who force
their wives to quit their war-era jobs only to ignore them, leaving the
women to tend house in boredom and isolation. Seeing their husbands
"growing fat" as they watch sports and swap war remembrances with their
buddies over beers, these wives realize that they are stuck in a monotonous
existence without end, propelling the smart ones to board the express train
to Reno and head back into the workforce. Instead of wondering about
the unintended consequences of marital instability, Parrott was now making a case for divorce for a new generation of women, urging them not to
waste their lives in dead-end servitude. Her argument had become sharper
and less tentative: divorce was a tool that women could use to set themselves free.

On September 24, 1957, the headline for Leonard Lyons' syndicated column,
The Lyons Den, was "Groucho Has a Theory." Lyons led the column with a
story of the extravagant construction costs of the comedian Groucho Marx's
new home and the Broadway debut of his recent play. Next came a bit about
the actor Tab Hunter's voice coach. Then a few words about the new Joe E.
Lewis film biography, *The Joker Is Wild*, starring Frank Sinatra. Buried halfway through the column are two paragraphs under the heading "FINANCE
DEPT.": "It was only a brief mention in the papers last week, that Ursula
Parrott had died, destitute. There was a time, soon after the publication of
her 'Ex-Wife,' that she could dictate her own terms to publishing houses and
movie companies. She had a town house as well as a country estate, jewels,
furs, and chauffeur-driven car. Once she carried in her purse a $50,000 check
from the Fox Studios as down payment for a story. It all went."

Not one US newspaper published an obituary for Parrott, even in her
hometown of Boston, where she was buried in the family plot at Holyhood Cemetery. Walter Winchell dedicated a mere sentence to her demise,
though he had given space generously to her setbacks in his column for years:
"Author Ursula Parrott passed away in a local hosp last week." Los Angeles
newspapers barely acknowledged Parrott's passing, though one pointed out

the paucity of attention her death had generated: "New York papers recently devoted a scant few lines of the death of destitute novelist Ursula Parrott." Five months after Parrott's passing, Dorothy Kilgallen's column reported that John Wildberg had just learned about his ex-wife's death "in poverty and obscurity" when he "arrived in New York on business."[4] Although there was no mention of Parrott's age, which would most certainly have been incorrect, in any of these brief notices, she had managed, despite years of hard knocks, to survive into her fifty-eighth year.

Marc Parrott described his mother's death as having taken place "in a charity ward of a New York hospital," where she had checked in "under a false name" and died as a result "of a mercifully fast cancer." Were Marc or her sister Lucy, whom she had supported for so many years and then hid from as she declined, by her side in those final days? There is no way to know. Traces of Parrott, private or public, are almost nonexistent after 1952. "Living's a fundamentally lonely business," one of her characters stated, well before Parrott's own life played out this declaration to its heartbreaking conclusion. Perhaps she took comfort in what her beloved childhood caretaker Dado had told her when she was on her deathbed: "There is nothing to be frightened of, my dear. This is only death."[5]

In a letter she wrote to British author Alec Waugh on the eve of World War II, Parrott wistfully described her generation, though she was certainly speaking first and foremost of herself: "We saw so many things without faith in anything. We loved so many people, meaning only to love one—the one we usually never met."[6] What Parrott wanted—for herself and for women of her time—was security, stability, and constancy without settling for dullness or a life without passion or achievements. Because women like her had raised their ambitions as well as their expectations, they also complicated their paths. This, of course, became clearer with the passage of time when the wreckage of their mistakes and the degree of their disappointments became fully evident.

Over thirty years after her death, Ursula Parrott's son turned to the philosopher George Santayana, a former professor at his alma mater, Harvard, to sum up his mother's complicated life. Marc credited Santayana with an observation that he believed could serve as an "epitaph on my mother": "We get in awful trouble...because some of us are drawn to live dramatically in a world which isn't at all dramatic." It seems likely that Ursula Parrott would have appreciated this characterization. She had certainly seen her own crash coming for a long time, having declared at the midpoint of her life,

"Maybe I'll die of living on black coffee, Scotch, and excitement after all, like a member in good standing of the Lost Generation everyone's forgotten ever existed." She added, "But not for a long time.... For better or worse, like the words of that ceremony with which I have been indecently familiar, one's Irish vitality is always there, an extremely mixed blessing."[7]

Remembering a "Leftover Lady"

If you were to sit down and read reviews of Parrott's novels and stories by many critics of her day or casual characterizations of her by commentators and columnists, you would expect her writing to be maudlin and romantic, her plots filled with champagne and late nights dancing at the smartest nightclubs, flowers and weddings, babies and country homes. But her plots are possessed of these elements only to prime her characters—and her readers—for disappointment. The often trivializing evaluations of her work by critics of her time indicate how much she was misunderstood, making it less surprising that she is all but forgotten today.

Parrott published around 130 novels, stories, novelettes, articles, and serials—none of which are currently in print. At the peak of her career, she made $100,000 a year—the equivalent of roughly two million dollars today.[1] Although most of her stories depicted romance of some sort, usually of the failed variety, she also wrote about people (indeed, a man and a woman) stranded following a small plane crash in the Canadian wilds during winter, escape plots about people (indeed, a man and a woman) captured by Nazis and held prisoner on a West Indies island during World War II, and stories of young men leaving comfortable lives to fight a war they believed in (indeed, men leaving women behind). Coupling and decoupling play out in most of her stories, but this was just the tip of Parrott's literary iceberg.

Like many of her female contemporaries, she was categorized as a woman who wrote trivial and sentimental romances, although her tales were about much more: difficult divorces, phenomenally successful women's careers, and single parenting; female piloting, adventuring, and traveling; risk-taking on the Underground Railroad, combat, and labor organizing; World War II veterans returning to civilian life and nefarious Nazi plots. Romance writing is a dubious corral in which to contain someone who used the genre to think about women's place in the modern world, and much more.

Of course, she wrote her fair share of tales for the marketplace and made concessions in the process, and she was never able to dedicate herself to the craft of writing in the fashion she had dreamed of. It is certain that Parrott could not have sold stories for such high sums to the mass market magazines that kept her afloat during the 1930s and the 1940s without nesting them inside of a familiar guise and adhering to certain editorial expectations. But most critics never bothered to get past the surface, not noticing, for example, that it was almost always the men in Parrott's stories who experienced unrequited love, wringing their hands over how to convince women to accept their proposals. When the United States rolled out its first World War II–era Victory Book Campaign in the fall of 1942, it warned potential donors to desist from donating any "women's love stories," listing Ursula Parrott—along with Kathleen Norris, Faith Baldwin, and Elinor Glyn—as authors to be avoided.[2] The limiting lasso of the woman writer had already been firmly drawn around Parrott while she was alive; without anyone tending to her legacy, there was no escaping it.

There is much to admire about Parrott's writing, including many of her stories and novels that receive woefully inadequate attention in these pages, like her 1933–34 "Breadwinner," a serialized novel that is a profound snapshot of a time, place, and worldview centered around a successful writer and single mother who cannot convince the unsuccessful man she adores to get over his preposterous inferiority syndrome. In it, Parrott enacts a stunning takedown of male privilege in the workplace when Mark learns that his office will be laying off workers and tells Linda about his likely disposability: "Most of the smaller agencies, like mine, have been too well filled for years, with a good many allegedly bright young men like me, who did a half-days' work for a good day's wage, because we wore our clothes well, or because the daughter of the senior partner liked the way we danced. We didn't need particularly marked abilities." In a mere two sentences, Parrott eviscerated an entire generation of entitled white-collar workers by cutting them down to size in the voice of one of their own. No wonder Mark was so insecure—he had no legs to stand on, except for those granted by virtue of his maleness.

Her second novel, *Strangers May Kiss*, contains some exceptionally interesting and adventurous writing, as when the novel's long-suffering female protagonist imagines New York City itself delivering her a pep talk:

> March on. It don't matter where or why—you had your fun, didn't you? It's finished? What of it and who cares? March on. Don't block traffic. You have a broken heart? Forget it. Applesauce. Bologna. March on. You're tired? Who isn't, sometimes? March on. You didn't get what you want? Nobody does in the end. All things pass, some slowly, some fast. It don't matter. The parade's the thing. Watch the parade. The band keeps playing. Keep step. March on, baby, somewhere or nowhere, in the end you won't know the difference. If you don't want to look at tomorrow, and you don't like today—hell, you had yesterday. And you can always watch the parade.

Written in a stylish staccato beat, this rallying cry brims with the forward-thinking ethos that carried its author through so many years of her life. It is sophisticated, witty, playful, and insightful. I wish I could go back in time to 1949 and scoop up the stack of Parrott's manuscript pages, which were so important to her that she dragged them around even as her life was falling apart, before they hit the dumpster at the Henry Hudson Hotel. Was a draft of her important novel among those pages? We will never know.

Parrott's life cannot be told as an inspirational feminist story. She was complicated, embodying and espousing many contradictions. A wildly successful woman who saw careers as impediments to women's happiness, especially of the marital variety. A romantic who pursued love and marriage in a serial fashion because she believed that a long-lasting relationship was the ideal path and the next walk down the aisle might lead her to it. A woman who craved stability but who could not resist making decisions that resulted in chaos. A radical who sometimes advocated for conservative values. Parrott did not always make sense, including to herself—but she tried her best to reckon with and explain her bewilderment. She was a skilled dismantler of dreams, her own included.

Parrott once predicted, "Women like me will be better off in a hundred years": "We hunt about among the wreckage of old codes for pieces to build an adequate shelter to last our lifetime…and the building material's just not there." "I do believe," she continued with equal parts hope and resignation, "that out of all this will come a comradeship between men and women… fairer to men…fairer to women. But not in time for us." She acknowledged, with a sense of defeat, "Women like me, here and now, feel one way, believe another…and on neither side is happiness to be reckoned among the spoils."[3]

I am convinced that Ursula Parrott was right, that it would have been significantly easier to be her now than it was a hundred years ago when many of her ideas and actions seemed untenable, off-putting, even outlandish. But as she struggled to make sense of the messy modern world and her place within it, she helped shape a conversation about women's lives during turbulent years of consequential change. If her inconclusiveness on these matters was as unsatisfying on the page as it was in her life, perhaps we should recall how she accepted this uncertainty but marched on nonetheless. "I'm sure I cannot tell whether the professional woman is happier than the wife or less so," she admitted. "But of one thing I'm sure—if we are able to make anything out of our mad era we must face the facts as we see them and piece out the salvation of our individual existence."[4]

ACKNOWLEDGMENTS

This book had a wonderfully circuitous genesis. A dinner table conversation with Jim West after a talk I gave at Penn State University in 2015 led me to F. Scott Fitzgerald's screenplays at the University of South Carolina (USC) archives. During a subsequent visit to USC, the associate dean of special collections, Elizabeth Sudduth, showed me Fitzgerald's screenplay manuscripts, one of which I was immediately intrigued by, no doubt because of its catchy title, "Infidelity." It was an adaptation of a magazine story written by a woman I had never heard of, Ursula Parrott. This book exists because of this fortuitous series of encounters, a reminder that we never know where our next projects will come from.

I was able to research and write this book because of the time and support provided by two fellowships. I had an M. H. Abrams Fellowship at the National Humanities Center (NHC) in 2019–20, where I experienced the unsurpassable quality of life as an NHC fellow: the beautiful building in the woods, the convivial community of scholars, the food prepared with care by James Gekin and Tom Reed, and the tireless assistance from in-house librarians Brooke Andrade, Sarah Harris, and Joe Milillo. I am especially indebted to my trade book working group: Kat Charron, Ann Rowland, Angela Steusse, Christina Snyder, and Ian Burney. I have never been as productive as I was at the NHC.

A National Endowment for the Humanities Public Scholar Fellowship in 2020–21 gave me a second full year of research, writing, and editing. This program, which supports academics who write with a general readership in mind, is a tremendous gift. It allowed me to complete a full draft of this book and start the long process of editing and revisions. Any views, findings, conclusions, or recommendations expressed in this book do not necessarily reflect those of the National Endowment for the Humanities.

The unsung heroes of any fellowship experience are those who write letters in support of a project as it is taking shape, and my trio of relentlessly generous supporters—Chris Holmlund, Eric Smoodin, and Kathy Fuller-Seeley—deserve gold medals for their collegiality.

For the ability to tell Ursula Parrott's story, I am indebted to the two men who had the foresight to save her letters, George Bye and Hugh O'Connor, and the institutions that have cared for the letters and made them accessible to researchers, Columbia University's Rare Book & Manuscript Library and University of Oregon, Special Collections & University Archives. Their archives constitute the sole surviving records of Parrott's private voice, which both helped me understand her and allowed me to let her speak for herself throughout this book. People who believe they are important keep records of their lives, and when they die these records are enshrined in "Important Archives," as Parrott might have put it. Ursula spent the last years of her life completely unaware of her achievements. It is our loss that more of her personal papers do not survive, making those that do even more precious.

I am thankful for the support I have received from North Carolina State University, especially from my department head, Laura Severin; the dean of the College of Humanities and Social Sciences, Jeff Braden; and the college research office, led by Tom Birkland. Sarah Guy knocked it out of the park as my undergraduate research assistant during the 2016–17 academic year, which was supported by the Provost's Professional Experience Program. This book is richer because of the unparalleled library services at NC State that are at my disposal year-round, day and night. I am especially grateful to the library's Tripsaver staff, who never balked at my unending barrage of requests for materials that were often difficult to find, and especially for the support of Stacey Amundson, Will Cross, Jason Evans Groth, and Cindy Levine.

I had significant assistance from a host of librarians and archivists, including Jennifer Fauxsmith, Sarah Hutcheon, and Laura Peimer at Harvard University's Schlesinger Library and Dr. Emily Meineke, who dipped into their archives on my behalf during a postdoc there; Jennifer Comins from Columbia University's archives; Shelley Barber from the John J. Burns Library at Boston College; Lauren Loftis at Simmons University; Genevieve Maxwell and Kristine Kreuger from the Margaret Herrick Library of the Academy of Motion Picture Arts and Sciences; Rich Remsberg; Buckey Grimm; Steve Wilson at the Harry Ransom Center at the University of Texas, Austin;

Grace Malloy at the Connecticut Historical Society; Rosemary Hanes at the Library of Congress; Patrick Raftery at the Westchester County Historical Society; Thomas Birkhead from the Penguin Random House UK Archive; Ed Richi at the Delaware Historical Society; Rebecca Aldi from Yale University Libraries; and Haley Maynard from the National Archives and Records Administration.

At the start of my research, I corresponded with Susan Berntson, whose 1999 master's thesis bio-bibliography, submitted under the name Susan Westall, first exposed me to Parrott's publication record. I am grateful for the resources Susan shared with me, and for her trailblazing work. Belle Boggs and Tift Merritt, with whom I had an informal writing group, helped me get this book started, and Belle patiently counseled me through the entire publishing process. Many others offered advice or read drafts, especially Matthew Booker, Louis Cherry, Allyson Nadia Field, Therese Fowler, Paul Fyfe, Sarah Gleeson-White, Nancy Gordon, Sarah Gordon, Doni Kay, Steve Levitus, Graham Moore, Kristine Stiles, and Sam Wasson. My profound gratitude goes to editor extraordinaire Michelle Weber of *Pipe Wrench* magazine, who gave me phenomenal, book-altering advice and editorial guidance during the home stretch.

My agent, Alexa Stark, guided me with great care through the publishing process and was a staunch advocate for the book. At University of California Press, I was energized and inspired by Raina Polivka's enthusiasm, sensitivity, and dedication to seeing this project through. Working with her—and her amazing editorial assistants Madison Wetzell and Sam Warren—has been a true pleasure. UC Press production editor Jeff Anderson, Dave Peattie of BookMatters, and crack copyeditor Athena Lakri expertly aided in the laborious process of polishing the final manuscript.

As I researched and wrote this book—including reading all the stories and novels Ursula Parrott published along with every available surviving letter she wrote—I developed tremendous admiration and empathy for my book's subject. I have tried to approach this retelling of her life guided by those sentiments, as well as with respect and honesty.

Any errors or omissions contained within these pages are my own.

CHRONOLOGY

1884   January 5, birth of Margaret Towle (Ursula's half-sister by her father, Henry Towle, and his first wife, Elizabeth, who died shortly after childbirth). Changes name to Madge Tyrone in adulthood.

1887   September 27, marriage of Henry Towle to Mary Flusk (Ursula's mother).

1888   August 4, birth of Lucy Inez Towle (Ursula's sister).

1899   March 26, birth of Katherine Ursula Towle in Boston. Nicknamed Kitty.

1916   June 25, death of mother, Mary Towle.

1920   June 23, graduates from Radcliffe.

1922   August 31, marries Lindesay Mark Parrott. Nicknamed Lin.

1923   October 28, gives birth to Lindesay Marc Parrott Jr. Nicknamed Marc.

1928   January, divorces Lindesay Marc Parrott.

1929   July, publishes *Ex-Wife* (at first anonymously). Starts using Ursula as her first name.

1930   September 5, death of father, Dr. Henry Towle.

1931   Buys first Connecticut house, Twin Elms, in Wilton.

1931   April, first trip to Hollywood.

1931   October 14, marries Charles Greenwood. Nicknamed Charlie.

1932   October 14, divorces Charles Greenwood.

1937   Sells Twin Elms and purchases estate in New Canaan, Connecticut.

1934   March 29, marries John Jacob Wildberg. Nicknamed Jack.

1938   June 17, divorces John Jacob Wildberg.

1939   March 4, marries Alfred Costar Schermerhorn. Nicknamed Fred.

1940   Sells Connecticut house.

1942   December 29, arrested for taking Private Michael Neely Bryan out of military stockade in Miami, Florida.

1943   February 27, acquitted in Michael Neely Bryan trial.

1944   February 10, divorces Alfred Costar Schermerhorn.

1950   May 31, arrested in Delaware over unpaid bill from the George Washington Hotel (in Princess Anne, Maryland).

1952   March, accused of stealing silverware from home of retired brigadier general Donald B. Adams.

1952   May, Walter Winchell reports in his column that Parrott is homeless.

1957   September, dies in New York City. Ancestry.com provides a September 14 date of death.

NOTES

In the service of readability, I have reduced the number of in-text endnotes by combining them whenever possible. Combined notes typically appear with the last note in a given paragraph. To reduce the overall number of notes, I have also chosen not to cite page numbers for quotations of Parrott's published writing if the source of the quotation is clearly stated in the text.

ABBREVIATIONS IN NOTES

AC, Alan Collins

GB, George Bye

HO, Hugh O'Connor

UP, Ursula Parrott

INTRODUCTION

1. UP to HO, August 17, 1929. Correspondence between Ursula Parrott and Hugh O'Connor is from the University of Oregon, Special Collections & University Archives, Hugh O'Connor papers.

2. Parrott, "Leftover Ladies," 61. The only Parrott novel that has been republished is *Ex-Wife*, reissued by Plume Books in 1988 and now out of print. The only recent writing about Parrott is Susan Westall's 1999 master's thesis bio-bibliography and Michael LaPointe's "The Racy Jazz Age Best Seller You've Never Heard Of" in the February 2019 *Paris Review*.

3. UP to HO, undated letter (circa 1930/1931).

4. Review of *Ex-Wife*, *New York Times*, August 11, 1929. Ruth Burns, "Living Up to the Title of Her 'Best Seller,'" *Boston Herald*, March 6, 1939. E. V. Durling, "On the Side," *Los Angeles Times*, January 1, 1938.

5. Mayme Ober Peak, "Boston Author in Hollywood Finds Great Demand

for Service," *Boston Globe*, April 28, 1931. Helen Welshimer, "What the Best Known 'Ex-Wife' Thinks of Marriage," *Santa Cruz News*, December 3, 1932.

6. Douglas, *Terrible Honesty*. Douglas makes no mention of Parrott in her book. Parrott quoted in Strider, "Sex and the Talkies," 21.

7. Katherine Ursula Parrott to Nickolas Muray, February 25, (no year), Smithsonian Archives of American Art, Nickolas Muray collection. Elizabeth Towle, Death Register, City of Boston, January 20, 1884, Ancestry.com. Cooper, *Technique of Contraception*, 34.

8. Parrott quoted in York, "Should Women Work?," 45. Showalter, *These Modern Women*, 8–10. Cott discusses the ex-feminist movement in "The Enemy of Society" chapter of *Grounding of Modern Feminism*, 175–212.

9. UP to HO; quotations are from three different undated letters.

10. Advertisement for *Next Time We Love*, *Universal Weekly*, March 21, 1936.

11. Parrott, "Breadwinner," December 1933, 36.

12. Parrott quoted in Strider, "Sex and the Talkies," 128. Brown, *Sex and the Single Girl*, 5–6.

13. Relevant literature about magazine publishing in this era includes Bothson and Goldsmith, *Middlebrow Moderns*; Keyser, *Playing Smart*; Rubin, *Making of Middlebrow Culture*; Sumner, *Magazine Century*; and Zuckerman, *History of Popular Women's Magazines*.

14. UP to GB, undated letter (likely 1929). Correspondence between Ursula Parrott and George Bye is from the Columbia University, Rare Book & Manuscript Library, James O. Brown Associates records.

CHAPTER 1. THE LIMITED LIFE OF A DORCHESTER GIRL

1. "Is Your Age a Secret?" New York *Daily News*, June 6, 1925.

2. FBI file obtained under the Freedom of Information Act, Department of Justice records, National Archives and Records Administration, Washington, DC. Henry Towle, "The Pioneer Days at Boston College," *Boston College Stylus* 11, no. 6 (June 1897), Boston College, John J. Burns Library, University Archives. "Dr. Henry C. Towle" obituary, *New York Times*, September 6, 1930, 15. "Death of Dr. Henry C. Towle," *Boston Globe*, September 5, 1930.

3. "Dr. Henry C. Towle" obituary, *New York Times*, September 6, 1930. UP to HO, June 28, 1928.

4. Marriage and death records sourced from Ancestry.com. Marriage announcement in "Wedding Bells," *Boston Pilot*, April 21, 1883. "Death of Dr. Henry C. Towle," *Boston Globe,* September 5, 1930.

5. Later in life, when asked about her family, Ursula Parrott discussed only one older sister, Lucy, with whom she shared a mother. Schaffer, "The New York Woman Suffrage Party." Information about Margaret's marriage and divorce derive from her marriage certificate, accessed on Ancestry.com, and from the Superior Court of the State of Washington records pertaining to complaint no.

2685 in Klickitat County in the Washington State Archives. She is referred to as Madge Towle in "Miss Madge Towle, Who Pleases in an Old Corbett Play," *San Francisco Examiner*, September 21, 1909. Review of "Old Dad," *The Pioneer* (Bemidji, Minnesota), February 15, 1921.

6. Untitled column, *Los Angeles Evening Express*, January 21, 1921, 29.

7. Frank, *Louise Bogan*, 26.

8. *The Microcosm* yearbook, 1911, Simmons University Archives, 65. "General Science," Simmons College catalog, 1911, 58, Simmons University Archives.

9. According to the 1910 federal census, Mary Towle gave birth to five children, only two of whom survived. These were not unusual infant mortality rates; on just the one census page on which the Towle family is recorded (Ancestry.com), their neighbors reported losing a total of twelve children.

10. Parrott, "Dado," 87.

11. UP to HO, undated letter.

12. Parrott, "It Must Be the Climate." UP to HO, undated letter (circa August 1930).

13. All quotations in this paragraph derive from Parrott, "Dado."

14. UP to HO, undated letters (circa 1928 and spring 1929).

15. UP to HO, June 28, 1928, and undated letter (circa 1928).

16. UP to GB, March 16, 1934 (letter is incorrectly dated 1933).

17. UP to HO, undated letter (circa August 1928).

18. School document no. 6—1911, Boston Public Schools, course of study for the Latin Schools (City of Boston Printing Department, 1911), 4. The history of the Boston Girls' School is derived primarily from Curran, *Her Greatness Proclaim*.

19. School document no. 6—1911, Boston Public Schools, 5.

20. Frank, *Louise Bogan*, 26.

21. Katherine Ursula Towle, application to Radcliffe College, 1916, Harvard University, Schlesinger Library, RG XXI, Series 1.

22. The quotations are from Parrott, "Dado." Mary Towle died on June 25, 1916.

23. "Wife of Sick Doctor Buried," *Boston Journal*, June 29, 1916.

24. Parrott, "Dado," 73.

25. "Dr. Henry. C. Towle" obituary, *New York Times*, September 6, 1930. "Madge Tyrone," death notice, *New York Times*, April 14, 1955.

CHAPTER 2. AT RADCLIFFE

1. Harvard University, Schlesinger Library, Radcliffe College Archives: *The Jabberwock* (monthly publication of the Girls' Latin School), October 1915 and June 1916; alumnae directories from 1922 and 1937; Margaret Elizabeth Towle, transcript, 1901–1904. Irwin, *Angels and Amazons*, 125–26.

2. Harvard University, Schlesinger Library, Radcliffe College Archives: "Late

List," *Radcliffe News*, February 16, 1917; "Lateness Statistics," *Radcliffe News*, February 15, 1918.

3. *The Red Book Student's Handbook of Radcliffe College*, 1921, 42–43, Harvard University, Schlesinger Library, Radcliffe College Archives.

4. UP to HO, June 28, 1928.

5. Parrott, *Tumult and the Shouting*, 34. UP to HO, June 28, 1928.

6. Quotations through the next note are from UP to HO, June 28, 1928.

7. Lynd and Lynd, *Middletown*.

8. UP to HO, June 28, 1928.

9. Quotations through the next note are from UP to HO, June 28, 1928.

10. UP to HO, undated letter (circa 1933). Marc Parrott, "Afterword," *Ex-Wife* (New York: Plume 1989), 221.

11. All quotations in this section are from UP to HO, June 28, 1928. Radcliffe Yearbook, 1920, Harvard University, Schlesinger Library, Radcliffe College Archives.

12. Harvard University, Schlesinger Library, Radcliffe College Archives: the "hotbed of Bolshevism" quote is from the 1920 Radcliffe yearbook, p. 198; the Liberal Club's mission is in *The Red Book Student's Handbook of Radcliffe College*, 1921.

13. Harvard University, Schlesinger Library, Radcliffe College Archives: Radcliffe College student files, 1890–1985; letter from the secretary of Radcliffe to Dr. Henry Towle, July 2, 1918; Katherine Ursula Towle, transcript, class of 1920, RG XXI, Series 1.

14. Harvard University, Schlesinger Library, Radcliffe College Archives: "Class Gifts," Radcliffe Yearbook, 1920; "Tutoring School Found for Student Government Exams," *Radcliffe Daily*, November 17, 1927. For more on The Widow's, see Ronald Kriss, "Exiled Tutoring Schools Once Fought College for Control of Educating Students, but Lost," *Harvard Crimson*, February 4, 1952.

15. UP to HO, June 28, 1928. Parrott references working for two specific newspapers in her postcollege years, although none of her articles are traceable (her writing would almost certainly not have been bylined): the *Ledger*, for which she wrote some Atlantic City stories, and the *New York World*. "Boston Novelist Seeks 2D Divorce," *Boston Globe*, September 28, 1932. UP to HO, undated letter (circa 1929).

16. Harvard University, Schlesinger Library, Radcliffe College Archives, RG XXI, Series 1: Katherine Ursula Towle, application to Radcliffe College master's degree program, February 13, 1922; Katherine Ursula Towle, transcript, Graduate School of Arts and Sciences, 1921–22.

CHAPTER 3. FIRST HUSBAND, LINDESAY PARROTT

1. Information about Parrott family history is from the 1920 Federal Census, Ancestry.com. "Dr. Parrott Is Honored at Princeton Fete; Elizabethan Specialist

to Be 90 Saturday," *New York Times,* December 16, 1956. "Lindesay Parrott, Ex-Times Reporter," *New York Times*, September 21, 1987.

2. Information about the Princeton prom is from Mayme Ober Peak, "Boston Author in Hollywood Finds Great Demand for Service," *Boston Globe*, April 28, 1931.

3. Their common interests are discussed in Helen Welshimer, "What the Best Known 'Ex-Wife' Thinks of Marriage," *Santa Cruz News*, December 3, 1932. "'Obeyists' Scarce: Women in Favor of Change in Marriage Vow Apparently in Large Majority," *New York Times*, April 23, 1922.

4. UP to HO, undated letter (circa 1928). Parrott, "Dado," 91.

5. State of New York Certificate and Record of Marriage, Certificate 24502, August 31, 1922.

6. Parrott, "Dado," 92.

7. Parrott, *Next Time We Live*, 6–7.

8. Darnton, "Old-Girl Network," 165.

9. Katherine Ursula Parrott, Passport #240033, stamped December 20, 1922, National Archives and Records Administration. Cunard's SS *Albania* passage from New York to Southampton, May 18, 1923, Ancestry.com.

10. UP to Alec Waugh, September 12, 1939, University of Texas, Harry Ransom Center, Alec Waugh collection. List of passengers, SS *Andania*, Liverpool to New York, April 11, 1923, Ancestry.com.

11. List of passengers, SS *Albania*, Liverpool to New York, May 28, 1923, Ancestry.com.

12. Lindesay Marc Parrott II, record of birth, October 28, 1923, Commonwealth of Massachusetts Office of the Secretary of State Archives Division, Boston Records of Birth, Volume 2, p. 142, No. 15669. Katherine occasionally referred to her son as Marc Dudley. Parrott, "Dado," 92.

13. Susan Westall's master's thesis, "The Development of a Bio-bibliography for Ursula Parrott," claims that Lindesay did not know that his wife was pregnant or had given birth for "about two years" after Marc was born. However, it is doubtful that she would or could have kept her son's existence a secret for so long. Westall cites no source for this claim and incorrectly provides a 1924 birth date for Marc. She also claims that "Marc was almost seven years old before she acknowledged being his mother," which is contrary to all other evidence.

14. UP to HO, August 31, 1928. The address appears in a letter from UP to Alice T. Kelley (circa 1924), student files, Harvard University, Schlesinger Library, Radcliffe College Archives, RG XXI, Series 1.

15. UP to HO, August 31, 1928, and undated letter (circa 1928). Mayme Ober Peak, "Boston Author in Hollywood Finds Great Demand for Service," *Boston Globe*, April 28, 1931.

16. UP to HO, August 31, 1928.

17. Parrott, *Ex-Wife*, 52. Parrott, "Brilliant Marriage," 147.

18. UP to HO, undated letter.

19. UP to HO, August 31, 1928.

20. "Real 'Ex-Wife' Married Again," *Los Angeles Times*, October 15, 1931. "Ex-Wife Author Now Is a Wife for Second Time," *Reading Times*, October 15, 1931. "'Ex-Wife' Author Is an 'Ex' Again," *Decatur Illinois Daily Review*, October 15, 1932. Helen Welshimer, "What the Best Known 'Ex-Wife' Thinks of Marriage," *Santa Cruz News*, December 3, 1932.

21. UP to HO, undated letter.

22. UP remarks on their two years together in a letter to HO, August 17, 1929. Lindesay Parrott, passenger manifest, SS *Fort St. George*, Bermuda to New York, November 15, 1927, Ancestry.com. UP to HO, August 19, 1928, and undated letter (circa 1928).

23. "City Room Crowded as Death Reported," *Corsicana Texas Daily Sun*, February 27, 1931. Lindesay began working as a foreign correspondent for the *New York Times* in 1937, covering World War II in the Pacific and General MacArthur's Philippine campaign, where he was injured at Leyte in November 1944. He headed the Tokyo bureau for the *Times* for ten years, starting in 1945, and covered the United Nations in the 1950s until his retirement. Lindesay died of heart failure in September 1987. "Lindesay Parrott, Ex-Times Reporter," *New York Times*, September 21, 1987.

24. James R. Daniels, "Manhattan Kaleidoscope," *Raleigh News and Observer*, March 8, 1931. "World Staff Will Write Obituary," *Montgomery Alabama Advertiser*, March 6, 1931.

25. Adler, *Marriage and Divorce*, 7, 15, 63–91. For more on this subject see Coontz, *Marriage, a History* and Simmons, *Making Marriage Modern*.

26. Lindsey and Evans, *Companionate Marriage*, v–vii. Wells, "Experimenting with Marriage." UP to HO, undated letter (circa 1928).

27. "One Pair Divorced of Seven Married," *New York Times*, October 4, 1923. Lynd and Lynd, *Middletown*, 121. "100 Years of Marriage and Divorce Statistics," 8.

28. Blanchard and Manasses, *New Girls for Old*, 180. Roosevelt, "Divorce," 16.

29. UP to HO, August 17, 1929. UP quoted in Muriel Babcock, "Anonymity Embarrasses," *Los Angeles Times*, April 26, 1931.

30. UP to GB, undated letter (circa 1930s).

CHAPTER 4. MODERN PARENTING

1. Parrott, "Dado," 91. UP to HO, undated letter (circa 1928).

2. Parrott, "Good-By at the Station," 117.

3. Quotations in this section through the next endnote derive from UP to HO, undated letter (circa summer 1928).

4. Nina Purdy, "Divorce and the Child," *Children: The Magazine for Parents*, January 1928, 10.

5. G. Stanley Hall, "What Is to Become of Your Baby," 661. For more on

the surge in child-rearing advice in the 1920s and 1930s, see Hulbert, *Raising America*.

6. UP to HO, undated letter (circa summer 1928). All quotations until the next note derive from UP to HO, August 7, 1928.

7. Dr. Katherine Bement Davis quoted in Purdy, "Divorce and the Child."

8. Marc Parrott, "Afterword," 222. Ursula Parrott, "This and That," *Connecticut Nutmeg*, July 14, 1938. Helen Welshimer, "What the Best Known 'Ex-Wife' Thinks of Marriage," *Santa Cruz News*, December 3, 1932.

9. Ursula Parrott notes, ca. 1940–41, University of Wyoming, American Heritage Center, Joseph Patrick McEvoy and Margaret Santry papers. Parrott, "Appointment with Tomorrow," 205. York, "Should Women Work?," 102.

10. Levine, "Rise of American Boarding Schools."

11. UP to HO, undated letters (circa spring 1928 and 1928/1929).

12. "Screen News," *Screenland*, September 1931, 88. Rosalind Shaffer, "Tiny Masseuse Makes a Call on Pola Negri," *Chicago Sunday Tribune,* May 31, 1932. ACME Newspictures, photograph, February 26, 1935, collection of the author.

13. Helen Welshimer, "What the Best Known 'Ex-Wife' Thinks of Marriage," *Santa Cruz News*, December 3, 1932. Charles Driscoll, New York Day by Day (syndicated), undated, unsourced clipping, Harvard University, Schlesinger Library, Radcliffe College Archives, RG IX, Series 2, Newspaper Clippings, Class of 1930—Dodge-Parrott. Manifest for SS *Corte di Savoia*, Cannes to New York, April 25, 1933, to May 2, 1933, Ancestry.com.

14. "Noted Novelist Hold-Up Victim Near Oracle Junction Monday," *Arizona Blade Tribune*, March 26, 1937.

15. Arizona State Library, Archives and Public Records, Johnnie Quantrell State Prison Records. "Ursula Parrott Sued," *Bloomington Illinois Pantagraph*, March 28, 1937.

16. Mrs. O.G., published letter to the editor, *Redbook*, March 1946, 58.

CHAPTER 5. GREENWICH VILLAGE

1. "Vogue of Bobbed Hair," *New York Times*, June 27, 1920. Parrott, "Though You Be Far," March 1936, 31.

2. Leuchtenburg, *Perils of Prosperity*, 225. Thompson, *Urbanization*, 479.

3. Cowley, *Exile's Return*, 59–60, 67, 78–79, 210.

4. Parrott, "Forever, Perhaps!" December 1933, 31. Fitzgerald, "Echoes of the Jazz Age," *The Crack-Up*, 16. Hecht, *Child of the Century*, 357, 358.

5. Stansell, *American Moderns*, 43. For more on the Greenwich Village and New York publishing scene, see "Market Place for Words," 162–80, and Stansell, *American Moderns*.

6. Ware, *Greenwich Village*, 40–46. Cowley, *Exile's Return*, 60. Parrott, "Leisure to Repent," 136.

7. In 1920, the US census documented almost two million married working women, a figure that had nearly doubled since 1910. Collier, *Marriage and Careers*, 9–10. Adams, *Women Professional Workers*, 18, 19, 31.

8. Collier, *Marriage and Careers*, 37. Woodward, *Through Many Windows*, 238.

9. See, for example, Rose Feld, "Vassar Girls to Study Home-Making as Career," *New York Times*, May 23, 1926.

10. UP to HO, undated letter (circa 1928). Cowley, *Exile's Return*, 64. Leuchtenburg, *Perils of Prosperity*, 165.

11. Muray later had relationships with both Martha Graham and Frida Kahlo. For more on Muray, see Hinzelman, *Covarrubias Circle*. The reference to Muray's work is from Ursula Parrott, "A Profile (but not for the New Yorker just for one New Yorker)," Smithsonian Archives of American Art, Nickolas Muray collection, Roll 4392, 4. Gallico, "Memento Muray," xvi. The studio location appears in Panzer, "Essential Tact of Nickolas Muray," 25.

12. Quotations until the next note derive from a February 25 (no year, but likely 1927) letter from Katherine Ursula Parrott to Nickolas Muray, Smithsonian Archives of American Art, Nickolas Muray collection.

13. Parrott quoted in Strider, "Sex and the Talkies," 21.

14. "Five Divorce Remedies," *New York Times*, June 5, 1921. Blanchard and Manasses, *New Girls for Old*, 196, 233–34.

15. Letter from Katherine Ursula Parrott to Nickolas Muray (February 25, no year), Smithsonian Archives of American Art, Nickolas Muray collection.

16. Alice Hughes, As a Woman Looks at It (syndicated), *Minneapolis Star Tribune*, November 6, 1929. UP to HO, undated letters (unknown and circa 1928).

17. UP to HO, undated letter (circa 1928).

18. Mayme Ober Peak, "Boston Author in Hollywood Finds Great Demand for Service," *Boston Globe*, April 28, 1931. Unless otherwise noted, all quotations until note 21 are from UP to HO, undated letter (circa 1928).

19. Mayme Ober Peak, "Boston Author in Hollywood Finds Great Demand for Service," *Boston Globe*, April 28, 1931.

20. This figure was derived by using the U.S. Bureau of Labor Statistics online Consumer Price Inflation Calculator.

21. UP to HO, undated letter (circa 1928/1929).

22. UP to HO, June 28, 1928, and undated letter (circa 1928/1929).

23. UP to GB, undated letter (likely 1931). Tolman, *Positions of Responsibility*, 44, 46, 47.

24. Parrott, *Ex-Wife*, 71.

25. UP to HO, undated letters (circa 1928/1929).

26. UP to HO, undated letter (circa spring or summer 1928).

CHAPTER 6. HUGH O'CONNOR

1. Information about Hugh O'Connor's early years is taken from United States and New York census records, Ancestry.com. United States passport application #160097, January 12, 1920, National Archives and Records Administration. Wedding announcement, O'Connor-Kelsey, *New York Times*, April 13, 1934. Hugh O'Connor, honorable discharge records, National Archives and Records Administration, Ancestry.com. Pitt, *1918: The Last Act*. "Hugh O'Connor," obituary, *New York Times*, July 4, 1967.

2. Dorothy Brenner is mentioned by name in O'Connor's *New York Times* obituary, July 4, 1967, and in O'Connor's marriage announcement to his second wife, Hope Kelsey, in the *New York Times*, April 13, 1934. Dot and Hugh divorced in 1930 through a legal proceeding in Texas, likely undertaken in that remote state because of New York's notoriously stringent divorce laws.

3. UP to HO, January 1, 1939, and undated letter (circa summer 1928).

4. UP to HO, undated letters (circa summer 1928 and summer 1931).

5. UP to HO, undated letter (circa spring 1929).

6. Hugh O'Connor, "Mr. Coolidge Silent on Hoover Offer to Resign," *New York Herald Tribune*, July 9, 1928; "President Gets Political News of R.O. West," *New York Herald Tribune*, July 15, 1928.

7. UP to HO, undated letter (circa summer 1928), Androy Hotel stationery.

8. UP to HO, July 9, 1928.

9. UP to HO, undated letter (circa summer 1928).

10. UP to HO, undated letter (circa summer 1928).

11. UP to HO, June 28, 1928, and undated letter (circa spring 1929).

12. UP to HO, undated letter (circa spring 1929).

13. The contract is discussed in an undated letter (circa 1931), UP to HO. UP to HO, undated letters (circa 1928/1929).

14. UP to HO, undated letter (circa 1928). Parrott also quotes these words verbatim in *Ex-Wife* during the epistolary exchange scenes in that novel, p. 229. UP to HO, undated letters (circa 1928/1929).

15. UP to HO, undated letters (circa 1928). Showalter, "Introduction," *These Modern Women*, 18.

16. UP to HO, undated letter (circa 1931).

17. UP to HO, August 17, 1929.

18. Quotations in this section derive from UP to HO, undated letter (circa January 1929).

19. UP to HO, August 17, 1929, and undated letter.

20. UP to HO, August 17, 1929.

21. UP to HO, undated letters (circa 1929/1934).

1. UP to HO, undated letter (circa summer 1929). York, "Should Women Work?," 102.

2. UP to HO, December 30, 1932, and January 1, 1939. Jessie Henderson, "Author of 'Ex-Wife' Tells How She Wrote Best Seller," *Appleton Post-Crescent*, April 23, 1931.

3. UP to HO, undated letters (circa 1931 and 1933/34).

4. Parrott quoted in Strider, "Sex and the Talkies," 128. Mayme Ober Peak, "Boston Author in Hollywood Finds Great Demand for Service," *Boston Globe*, April 28, 1931. York, "Should Women Work?"

5. Associated Press photo caption, "A New Year's Resolution Made Good," May 6, 1931, collection of the author. Charles Driscoll, New York Day by Day (syndicated), undated, unsourced clipping, Harvard University, Schlesinger Library, Radcliffe College Archives, RG IX, Series 2, Newspaper Clippings, Class of 1930—Dodge-Parrott.

6. "Women in Industry," in United States Department of Labor, Bureau of Labor Statistics, *Handbook of Labor Statistics: 1936 edition, Bulletin No. 616*. "Situation in New York City," 1929–1930, 1104. The figure was derived by using the U.S. Bureau of Labor Statistics online Consumer Price Inflation Calculator.

7. UP to HO, undated letter (circa 1931).

8. Charles Driscoll, New York Day by Day (syndicated), undated, unsourced clipping, Harvard University, Schlesinger Library, Radcliffe College Archives, RG IX, Series 2, Newspaper Clippings, Class of 1930—Dodge-Parrott.

9. Mayme Ober Peak, "Boston Author in Hollywood Finds Great Demand for Service," *Boston Globe*, April 28, 1931. "Harrison Smith Organizing New Publishing Firm," *New York Herald Tribune*, November 17, 1931.

10. UP to HO, undated letter (circa spring 1929).

11. UP to HO, undated letter (circa late 1929 / early 1930). Hackett, *60 Years of Best Sellers*, 110. Table of contents, *Smart Set*, March 1927. George Currie, "Passed in Review," *Brooklyn Daily Eagle*, October 30, 1929.

12. HP to HO, undated letters (circa spring 1929). The Crillon is described in Brooks, *New York: An Intimate Guide*, 111. Walter Winchell, On Broadway (syndicated), *Pittsburgh Sun Telegraph*, August 14, 1929. "About the Latest Books," *Tarrytown Daily News*, August 20, 1929. UP to HO, undated letter (circa late 1929 / early 1930).

13. UP to HO, undated letter (circa 1929).

14. "Boston Novelist Seeks 2d Divorce," *Boston Globe*, September 28, 1932. "Anonymous Author Can't Stay That Way," *China Press*, November 19, 1929. Parrott quoted in Strider, "Sex and the Talkies," 128. Jessie Henderson, "Author of 'Ex-Wife' Tells How She Wrote Best Seller," *Appleton Post-Crescent*, April 23, 1931.

15. Walter Winchell, On Broadway (syndicated), *Pittsburgh Sun Telegraph*, October 10, 1929.

16. UP to HO, undated letter (circa fall 1929). *Ex-Wife* is not included in Zechariah Chafee's Appendix of "the majority of those [books] that have been suppressed during the current Boston frenzy of censorship," *Censorship in Boston*. Boyer, *Purity in Print*, 183. Marks, *Plastic Age*.

17. Robert B. Macdougall, "This Freedom," *Saturday Review of Literature*, August 31, 1929. Lillian C. Ford, "Ex-Wives Reveal Their Woes," *Los Angeles Times*, August 25, 1929. Review of *Ex-Wife*, *Bookman Advertiser*, September 1929, xx.

18. UP to HO, undated letter (circa fall 1929).

19. "The Month's Best Sellers," *Los Angeles Times*, January 26, 1930. The detail about Chumley's is in Darnton, "The Old-Girl Network," 164. Anonymous, *Ex-Mistress*, attributed to Grace Perkins Oursler in the *Catalog of Copyright Entries*, Third Series, Vol. 12, Part 1, No. 2 (Washington, DC: Copyright Office, Library of Congress, July–December 1958), 1637. Anonymous, *Ex-"It."* Kandel, *Ex-Baby*, 7.

20. UP to HO, August 17, 1929, and undated letter (circa fall 1929). The figure was derived using the U.S. Bureau of Labor Statistics online Consumer Price Inflation Calculator.

21. George Currie, "Passed in Review," *Brooklyn Daily Eagle*, October 30, 1929.

22. Quotations until the next note derive from UP to HO, August 17, 1929.

23. UP to HO, undated letter (circa 1929).

24. UP to HO, undated letter (circa late 1929). Review of *Ex-Wife*, *The Nation*, September 18, 1929, 310. Florence Haxton, "Wisecracks and Some Wisdom," *New York Herald Tribune Books*, August 11, 1929. Anonymous, "A Glib Footnote to Local Sociology," *New York Times*, August 11, 1929.

25. There are around 250 uses of the term *ex-wife* in a search of *New York Times* articles from 1920 to 1929, an increase from the decade prior, during which the term was, however, already being used with some frequency.

26. Coontz, *Marriage, a History*, 211. Baker, "Says There Will Be No Marriage 50 Years Hence," 1.

27. "A Sordid New York Narrative," review of *Ex-Wife*, *Springfield Daily Republican*, August 25, 1929. UP to HO, undated letter (circa late 1929 / early 1930). Lewis Gannett, "Books and Other Things," *New York Herald Tribune*, August 8, 1930.

28. "Best Sellers," *Variety*, October 30, 1929, 76. "Hollywood's Reading," *Variety*, December 11, 1929. "Ursula Parrott Arrested," *Publisher's Weekly*, January 9, 1943.

29. All remaining quotations derive from Blanchard and Manasses, *New Girls for Old*, 223, 231.

1. September 4, 1929, (signed) Metro-Goldwyn-Mayer contract with Ursula Parrott for *Ex-Wife*, Columbia University, Rare Book & Manuscript Library, Ann Watkins Loomis Papers Collection. Parrott did not have a hand in the script, which was cocredited to screenwriters Nick Grinde, Zelda Sears (who also played a small part in the film), and John Meehan. "Garbo Refuses 'Ex-Wife,'" *Billboard*, November 30, 1929. Eleanor Packer, "What's Ahead for Norma Shearer?," *Modern Screen*, December 1936, 98. See also Vieira, *George Hurrell's Hollywood*.

2. For more on this subject see Doherty, *Pre-Code Hollywood*.

3. "M-G-M Abandons 'Ex-Wife' Picture," *The Billboard*, January 18, 1930. "In Hollywood," *Reading Times,* May 20, 1930. *The Divorcee* file, Margaret Herrick Library of the Academy of Motion Picture Arts and Sciences.

4. "'Divorcee' Story of 'Ex-Wife,'" *Los Angeles Times*, May 11, 1930. Parrott quoted in Strider, "Sex and the Talkies," 128.

5. Hubbard Keavy, "Screenlife in Hollywood," *Sandusky Register*, May 14, 1931. Edwin Schallert, "Shearer Film Ultra in Plot," *Los Angeles Times*, May 16, 1930. "Picture Grosses," *Variety*, May 21, 1930.

6. "Buy Unpublished Book," *Billboard*, July 19, 1930. "M.-G.-M. Buys Parrott Story," *Los Angeles Times*, July 11, 1930. Advertisement for *Strangers May Kiss*, *Screenland*, May 1931, 11.

7. Margaret Herrick Library, Motion Picture Association of America Production Code Administration Records: Lenore Samuels, "Strangers May Kiss" synopsis, June 6, 1930; Lamar Trotti Production Code Administration memorandum on "Strangers May Kiss," August 12, 1930.

8. January 12, 1931, Jason S. Joy to Irving Thalberg, Margaret Herrick Library, Motion Picture Association of America Production Code Administration Records for "Strangers May Kiss."

9. Edwin Schallert, "Shearer Film Smart Event," *Los Angeles Times*, March 16, 1931.

10. L.A.W. to C.E.M. and McK., Production Code Administration inter-office memorandum on "Strangers May Kiss," April 13, 1931, Margaret Herrick Library, Motion Picture Association of America Production Code Administration Records. Quigley, *Decency in Motion Pictures*, 40.

11. "Writers' Council for Paramount," *New York Herald Tribune*, August 10, 1930. "Grace Kingsley, "Lasky Signs Ursula Parrott," *Los Angeles Times*, August 15, 1930. UP to GB, undated letters (likely 1931 and October 1, no year).

12. UP to HO, undated letter (circa 1929/1930). Richard Watts Jr., "On the Screen," *New York Herald Tribune*, June 29, 1931.

13. "Two Will Costar in Parrott Story," *Los Angeles Times*, October 1, 1930. Pitkin and Marston, *The Art of Sound Pictures*. Parrott mentions reading *The Art of Sound Pictures* in Strider, "Sex and the Talkies."

14. For more about William Moulton Marston, see Lepore, *Secret History of Wonder Woman*. Pitkin and Marston, *Art of Sound Pictures*, 159–61.

15. GB to UP, August 7, 1930. UP to GB, July 19, 1930.

16. Grace Kingsley, "Story Pendulum Swings Back," *Los Angeles Times*, April 18, 1931.

17. UP to HO, undated letter (circa 1930). UP to GB, October 1 (no year).

18. Mollie Merrick, "Stars and Talkies of Hollywood," *Semi-Weekly Spokesman-Review*, May 16, 1931. Mayme Ober Peak, "Boston Author in Hollywood Finds Great Demand for Service," *Boston Globe*, April 28, 1931. Peak became the founder and first president of the Hollywood Women's Press Club.

19. UP to GB, April 19, 1931, and April 21, 1931, Beverly-Wilshire Hotel stationery. Mollie Merrick, "Lowell Sherman Is Director and Actor," *Lincoln Journal Star*, April 27, 1931.

20. UP to GB, April 19, 1931. Jessie Henderson, "Author of 'Ex-Wife' Tells How She Wrote Best Seller," *Appleton Post-Crescent*, April 23, 1931. UP to Mr. Spock, undated letter (likely April 1931), Beverly-Wilshire stationery, Columbia University, Rare Book & Manuscript Library, James O. Brown Associates records.

21. UP to GB, May 1, 1931. UP to HO, undated letter.

22. UP to GB, April 19, 1931, Beverly-Wilshire Hotel stationery. UP to GB, May 21, 1931, telegram.

23. Mollie Merrick, "Lowell Sherman Is Director and Actor," *Lincoln Journal Star*, April 27, 1931. "Screen News," *Screenland*, September 1931, 88.

24. UP to GB, April 19, 1931. UP to HO, undated letter (circa April 1931), Beverly-Wilshire Hotel stationery. UP to GB, April 21, 1931, Beverly-Wilshire Hotel stationery. UP to GB, April 15, 1931, telegram.

25. UP to GB, April 23, 1931, telegram. James Smith, Review of "Love Affair," *Liberty*, April 23, 1932.

26. Mollie Merrick, "Hollywood in Person," *Los Angeles Times*, May 6, 1931. UP to GB, April 19, 1931, Beverly-Wilshire Hotel stationery. UP to GB, May 3, 1931.

27. UP to GB, May 3, 1931. Mayme Ober Peak, "Reel Life in Hollywood," *Boston Globe*, May 21, 1933.

28. Mollie Merrick, "Gloria Soon to Start on New Picture," *Hartford Courant*, July 8, 1931. *Love Goes Past* was never produced.

29. UP to HO, undated letter (circa 1931).

30. Gerladine G. Lackey to UP, May 27, 1931, telegram, and California Bank to UP, June 1, 1931, telegram, Columbia University, Rare Book & Manuscript Library, James O. Brown Associates records.

31. Geraldine G. Lackey to UP, June 3, 1931, telegram, Columbia University, Rare Book & Manuscript Library, James O. Brown Associates records.

32. Rosalind Shaffer, "Tiny Masseuse Makes a Call on Pola Negri," *Chicago Sunday Tribune*, May 31, 1931. UP to HO, August 17, 1929.

33. UP to GB, April 19, 1931, Beverly-Wilshire Hotel stationery. Mayme Ober Peak, "Socks Film Stars and They Like It," *Boston Globe*, May 31, 1931.

34. Quotations through "Laurel and Hardy" derive from Sylvia of Hollywood, *No More Alibis!*.

35. UP to HO, undated letter.

36. UP to GB, undated letter (likely 1929).

37. Quotations in the remainder of this chapter derive from Parrott quoted in Strider, "Sex and the Talkies." For the definitive book on the subject of marriage in the movies, see Basinger, *I Do and I Don't*.

CHAPTER 9. SECOND HUSBAND, CHARLES GREENWOOD

1. UP to GB, undated letter (handwritten note, 1932); GB to UP, August 10, 1931.

2. This figure was derived by using the U.S. Bureau of Labor Statistics online Consumer Price Inflation Calculator. UP to GB, undated letter (circa 1933), Barbizon Plaza Hotel stationery. UP to GB, undated letter (handwritten notation, circa 1932). Otto H. Kahn to UP, October 31,1933, Princeton University, Firestone Library, Otto H. Kahn Papers.

3. York, "Should Women Work?," 101–102. UP to Bank of Manhattan Trust Co., November 21, 1930, Columbia University, Rare Book & Manuscript Library, James O. Brown Associates records.

4. UP to HO, February 15, 1931. Parrott quoted in Strider, "Sex and the Talkies," 128.

5. "Capt. Greenwood, War Veteran, Dies," *Brooklyn Daily Eagle*, December 28, 1939. Rodengen, *Polytechnic University Changing the World*. "Brooklyn Society," *Brooklyn Daily Eagle*, December 22, 1911. Yale University Yearbook, 1912, Ancestry.com.

6. April 6, 1918, passenger list from United States Army Transport Service, Port of New York, Ancestry.com. "Charles T. Greenwood Promoted to Captain," *Brooklyn Daily Eagle*, November 12, 1918. "Rites for Charles Greenwood, World War Captain, Tonight," *Brooklyn Citizen*, December 28, 1939. "Application for Headstone or Marker," War Department, Charles Greenwood, August 12, 1941, Ancestry.com. Passenger list, Brest, France, to New York City, July 18, 1919, Ancestry.com.

7. "Bank of Manhattan Opens New Branch," *New York Times*, February 10, 1924. "Charles T. Greenwood," *New York Times*, December 28, 1939. "Charles Terry Greenwood Weds Mrs. Katharine Parrott," *Brooklyn Daily Eagle*, October 15, 1931. UP to HO, undated letter (circa 1929). UP to HO, undated letter (circa 1928).

8. UP to GB, May 1, 1931. "Ursula Parrott Wed to Brooklyn Banker," *New York Times*, October 15, 1931.

9. "Scenarist Weds Brooklyn Banker," *Los Angeles Times*, October 15, 1931. UP to Elizabeth Parrott, October 14, 1931, Columbia University, Rare Book &

Manuscript Library, James O. Brown Associates records. UP to GB, undated letter (circa November 1931).

10. UP to GB, undated letter (circa December 1931). "Divorce Is Granted to Ursula Parrott," *Boston Globe*, October 15, 1932. UP to GB, undated letter (circa December 1931).

11. UP to GB, undated letter (handwritten note).

12. Ernst and Lorentz, *Censored*, 88. "Divorce," *Liberty*, January 24, 1931.

13. Joyce, *Men, Marriage, and Me*, 210. Mackay, *Marriage and Divorce Law Simplified*, 1, 37. Parrott, "Too Busy for Love," 16.

14. Roosevelt, "Divorce," 16. Macfadden, "Reform Needed in Our Ancient Divorce Laws," 4. UP to HO, undated letter (circa 1928).

15. UP to GB, undated letter (handwritten note, circa June 1932).

16. UP to HO, undated letter (circa 1932). Lucy Towle to HO, undated letter (circa 1933), University of Oregon, Special Collections & University Archives, Hugh O'Connor papers.

17. UP to GB, undated letter. "Ursula Parrott Suing Greenwood for Divorce," *New York Herald Tribune*, September 28, 1932. "Referee Backs Ursula Parrott in Divorce Plea," *Brooklyn Daily Eagle*, October 11, 1932.

18. Hecht, *Child of the Century*, 384.

19. Gabler, *Winchell*, xii–xi.

20. "Divorce Is Granted to Ursula Parrott," *Boston Globe*, October 15, 1932.

21. "Referee Backs Ursula Parrott in Divorce Plea," *Brooklyn Daily Eagle*, October 11, 1932.

22. "Favors Ursula Parrott," *New York Times*, October 11, 1932. "Referee Backs Ursula Parrott in Divorce Plea," *Brooklyn Daily Eagle*, October 11, 1932. "Authoress of 'Ex-Wife' Sues Mate," *Los Angeles Times*, September 28, 1932. "Ursula Parrott Suing Greenwood for Divorce," *New York Herald Tribune*, September 28, 1932.

23. "Divorce Is Granted to Ursula Parrott," *Boston Globe*, October 15, 1932. "Authoress of 'Ex-Wife' Sues Mate," *Los Angeles Times*, September 28, 1932.

24. UP to HO, December 30, 1932. Ursula Parrott, "Nice People Don't Eat," 58. UP to GB, undated letter (handwritten note, 1932).

25. Graham, *New York Nights*, 63. Sinclair, *Prohibition*, 230, 233.

26. Marc Parrott, "Afterword," *Ex-Wife*, 223. UP to HO, undated letters (circa 1929 and spring 1929). The essay is mentioned, but not contained, in UP to HO, undated letter (circa summer 1928). UP to HO, undated letters (unknown and circa 1929).

27. Ursula Parrott, "You Ride Success Alone," September 1938, 99.

28. UP to HO, undated letter (circa summer 1928). UP to GB, undated letter (circa February 1935). UP to GB, April 19,1931. Sylvia of Hollywood, *No More Alibis!*, 22.

29. UP to HO, December 30, 1932, and undated letter (circa 1933).

30. Parrott quoted in Strider, "Sex and the Talkies," 128. George T. Bye obit-

uary, *New York Herald Tribune*, November 25, 1957. UP to GB, undated letter (circa 1930s).

31. UP to HO, undated letter.

32. Parrott quoted in Strider, "Sex and the Talkies," 128. Hillis, *Live Alone and Like It*. For more on Hillis and the idea of embracing a live-alone lifestyle see Scutts, *Extra Woman*. Blanchard and Manasses, *New Girls for Old*, 175, 237.

33. Parrott quoted in York, "Should Women Work?."

CHAPTER 10. "EXTRAVAGANT HELL"

1. UP to GB, January 16, 1933, Barbizon Plaza Hotel stationery.

2. UP to HO, undated letter (circa spring 1929).

3. *Strangers May Kiss* was banned in Ireland; in the United States it sold out its advanced run of ten thousand copies even before it was published. "Banned Books," *Irish Times*, November 25, 1933. "Books New Yorkers Are Buying," *Book World*, August 24, 1930.

4. Review of *Strangers May Kiss*, *The Nation*, August 27, 1930, 228. Blanchard and Manasses, *New Girls for Old*, 232.

5. UP to HO, February 15, 1931.

6. UP to HO, December 11, 1932, and January 2, 1933. Brooks, *New York*, 24.

7. UP to HO, undated letter, and December 11, 1932.

8. UP to HO, undated letter (circa 1934).

9. UP to HO, undated letter (circa 1928). Sanger's legal troubles are discussed in McCann, *Birth Control Politics in the United States, 1916–1945*. Congressional act 35 Stat. L., 1129, sections 211 and 212, approved on March 4, 1909, and amended March 4, 1911. Cooper, *Technique of Contraception*, 248–52.

10. "One Hundred Years of Birth Control, an Outline of Its History." Cooper, *Technique of Contraception*, 224. Sanger and Stone, *Practice of Contraception*, 199. Hutchins, *Women Who Work*, 45. The study, published under the labor arm of the Communist Party of the United States of America, compiles data on women's work and living conditions in the United States.

11. UP to Mildred Gilman Wohlforth, July 1932, Princeton University, Firestone Library, Mildred Gilman Wohlforth Papers. Reagan, *When Abortion Was a Crime*, 24, lists phrases used to discuss abortion by women in Chicago and New York.

12. Reagan, *When Abortion Was a Crime*, 20, 23. Reagan refers to the quoted terms in her "Introduction." Cooper, *Technique of Contraception*, 197–98.

13. Levy-Lenz, "A New Non-Operative Method for the Interruption of Pregnancy," 180, 191, 193. Reagan, *When Abortion Was a Crime*, 156–57.

14. Blanchard and Manasses, *New Girls for Old*, 247.

15. Ware, *Greenwich Village*, 179.

16. Quotations through "fault of the system" derive from UP to HO, "Just a Full Day," undated letter (circa 1928).

17. UP to HO, undated letter (circa spring 1928).

18. UP to HO, undated letter (circa summer 1928).

19. UP to HO, undated letter (circa spring 1928).

20. UP to HO, undated letter (circa 1928).

21. UP to HO, undated letters (unknown and circa spring/summer 1928).

22. UP to HO, undated letter (circa 1931).

23. UP to HO, undated letter (circa 1932), Barbizon Hotel stationery. Quotations until the next note derive from UP to HO, undated letter (circa 1933).

24. UP to GB, undated letter (circa February/March 1933), French Hospital stationery, New York City.

25. According to a 1928 manual, sterilization techniques of the period included the discredited method of ovariotomy, double salpingectomy (removal of the fallopian tubes), hysterectomy, cautery of the uterus, and a new experimental method involving X-ray sterilization. Cooper, *Technique of Contraception*, 123–31. UP to HO, undated letter.

26. Quotations until the next note derive from Lucy Towle to HO, undated letter (circa 1933), University of Oregon, Special Collections & University Archives, Hugh O'Connor papers.

27. UP to HO, undated letter (circa 1934).

28. Wedding Announcement, O'Connor-Kelsey, *New York Times*, April 13, 1934. UP to GB, undated letter (circa 1934).

CHAPTER 11. THE BUSINESS OF BEING A WRITER

1. UP to HO, undated letter (circa 1931).

2. Landers, *Improbable First Century of* Cosmopolitan *Magazine*. This figure does not take into account newsstand sales. Dora Copperfield (an editor's note explains that this "is a pseudonym of a woman writer"), "The Women's Magazines," *Vanity Fair*, January 1934, 22. The female-centric *Woman's Home Companion, Pictorial Review, McCall's, Good Housekeeping*, and *Ladies' Home Journal* collectively had over 10 million subscribers in 1934. In the 1930s, *Ladies' Home Journal* increased their circulation by 36 percent to 2.5 million subscribers; *Redbook* went from 561,000 readers to 1.2 million subscribers, an increase of over 120 percent. Sumner, *Magazine Century*, 77.

3. The dollar conversion was derived by using the U.S. Bureau of Labor Statistics online Consumer Price Inflation Calculator. Radway discusses these matters in "On the Gender of the Middlebrow Consumer."

4. Whitehead, "Edith Wharton and the Business of the Magazine Short Story," 50. Advertisement for Jonatan Cape & Harrison Smith, *New York Times*, November 10, 1929. For more on the women's magazines of this era, see Endres

and Lueck, eds., *Women's Periodicals in the United States*, and Whitehead, "Edith Wharton and the Business of the Magazine Short Story." For more on Ferber, see Smyth, *Edna Ferber's Hollywood*.

5. Widdemer, "Message and Middlebrow." Widdemer specifically mentions Ursula Parrott as a writer of middlebrow books "by and about other modern young women."

6. Faith Baldwin, *Week-End Marriage*. For more on this subject, see Wandersee, *Women's Work and Family Values*.

7. "A Little Love," *Cosmopolitan*, August 1946.

8. Woodward, *Lady Persuaders*, 60. "The New Ursula Parrott Story," *Time*, January 11, 1943, 21. The cultural critic Lauren Berlant has characterized writing about failed romance as "the female complaint," in which "flawed men and bad ideologies" are blamed for "women's intimate suffering." Berlant, *Female Complaint*, 1–2.

9. Widdemer, *Best American Love Stories of the Year*, vii, viii, xi.

10. Herbert R. Mayes, "Introduction," in *Editor's Choice: 26 Modern Short Stories from Good Housekeeping* (New York: Random House, 1956), v. UP to HO, undated letter (circa 1930/1931).

11. Mary Margaret McBride, "Eternal Triangle Revised!," *San Bernadino County Sun*, June 2, 1935. Unless otherwise noted, details about Parrott's writing methods derive from McBride's article or from typed notes from an interview with Parrott, circa early 1940s, University of Wyoming, American Heritage Center, Joseph Patrick McEvoy and Margaret Santry papers, Accession #681, Box 113.

12. UP to GB, July 17, 1933.

13. Parrott quotes William Butler Yeats in "Dream without Ending," Robert Browning in "Nowhere and Return," and Lewis Carroll in "Though Time Be Fleet." She mentions Galsworthy, Wells, and Thackeray in *Ex-Wife*; quotes John Gay's *Polly: An Opera* in UP to HO, August 17, 1929; and mentions Mussolini's biography and George Bernard Shaw's letters in different undated letters, UP to HO.

14. GB to UP, April 4, 1933. UP to GB, undated (circa spring 1933), Barbizon Plaza Hotel stationery.

15. UP to GB, April 15, 1935, and undated letter.

16. GB to UP, April 4, 1933, and April 1933.

17. UP to GB, March 16, 1934 (letter is incorrectly dated 1933). Cowley, *Exile's Return*, 62.

18. Marc Parrott, "Afterword," 220.

19. UP to GB, undated letter from Wilton, CT, and undated letter (circa August 1933).

20. GB to UP, April 4, 1933, and April 1933.

21. The statistics on employment are from 1932 in Leuchtenburg, *Perils of Prosperity*, 247, and magazines are from Landers, *Improbable First Century of Cosmopolitan Magazine*, 173–84.

22. UP to GB, April 16, 1935. Florey also served as Sinclair Lewis's private sec-

retary for many years. "Louis E. Florey Dies, Publications Specialist," *Washington D.C. Evening Star*, July 11, 1956.

23. UP to GB, undated letter (circa April 1935). UP to HO, undated letter.

24. UP to GB, undated letters (circa 1930s and circa May 1934). UP to HO, undated letter. UP to GB, January 31, 1935, Hotel Lombardy stationery. Mary Margaret McBride, "Eternal Triangle Revised!," *San Bernadino County Sun*, June 2, 1935.

25. UP to GB, undated letter (circa summer 1933).

26. GB to UP, January 8, 1935, and October 5, 1935.

27. UP to GB, October 5, 1935, and December 27, 1935.

28. "Script for Story Was Sent 19,800 Miles to Publishers," *Boston Globe*, February 19, 1933. Review of "The Woman Accused," *Film Daily*, March 11, 1933.

29. Charles Driscoll, New York Day by Day (syndicated), undated, unsourced clipping, Harvard University, Schlesinger Library, Radcliffe College Archives, RG IX, Series 2, Newspaper Clippings, Class of 1930—Dodge-Parrott. Marc Parrott, "Afterword," 220. Parrott mentions the word count in UP to GB, undated letter (circa 1930s), Hotel New Weston stationery. Honey, "Feminist New Woman Fiction in Periodicals of the 1920s," 89. Mary Margaret McBride, "Eternal Triangle Revised!" *San Bernadino County Sun*, June 2, 1935.

30. UP to HO, undated letter (circa April 1931), Beverly-Wilshire Hotel stationery, and April 30, 1933. UP to GB, undated letter.

31. UP to GB, undated letters (circa 1933, circa August 1933, and circa fall 1933, the latter on Sherman Square Hospital stationery).

32. John Chamberlain, "Books of the Times," Review of *The Tumult and the Shouting*, *New York Times*, November 7, 1933. Isabelle Keating, "Authoress Has New Aim—Garden Calls," *Brooklyn Daily Eagle*, November 1, 1933.

CHAPTER 12. THIRD HUSBAND, JOHN WILDBERG

1. UP and GB, June 30, 1933.

2. UP to GB, undated letter (circa 1933). B. Alsterlund, "Robert Carse," *Wilson Library Bulletin*, *19* (1944), 242.

3. UP to GB, undated letter (circa 1933).

4. UP to GB, undated letter (circa 1933). GB to UP, January 8, 1934.

5. "Robert Carse, 67, Wrote Sea Books," *New York Times*, January 15, 1971. The Carses remained married until his death in 1971. UP to HO, undated letter.

6. Marc Parrott, "Afterword," 221. UP to GB, undated letter (circa fall 1933), Sherman Square Hospital stationery.

7. UP to GB, undated letter (circa 1934).

8. UP to HO, January 1, 1939.

9. Wildberg's birth date and name are written on the travel manifest for the SS *Haiti*'s March 29, 1934, voyage to New York; his February 15, 1942, Selective

Service registration card; and on his British death certificate (Ancestry.com). His published obituaries shave a year off his age. Both he and his father used, on occasion, the name Jacques instead of Jack or Jacob. "Ursula Parrott to Wed," *New York Times*, March 28, 1934. "John Wildberg, a Producer, 55: Sponsor of 'Porgy and Bess' and 'Anna Lucasta' Dies—Was Copyright Lawyer," *New York Times*, February 9, 1959. "Weddings," "Wildberg-Untermeyer," *New York Times*, December 19, 1929. "Ursula Parrott to Wed," *New York Times*, March 28, 1934.

10. UP to GB, March 16, 1934 (incorrectly dated 1933). UP to GB, July 30, 1941.

11. All quotations in this paragraph and the next derive from UP to GB, March 16, 1934 (incorrectly dated 1933).

12. This figure was derived by using the U.S. Bureau of Labor Statistics online Consumer Price Inflation Calculator.

13. His greatest theatrical achievement was the revival of a play that had failed in its original production in the 1930s, "Porgy and Bess," which became what the *New York Times* called a "smash hit" when Wildberg produced it in 1942. "John Wildberg, a Producer, 55," *New York Times*, February 9, 1959.

14. Quotations until the next endnote derive from UP to GB, March 16, 1934 (incorrectly dated 1933).

15. "Ursula Parrott Weds Third Time," *Boston Herald*, March 30, 1934. "Ursula Parrott Wed," *New York Times*, March 30, 1934. "Ursula Parrott, Writer, Takes Third Husband," *Hartford Courant*, March 30, 1934.

16. SS *Haiti*, list of passengers sailing from New York, March 19, 1934, Ancestry.com. Quotations in this section (through "every single time since I've liked him better") derive from UP to GB, March 16, 1934.

17. For example, Parrott, "Brilliant Marriage." The quote is from Parrott, "Though You Be Far," April 1936, 146.

18. "O'Connor-Kelsey," *New York Times*, April 14, 1934.

19. Marjory Adams, "Wildberg Plans to Take 'Anna Lucasta' to London and Paris," *Daily Boston Globe*, June 1, 1947.

20. UP to GB, undated (circa late April 1934).

21. Remaining quotations in this paragraph and the next derive from UP to GB, undated (circa May 1934).

22. UP to GB, October 5, 1934, and October 11, 1934.

23. Lindesay Parrott, "Reds Urged to Wed Legally," *East Liverpool Evening Review*, December 17, 1934.

24. UP to GB, January 31, 1935, Hotel Lombardy stationery.

25. UP to GB, February 10, 1935, and undated letter (circa February 1935).

26. Walter Winchell, "Winchell Reports Troths and Rows," *Salt Lake Telegram*, December 30, 1937. "Marriage Fails: Ursula Parrott Seeks Divorce," *Los Angeles Times*, December 30, 1937. Louella Parsons, "Maestro Toscanini Now Screen Possibility," *Pittsburgh Sun-Telegraph*, January 3, 1938. Alice Hughes, As a Woman Looks at It (syndicated), *Minneapolis Star Tribune*, January 12, 1938.

27. "Divorce Makes Ursula Parrott Ex-Wife Again," *Hartford Courant*, June

18, 1938. "Ursula Parrott Asks for Divorce," *Pennsylvania Reading Times*, December 30, 1937.

28. "Ursula Parrott Divorces 3d Husband, Citing Gun," *New York Herald Tribune*, June 18, 1938. Divorce Makes Ursula Parrott Ex-Wife Again," *Hartford Courant*, June 18, 1938. "Ursula Parrott Freed," *New York Times*, June 18, 1938.

29. UP to GB, undated (circa 1938). UP to GB, November 21, 1938.

30. UP to Morris Ernst, November 21, 1938, Columbia University, Rare Book & Manuscript Library, James O. Brown Associates records.

31. Louella Parsons, "High School Blondes Gains Coveted Role amid Film Galaxy," *Camden New Jersey Morning Post*, April 17, 1939. "Wildberg Goes to the Coast," *New York Times*, September 14, 1939. Lawrence Langner to UP, December 13, 1939. Yale University, Beinecke Rare Book and Manuscript Library, Theatre Guild Archive, MSS 436, Box 158, Folder 4155.

32. "John Wildberg, a Producer, 55," *New York Times*, February 9, 1959. Walter Winchell, On Broadway (syndicated), *Pittsburgh Sun-Telegraph*, November 13, 1940. Dorothy Kilgallen, Broadway Bulletin Board, *Lowell Sun*, December 14, 1945.Walter Winchell, On Broadway (syndicated), *Madison Wisconsin State Journal*, February 25, 1948. Danton Walker, Broadway (syndicated), *New York Daily News,* March 8, 1949.

33. "John Wildberg, a Producer, 55," *New York Times*, February 9, 1959. "Divorces John Wildberg," *New York Times*, August 10, 1943. Marjory Adams, "Wildberg Plans to Take 'Anna Lucasta' to London and Paris," *Daily Boston Globe*, June 1, 1947. "John Wildberg's Wife Found Dead on Coast," *New York Times*, December 19, 1950. Florabel Muir, "Mrs. Wildberg Dies from Pills in Coast Hotel," *New York Daily News*, December 19, 1950.

CHAPTER 13. "THE MONOTONY AND WEARINESS OF LIVING"

1. Margaret Santry and Ursula Parrott, broadcast transcript, January 31, 1936, recorded at the Ritz-Carlton Hotel, University of Wyoming, American Heritage Center, Joseph Patrick McEvoy and Margaret Santry papers, 1898–1982.

2. Helen Welshimer, "What the Best Known 'Ex-Wife' Thinks of Marriage," *Santa Cruz News*, December 3, 1932.

3. Margaret Herrick Library of the Academy of Motion Picture Arts and Sciences, Motion Picture Association of America Production Code Administration Records, Joseph I. Breen to Harry Zehner, July 7, 1934; review of *There's Always Tomorrow*, unidentified source, clipping file for *There's Always Tomorrow*.

4. Margaret Santry and Ursula Parrott, broadcast transcript, January 31, 1936, recorded at the Ritz-Carlton Hotel, University of Wyoming, American Heritage Center, Joseph Patrick McEvoy and Margaret Santry papers, 1898–1982.

5. "Ursula Parrott Approves Change in 'Next Time We Love' Title," *Universal Weekly*, January 25, 1936. "Spreckles Gags 'Love' in Lobby," *Universal Weekly*,

March 21, 1936. Review of "Next Time We Love," *Motion Picture Daily*, January 29, 1936. "New Films," *Boston Globe*, February 21, 1936.

6. "Joan Crawford Will Be Heiress in Next Picture," *Los Angeles Times*, July 29, 1934. UP to GB, undated letter. UP to GB, May 15, 1934, and December 21, 1934.

7. Martin Dickstein, "Picture Parade," *Brooklyn Daily Eagle*, January 31, 1936.

8. "Two Famous Authors Have Works Filmed on Columbia Screen," *East Liverpool, Ohio Evening Review*, May 23, 1936. Review of "Brilliant Marriage," *Film Daily*, September 19, 1936. R.H. Gardner, "A Neglected Husband," *The Sun*, February 6, 1956.

9. Fitzgerald's weekly salary is from Bruccoli, *Life in Letters*, 325. "Fidelity" advertisements, *Motion Picture Herald*, May 28, 1938, and June 2, 1938.

10. F. Scott Fitzgerald to Frances Scott Fitzgerald, October 31, 1939. Reprinted in Turnbull, *Letters of F. Scott Fitzgerald*, 61.

11. F. Scott Fitzgerald to Hunt Stromberg, June 27, 1938. Reprinted in Bruccoli and Duggan, *Correspondence of F. Scott Fitzgerald*, 508–509.

12. Joseph I. Breen, Memorandum for the Files, April 27, 1938, "Infidelity," Margaret Herrick Library of the Academy of Motion Picture Arts and Sciences, Motion Picture Association of America Production Code Administration Records.

13. F. Scott Fitzgerald to Frances Scott Fitzgerald, spring 1938, reprinted in Turnbull, *Letters of F. Scott Fitzgerald*, 29.

14. F. Scott Fitzgerald to Leland Hayward, December 6, 1939. Reprinted in Bruccoli and Duggan, *Correspondence of F. Scott Fitzgerald*, 565. UP to GB, January 13, 1940.

15. "The Connecticut Nutmeg," *Evening News* (Harrisburg, Pennsylvania), June 16, 1938. Among the *Nutmeg*'s charter subscribers were some arts and letters heavy hitters, including Alfred Harcourt, George S. Kaufman, Lowell Thomas, and Frank Buck. "100 Subscribers!," *Connecticut Nutmeg*, May 26, 1938.

16. Parrott, "This and That," *Connecticut Nutmeg*, May 26, 1938, and July 28, 1938. Faith Baldwin, "Fable Farm," *Connecticut Nutmeg*, May 26, 1958.

17. Parrott, "This and That," *Connecticut Nutmeg*, June 23, 1938, and June 30, 1938.

18. UP to GB, July 29, 1938. "Nutmeg? Sugar!," *Connecticut Nutmeg*, October 20, 1938.

19. "I'm Thankful," *Connecticut Nutmeg*, November 24, 1938.

CHAPTER 14. FOURTH HUSBAND, ALFRED COSTER SCHERMERHORN

1. UP to GB, October 6, 1938.
2. UP to GB, October 11, 1938.

3. UP to GB, December 27, 1938.

4. Quotations through "as if all the things that happened happened to a different person" derive from UP to HO, January 1, 1939.

5. *Radcliffe Quarterly*, May 1939, 75, Harvard University, Schlesinger Library, Radcliffe College Archives. UP to HO, undated letter (circa 1939).

6. Schermerhorn's age is listed on the ship's manifest for the SS *Queen of Bermuda*, March 15, 1939, Ancestry.com. "Ursula Parrott Held on Charge She Helped Soldier to Desert," *New York Herald Tribune*, December 30, 1942. The quotation is from "A.E. Schermerhorn, Clubman, Dies, 60," *New York Times*, May 12, 1932.

7. "Woman Novelist to Wed Socialite," *Scranton Tribune*, February 16, 1939. Pringle, "What Do the Women of America Think about Marriage and Divorce," 14.

8. "Ruth Fahnestock Engaged to Marry," *New York Times*, May 4, 1926, 32. "A. C. Schermerhorn Is Divorced at Reno," *New York Times*, November 28, 1937.

9. "Divorces John Kirkland," *New York Times*, March 26, 1937. "Schermerhorn-Kirkland," *New York Times*, January 3, 1938. "Ursula Parrott to Be Wed," *New York Herald Tribune*, February 28, 1939). *New York, New York, Extracted Marriage Index, 1866–1937*, marriage and divorce records, Ancestry.com.

10. "Ursula Parrott to Be Wed," *New York Herald Tribune*, February 28, 1939. Marriage Column, "Author and Photographer Too," *Minneapolis Star-Journal*, December 24, 1939. "Ursula Parrott Held on Charge She Helped Soldier to Desert," *New York Herald Tribune*, December 30, 1942.

11. "Woman Novelist to Wed Socialite," *Scranton Tribune*, February 16, 1939. Alice Hughes, As a Woman Looks at It (syndicated), *Minneapolis Star Tribune*, November 6, 2019.

12. GB to UP, April 11, 1939, and April 19, 1939.

13. GB to UP, April 28, 1939.

14. GB to UP, quoting Otis Wiese to GB, July 18, 1939.

15. GB to UP, August 4, 1939. UP to GB, August 21, 1939.

16. *Radcliffe Quarterly*, May 1939, 75–76, Harvard University, Schlesinger Library, Radcliffe College Archives.

17. Walter Winchell, On Broadway (syndicated), *Daily Times* (Davenport, Iowa), May 17, 1939. Walter Winchell, On Broadway (syndicated), *The Tribune* (Scranton, PA), May 23, 1939. Harry Neigher, "Nite Life," *Bridgeport Sunday Herald*, May 28, 1939.

18. GB to UP, June 2, 1939.

19. GB to UP, June 28, 1940; July 22, 1940; August 13, 1940. UP to GB, October 17, 1940.

20. GB to UP, July 31, 1940. F. Scott Fitzgerald, "Echoes of the Jazz Age," 20.

21. Wilson, *Turbulence Aloft*, 25. "Journal about Town," *Ladies' Home Journal*, February 1942, 11.

22. GB to UP, October 1, 1940. UP to GB, December 10, 1940.

23. GB to UP, November 25, 1940, telegram, and November 29, 1940.

24. GB to UP, June 24, 1941.

25. GB to UP, March 15, 1944, and May 19, 1944.

26. Mrs. B.S., "A War Wife," *Redbook*, August 1944, 12.

27. Statement of Account, December 6, 1940, and October 13, 1941, Columbia University, Rare Book & Manuscript Library, James O. Brown Associates collection.

28. Alfred Coster Schermerhorn Report of Interment, May 9, 1946, Ancestry.com. "Ursula Parrott Suiting for Her Fourth Divorce," *New York Herald Tribune*, February 18, 1943. "Ursula Parrott Obtains Divorce" *New York Times*, February 11, 1944.

29. David V. Felts, "Second Thoughts," *Decatur Herald* (Illinois), February 21, 1939. Charles Driscoll, New York Day by Day (syndicated), undated, unsourced clipping, Harvard University, Schlesinger Library, Radcliffe College Archives, RG IX, Series 2, Newspaper Clippings, Class of 1930—Dodge-Parrott.

CHAPTER 15. SAVING PRIVATE BRYAN

1. Hedda Hopper's Hollywood (syndicated), *Los Angeles Times*, December 30, 1942. George Cukor to Hedda Hopper, February 15, 1943, Margaret Herrick Library, Hedda Hopper Collection.

2. Michael Neely Bryan was born August 9, 1916. All Bryan family history is taken from federal census documents dated 1920, 1930, and 1940, along with his induction papers, courtesy of the National Archives and Records Administration, accessed through Ancestry.com. A thorough account of Parrott's relationship with Bryan appears in "Tea Scandal Stirs Musicdom," *DownBeat*, January 15, 1943, 1. *DownBeat* was concerned with the way musicians were being associated with illegal substances, marijuana in particular, and carefully reported the facts of this case. Bryan's musical resume is laid out in his FBI testimony: FBI interrogation summary, January 4, 1943, 8, National Archives and Records Administration, Department of Justice case files for Michael Neely Bryan and Ursula Parrott.

3. Quotations and details are from "Tea Scandal Stirs Musicdom," *DownBeat*, January 15, 1943, as well as FBI testimony: FBI interrogation summary, January 4, 1943, 9, 17–18, National Archives and Records Administration, Department of Justice case files. Parrott's "surfside" winter home in Miami is mentioned in "The New Ursula Parrott Story," *Time*, January 11, 1943.

4. Details about the case come from the comprehensive account of the chronology of events in the Department of Justice file for the case: National Archives and Records Administration, NY 42-160.

5. "Drug Charge Lodged against Ursula Parrott's Soldier Friend," *Los Angeles Times*, January 1, 1943. "Ursula Parrott Puts All Blame for Army Scrape on 'Impulse,'" *Boston Herald*, December 31, 1942. "Tea Scandal Stirs Musicdom," *DownBeat*, January 15, 1943. Parrott's testimony is from her sworn statement to

FBI Special Agent John P. Lair, National Archives and Records Administration, Department of Justice case files.

6. "Ursula Parrott Puts All Blame for Army Scrape on 'Impulse,'" *Boston Herald*, December 31, 1942. FBI interrogation summary, January 4, 1943, 13, National Archives and Records Administration, Department of Justice case files. "Love Scene Staged in Flight Plot," *Boston Post*, February 26, 1943.

7. FBI file for Ursula Parrott, obtained under the Freedom of Information Act, National Archives and Records Administration. "Ursula Parrott Seized by Federal Agents," *Los Angeles Times*, December 30, 1942.

8. "Ursula Parrott Puts All Blame for Army Scrape on 'Impulse,'" *Boston Herald*, December 31, 1942. "Mrs. Parrott Takes Army Case Blame," *New York Times*, December 31, 1942. Bryan's marriage is noted in the January 4, 1943 FBI investigation report, Agent Robert Seaburn Moore, National Archives and Records Administration, Department of Justice case files, 3. "Aging" is used in "The New Ursula Parrott Story," *Time*, January 11, 1943, 21.

9. "Ursula Parrott Takes Blame for Desertion," *Los Angeles Times*, December 31, 1942. "Miss Parrott's Soldier Sought in Drugs Case," *New York Herald Tribune*, December 31, 1942.

10. "Woman Faces Grave Charge," *Daily Chronicle* (DeKalb, Illinois), December 30, 1942. "Ursula Parrott Admits Smuggling Army Deserter out of Camp," *St. Louis Post-Dispatch*, December 30, 1942. FBI interrogation summary, January 4, 1943, 7–8, National Archives and Records Administration, Department of Justice case files.

11. "Ursula Parrott Puts All Blame for Army Scrape on 'Impulse,'" *Boston Herald*, December 31, 1942.

12. George Gallup, "Jury Indicts Ursula Parrott," *Los Angeles Times*, January 9, 1943.

13. "Move Hits Indictment of Writer," *Hartford Courant*, January 17, 1943. "February 25 Trial Is Set for Novelist," *Hartford Courant*, January 25, 1943. Frydl, *Drug Wars in America*, 55. "Ursula Parrott Is Indicted on Three Federal Charges," *St. Petersberg Times*, January 9, 1943.

14. "This Should Be Probed," *Cumberland Evening Times*, December 31, 1942.

15. "Ursula Parrott's Army Friend Sentenced at Court-Martial," *Los Angeles Times*, January 24, 1943. "Four Are Indicted in Tax Violation," *Wilkes-Barre Evening News*, January 23, 1943. "Miss Parrott's Soldier Sought in Drugs Case," *New York Herald Tribune*, December 31, 1942. "Soldier Indicted Here," *New York Times*, January 23, 1943.

16. Information about marijuana legislation in this era comes primarily from Ferraiolo, "From Killer Weed to Popular Medicine," and McAllister, "Harry Anslinger Saves the World." Anslinger, "Marijuana, Assassin of Youth," 18.

17. Memorandum from Mathias F. Cornea, United States attorney, to judge advocate general, February 12, 1943, National Archives and Records Administration, Department of Justice case files. "Service Men's Marijuana Den Was Run in N.Y.," *New York Herald Tribune*, January 1, 1943.

18. "Ursula Parrott Asks Divorce," *New York Times*, February 18, 1943. "Love Scene Staged in Flight Plot," *Boston Post*, February 26, 1943.

19. "Ursula Parrott Puts All Blame for Army Scrape on 'Impulse,'" *Boston Herald*, December 31, 1942. Remaining quotations in this paragraph and the next derive from FBI interrogation summary, January 4, 1943, 6, National Archives and Records Administration, Department of Justice case files.

20. "Love Scene Staged in Flight Plot," *Boston Post*, February 26, 1943. "Miss Parrott's Soldier Sought in Drugs Case," *New York Herald Tribune*, December 31, 1942.

21. "All-Male Jury Chosen to Try Ursula Parrott," *Kingston Daily Freeman*, February 25, 1943.

22. National Archives and Records Administration, Department of Justice case files: FBI case file, Michael Neely Bryan et. al., February 26, 1943; Robert Carey, Jr. to Lieut. Colonel E.M. Barron of the Litigation Division, Office of the Judge Advocate General, February 18, 1943.

23. "Parrott Told about Bryan Escape," *Hartford Courant*, February 26, 1943. FBI interrogation summary, January 4, 1943, 5–6, National Archives and Records Administration, Department of Justice case files.

24. "Miss Parrott Sobs as Her Confession Is Introduced," *Dunkirk Evening Observer*, February 26, 1943. "Ursula Parrott Sheds Tears to Hear Her Own Confession," *Daily News*, February 27, 1943.

25. "Mrs. Parrott Freed on Army Charge," *Los Angeles Times*, February 28, 1943. "Ursula Parrott Freed of Federal Charges," *Tuscaloosa News*, February 28, 1943.

26. "The New Ursula Parrott Story," *Time*, January 11, 1943.

27. "Bigtown Smalltalk," *Wilkes-Barre Times Leader*, February 17, 1943.

28. "Ursula Parrott Freed of Federal Charges," *Tuscaloosa News*, February 28, 1943. "Ursula Parrott, Acquitted by Jury, Weeps at Verdict," *Coshocton Tribune*, February 28, 1943. UP to GB, undated letter (likely 1929). Walter Winchell, In New York (syndicated), February 26, 1943.

29. Charles Driscoll, New York Day by Day (syndicated), undated, unsourced clipping, Harvard University, Schlesinger Library, Radcliffe College Archives, RG IX, Series 2, Newspaper Clippings, Class of 1930—Dodge-Parrott.

CHAPTER 16. HER "BREAKS WENT BAD"

1. U.S. Department of the Treasury: "Notice of Levy," February 9, 1943; "Warrant for Distraint," July 10, 1942. Dodd, Mead & Company to Mr. John J. McCloskey, May 20, 1942, Indiana University, Lilly Library, Dodd, Mead & Company collection, LMC 245, account of Ursula Parrott as of October 1, 1942.

2. Ursula Parrott judgment ledger, November 18, 1943. Accounting Department, Dodd, Mead & Company to Mr. Jerome Sherman, Brodsky and Lieber-

man, July 14, 1944, Indiana University, Lilly Library, Dodd, Mead & Company collection, LMC 245.

3. Louella Parsons, "Gene Tierney to Star in U. Parrott's 'Army Wives,'" *Waterloo Courier*, May 15, 1942. "Conover Models Test for Film," *Nebraska State Journal*, December 9, 1945. The Lyons Den (syndicated), *Oakland Tribune*, August 31, 1947.

4. Ruark, "Roaring 20's," 32.

5. Parrott, "Your Picture and My Love," 77, 94.

6. Walter Winchell, syndicated column, *Pittsburgh Sun-Telegraph*, May 1, 1952.

7. UP to HO, undated letter.

8. Indiana University, Lilly Library, Dodd, Mead & Company collection: Dodd, Mead & Co. to Mr. Gaetano C. Carretta, lawyer for W. & J. Sloane, November 22, 1948; Paul Slota to Gaetano C. Carretta, list of judgment creditors, November 26, 1948.

9. Jessica Weisburg, "Mavis Gallant's Double-Dealing Literary Agent," *New Yorker*, July 11, 2012.

10. Information and quotations in this paragraph through the next endnote derive from Alfred Albelli, "Ursula's New Episode—'Ex-Guest,'" *New York Daily News*, March 14, 1949.

11. Information and quotations in this paragraph to the next endnote derive from "Ursula Parrott Jailed for Skipping Sho' Hotel Bill," *Salisbury Daily Times*, May 31, 1950, and "Novelist Is Held in Dispute over Paying Hotel Bill," *Miami Daily News-Record*, May 31, 1950.

12. "N.Y. Friends to Air Ursula Parrott," *Baltimore Sun*, June 1, 1950.

13. "Hotel Jails Ursula Parrott over Six-Month-Late Rent," *New York Daily News*, June 1, 1950. "Miss Parrott Jailed over $255 Hotel Bill," *New York Herald Tribune*, June 1, 1950. "N.Y. Friends to Aid Ursula Parrott," *Baltimore Sun*, June 1, 1950.

14. "Friend Pays Bill," *Baltimore Sun*, June 2, 1950.

15. "Charge Ursula Robbed Brass of Some Silver," *New York Daily News*, March 20, 1952. The quotations in this paragraph and the next derive from "Ursula Parrott Sought in Theft of $1,000 Silver," *New York Herald Tribune*, March 20, 1952.

16. "Ursula Parrott Eludes Police in Theft of Silver," *Minneapolis Morning Tribune*, March 20, 1952.

17. Harvard University, Schlesinger Library, Radcliffe College Archives, RG IX, Series 2, Newspaper Clippings, Class of 1930—Dodge-Parrott.

18. UP to AC, August 21, 1952. Correspondence between Ursula Parrott and Alan Collins is from the Columbia University, Rare Book & Manuscript Library, Curtis Brown Ltd. collection.

19. AC to Sara March (a.k.a. Ursula Parrott), July 17, 1952. UP to AC, undated letter (circa July 1952).

20. UP to AC, August 21, 1952, undated letter (circa September 1952), and August 21, 1952.

21. UP to AC, undated letters (circa September 1952 and July 1952). Parrott, "Love Song—1939," 23.

22. AC to John Wildberg, November 20, 1952, Columbia University, Rare Book & Manuscript Library, Curtis Brown Ltd. collection. UP to AC, undated letter. AC to Sarah March (UP), October 3, 1952.

23. AC to Sarah March (UP), October 31, 1952. UP to AC, undated letter (circa October 1952).

24. UP to AC, undated letter (circa October 1952), Standish Arms Hotel stationery. UP to AC, August 21, 1952, and undated letter (circa September 1952).

25. UP to AC, undated letters (circa September 1952 and circa October 1952).

26. UP to AC, undated letter (circa November 1952).

27. UP to AC, undated letter (circa November 1952), Standish Arms Hotel stationery.

28. AC to John Wildberg, November 20, 1952. John Wildberg to AC, November 25, 1952.

29. AC to John Wildberg, November 28, 1952.

30. Review of "One More Such Victory," *Item of Millburn and Short Hills*, September 25, 1942. Advertisement for "One More Such Victory," *Cosmopolitan*, August 1941, 172.

CHAPTER 17. "BLACK COFFEE, SCOTCH,
AND EXCITEMENT"

1. UP to HO, undated letters (unknown and circa 1933/34).

2. UP to HO, undated letter (circa 1933). UP to GB, July 25, 1941, and undated letter (circa 1941). Marc Parrott, "Afterword," 220.

3. Quotations through "'career woman' became a dirty word" derive from Friedan, *Feminine Mystique*.

4. Leonard Lyons, "Groucho Has a Theory," Lyons Den (syndicated), *Boston Herald*, September 24, 1957. Walter Winchell, "Mutes on 42nd St., Do Speeches in Sign," *Jackson Mississippi Clarion-Ledger*, September 23, 1957. "Line of Type or Two on Filmland's Folks, Affairs," *North Hollywood Valley Times*, October 16, 1957. Dorothy Kilgallen, "Voice of Broadway," *Weirton West Virginia Daily Times*, January 21, 1958.

5. Marc Parrott, "Afterword," 222. Ursula Parrott, "You Ride Success Alone," October 1938, 62. Ursula Parrott, "Dado," 93.

6. Ursula Parrott to Alec Waugh, September 12, 1939. University of Texas, Harry Ransom Center, Alec Waugh collection.

7. Marc Parrott, "Afterword," 222. UP to HO, undated letter (January 14, circa late 1930s).

1. Parrott's income is noted in Alice Hughes, As a Woman Looks at It (syndicated), *Minneapolis Star Tribune,* March 1, 1939. The dollar equivalency was derived by using the U.S. Bureau of Labor Statistics online Consumer Price Inflation Calculator.

2. "Librarian Gives Do's and Don'ts for Donors in New Campaign to Provide Books for Service Men," *Moberly Monitor-Index,* October 3, 1942, 6.

3. UP to HO, undated letters (unknown and circa 1929).

4. York, "Should Women Work?," 102.

PUBLISHED WRITINGS BY URSULA PARROTT

This bibliography details Ursula Parrott's known published writings. I began by drawing from Susan Westall's bio-bibliography of Parrott, which she completed as a master's thesis at Kent State University in 1999. I verified and, when necessary, updated Westall's entries, limiting my scope to US editions of Parrott's novels. Using digital periodical and newspaper databases, I added forty-three Parrott stories and essays beyond what Westall documented in 1999. I suspect that there are other Parrott publications still to be found, perhaps published under pseudonyms or in magazines that cannot yet be searched digitally. When her novels also appeared in serialized form in newspapers or magazines, I indicate the publication venue in brackets.

NOVELS

1929   *Ex-Wife.* Originally anonymous. Parrott's name attached after the October 1929 seventh printing. Jonathan Cape & Harrison Smith.
[Also New York *Daily Mirror*]

1930   *Strangers May Kiss.* Jonathan Cape & Harrison Smith.

1931   *Gentleman's Fate.* As K.U.P. Jonathan Cape & Harrison Smith.
[Also *Household Magazine*]
Love Goes Past. Jonathan Cape & Harrison Smith.
[Also *College Humor*]

1933   *The Tumult and the Shouting.* Longmans, Green and Co.
The Woman Accused. Ray Long & Richard Smith, Inc. Contributing author with Rupert Hughes, Vicki Baum, Zane Grey, Viña Delmar, Irvin S. Cobb, Gertrude Atherton, J. P. McEvoy, Pola Banks, and Sophie Kerr.
[Also *Liberty*]

1935	*Next Time We Live*. Longmans, Green and Co.
	[Also *Los Angeles Times* as "Next Time We Live"]
	Dream without Ending. Longmans, Green and Co.
	[Collection of eight stories. "Dream without Ending," "A King in Caribbea," "Salute! There Goes Romance," "Remember Me," "Death Is a Dream," "Forever, Perhaps," "Whenever Spring" also appeared in magazines; "A Princess Goes Home" is original to the book.]
1936	*Though You Be Far* and *When Summer, Returning*. Longmans, Green and Co.
	[Also *McCall's* and *Good Housekeeping*]
1938	*For All of Our Lives*. Dodd, Mead & Company.
	[Also *McCall's*]
1939	*Life Is for the Living*. Dodd, Mead & Company.
	[Also *Redbook*]
1941	*Road Leading Somewhere*. Dodd, Mead & Company.
	[Also *Ladies' Home Journal*]
	Marry Me before You Go. Dodd, Mead & Company.
	[Also *Redbook*]
1942	*Nothing Ever Ends*. Dodd, Mead & Company.
	[Also *Redbook*]
	Heaven's Not Far Away. Dodd, Mead & Company.
	One More Such Victory. Smith & Durrell.
	[Also *Cosmopolitan*]
1943	*Storm at Dusk*. Dodd, Mead & Company.
	[Also *Redbook*]
	Navy Nurse. Dodd, Mead & Company.
	[Also *Redbook*]
	Island of Fear. Dodd, Mead & Company.
	[Also *Redbook* as "Tomorrow We'll Be Free"]
1944	*Even in a Hundred Years*. Dodd, Mead & Company.
	[Also *Redbook* as "One Day, There You Will Be!"]

STORIES AND ARTICLES

1929	"Ex-Wife," *Daily Mirror* (New York), October 3–November 16
	"Leftover Ladies," *The Mentor*, December
1930	"Love Affair," *College Humor*, August

1931   "Gentleman's Fate," *Household Magazine*, March–May

"Love Goes Past," *College Humor*, May–August

"Meeting at Midnight," *Liberty*, May 23

"First Love," *Redbook*, August

1932   "Dream without Ending," *Good Housekeeping*, August

1933   "The Bottle of Pills," (chapter 8 of the book *The Woman Accused*), *Liberty*, February

"Thirtieth Birthday," *Hartford Courant*, February 26

"Peter Keeps Memorial Day," *Ladies' Home Journal*, May

"Remember Me," *Good Housekeeping*, June

"It Must Be the Climate," *American Magazine*, July

"A King in Caribbea," *American Magazine*, August

"Breadwinner," *Redbook*, October 1933–February 1934

"Forever, Perhaps," *Liberty*, November 1933–January 1934

"In Heaven Surely," *Ladies' Home Journal*, December

1934   "Smile Painted On," *Good Housekeeping*, February

"For No Earthly Reason," *Good Housekeeping*, March

"Merchant Princess," *American Magazine*, April–August

"Salute! There Goes Romance," *McCall's*, August

"There's Always Tomorrow," *New York Herald Tribune*, September

"Nowhere and Return," *Redbook*, October

"Last Love," *American Magazine*, October

"Though Time Be Fleet," *Good Housekeeping*, November

"Say Goodbye Again," *McCall's*, December 1934–March 1935

1935   "Ina Claire," *Saturday Evening Post*, January

"Whenever Spring," *Fiction Parade*, May

"When Summer, Returning," *Good Housekeeping*, May–October

"Brilliant Marriage," *Redbook*, July

"Next Time We Live," *Los Angeles Times*, September–November

"The Unscientific Gardener," *Arts and Decoration*, October

1936   "Leisure to Repent," *Redbook*, February

"Though You Be Far," *McCall's*, February–June

"The Second Mink Coat," *Cosmopolitan*, May

"Manhattan Dawn," *Redbook*, May

"Death Is a Dream," *Pittsburgh Sun Telegraph*, May 29

"Love Comes but Once," *Good Housekeeping*, June

"Never See Snow Again," *Cosmopolitan*, August

"We Shall Never Meet Again," *Redbook*, September

"Westport Week End," *Cosmopolitan*, September

"Tomorrow's Sun," *McCall's*, September–January 1937

"Some Day You'll Find Him," *Pictorial Review*, November

"Second Choice," *American Magazine*, December

1937   "Love Is Forever," *Pictorial Review*, May

"Some Other Springtime," *Ladies' Home Journal*, May

"No Answer Ever," *Cosmopolitan*, July

"She Married for Money," *Redbook*, October

"Spring Singing," *Good Housekeeping*, November–April 1938

"Life Sentence," *Redbook*, December

1938   "Brief Encore," *Ladies' Home Journal*, January

"For All of Our Lives," *McCall's*, January

"That Wife of Hugo's," *Ladies' Home Journal*, February

"Grounds for Divorce: Infidelity," *Cosmopolitan*, February

"Ground for Divorce: Desertion," *Cosmopolitan*, March

"Grounds for Divorce: Nonsupport," *Cosmopolitan*, May

"This and That," recurring column in *Connecticut Nutmeg*, May–October

"Revoir," *Ladies Home Journal*, August

"Til I Forget to Love," *McCall's*, August

"You Ride Success Alone," *Redbook*, September–October

"Life Is for the Living," *Redbook*, December

1939   "Dusk over Manhattan," *Redbook*, January

"And Tomorrow to You," *Ladies Home Journal*, January

"Appointment with Tomorrow," *Good Housekeeping*, March–August

"The Boy Next Door" *Ladies' Home Journal*, April

"World's Fair," *Redbook*, June

1940   "Love Song—1939," *McCall's*, February

"Nothing Ever Ends," *Redbook*, April

"Road Leading Somewhere," *Ladies' Home Journal*, August–December

"Grounds for Divorce: Incompatibility," *Cosmopolitan*, October

1941   "Nice People Don't Eat," *Ladies' Home Journal*, March

"Marry Me before You Go," *Redbook*, June

"Hour of Departure," *Cosmopolitan*, July

"Hour of Departure II, Today Is All" *Cosmopolitan*, August

"Somewhere East of Sunrise," *Redbook*, November–February 1942

1942   "Promise to Forget," *Ladies' Home Journal*, February

"One More Such Victory," *Cosmopolitan*, February

"Storm at Dusk," *Redbook*, April

"A Far Off Music," *Ladies' Home Journal*, April

"This Is Our Day," *McCall's*, May

"Happy Ending," *Cosmopolitan*, June

"Postscript to a Love Affair," *Cosmopolitan*, August

"Never Grow Old Darling," *Cosmopolitan*, September

"Navy Nurse," *Redbook*, October

"Tomorrow We'll Be Free," *Cosmopolitan*, December

"You Can't Find Yesterday," *Woman's Home Companion*, October

1943 "The Last Time We Meet," *Redbook*, March–June

"One Day, There You Will Be!," *Redbook*, October

1944 "Sorrow Always Passes," *Redbook*, February

"The Years I'll Spend without You," *Redbook*, May

"Until Some Other Year," *Redbook*, July

"Good-by at the Station," *Redbook*, October–November

1945 "This Wonderful Moment," *Redbook*, January

"If We Could Be Alone," *Redbook*, February

"And Then For Always," *Redbook*, March

"And Throw the Key Away," *Cosmopolitan*, March–May

"Sleighbells in the Night," *Redbook*, April

"The Beauty of the Family," *Redbook*, May–June

"Let Go of Yesterday," *Redbook*, August

"His Broken Promise," *Redbook*, October

"Love Is So Universal," *Redbook*, November

"Your Picture and My Love," *Redbook*, December–March 1946

1946 "Our Footsteps Echo," *Cosmopolitan*, February–March

"Too Busy for Love," *Liberty*, May 11

"Dado," *Woman's Day*, November

"Until Moonrise," *Liberty*, December

"You Call That Work?" *New York Journal-American*, December 14, 1946

"Parked Wives," *New York Journal-American*, December 21, 1946

"Of Course, She's Older," *Redbook*, December–February 1947

1947 "Let's Just Marry," *Redbook*, November

FILMOGRAPHY

This filmography aggregates the film adaptations of Parrott's published writing, as well as the known scripts that Parrott worked on for hire, none of which appear to have been produced.

PRODUCED

1930   *The Divorcee*. Metro-Goldwyn-Mayer (MGM). Based on *Ex-Wife*. Dir. Robert Z. Leonard. Starring Norma Shearer, Chester Morris, Conrad Nagel. Best Actress Academy Award, 1930, for Norma Shearer.

1931   *Strangers May Kiss*. MGM. Based on novel of same name. Dir. George Fitzmaurice. Starring Norma Shearer, Robert Montgomery, Ray Milland. Parrott worked on script with John Meehan.

    Gentlemen's Fate. MGM. Based on serial and novel of same name. Dir. Mervyn LeRoy. Starring John Gilbert, Louis Wolheim, Leila Hyams, Anita Page.

    Leftover Ladies. Tiffany Pictures. Loosely based on "Leftover Ladies." Dir. Erle Kenton. Produced by Sam Bischoff. Starring Claudia Dell, Marjorie Rambeau, Walter Bryon, Roscoe Karns.

1932   *Love Affair*. Columbia. Loosely based on story of the same name. Dir. Thornton Freeland. Starring Humphrey Bogart, Dorothy Mackail.

1933   *The Woman Accused*. Paramount. Serialized novel of same name written by ten contributing authors. Dir. Paul Sloane. Starring Nancy Carroll and Cary Grant.

1934   *There's Always Tomorrow*. Universal. Based on story of same name. Dir. Edward Sloman. Starring Binnie Barnes, Alan Hale, Robert Taylor, Frank Morgan.

1936   *Next Time We Love*. Universal. Based on novel, *Next Time We Live*. Dir. Edward H. Griffith. Starring Jimmy Stewart, Margaret Sullivan, Ray Milland.

        Brilliant Marriage. Invincible Pictures. Based on story of same name. Dir. Phil Rosen. Starring Joan Marsh, Ray Walker, Hugh Marlowe.

1956   *There's Always Tomorrow*. Universal. Dir. Douglas Sirk. Starring Barbara Stanwyck, Fred Mac Murray.

UNPRODUCED (OPTIONED, COMMISSIONED, OR REPORTED IN THE PRESS)

1931   "Love Goes Past." Samuel Goldwyn, United Artists, for Gloria Swanson.

1932   "Two Kinds of Love." Worldwide Pictures. Based on Parrott story "Thirtieth Birthday." (Discussed again in 1938.)

1934   "Salute! There Goes Romance." MGM, for Joan Crawford.

1937   "Trailer Romance." RKO, for Ginger Rogers and Herbert Marshall. Adapted from Parrott story "She Married for Money."

1938   "Infidelity." MGM. Based on Parrott story "Grounds for Divorce: Infidelity." Screenplay by F. Scott Fitzgerald. Blocked by Production Code Administration. Drafts and related correspondence in the Warner Bros. / Turner Entertainment, F. Scott Fitzgerald screenplay collection at the University of South Carolina, Ernest F. Hollings Special Collections Library.

1939   "Love Song—1939." Purchased by United Artists. Based on Parrott story of the same name.

        "For All of Our Lives." Based on Parrott story of the same name. Slated for production by Eastern Service Studios, Astoria (John Wildberg, producer; Ursula Parrott and Worthington Miner, screenwriters). Starring Herbert Marshall. Plan was for distribution by Columbia after theatrical run of the play in New York.

1940   "Love and Song." Based on Parrott story of the same name. Purchased by James Roosevelt, Globe Productions, for their second production.

1942   "A Far Off Music." Based on Parrott story of the same name. Purchased by 20th Century-Fox for $50,0000 for Gene Tierney, to be retitled "Army Wives."

1945   "The Conover Girl." Based on Parrott's unpublished story about the Harry Conover Advertising Agency in New York. Purchased by Republic Pictures as "top budget musical romance," slated to start in December.

1962   *Next Time We Love*. Ross Hunter reported to produce a remake with Sandra Dee in leading role.

BIBLIOGRAPHY

ARCHIVAL COLLECTIONS

Ancestry.com. The searchable database contains a wealth of resources including state and federal censuses; ships' records; passport applications; and birth, death, and marriage certificates.

Arizona State Library, Archives and Public Records. Johnnie Quantrell State Prison Records, Florence, Arizona.

Boston College, John J. Burns Library. Chestnut Hill, Massachusetts. University Archives. Information about Parrott's father, Henry Towle.

Columbia University, Rare Book & Manuscript Library. New York, New York. Correspondence between Ursula Parrott (UP) and George Bye (GB) are in the James O. Brown Associates records, Box C33. Most of Parrott's letters to Bye are undated, and I have attempted to estimate dates where the contents of the letters make this possible. Additional materials are from the Ann Watkins Loomis Papers Collection, uncatalogued contracts, Box 151, and the Curtis Brown Ltd. collection, which contains correspondence between Ursula Parrott (UP) and her last agent, Alan Collins (AC).

Connecticut Historical Society. Hartford, Connecticut. Copies of the *Connecticut Nutmeg* (later known as *Broun's Nutmeg*), which Parrott cofounded.

Delaware Historical Society. Wilmington, Delaware. Information pertaining to Parrott's 1950 arrest.

Harvard University, Schlesinger Library, Radcliffe Institute, Radcliffe College Archives. Cambridge, Massachusetts. RG XXI, Series 1: student files, 1890–1985, Katherine Ursula Towle (Mrs. Ursula Parrott). RG IX, Series 2: records of the Radcliffe College Alumnae Association, ca. 1894–2004. RG IX, Series 7: class collections of the Radcliffe College Alumnae Association, 1893–2001. *The Jabberwock* (monthly publication of the Girls' Latin School). *Radcliffe News. Radcliffe Quarterly.* Radcliffe College yearbook. *The Red Book Student's Handbook of Radcliffe College.*

Indiana University, Lilly Library. Bloomington, Indiana. Dodd, Mead & Company collection.

Library of Congress, Moving Image Research Center. Washington, DC. Film and film-related archival materials, including the only known 35 mm print in North America of *Leftover Ladies.*

Margaret Herrick Library of the Academy of Motion Picture Arts and Sciences. Beverly Hills, California. Motion Picture Association of America Production Code Administration Records. Hedda Hopper Collection. Joseph L. Mankiewicz Collection. Motion picture files for Ursula Parrott adaptations.

Media History Digital Library. Online. A free, full-text searchable digital archive "featuring millions of pages of books and magazines from the histories of film, broadcasting, and recorded sound," Wisconsin Center for Film and Theater Research at the University of Wisconsin-Madison

National Archives and Records Administration. Department of Justice case files for Michael Neely Bryan and Ursula Parrott, Record Group 60: Records of the Department of Justice, Entry A1 COR 42, Box 1, 42-18-1, 230/14/40/06. FBI file for Ursula Parrott obtained through Freedom of Information Act request. Passport applications pre-1925 are held in the textual reference division in College Park, Maryland.

New York Public Library. New York, New York. General Research Division, including information about Margaret Towle (a.k.a. Madge Tyrone).

New York University, Tamiment Library and Robert F. Wagner Labor Archives. New York, New York. Veterans of the Abraham Lincoln Brigade Photograph Collection.

Princeton University, Firestone Library, Department of Special Collections. Princeton, New Jersey. Mildred Gilman Wohlforth Papers, Box 3, Folder 12. Otto H. Kahn Papers, TC032, Box 208, Folder 7. Undergraduate Alumni Records.

Simmons University Archives. Boston, Massachusetts. Information pertaining to Parrott's sister, Lucy Towle.

Smithsonian Archives of American Art. Washington, DC. Nickolas Muray collection, Roll 4392.

University of Oregon, Special Collections & University Archives. Eugene, Oregon. Letters from Ursula Parrott (UP) to Hugh O'Connor (HO) are in the Hugh O'Connor papers, Ax 620. Most of this correspondence is undated. I have attempted to estimate dates where the contents of the letters make this possible.

University of Reading, Penguin Random House UK Archive. Special Collections Library. Jonathan Cape records.

University of South Carolina, Ernest F. Hollings Special Collections Library, Rare Books & Special Collections. Columbia, South Carolina. Warner Bros. / Turner Entertainment, F. Scott Fitzgerald screenplay collection.

University of Texas, Harry Ransom Center. Austin, Texas. Alec Waugh collection.

University of Wyoming, American Heritage Center. Laramie, Wyoming. Joseph Patrick McEvoy and Margaret Santry papers, 1898–1982.

Washington State Archives. Olympia, Washington. Superior Court of the State of Washington records pertaining to complaint no. 2685 in Klickitat County, Margaret Towle (a.k.a. Madge Tyrone) divorce.

Westchester County Historical Society. Westchester, Connecticut. Donald Adams file.

Yale University, Beinecke Rare Book and Manuscript Library. New Haven, Connecticut. Theatre Guild Archive.

SYNDICATED COLUMNISTS

Driscoll, Charles	Kilgallen, Dorothy	Peak, Mayme Ober
Hopper, Hedda	Lyons, Leonard	Walker, Danton
Hughes, Alice	Parsons, Louella O.	Winchell, Walter

SELECTED BIBLIOGRAPHY

What follows provides a bibliographic record for primary and secondary sources that informed the writing of this book. I have excluded materials that are limited in scope, such as reviews of Parrott's writings or articles about her and her associates' lives; these are cited in full in the book's endnotes.

"100 Years of Marriage and Divorce Statistics Unites States, 1867–1967." Series 21, Number 24. National Center for Health Statistics, Department of Vital Statistics. DHEW publication no. (HRA) 714–1902.

Adams, Elizabeth Kemper. *Women Professional* Workers. New York: Macmillan, 1921.

Adler, Felix. *Marriage and Divorce.* New York: D. Appleton, 1923.

Anslinger, H. J. "Marijuana, Assassin of Youth." *American Magazine,* July 1937.

Anonymous. *Ex-'It.'* New York: Vanguard Press, 1930.

———. *Ex-Mistress.* New York: Brentano's, 1930.

Anti-Suffrage Essays by Massachusetts Women. Boston: Forum Publications of Boston, 1916.

Baker, Gladys. "Says There Will Be No Marriage 50 Years Hence." *The World,* Woman's Section, August 10, 1930.

Baldwin, Faith. *Week-End Marriage.* New York: Balkiston, 1932.

Barnett, Vincent. "The Novelist as Hollywood Star: Author Royalties and Studio Income in the 1920s." *Film History* (2008).

Basinger, Jeanine. *I Do and I Don't: A History of Marriage in the Movies.* New York: Vintage, 2014.

Berlant, Lauren. *The Female Complaint: The Unfinished Business of Sentimentality in American Culture.* Durham: Duke University Press, 2008.

Blanchard, Phyllis, and Carlyn Manasses. *New Girls for Old*. New York: Macaulay, 1930.

Bond, Helen Judy. "Foreword," *The Good Housekeeping Marriage Book: Twelve Ways to a Happy Marriage*. New York: Prentice Hall, 1938.

Bothshon, Lisa, and Meredith Goldsmith. *Middlebrow Moderns: Popular American Writers of the 1920s*. Boston: Northeastern Press, 2003.

Boyer, Paul. *Purity in Print: Book Censorship in America from the Gilded Age to the Computer Age*. Madison: University of Wisconsin Press, 2003.

Brace, Blanche. "Suffrage Lapboards Make Subway Grin, Then Think," *New York Tribune*, October 31, 1915.

Brooks, Walter. *New York: An Intimate Guide*. New York: Alfred Knopf, 1931.

Brown, Helen Gurley. *Having It All*. New York: Simon & Schuster, 1982.

———. *Sex and the Single Girl*. New York: Bernard Geis, 1962.

Bruccoli, Matthew, ed. *A Life in Letters: F. Scott Fitzgerald*. New York: Charles Scribener's Sons, 1994.

Bruccoli, Matthew, and Margaret Duggan, eds. *Correspondence of F. Scott Fitzgerald*. New York: Random House, 1980.

Chafee, Zechariah. *The Censorship in Boston*. Boston: Civil Liberties Committee of Massachusetts, 1929.

Collier, Virginia MacMakin. *Marriage and Careers: A Study of One Hundred Women Who Are Wives, Mothers, Homemakers and Professional Workers*. Bureau of Vocational Information, 1926.

Coontz, Stephanie. *Marriage, a History: From Obedience to Intimacy or How Love Conquered Marriage*. New York: Viking, 2005.

Cooper, James. *Technique of Contraception*. New York: Day-Nichols, 1928.

Copperfield, Dora. "The Women's Magazines," *Vanity Fair*, January 1934.

Cott, Nancy. *The Grounding of Modern Feminism*. New Haven: Yale University Press, 1987.

Cowley, Malcolm. *Exile's Return: A Narrative of Ideas*. New York: W. W. Norton, 1934.

Curran, Karen Mastrobattista. *Her Greatness Proclaim: The History of the Girls' Latin School*. Self-published: 2014.

Darnton, Robert. "The Old-Girl Network." *Raritan* (Summer 2011).

Davis, Clare Ogden. *The Woman of It*. New York: J. H. Sears, 1929.

Delafield, E. M. *I Visit the Soviets: The Provincial Lady Looks at Russia*. New York: Harper & Brothers, 1937.

Doherty, Thomas. *Pre-Code Hollywood: Sex, Immorality, and Insurrection in American Cinema 1930–1934*. New York: Columbia University Press, 1999.

Douglas, Ann. *Terrible Honesty: Mongrel Manhattan in the 1920s*. New York: Noonday Press, 1995.

Dickinson, Robert Latou, and Louise Stevens Bryant. *Control of Conception: An Illustrated Medical Manual*. Baltimore: Williams & Wilkins, 1931.

Endres, Kathleen L., and Therese L. Lueck, eds. *Women's Periodicals in the United States: Consumer Magazines*. Westport: Greenwood Press, 1995.

Ernst, Morris, and Pare Lorentz. *Censored: The Private Life of the Movie.* New York: Jonathan Cape & Harrison Smith, 1930.

Fass, Paula S. *The Damned and the Beautiful: American Youth in the 1920's.* New York: Oxford University Press, 1977.

Ferraiolo, Kathleen. "From Killer Weed to Popular Medicine: The Evolution of American Drug Control Policy, 1937–2000." *Journal of Policy History* 19, no. 2 (2007).

Fitzgerald, F. Scott. "Early Success" (1937), "Echoes of the Jazz Age" (1931), "My Lost City" (July 1932). In *The Crack-Up,* edited by Edmund Wilson. New York: New Directions, 1945.

———. *The Last Tycoon.* New York: Scribner and Sons, 1941.

Francke, Lizzie. *Script Girls: Women Screenwriters in Hollywood.* London: British Film Institute, 1994.

Frank, Elizabeth. *Louise Bogan: A Portrait.* New York: Alfred A. Knopf, 1985.

Friedan, Betty. *The Feminine Mystique.* New York: W. W. Norton, 1963.

Frydl, Kathleen. *The Drug Wars in America, 1940–1973.* Cambridge: Cambridge University Press, 2013.

Gabler, Neal. *Winchell: Gossip, Power and the Culture of Celebrity.* New York: Alfred. A. Knopf, 1995.

Gallico, Paul. "Memento Muray." *The Revealing Eye.* New York: Atheneum, 1967.

Hackett, Alice Payne. *60 Years of Best Sellers, 1895–1955.* New York: R. R. Bowker, 1956.

Hall, G. Stanley. "What Is to Become of Your Baby." *Cosmopolitan,* April 1910.

Hillis, Marjorie. *Live Alone and Like It: A Guide for the Extra Woman.* New York: Bobbs-Merrill, 1936.

Honey, Maureen. "Feminist New Woman Fiction in Periodicals of the 1920s," *Middlebrow Moderns: Popular American Women Writers of the* 1920s, edited by Lisa Botshon and Meredith Goldsmith. Boston: Northeastern University Press, 2003.

Graefenberg, Ernest. "Intrauterine Methods." In *The Practice of Contraception: An International Symposium and Survey,* edited by Margaret Sanger and Hannah Mayer Stone, 33–47. Baltimore: Williams & Wilkins, 1931.

Graham, Stephen. *New York Nights.* New York: George H. Doran, 1927.

Hecht, Ben. *A Child of the Century.* New York: Simon & Schuster, 1954.

Hinzelman, Kurt, ed. *The Covarrubias Circle: Nickolas Muray's Collection of Twentieth-Century Mexican Art.* Austin: University of Texas Press, 2004.

Hulbert, Ann. *Raising America: Experts, Parents, and a Century of Advice about Children.* New York: Alfred A. Knopf, 2003.

Hurst, Fannie. *No Food with My Meals.* New York: Harper & Brothers, 1935.

Hutchins, Grace. *Women Who Work.* New York: International Publishers, 1934.

Irwin, Inez Haynes. *Angels and Amazons: A Hundred Years of American Women.* New York: Doubleday, 1933.

Joyce, Peggy Hopkins. *Men, Marriage, and Me.* New York: Macaulay, 1930.

Kandel, Aben. *Ex-Baby.* New York: Covici Friede, 1930.

Keyser, Catherine. *Playing Smart: New York Women Writers and Modern Magazine Culture*. New Brunswick: Rutgers University Press, 2010.

Landers, James. *The Improbable First Century of Cosmopolitan Magazine*. Columbia: University of Missouri Press, 2010.

LaPointe, Michael. "The Racy Jazz Age Best Seller You've Never Heard Of." *Paris Review*, February 2019.

Latham, Aaron. *Crazy Sundays*. New York: Viking Press, 1970.

Lee, Henry. *How Dry We Were: Prohibition Revisited*. Englewood Cliffs: Prentice-Hall, 1963.

Lepore, Jill. *The Secret History of Wonder Woman*. New York: Vintage Books, 2015.

Leuchtenburg, William. *The Perils of Prosperity 1941–1932*. Chicago: University of Chicago Press, 1958.

Levine, Steven. "The Rise of American Boarding Schools and the Development of a National Upper Class," *Social Problems* 28, no. 1 (October 1980): 63–94.

Levy-Lenz, Ludwig. "A New Non-Operative Method for the Interruption of Pregnancy." In *The Practice of Contraception: An International Symposium and Survey*, edited by Margaret Sanger and Hannah Mayer Stone. Baltimore: Williams & Wilkins, 1931.

"Librarian Gives Do's and Don'ts for Donors in New Campaign to Provide Books for Service Men." *Moberly Monitor-Index,* October 3. 1942.

Lindsey, Ben B., and Wainwright Evans. *The Companionate Marriage*. New York: Brentano's, 1928.

Lynd, Robert, and Helen Merrell Lynd. *Middletown: A Study in Contemporary American Culture*. New York: Harcourt, Brace and Company, 1929.

Macdougall, Robert B. "This Freedom." *Saturday Review of Literature,* August 31, 1929.

Macfadden, Bernarr. "Reform Needed in Our Ancient Divorce Laws." *Liberty* (February 9, 1935).

Mackay, Richard. *Marriage and Divorce Law Simplified*. New York: Legal Almanac, 1940.

Marguiles, Lazar. "History of Intrauterine Devices." *Bulletin of the New York Academy of Medicine*, May 1975.

"Market Place for Words." In *New York Panorama*, presented by Federal Writers' Project, 162–80. New York: Random House, 1938.

Marks, Percy. *The Plastic Age*. New York: Century, 1924.

Mayes, Herbert R. "Introduction." In *Editor's Choice: 26 Modern Short Stories from* Good Housekeeping. New York: Random House, 1956.

McAllister, William. "Harry Anslinger Saves the World: National Security Imperatives and the 1937 Marihuana Tax Act." *Social History of Alcohol and Drugs* 33, no. 1.

McCann, Carole R. *Birth Control Politics in the United States, 1916–1945*. Ithaca: Cornell University Press, 1994.

Meade, Marion. *Lonelyhearts: The Screwball World of Nathanael West and Eileen McKenney*. New York: Mariner Books, 2011.

Morey, Anne. "Elinor Glyn as Hollywood Labourer." *Film History* 18 (2006): 110–18.

Newcomer, Mabel. *A Century of Higher Education for American Women*. New York: Harper & Brothers, 1959.

Okrent, Daniel. *Last Call: The Rise and Fall of Prohibition*. New York: Scribner, 2010.

"One Hundred Years of Birth Control, an Outline of Its History." New York: The American Birth Control League, Third Printing, 1927.

Panzer, Mary. "The Essential Tact of Nickolas Muray." In *The Covarrubias Circle: Nickolas Muray's Collection of Twentieth-Century Mexican Art*, edited by Kurt Hinzelman. Austin: University of Texas Press, 2004.

Parrott, Marc. "Afterword." In *Ex-Wife*, by Ursula Parrott. New York: Plume, 1989 reprint.

Pitkin, Walter B., and William M. Marston. *The Art of Sound Pictures*. New York: D. Appleton, 1930.

Pitt, Barrie. *1918: The Last Act*. New York: W. W. Norton, 1962.

Pringle, Henry. "What Do the Women of America Think about Marriage and Divorce." *Ladies' Home Journal*, February 1938.

Quigley, Martin. *Decency in Motion Pictures*. New York: Macmillan Company, 1937.

Radway, Janice. "On the Gender of the Middlebrow Consumer and the Threat of the Culturally Fraudulent Female," *South Atlantic Quarterly* (Fall 1994), 871–93.

Reagan, Leslie J. *When Abortion Was a Crime: Women, Medicine, and Law in the United States, 1867–1973*. Berkeley: University of California Press, 1997.

Robinson, William J. *Fewer and Better Babies or the Limitation of Offspring by the Prevention of Conception*. New York: Critic and Guide, 1915.

Rodengen, Jeffery. *Polytechnic University Changing the World: The First 150 Years*. Fort Lauderdale: Write Stuff, 2005.

Roosevelt, Eleanor. "Divorce." *Ladies' Home Journal*, April 1938.

———. "Should Wives Work?" *The Good Housekeeping Marriage Book: Twelve Ways to a Happy Marriage*. New York: Prentice Hall, 1938.

Ruark, Robert. "Roaring 20's Were Really Dull." *Detroit Free Press*. July 17, 1952.

Rubin, Joan Shelley. *The Making of Middlebrow Culture*. Chapel Hill: University of North Carolina Press, 1992.

Ryan, Dennis. *Images of America: A Journey through Boston Irish History*. Charleston: Arcadia Publishing, 1999.

Sanger, Margaret, and Hannah Mayer Stone, eds. *The Practice of Contraception: An International Symposium and Survey*. Baltimore: Williams & Wilkins, 1931.

Schaffer, Ronald. "The New York Woman Suffrage Party, 1909–1919." *New York History* 42, no. 2 (July 1962).

School Document No. 6—1911, Boston Public Schools, Course of Study for the Latin Schools. Boston: City of Boston Printing Department, 1911.

Scutts, Joanna. *The Extra Woman: How Marjorie Hillis Led a Generation of Women to Live Alone and Like It*. New York: Liveright, 2018.

Showalter, Elaine. *These Modern Women: Autobiographical Essays from the Twenties*. Old Westbury: Feminist Press, 1978.

Simmons, Christina. *Making Marriage Modern: Women's Sexuality from the Progressive Era to World War II*, New York: Oxford University Press, 2009.

Sinclair, Andrew. *Prohibition: The Era of Excess*. Boston: Little Brown and Company, 1962.

Slide, Anthony. *Inside the Hollywood Fan Magazine*. University Press of Mississippi, 2010.

Smyth, J. E., *Edna Ferber's Hollywood: American Fictions of Gender, Race, and History*. Austin: University of Texas Press, 2009.

Sochen, June. *The New Woman: Feminism in Greenwich Village, 1910–1920*. New York: Quadrangle Books, 1972.

Stansell, Christine. *American Moderns: Bohemian New York and the Creation of a New Century*. New York: Henry Holt, 2000.

Strider, Gray. "Sex and the Talkies." *Screenland*, February 1931.

Sumner, David E. *The Magazine Century: American Magazines Since 1900*. New York: Peter Lang, 2010.

Sylvia of Hollywood. *No More Alibis!* New York: Macfadden, 1935.

Tebbel, John. *The American Magazine: A Compact History*. New York: Hawthorn Books, 1969.

Thompson, John Giffen. *Urbanization: Its Effects on Government and Society*. New York: Dutton & Company, 1927.

Tolman, Mary. *Positions of Responsibility in Department Stores and Other Retail Selling Organizations*. New York: Bureau of Vocational Information, 1921.

Turnbull, Andrew, ed. *The Letters of F. Scott Fitzgerald*. London: Bodley Head, 1963.

United States Department of Labor, Bureau of Labor Statistics. "Women in Industry." In *Handbook of Labor Statistics: 1936 edition*, Bulletin No. 616, 1104. Washington, DC: United States Government Printing Office, 1936.

Vanderbilt, Cornelius. "Rollicking Reno." *Liberty*, July 25, 1931.

Vieira, Mark. *George Hurrell's Hollywood*. New York: Running Press Adult, 2013.

Wandersee, Winifred D. *Women's Work and Family Values: 1920–1940*. Cambridge, Harvard University Press: 1981.

Ware, Caroline. *Greenwich Village: 1920–1930*. New York: Harper & Row, 1965. First printed 1935.

Wells, H. G. "Experimenting with Marriage." *The Way the World Is Going: Guesses and Forecasts of the Years Ahead*. New York: Doubleday, 1929.

Westall, Susan. "The Development of a Bio-bibliography for Ursula Parrott with Indexing and Navigation Tools in Printed and Web-Based Versions." Master's thesis, Kent State University School of Library and Information Science, 1999.

Whitehead, Sarah. "Edith Wharton and the Business of the Magazine Short

Story." In *The New Edith Wharton Studies*, edited by Jennifer Haytock and Laura Rattray. Cambridge: Cambridge University Press, 2019.

Widdemer, Margaret, ed. *The Best American Love Stories of the Year*. New York: Tudor, 1932.

———. "Message and Middlebrow," *Saturday Review of Literature*, February 18, 1933.

Wilson, Edmund. "F. Scott Fitzgerald" (originally published March 1922), *The Shores of Light: A Literary Chronicle of the Twenties and Thirties*. New York: Farrar, Straus and Young, 1952.

Wilson, John R. M. *Turbulence Aloft: The Civil Aeronautics Administration Amid Wars and Rumors of Wars, 1938–1953*. Washington, DC: U.S. Department of Transportation, 1979.

Woodward, Helen. *The Lady Persuaders*. New York: Ivan Obolensky, 1960.

———. *Through Many Windows*. New York: Harper & Brothers Publishers, 1926.

Wylie, Philip. *Generation of Vipers*. New York: Farrar & Rinehart, 1942.

York, Cal. "Should Women Work?" *Photoplay*, August 1931.

Zuckerman, Mary Ellen. *A History of Popular Women's Magazines in the United States, 1792–1995*. New York: Prager, 1998.

INDEX

Note: page numbers in italics refer to figures. Those followed by n refer to notes, with note number.

diet article by Parrott (*Ladies' Home Journal*), 101, *102*

divorce: acceptable grounds for, 78, 83; acceptance of, at Parrott's son's progressive school, 45; concerns about effects on child, 45, 46; destigmatization in 1930s, 41, 110–11, 178; as difficult to obtain, by design, 110; Eleanor Roosevelt on, 41, 110; *Liberty* magazine issue on, 109–10; Parrott's "Men as Marriage Killers" series on, 221–23, *222*; rigid New York laws on, 78, 109–10; rising rate of, as perceived crisis, 41, 53, 83; as routine, in *Ex-Wife*, 78; women's new independence and, 41

divorced women: increased number in early 20th century, 3, 41; Parrott as recognized expert on, 3; Parrott's recognition of large number of, 74

The Divorcee (*Ex-Wife* film version), 86–87; fee paid to Parrott for rights, 86; happy ending added to, 90; Parrott on, 87; publicity for, 87; rewrite of, to satisfy censors, 86–87, 90; Shearer's academy award for, 87, *89*

Dodd, Mead & Co., 202, 207

Dodge, Mabel, 54–55

Donahue, Mary "Dado": at birth of Parrott's son, 34–36; as caregiver for Parrott's son, 43; on death, 224; as housekeeper for Parrott family, 16; with Parrott family on vacation, 20; on Parrott's lack of skill in sewing and knitting, 43; Parrott's marriage and, 32–33; at Twin Elms estate, 46, *47*

double standard: *Ex-Wife* on, 77; film version of *Ex-Wife* on, 87; in Parrott's first marriage, 38

Dove, Billie, 98

Dream without Ending (Parrott), 157

Dressler, A. C., *198*

drinking, and alcoholism treatment, 116

drinking by Parrott, 114–17; brief periods of abstinence, 16, 71, 114, 116–17, 129; as cause of ill-advised second marriage, 114; and New York speakeasy circuit, 16, 56, 65, 67, 74, 80–82, 108, 114; to numb psychological pain, 71–72, 114, 116; and

rise in women's drinking during Prohibition, 114; as significant problem, 114; and writing about drinking, 114–16

Driscoll, Charles, 49–50, 145, 188, 201

Duhaime, Ernest, 193

Earhart, Amelia, 184

education. *See* Girls' Latin School (Boston); Radcliffe College

employment: at advertising firm, 60; after divorce from Lindesay Parrott, 58–62; in department store advertising department, 58, 60–62; as model, 58–59, 65; Parrott's aversion to routine and, 60; search for newspaper job, 58–59

Ernst, Morrie, 160–61

Erskine, John, 171

Even in a Hundred Years (Parrott): echoes of Parrott's affair with O'Connor in, 68; publication of, 202; themes in, 202–3

Ex-Wife (Parrott): abortion in, 124–25; anonymous publication of, 73, 75; on birth control, 124; critics' response to, 77; dedication to O'Connor, 73; Dell edition of (1949), *204*; drinking to numb psychological pain in, 116; echoes of Parrott's advertising work in, 61; echoes of Parrott's affair with O'Connor in, 67–68, 78, 120, 130; echoes of Parrott's housekeeper in, 16; echoes of Parrott's marital problems in, 39, 90; as embarrassment to Parrott's father, 79; exposure of Parrott as author of, 75–76; and line between high and low culture, 135; marketing as sociological document, 80, 84; newspaper's censoring of plot description, 84; parodies of, 80–82; and Parrott's financial success, 73, 82; Parrott's life during writing of, 1; and Parrott's notoriety, 79–80; Parrott's public appearances to deny autobiographicality of, 79; plot of, 76–79; publication of, 75; publicity surrounding, 75–76, 79; on regret about aborted children, 125; reviews, Parrott's interest in, 83; reviews of, 83, 84; serialization in *New York Daily Mirror*,

80, *81*; smoking in, 16; success of, 80, 84; suffering of women in, 84–85; title choice for, 75; ugly side of modern life portrayed in, 78, 79; violence against women in, 77; as warning about new morality, 85; wife's threat of suicide in, 130; on women's new freedom as benefit only to men, 83–84; writing of, 73–75; writing of, money borrowed for, 74. *See also The Divorcee* (*Ex-Wife* film version)

Ex-Wife (Parrott's dog), 95

ex-wife, Parrott's popularization of term, 3, 83

Fahnestock, Ruth, 178

"A Far Off Music" (Parrott), 187; sale to Hollywood, 203

feminism of early 20th century: and birth control activism, 5, 122–23; and drinking as sign of new freedom, 114; goals and frustrations of, 5–6; Greenwich Village and, 70, 122; and husbands' resentment, 6; Parrott's life and, 229; Parrott's views on, 5–6, 70

Ferber, Edna, 135

financial difficulties: arrest for nonpayment of hotel bill, 209–10; back taxes, and attachment of income, 202, 203, 207; creditors' court actions, 202, 208; and cutting of ties to family and friends, 213; death under false name in charity ward, 224; debt owed to literary agent, 207; debt owed to publisher, 207; disappearance from public view in early 1950s, 210; drop in demand for her work and, 207; events leading to, as not fully known, 206–7; flights from hotels without paying bills, 208–9; letter to O'Connor asking for money, 207; letter to Walter Winchell describing her poverty, 206; and loss of friends, 214; manuscripts lost during, 208, 229; part-time work at dry cleaner, 213; and reputation for bouncing checks, 203; and research for novel, 209, 210; residence in shelters and cheap hotels, 211–13; short stories written under pseudonym, 213–14; stealing of silver from friend's home,

210–11, *212*; Wildberg's assistance during, 214–15

financial difficulties, and attempt to write autobiography: borrowing of typewriter to work on, 211–12, 215; inability to produce, 213, 215; Wildberg's support in writing of, 215

financial life: complexity of, 140–41; cost of second divorce, 114; debts owed by 1942, 202; difficulties following first divorce, 58–59, 82; lack of productivity after marriage to Schermerhorn and, 180–81; missed deadlines and, 185; money management, early training in, 17; mounting debts in 1938, 175; mounting debts of 1940s, 187; sale of Connecticut estate to reduce expenses, 187; success in movie industry and, 2, 103, 105; success of writing career and, 2, 3, 73, 82, 227; tax debts and, 141, 160, 175, 187. *See also* spending; wealth of Parrott

"First Love" (Parrott): in *Best American Love Stories of the Year* (1932), 136; echoes of Parrott's child-rearing anxieties in, 50

Fitzgerald, F. Scott, 54, 168–70, 183–84

Florey, Louis, 142

For All Our Lives (Parrott), 161

Forever, Perhaps! (Parrott), 48

fortune teller, on Parrott's future, 73

Friedan, Betty, 4, 221

Friends of Abraham Lincoln Battalion, Parrott's fundraising for, 173, *174*

Gabler, Neal, 112

Gannett, Lewis, 84

Garbo, Greta, 86

gender equality, Parrott on, 174, 205

generation, Parrott's. *See* Parrott's generation

generation following Parrott's, in Parrott's fiction: efforts to repair her generation's damage, 185; women's lives of purpose and meaning, 186–87; women's self-sufficiency in, 187

Gentlemen's Fate (Parrott): film version of, 91, 98; publication under pseudonym, 91, *93*; serial publication of, 91, *93*

Gilbert, John, 91

Girls' Latin School (Boston): colleges attended by graduates, 22; Parrott's education at, 17–19, *19*

Goldman, Emma, 27, 54–55

Goldwyn, Samuel, 98–99

Good Housekeeping magazine: Parrott's missed deadlines for, 139; Parrott's stories in, 3, 133; and Parrott's willingness to edit submissions, 143–44; popularity of, 133; types of fiction published in, 137

Goodman, Benny, 189–90

Goodwin, Wilder, 109

gossip columnists, 112; as help and danger to celebrities, 112; Parrott's fear of, 112. *See also* Hopper, Hedda; Lyons, Leonard; Parsons, Louella; Winchell, Walter

Gould, Bruce, 184

Grable, Betty, 97, *97*

Graham, Martha, 244n11

Grant, Cary, 144

Great Depression: drop in magazines' revenue during, 141; film version of *Ex-Wife* and, 87; and Park Row newspapers, 39–40; Parrott's financial success during, 2, 73, 82; and publication of *Ex-Wife*, 80; unemployment in, 141

Green, John, 154

Greenwich Village: as haven for artists and writers, 54; liberal thinkers and culture changers frequenting, 54–55; "live for the moment" lifestyle in, 54; Parrott's attraction to writer's life in, 70; Parrott's dates with first husband in, 31–32; Parrott's partying in, 56–57; Parrott's research for O'Connor's book on, 69–70, 122; repudiation of traditional values in, 53–54, 55; and women's equality in work, leisure, and sex, 55, 56; young people seeking thrills in, 54

Greenwich Village Feminist Alliance, 70

Greenwood, Charles Terry (second husband): background and education, 107; career of, 108; courting of Parrott in Hollywood, 107, 108; death of, *115*; as Parrott's friend after divorce, 108; Parrott's lack of romantic interest in, 108; in World War I, 107–8

Greenwood, Parrott's divorce from: as acrimonious, 111; cost of, 114; court hearing, Parrott's claims of abuse in, 112–13; and fear of Greenwood's reprisal, 109–10, 111; granting of, 113; Greenwood's refusal to comment on, 113; Parrott's depression following, 117; Parrott's search for quickest venue for, 109–10; press coverage of, 111–14; venue for, 111

Greenwood, Parrott's marriage to: ceremony, 108; as means of breaking ties to O'Connor, 111; Parrott's drinking and, 114; Parrott's immediate regret of, 108–9; Parrott's trip to West Indies to escape, 109; press coverage of, 108; as sudden decision, 108

"Grounds for Divorce: Infidelity" (Parrott), 169. *See also* "Infidelity" (film)

"Grounds for Divorce: Nonsupport" (Parrott), 118–19

"Grounds for Divorce" series (Parrott), 169

hair, bobbed, and modern women, 53

Hall, G. Stanley, 45

Halton, Mary, 128–29

Hapgood, "Happy," 18–19

Harding, Ann, 98

Haxton, Florence, 83

Hays, Will, 86–87

Hays Code. *See* Motion Picture Production Code (Hays Code)

Hayward, Leland, 90

health: complications from abortion, 129, 130–31; depression, periods of, 77, 82, 117, 120, 142, 218; diagnosis of probable infertility, 126; exercise regimen and, 100; fall from horse, 114; ill health, comebacks from, 218; ill health, periods of, 120, 145, 159–60; ill health in later life, 213; low point of physical and mental resilence in 1932, 120; rape, suicidal depression following, 77; sterilization surgery considered, 131, 252n25; suicidal thoughts and incidents, 78, 82, 129–30, 142; and Sylvia of Hollywood lifestyle regimen, 100–101, *102. See also* drinking by Parrott

Hearst, William Randolph, 80, 98, 141, 169

Lowell, Joan, *106*
Lynd, Robert and Helen, 41
Lyons, Leonard, 112, 223

Macfadden, Bernarr, 110
Mackaill, Dorothy, 98
MacMurray, Fred, 168, 203
magazines: boom in 1920s, 133, 253n2; high compensation to writers, 133–35; and high vs. low culture, 135–37; notable authors publishing work in, 135; Parrott's nonfiction in, 171; revenue drop in Great Depression, 141
magazines, Parrott's stories in: *American Magazine* editor's demand for rewrites, 143–44, 149; and constant deadline pressures, 144, 145; income from, *134*, 135; magazines published in, 133; as way of remaining in public eye, *134*, 144; willingness to take advice from editors, 143–44; and "The Woman Accused" all-star serial, 144, *145*. *See also specific magazines*
male-female relations: as focus of middlebrow writers, 135–36; inequitable relationship exposed by Parrott, 122; Parrott on common failings of men, 4, 6–7; Parrott's rethinking of, 121; and women's equality, 3. *See also* marriage; women, modern; women, working
Mankiewicz, Herman, 91, *92*
marijuana: federal campaign to stigmatize, 194; laws against, 194. *See also* Bryan, Michael Neely
Marijuana Tax Act of 1937, 194
Marks, Percy, 80
marriage: calls in 1930s for women to reject, 118; failure of, Parrott's advice on, 39; formal, in Parrott's fiction, 155; formal, Parrott's marriage to Wildberg as, 155; happy, as Parrott's greatest desire, 117–18, 119; Parrott's cynicism after three failed marriages, 177; Parrott's expectations for, 30; Parrott's hope to use movies to educate women about, 103–4; second, lower divorce rates for, 107; second, Parrott's optimism about, 107; successful, Parrott on requirements for, 38;

Sylvia of Hollywood on, 101; transformation of, in early 20th century, 40–41; women's resurgent interest in, in 1930s, 118. *See also* divorce
marriage in modern age: erosion, critics of, 83; and "New Morality," Parrott on, 40–41; proposed "companionate marriage," 40–41; as subject of *Ex-Wife*, 76–78
marriages of Parrott. *See* Greenwood, Charles Terry (second husband); Parrott, Lindesay Marc (first husband); Schermerhorn, Alfred Coster (fourth husband); Wildberg, John J. "Jack" (third husband)
Marry Me Before You Go (Parrott), echoes of Parrott's affair with O'Connor in, 68
Marston, William Moulton, 93–94
Maugham, W. Somerset, 207
Mayer, Louis B., 12
McCall's magazine: income from stories sold to, 187; Parrott's missed deadlines for, 139, 154, 180–81; Parrott's stories in, 153, 157
McCollister, Alice, 39
McKeogh, Elsie, 185
Mead, Dodd, 175
melodrama, Parrott on, 136
Men, Marriage, and Me (Joyce), 110
"Men as Marriage Killers" series (Parrott), 221–23, *222*
Merchant Princess (Parrott), serial publication of, *134*
Merrick, Mollie, 94
Metro-Goldwyn-Mayer (MGM): and film version of *Ex-Wife*, 86–87, *89*, 90; and film version of *Gentlemen's Fate*, 91, 98; and film version of "Grounds for Divorce: Infidelity," 168–70; and film version of *Strangers May Kiss*, 87–89, 90; Parrott's movie writing deal with, 91, 98; stories sold to MGM in mid-1930s, 168
middlebrow writers: focus on male-female relations, 135–36; Parrott as, 135
Millay, Edna St. Vincent, 57, 69
Mindell, Fania, 123
Miner, Worthington, 161

father after, 39, 43; time required for recovery from, 38

Parrott, Lindesay (first husband), marriage to: apartments in New York, 33, 36; certificate of marriage, 32, *32*; early married life, 33; echoes of, in her fiction, 90; elopement, 32; and end of her graduate studies, 29; infidelity leading to end of, 36–38, *38*; as inspiration for fiction, 41–42; Lin and Parrott's romantic involvements following, 39; and Lin's aversion to children, 34–36, 43, 241n13; Lin's transfer to London and, 33–34; memories of, 42; move to London, 33–34; Parrott on failure of, 36, 38, 39; Parrott's attempts to repair marriage, 38, 42; and unexpected pregnancy, 34–36; as volatile relationship, 33

Parrott, Lindesay Marc II (son). *See* Parrott, Marc [Lindesay Marc II] (son)

Parrott, Marc [Lindesay Marc II] (son), *49*; birth of, 34; child support paid by father, 43–44; custody awarded to Parrott, 39; education at progressive Shady Oak School, 44–45, 46; father's limited contact with, 43–44; Harvard degree, as culmination of Parrott's hopes, 218–19; as Marine in World War II, 185, 188, 190; on mother's death, 224; on mother's drinking, 114; on mother's fast-paced life, 224–25; on mother's hard work as writer, 145; on mother's life, 224; on mother's spending, 139; Parrott's knitting of sweaters for, 43; Parrott's lack of maternal instinct and, 43; Parrott's visits to, 44; residence with Parrott's father after her divorce, 39, 43, 44; work around Connecticut farm to cut expenses, 142

Parrott, Marc (son), Parrott's raising of: admirers of, 49–50; concern about spoiling him, 46; concerns about lack of father, 47–48; critics of, 48; echoes of, in Parrott's stories, 50; minimal contact before age 6, 45–46; money spent on lessons, 49–50; Parrott's anxieties about, 50; Parrott's sudden wealth and, 48–49, *49*; and pride in parenthood,

49; as similar to other wealthy families, 48; summers spent at camps, 45–46; and travel, 50, 156–57

Parrott, Marc (son), at Parrott's country estate, *47*; greater time spent with mother, 46–47; money spent on, 47–48; move to, after grandfather's death, 46

Parrott, Mary Adamson (mother-in-law), 30; and care for Parrott's son, 36, 43, 44, 48; Parrott's friendly relations with, 44, 66

Parrott, Thomas Marc (father-in-law), 30; and care for Parrott's son, 44, 48; Parrott's friendly relations with, 48, 66

Parrott, Ursula [Katherine Ursula] "Kitty": birth name vs. chosen name, 11, 12, 30, 79; birth of, 14–15; casual anti-Semitism of, 95, 152; death of, 223–24; happy marriage as greatest desire, 117–18, 119; hiding of true age, 11, 32, 154, 179, 192; "Kitty" as nickname of, 11; life of, as more-easily lived today, 229–30; permanence and stability as goal of, 218, 224, 229; on persona created by her publisher and agent, 218; signature cropped hairstyle of, 19, *19*. *See also* childhood and youth; college years; drinking by Parrott; employment; financial difficulties; financial life; health; writing career; writings of Parrott; *other specific topics*

Parrott's family. *See entries under* Towle

Parrott's generation: following generation's efforts to repair damage from, 185; formative events of, 2; Parrott on disillusionment of, 224; postwar hedonism of, 2, 24, 54, 64; in stories of 1940s, 186; *The Tumult and the Shouting* as critique of, 147; and working women, large increase in, 55. *See also* generation following Parrott's

Parsons, Louella, 112, 159

passport application (1922), 34, *35*

Pathé, Parrott's movie writing deal with, 98, 108

Peak, Mayme Ober, 94

Pegler, Westbrook, 171

"Peter Keeps Memorial Day" (Parrott), 50

sex and romance: and birth control, 5;
feminist views on, 5; novels about, and
spread of big-city mores, 58; Parrott's
rape, suicidal depression following, 77;
spread of big-city ideas about, 58. *See
also* abortions; birth control
sex and romance, Parrott on: cost of freedom in, 9; extramarital, pessimism
about, 120–21; frankness in discussing, 5, 58; learning to negotiate, in age
of impermanence, 56, 57, 58; pressure
on modern women to have sex, 56; and
sexual aggressiveness of men, 56. *See also*
affairs
"Sex and the Talkies" (Strider), 87, *88*
sexism: Parrott's search for newspaper job
and, 59; in press coverage of Parrott's aid
in lover's escape from military stockade,
198–200
sexual harassment, Parrott on, 6
sexual liberation, Parrott's views on, 5–6
Shady Oak School (Boston), 44–45, 46
Shearer, Norma: in *The Divorcee*, 86, 87, *89*;
as embodiment of Parrott protagonist,
90; in *Strangers May Kiss*, 87–88; and
Sylvia of Hollywood, 100–101
"She Owed Him Everything" (Parrott
screenplay), 94
Showalter, Elaine, 6
Sirk, Douglas, 168
Skolsky, Sidney, 112
Smith, Harrison "Hal," 75, 133, 146
smoking by Parrott: in childhood, 15–16;
Ex-Wife and, 16; hiding of, from father,
79
So Big (Ferber), 135
socialism, Parrott's interest in, 69
"Somewhere East of Sunrise" (Parrott), 205
Spanish Civil War, Parrott's fundraising
for Americans fighting in, 173, *174*
Spelke, Max, 112
spending: as always in excess of her income,
96–97, 105–6, 131–32, 139–41; cost of
Connecticut estate and, 97, 105–6, 173;
efforts to control, 106–7, 139–42; exces-
sive, "One More Such Victory" on, 216;
Great Depression and, 141–42; on New

York hotel rooms, for writing space,
138; and penchant for nice clothes, 60,
74, 75, 82, 159; as spur to writing, 105,
142–43
Stansell, Christine, 54
Stanwyck, Barbara, 168, 203
Steuer, Aaron, 154
Stewart, Donald Ogden, 91, *92*
Stewart, Jimmy, 7, 167
Strangers May Kiss (film version), 87–88;
banning in Ireland, 252n3; as box office
success, 89; criticisms of moral tone of,
90; happy ending added to, 90; rewrite
of, to satisfy censors, 87–88, 90; as
undervalued work, 228–29
Strangers May Kiss (Parrott): drinking to
numb psychological pain in, 116; echoes
of affair with O'Connor in, 90; as Parrott's second novel, 87; pessimism about
extramarital love, 120–21; reviews of,
120
Strider, Gray, 87, *88*
Sturges, Preston, *92*
suicide threats: to O'Connor, 129–30; during time of financial stress, 142
Sullivan, Ed, 112
"Sunlit" (unfinished Parrott novel), 201
Swanson, Gloria, 98–99, 100–101
Sylvia of Hollywood, 100–101, *102*, 116–17

Terrett, Courtenay "Terry" "Brick," *37*; and
closing of newspapers in Great Depres-
sion, 40; Parrott's affair with, 36–37,
60; and Parrott's search for newspaper
work, 59–60
Thalberg, Irving, 86, 89, 98
"There's Always Tomorrow" (Parrott): film
versions of, 165, 168, 203; on happy mar-
riage, 117; plot of, 163–65
Thompson, Dorothy, 112
"Though You Be Far" (Parrott), echoes of
Parrott's life in, 131
Time magazine, sexism in coverage of
Parrott's trial for aiding soldier's escape,
198–200
Tonight or Never (film), 99–100
"Too Busy for Love" (Parrott), 206

writing career *(continued)*
last works sold to movie industry,
203; missed deadlines, 10, 130, 139,
153–54, 173, 180–81, 182–83, 184–85,
202; numerous comebacks in, 218;
O'Connor's efforts to profit from, 74;
O'Connor's encouragement of, 62,
63, 73–74; periods of high and low
productivity, 142–43; preparations
for, in research for O'Connor's book,
69–70, 122; and procrastination and
distractions, 138–39; resignation of Bye
as literary agent, 184–85; search for
literary agent to replace Bye, 184–85;
success of, as little comfort to Parrott,
82–83; willingness to accept advice from
editors, 143; writing habits, 137–38
writings of Parrott: basis in personal
experience, 3, 4, 10; best sellers, 2; broad
range of subjects besides romance, 227–
28; characters in, as smart and literate,
138; and concessions made to mass
market, 228; defining of Parrott by, 3;
and line between high and low culture,
135–37; list of, 267–71; magazines
published in, 3; as middlebrow, 135;
modern women's life as focus of, 2–3;
as now forgotten, 10; number of, 2, 227;
rarity of happy endings in, 5; research for,
138; "tomorrow" stories about deferred or
dashed hopes, 176; as undervalued, 227–
28; "Until Sundown" proposal for, 175;
women's interest in, 3–4
writings of Parrott in 1930s: as better suited
to Hollywood adaptation, 165; female
characters resigned to compromise in,
163–65, 169; loneliness of career women
in, 163–65; maturity of characters as
reflection of her own life, 165–66, 169
writings of Parrott in 1940s: characters in,
as more responsible and thoughtful,
203–6; more women in domestic life
in, 205–6; women's lives of purpose and
meaning in, 186–87, 205; World War II
themes in, 185–88, 205
writing style of Parrott, similarity to
contemporaries, 5

"The Years I'll Spend without You"
(Parrott), 186–87
"You Call That Work?" (Parrott), 221, *222*
"You Love But Once—or Twice" (Parrott),
181
"You Ride Success Alone" (Parrott), 118

Founded in 1893,
UNIVERSITY OF CALIFORNIA PRESS
publishes bold, progressive books and journals
on topics in the arts, humanities, social sciences,
and natural sciences—with a focus on social
justice issues—that inspire thought and action
among readers worldwide.

The UC PRESS FOUNDATION
raises funds to uphold the press's vital role
as an independent, nonprofit publisher, and
receives philanthropic support from a wide
range of individuals and institutions—and from
committed readers like you. To learn more, visit
ucpress.edu/supportus.